Reviewing Qualitative Research in the Social Sciences

Foundational characteristics of qualitative research include flexibility, variation in application, critique, and innovation, all of which derive from its subjective roots in interpretivism and constructivism. While the scholars who design qualitative research projects envision these qualities as strengths, such a breadth of practices and the assumptions that undergird them may present challenges during the peer review process. As a result, those who review and consume qualitative research often have important and difficult-to-answer questions about the project's design, strategies/tools, and analysis, with few guidelines for gauging the merit of the work.

The mission of this book is to provide a useful guide for researchers, reviewers, and consumers who are charged with judging the quality of qualitative studies. In order to embrace the challenges and controversies that accompany this goal, the editors have solicited experts representing multiple disciplines and methods of qualitative inquiry. Their contributions represent the rich diversity in the field while simultaneously producing a pragmatic and useful guide. While it is neither possible nor desirable to compartmentalize qualitative approaches and issues into neatly organized categories, the construct of *method* has been chosen as a common organizing device.

The introductory chapter explains the need for such a book and underscores the foundational strengths of qualitative research: flexibility, variation, critique, and innovation. The remaining chapters review the principal approaches to qualitative research with care taken not to standardize, rigidly define, or oversimplify any approach. For ease of use, all methodological chapters are organized around the following elements of inquiry which reviewers tend to examine: definition, sampling, data collection, data analysis, representation, and congruency.

Audrey A. Trainor and **Elizabeth Graue** have been interdepartmental colleagues at the University of Wisconsin, Madison for seven years. Together, with their colleagues and co-members of the Qualitative Research Committee in the School of Education, they have designed a qualitative research minor for doctoral students. Both are members of QSIG, the qualitative research special interest group of the American Education Research Association. Elizabeth is a former chair of QSIG.

Reviewing Qualitative Research in the Social Sciences

Edited by
Audrey A. Trainor and Elizabeth Graue

Routledge
Taylor & Francis Group

NEW YORK AND LONDON

First published 2013
by Routledge
711 Third Avenue, New York, NY 10017

Simultaneously published in the UK
by Routledge
2 Park Square, Milton Park, Abingdon, Oxon OX14 4RN

Routledge is an imprint of the Taylor & Francis Group, an informa business

© 2013 Taylor & Francis

Library of Congress Cataloging in Publication Data
CIP data has been applied for

ISBN: 978-0-415-89347-3 (hbk)
ISBN: 978-0-415-89350-3 (pbk)
ISBN: 978-0-203-81332-4 (ebk)

Typeset in Minion Pro
by Florence Production Ltd, Stoodleigh, Devon

Printed and bound in the United States of America
by Edwards Brothers, Inc.

Contents

Foreword

The Past, Present, and Future of Qualitative Research and the Need for this Book

James Joseph Scheurich

Qualitative research. Qualitative research in education. Reviewing qualitative research in education. What a fascinating trajectory it has been since Lincoln and Guba's "fighting" book, *Naturalistic Inquiry*, came out in 1985 (nearly 30 years ago!!) as part of the paradigm (and methodology) wars. I call it a fighting book because when I read it, my interpretation of it is that they were giving no quarter to those who had condemned qualitative research and its attendant epistemologies. To me, they wanted to fight and so did many other scholars. It was definitely a fractious fray with scholars on both sides scorching each other in various scholarly venues.

I came into this furor in the late 1980s, especially when I went to Ohio State University in 1990 to work with Patti Lather and Bob Donmoyer, two participants in this battle, both qualitative researchers. In my view, Patti, with her feminist poststructuralism, was trying to move epistemology far beyond what Lincoln and Guba were arguing for, but Patti was definitely and strongly on the proqualitative side. Bob was more willing to try to bridge across the disputational divide, but he was also strongly proqualitative.

While I had had extensive doctoral training in quantitative methodologies before going to Ohio State, I had begun to learn qualitative and went to Ohio State specially to work with Patti and Bob. Not surprisingly, then, I jumped into the battle on the same side on which they were. I particularly began to apply a critical poststructuralism to qualitative methodological issues, much like Patti was doing. This poststructuralist endeavor, in general, made many scholars on both sides uncomfortable. We probably seemed totally insane to the quantitative folks, and our epistemological position, poststructuralism, particularly drawing from the French poststructuralists, made many qualitative advocates uncomfortable, as it problematized many of the qualitative adherents' favorite epistemological assumptions. However, these epistemological differences, even among qualitative researchers, were emblematic of what was to come. What the once-famous paradigm wars actually did was open the doors not to just one additional epistemology, but to many, opening the door to what was later called a proliferation of paradigms and methodologies, the underlying basis of this book with its fifteen different qualitative approaches.

The problem with fighting wars is that the sides tend to get simplistically reduced to easy stereotypes, and in many regards this certainly happened. For instance, "positivism" became the derogatory word that qualitative advocates laid hostilely at the door of those who fought on the side of quantitative methodologies. For those who looked a little deeper, "positivism" had had its own internal wars and disputations for most of the twentieth century and over time experienced significant revisions, many of which moved in the direction that the qualitative folks and Lincoln and Guba were recommending.

Nonetheless, the dominant discourse, the dominant truth, in education and the social sciences (still is in some social sciences, political science for one) at that time was some kind of revized positivism or postpositivism, deeply built upon quantitative methodologies and the scientific method (often a needlessly restricted view of the scientific method, one more restricted than that often used by those in the physical sciences). Much of this methodological and epistemological dominance in education came out of departments of educational psychology, whose faculties in many colleges of education controlled the methodology courses and who, in my opinion, were insecure in their claim to be scientists in comparison to the physical scientists. As a result, they built a view of science that was overly restrictive and limited, whereas science as practiced by physical scientists is often more free form, creative, loose, focused on the issues at hand rather than on adherence to some strict definition of method or epistemology, though this certainly does not mean anything goes or that there are not physical scientists who advocate a fairly strict version of the scientific method and its assumptions.

There are several points, then, that I am making at this point. First, there was a methodological and epistemological war in the 1980s and 1990s in education, and *Naturalistic Inquiry* was at the center of this as the main fighting book on the qualitative side. Second, each side tended to simplify the nature of the other side, creating straw epistemologies and overlooking the complexities and difficulties of the range of possible epistemological assumptions on both sides. Third, some of why it went this way in education—and this is just my view—was that faculty in educational psychology departments, who generally at that point in time had control of methodology courses, were afraid of not being seen as real scientists and thus attached themselves to a more restricted or limited view of the practice of science. Fourth, the largely inadvertent outcome of all of this was that it opened up a much broader epistemological and methodological discussion, one result of which is this book, along with, most famously, the different editions of Denzin and Lincoln's *Sage Handbook of Qualitative Research*.

Where I began to play a larger role in this history is that in 1995, I became the lead editor of the *International Journal of Qualitative Studies in Education*, often known as QSE. This journal had been started in 1988 by British scholars (Stephen Ball and Ivor Goodson played key roles in this endeavor, though it had two sets of U.S. editors before I came on board) who wanted to support the emergence of qualitative research. Indeed, when QSE first started in 1988, most mainline journals in education would not accept qualitative research articles. This was especially true of the AERA journals, which were often considered some of the most prestigious ones. Thus, QSE was a key part in the battle of qualitative versus quantitative as it provided a scholarly journal for qualitative researchers.

I was a fairly radical choice as the lead editor for QSE, a choice in which Stephen Ball played a major role. I was an assistant professor, and I was mostly known to Stephen and others as a poststructuralist who had studied with Patti Lather. I had just published two articles in QSE based on a poststructuralist take on interviewing and validity. Based, then, on these two articles, I was given a chance to be the editor of QSE and have remained the same since then, helped along with several excellent co-editors—Doug Foley, Angela Valenzuela (both at the University of Texas at Austin), Carolyn Clark, and now Kathryn McKenzie (the latter two at Texas A&M University, where I moved to in 2004), in that order. Together, we created a journal representative of the same paradigm and methodological proliferation that drives this book.

Where Are We Now with Qualitative Research?

What I have provided to this point is a brief, somewhat personal history of qualitative research in education since the mid-1980s. (Other social sciences, including nursing, have their own histories.)

We fought a war with the result being a loud, loose, far-ranging, messy discussion of many different paradigms (epistemologies) and many different methodologies for applying qualitative research. Not incidentally, along the way, qualitative basically won the war. Now *some* qualitative methodologies are widely accepted, even in the most mainline journals, including most AERA ones, while *other* qualitative methods, such as poststructuralist ones or poetry as a representation of qualitative research, find it difficult to impossible to publish in mainline journals, though QSE and some other journals do publish this work.

Of course, some scholars would argue that we went backwards during the Bush administration's push toward experimental research in education, a push that still holds significant influence. It is certainly true that there was some of that, especially in terms of IES grants (the U.S. Department of Education's Institute for Education Sciences, one of the main sources, along with National Science Foundation [NSF] of federal education grants). I know many got into fighting all over again, and this showed up in many journals, including *Educational Researcher*, AERA's journal that everyone belonging to AERA gets.

What was provocative to me was that though there were efforts among some education scholars to once again narrow what was epistemologically and methodologically acceptable, I found those efforts to be fairly limited. Most mainline journals, including AERA ones, have continued to welcome qualitative research as do NSF and IES to some extent. Indeed, I was pleasantly surprised that we moved backward very little (in my view) and then only in a few spaces. If that was the best the quantitative restorationists could do, their days of dominance were clearly over.

What this limited success to move backward also reinforced to me was that qualitative is here to stay. Indeed, my experience has been that most younger scholars, many of whom did not even experience the paradigm wars, believe that qualitative research gets at some results that quantitative cannot and quantitative research gets at some results that qualitative cannot. Thus, they see both as highly valuable; they just provide different kinds of results or insights.

For those, though, who are ruled by a particular epistemology, this is not a particularly good result as it comes off as a kind of naïve realist version of holding hands together and singing *kum ba yah*. These latter folks claim that there is a deep epistemological divide here, and thus this naiveté is a papering over of this division. They tend to be skeptical of most mixed methods approaches, wanting rigorous discussions that address the epistemological differences.

One solution to this dilemma—in my view—is to adopt a pragmatic approach, not the everyday American version of being "pragmatic," but the philosophical version of pragmatism, which has many of the same general assumptions as does poststructuralists. In this view, epistemology is no longer the dominant question or issue. Indeed, I would suggest that pragmatism is nonepistemological, taking that issue completely off the table. The main question becomes what human social purposes does research serve. What methodology will help us address the issues we face? Of course, this does not mean that everyone would agree any more on these issues than they do on epistemology. In fact, I am sure we could have as large of battles about this as we have had about epistemology. However, I for one am much more interested today in fighting about the social purposes of education research than about epistemology and methodology, much to the unhappiness of some of my poststructuralist friends. It is also important to note, though, in this regard, that there has to date been little discussion of this kind of viewpoint. Cherryholmes does some work in this area, but we have had no submissions to QSE on this, though I have tried to prompt some.

The result of all of this history is we have a book like this one. To me, having a book focused on the reviewing of different qualitative approaches means that we are no longer fighting over the existence of qualitative research. Now, we are worried about doing good reviewing of these different approaches. In other words, as Trainor and Graue state in their Introduction, we are concerned with the quality criteria for each different approach to qualitative research. However, as they also point out in their

Introduction, they are not focused on any final, correct list for such quality criteria. Nor are there any solid, stable, agreed-upon definitions of major terms in qualitative research. Instead, Trainor and Graue want an open, dynamic, ongoing discussion, which is appropriate given the broad array of different epistemological perspectives, the different ways of taking up even a single qualitative methodology, and the different definitions of a variety of commonly used terms. In other words, qualitative research is a radically open endeavor, though this may disturb some researchers and some consumers of research.

As the editor of QSE for over fifteen years, I have directly experienced all of what Trainor and Graue discuss. Over that time period, I have literally read hundreds and hundreds, maybe thousands, of qualitative research manuscripts for QSE and other journals. It is a radically open endeavor with even more methodological approaches than they cover in this book, though they have certainly addressed most of the main ones. However, one thing I see, and I do not see Trainor and Graue addressing this, is that a high percentage of qualitative research published in QSE and other journals does not use these specific methodologies as much as simply being qualitative research based on collecting data through interviewing, observing, and examining documents. Of course, QSE tends to get more of the type of approaches covered in this book than more general journals, but even with QSE, most qualitative research could be simply described as qualitative research without any epistemological or methodological specificity. In other words, I am suggesting that in practice a very high percentage of published qualitative research does not do much to address epistemological issues and does not engage in the wide array of methodological possibilities. If I am largely correct, why this is and what it means could be the source of some fruitful discussions.

Another issue I see as a QSE editor is that many qualitative researchers have little in-depth understanding of the different approaches addressed in this book. For example, we see many manuscripts that claim to be grounded theory though the only aspect of their work that alludes to grounded theory is the way they took their analyses method from books on grounded theory. Another common error we see is a claim to be doing autoethnography though the manuscript in no way resembles what those with respected expertise say autoethnography should look like. We also see fairly superficial ideas of what phenomenology is or what narrative research is. Many will claim some epistemology or methodology at the beginning but not follow through with any depth. Thus, a useful purpose of this book is hopefully to educate qualitative researchers more deeply on the nature of these many different approaches.

A third issue we see at QSE is that 70–80 percent of manuscripts submitted to us are poorly done. This, of course, is not that different from any decent research journal. Most faculty and students submitting manuscripts simply do not know how to compose a good article. I truly hope this book helps with that, too, as this is the worst problem we have at QSE.

Where Are We Headed in the Future with Qualitative Research?

My first answer is more of the same. We will continue to have many different epistemologies and many different ways of doing qualitative research. We will continue to have most published qualitative research not claim some specific epistemology or methodology, other than interviewing, observing, or examining documents. We will continue to have false claims of the use of specific epistemologies and methodologies, and we will continue to have poorly done manuscripts, which hopefully do not get published.

My second answer is to hope for some to take on why most published qualitative research is done from a perspective that can be labeled naïve realism. The way I define this is that the qualitative researchers naively assume that what they find is simply real. In other words, most qualitative researchers have no serious understanding of epistemologies and their attendant complexities. Is this simply ignorance or is it something more? Yes, it is ignorance to a certain degree, but I think it is more than this. Nonetheless, I do not see anyone exploring this. (I would suggest some work with philosophical pragmatism might be helpful here, but I am not sure.)

My third answer is technology and the internet. I do not think that qualitative research has yet been strongly impacted by the new technologies and communication through the internet or smart phones and other devices. At QSE, we see very little exploration of this. Also, I see little exploration of qualitative research as websites that include voice, video, and multiple pathways through the website. Our journals are still overwhelmingly paper-based and a linear read. Even those online are still a paper-based format and a linear read. What will happen to qualitative when the currently dominant format starts to crumble? What will happen when those who are now youngsters using all this new communication technology become qualitative researchers? I for one look forward to the tumult and the gnashing of teeth of those trying to protect newly old boundaries.

My fourth answer is that the university itself, where most qualitative researchers live, is less and less a stable social form. It is being impacted by multiple forces, like new forms of technological communication, that are destabilizing it. For example, Foucault said that social science research was an institutional form that emerges in a certain historical context and thus may disappear as that context changes. To me, we in the university are very conservative about such potential changes. I think we are far away from comprehending the long-term impact on the university and social science research of the technological innovations that have become common place in the social world. Large waves are building, and we are largely ignoring them, and these waves are going to change the university and the nature of the social sciences themselves. Again, I look forward to riding some of these large waves.

Conclusion

Since the 1980s, those of us who have been doing qualitative research have lived through an intense trajectory. We were roundly rejected; we fought back; we largely won. Some versions of qualitative research are commonly accepted across education and most of the social sciences, and many, many social science faculty do qualitative research and get promoted with such. This book is emblematic of all of this. It is not a fighting book. It is a book that is meant to raise the quality of the different approaches to qualitative research and the reviewing of those approaches, which, based on my experience as the QSE editor, is badly needed. We are tending to a garden we were able to create and develop. We are trying to make it a better garden.

Nonetheless, I would suggest that we should have some concerns. First, we have a few people who have become experts in particular qualitative methods, but most do not follow them or follow them well. Hopefully, this book will help address this problem. Second, unfortunately, most qualitative research manuscripts submitted to the better journals are poorly done (the same is true of quantitative-based manuscripts), which means we have some serious quality problems in our university-based training. For example, at QSE we see many manuscripts done by professors of all ranks that are not that good. Hopefully, this book can help with this, too. Third, most published qualitative research is plainly based on a naïve realist position, contra to all of the sophisticated discussions of epistemology and methodology, like that by those in this book. Who is going to engage in a more in-depth way the reasons for this? Fourth, when are we going to seriously engage the techno-logical revolution of the internet and all of these new communication devices and media? No matter how slow or conservative we are, it is coming. Fifth, what about the university and social science knowledge? Will these continue to have the same social meaning and relevance they have had in the recent past? Probably not. They will likely morph into some new directions and forms.

In the meantime, we do have this book and its effort to raise the quality of qualitative research and, more specifically, the quality of the reviewing of qualitative research. At this moment in our history together, these are important. I recommend you read it, increase your expertise with specific epistemologies and qualitative methodologies, and subsequently do and publish better qualitative research. However, at the same time, we need to look beyond this book. We need to look at the future of qualitative research, of the universities that sponsor such research, and of the nature of the social sciences themselves. If you think the next thirty years of qualitative research will be like the past thirty years or even the past ten years, the odds are you will be wrong. In the end, though, I personally love doing qualitative research, and I hope you do, too. Further, I hope we all use this book to improve our qualitative work.

1

Introduction

Audrey A. Trainor and Elizabeth Graue

The room is packed—surprising for a session scheduled first thing in the morning. Audience members are jockeying for seats and the panel is chatting as they figure out the order of presentations. At 8:15 a.m. on the dot the chair of the session welcomes the group.[1]

Dr. Intro: I'd like to welcome you all to what I think will be a very exciting session today. As the title indicates, the topic is Quality in Qualitative Research. The crowd that has gathered today is an indication of the broad interest in this topic and I'm looking forward to a stimulating conversation. It was arranged by the head of the qualitative interest group as a way to publicly talk through an idea presented to the board last year—that we develop a reviewer's guide for qualitative research. We've gathered together a group of thinkers representing varied perspectives on qualitative research and posed the question of whether developing this kind of guide will enrich our work or constrain it. Why don't we begin with Dr. Lovett?

Dr. Lovett: I love the idea of this text. I teach a course on reading social science research, and having a text that could walk students through the processes of judging the quality of the research would be invaluable. Also I edit a journal, and some of our reviewers are not from social science fields, but they are reading and reviewing social science papers, and I think some of them would be very pleased to have a good resource to help guide them through the process. I also frequently chair dissertation studies and would love to have a resource that could help students understand and evaluate the work that they are reading; I think it would help make them more critical and selective. In short, I'm pretty much whom you'd think of to buy, and recommend, this book.

Prof. Subjective: I think successfully accomplishing this task may be more challenging than you think. By its very nature, qualitative approaches to research are varied, flexible, critical, and innovative. The idea that one might reduce each sub-discipline to a series of checklists would likely offend the very individuals for whom the book is meant to provide support. In contrast, should the book encourage "non-qualitative" reviewers to "let go" and embrace the variety within approaches, the potential consumers of the book will likely be disappointed.

Dr. Lovett: The key will be to think about what reviewers would need to know about qualitative research to make informed decisions about a study's quality. I worry that authors most likely will write methods chapters for researchers rather than informational chapters for reviewers.

Prof. Careful: I agree—the audience is paramount. My confusion is whether the book will be read as a "how to" manual for novice researchers or a guide for reviewers. *My sense is that it would be difficult to create an outstanding guide for reviewers that would also serve as an outstanding teaching guide—while the content overlaps the orientation to the text and reader would probably be different so as to serve its different purposes. A text that would guide reviewers would provide examples of how terminology might be used differently in different designs for the purpose of helping them make a decision as to appropriateness, rather than to elicit a critical discussion, which a teaching oriented text might do. Because a good book to guide reviewers is lacking and there are plenty of introductory texts on qualitative research, I would encourage the editors to keep the review orientation in the forefront when providing guidelines to chapter authors.*

Prof. Intro: Thanks—so far it seems that we're hearing that there is a need for this resource, with the caveat that doing it well will be difficult. I'd love to hear more from you Dr. Subjective.

Dr. Subjective: I may be the lone voice of dissent but I am not sure that this is a project that is doable. *Qualitative research ultimately reflects a subjectivist/subjective relationship to knowledge. Those unwilling to embrace qualitative research do so given a lack of trust and respect for the subjective nature of the approach, a decision that ultimately precedes one's respectful consideration of rigor and method. In short, qualitative research is less published because some reviewers do not trust it. I doubt a volume that argues for the flexibility of design would provide reviewers with any more trust in the approach. Similarly, a volume that reduces qualitative methodologies to a prescriptive set of structures would not be well aligned with the principles of the approach.*

Dr. Who are We?: I understand Dr. Subjective's position—does that mean we have intersubjective agreement? (laughter) *I think the success of a project like this will depend on the degree to which you keep the focus on evaluating quality within methods, under different theoretical and philosophical orientations.* Here's my concern—when do you call something methods, methodologies, or theoretical frameworks? I know that this sounds like a simple intro to qual methods question, but it has important implications for the organization and conceptualization of this kind of book. So if I brainstorm a list of chapters, I end up with a muddled mess. Some are methodologies (action research, case study, mixed methods), some are theoretical perspectives (critical theory, phenomenology), and some are methods (GT, DA, etc). Unlike a handbook for quantitative methods, qualitative researchers do not share a single epistemology—*ontological and epistemological views have major implications for assessing "quality." Any approach (focusing on analysis methods, methodologies, or even theoretical perspectives) becomes problematic because the number of possible epistemological/ methodological combinations (constructivist study with interviews and narrative analysis, constructivist study with visuals and semiotic analysis, etc.) is almost endless. I am not sure how to address, discuss, or illustrate this type of variance and diversity. I also wonder what enough detail is for this type of audience—how much nuances are needed and/or helpful.*

Prof. Intro: This is a classic problem—and one that is in dispute if you compare discussions across methodology texts. What are your thoughts on what should be included in such a text? What organizational structure will support the key ideas?

Dr. Who are We?: There are so many ways to cut the chapters—by methods, by various design elements rather than methods, around the more commonly used orientations and focus on how quality would be defined for different types of activities of different types of studies.

Prof. Careful: How you define the structure is all bound up with what you want it to be and with whom you would like to talk. *The main issue is developing a structure that speaks to qualitative researchers who are writing the chapters but also helps readers unfamiliar with the terrain navigate the vast amount of terms that each tradition brings with it.*

Dr. Subjective: If the goal is to support qualitative researchers in gaining access to research support from a new set of organizations, it seems to me that a more important contribution would be in the form of a book that helps qualitative researchers understand the language and values of these organizations. Rather than asking these institutions to change for us, perhaps it would be easier if we figured out how to communicate our findings to them in a way that they would view as more applicable. Translational research is something that is very "hot" in the large, scientific funding circles. Qualitative research in many forms seems very well suited to the demands and language of this paradigm. Wouldn't it make more sense to think about how qualitative researchers may frame their work in the language of a translational researchers, rather than trying to get NIH to change the way it thinks about the value of "performance" research?

Prof. Intro: So it seems that we are back to the question of meaning—how qualitative—what are the goals for this project, what ends are we working toward, and what are the appropriate means we'd use to get there. We've heard a variety of ideas this morning and it looks like the audience is ready to weigh in on the topic. Let's open things up for questions and comments . . .

Embarking on Unchartered Waters

When we first came together to discuss the possibility of a reviewer's guide, we thought such an endeavor would be a challenge, but we perhaps misjudged the extent to which other qualitative researchers would react, either with a healthy dose of skepticism or with enthusiasm, to the idea. But, really, how should we have known? Methods books sometimes include criteria for quality, and over the years, experts have provided the field with discussions about criteria (see, for example, Brantlinger et al., 2005; Caelli et al., 2003; Lincoln & Guba, 1986; Lincoln, 1995; Morrow, 2005). Yet no similar volume directed toward the art of reviewing exists as a thumbnail for comparison in the field of qualitative methods. In retrospect, of course, the absence of such should have been our first clue that the project would spark lively feedback from enthusiasts and skeptics alike.

The introductory script, constructed from our reflections and excerpts of the six reviews of the proposal for this volume, illustrates the divergent nature of the range of expert reviewers' opinions, matched by the intensity of the sentiments behind them. Obviously, albeit with tentative footing, we were able to advance our belief that such a volume could contribute to the field, and we present the culmination of the collective efforts of the editors, authors, and the reviewers herein.

The Promises and Perils of Consensus

The image of the big tent is rich. It may conjure up a sweaty crowd of diehard believers who frenetically shout a common response to a leader's call, or it may invoke the obedient who mechanistically follow unspoken rules and policed compliance. Similarly, the image may call to mind a blissful gathering of devotees who unquestioningly accept a philosopher's dogma. On the other hand, the big tent might represent common ground for political allies, a meeting place for friends and constituents, or a stage for fanfare, bragging, and showmanship. We follow Denzin (2008) and expand Tracy's (2010) subsequent use of the metaphor of the big tent as a place to house dialog across paradigms as we consider quality. We are interested in both the perils and the potentials of the big tent as pertains to coherence and divergence around quality, peer reviewing, and qualitative research dissemination. In this volume, we aim to avoid the perils of narrowly defined checklists of quality and what counts as educational research. Toward this end we strive to promote a discussion of quality that avoids mechanistic application of such checklists for the sake of purity, instead focusing on the value of the research endeavor. We aim to highlight the potential of qualitative research to innovatively and creatively address the most enduring challenges and questions in the social sciences.

Quality, as it has been conceptualized in the broad field of qualitative research, is neither easy to articulate nor commonly defined among researchers who engage a variety of methods and methodologies. The breadth of qualitative epistemological, ontological, and methodological approaches is a strength in that such diversity allows for creative and innovative strategies for addressing persistent problems in the social sciences (Lather, 2006). Nevertheless, the diverse philosophies and methodologies that inform researchers' qualitative research decisions share a common ancestry. Across methods, shared concerns about quality focus on validity, sample selection, participant and researcher relationships and positions, and the ecological frame of qualitative projects.

Coming to shared understandings about quality, as we argue, is important to redress the narrow conceptualizations of quality, evidence, and validity currently privileged in research (Chatterjui, 2008; Freeman et al., 2007). Additionally, we agree with Morrow (2005) that broad quality indicators (e.g., congruency between question and method, and ethical consideration of participants) span quantitative and qualitative methods and that any discussion of quality must be decipherable to all researchers. We also assert, however, that it is the work of qualitative researchers to define quality across internal epistemological, ontological, and methodological approaches from within the field rather than from a prescribed set of axioms that govern quantitative designs. Lincoln (1995) underscored this point in her discussion of "relational" indicators of quality that are outside of the realm of more "traditional inquiry, which posits a detached observer's distance" (p. 278). Articulating shared conceptualizations of quality, we believe, has the potential to initiate dialog among researchers who see themselves as insiders and experts, as well as researchers who see themselves as guests in the field, asked to review journal submissions and grant proposals for their expertise in content, but strangers to the logic of the methods and methodologies under scrutiny. Having a tent under which to gather, then, allows us to locate our work and each other. Ceglowski and colleagues (2011) have highlighted a type of censorship that results when reviewers perpetuate a master narrative in research through the application of narrow definitions of quality criteria that do not align with the methodology and the underlying epistemology and ontology of the inquiry under review. We put forth this guide as a tool for supporting those who wish to participate in the review of qualitative research, not as a tool designed to cut or exclude from participation those who do not comply with some set of arbitrary and predetermined rules. That said, we have encouraged chapter authors throughout the editing process to make claims about quality but to do so in contextualized ways that allow room for reviewers to understand the breadth and scope of the lack of consensus with which the field of qualitative research grapples and, indeed, invites and enjoys.

Our Intentions for this Reviewers' Guide

It is impossible for all researchers to have expertise in, or in some cases even familiarity with, a wide span of methods. The appeal of the *Reviewer's Guide to Quantitative Methods* edited by Hancock and Mueller (2010) caught our attention as an excellent resource for seeking additional information when we were unsure of how to judge the merit of a study whose researchers employed an approach with which we were unfamiliar. Coming to the idea that such a publication might be useful for those reviewing qualitative methodologies was neither obvious nor swift. Quantitative research, though diverse, shares common set of assumptions, tools for inquiry, and goals. These shared beliefs and practices promote coherence and adherence to rules, with debate relegated to the most esoteric methods. Clearly, a volume addressing qualitative research and quality would take on a different form. We questioned, as our proposal reviewers also did later, whether such a volume could be useful and we set about building a rationale for this project. We concluded that devoting consistent attention to the foundational aspects of qualitative research would allow the identification of criteria for quality.

We have multiple purposes for this edited volume. First, we have attempted to create a space for a discussion of quality indicators in qualitative research. This goal is not born of a discomfort for flexibility, variation in application, critique, or innovation in research. In fact, we see these as defining characteristics of qualitative research, as those from which great potential emerges in the construction of transformative knowledge. We understand the reluctance to endorse our endeavor by some scholars (with whom we sometimes agree) that benchmarks or guides can be overly prescriptive or simplistic when applied routinely without contextualization. Caution is prudent; in our own fields within educational research, ongoing efforts to define quality indicators of rigorous research have been narrowly interpreted and applied to the exclusion of funding and dissemination of qualitative research that strays afield from a postpositivist epistemology and a realist ontology.

Interestingly, both the narrow definition of science and conceptualizations of accountability led us to this project. Like many of our colleagues, we were concerned that constricted notions about value and rigor of social science research constrained the potential of qualitative methodologies. Our interest was in identifying some criteria that would allow, expand, affirm, and confirm qualitative work that was ontologically and epistemologically interpretivist and constructivist, rather than postpositivistic. So, although this might be counterintuitive to the recent standards applications, our motivation was to devise criteria that would be sufficiently broad yet identify a core group of quality indicators.

Controversies surrounding the role that qualitative research, rich in variety and flexibility, plays in the construction of knowledge throughout the social sciences affect researchers' methodological decisions, and as importantly, affect reviewers' evaluations of these choices as they help to determine that which is disseminated in publications and conferences, or that which is funded for future study. Moreover, while these controversies have played out across the social sciences in journals and at conferences (e.g., in the field of education, see Denzin, 2008; Brantlinger, Klingner & Richardson, 2005; Eisenhart & Towne, 2003; Lather, 2004; or, in the field of nursing, see Morse, Barrett, Mayan, Olsen & Spiers, 2002, Sandelowski, 1993, Thorne, 1991; or, in the field of communications, see Chesebro & Borisoff, 2007), few texts and presentations address an important link in the chain of dissemination that is the role of the reviewer.

Minding this gap, we wanted to find common conceptualizations of quality that served to acknowledge the value of research methodologies that, unlike their quantitative analogs, were not uniform or circumscript by linear and predetermined rules. What are the criteria or quality indicators for qualitative research? How are these articulated during the review process? How are flexibility, variation, critique, and innovation considered across methods? We are certainly not the first to pose these questions, yet we believe it is important to move beyond a philosophical discussion of quality and aid in its implementation and interpretation. The absence of such markers or criteria position qualitative researchers and the contributions of their work precariously. Researchers who review and consume qualitative research may have important and difficult-to-answer questions about the design, approaches, and tools used for data collection and analysis, with few guidelines as to how to gauge the merit of the work.

Finally, we also wanted to create a space for a multidisciplinary discussion of qualitative research designs in the social sciences beyond our respective fields in education. Expanding the exploration of qualitative touchstones across disciplines, we believe, will bring an expanded sense of familiarity and consensus about the breadth and scope of qualitative designs, allowing us to apply different lenses and adjusting any myopia that might predominate within pockets of fields of visions in the social sciences.

Our Approach and Organization

To address our multiple purposes, we built in several mechanisms to prompt complexity and richness that defy the dogma associated with such criteria. One of the greatest assets of interpretivist and constructivist research designs is an orientation toward multiplicity in perspectives. This, of course, emerged as an immediate challenge in this project. Should we organize the identification of qualitative touchstones around big ideas that crisscross methodologies (e.g., validity and triangulation) or should we focus on the qualitative touchstones researchers typically associate with traditions or approaches? To honor complexity in the field, we decided to do both. In Chapter 2, readers will find Graue and Karabon's broad description of qualitative touchstones that build on foundational and insightful works by Lincoln (Lincoln, 1995), Denzin and Lincoln (Denzin & Lincoln, 2000), and Denzin and colleagues (Denzin, Lincoln & Giardina, 2006) and have provided theoretical direction. Our aim is to begin a provocative conversation about the practical implications of these concepts and ideas and their meanings in the context of reviewing and disseminating qualitative research.

The second chapter stands alone, however, in its breadth. All subsequent chapters, arranged alphabetically by methodological label or moniker, encompass methods-focused approaches. When we identified chapter content and authors we attempted to be as inclusive as possible. As we learned, though, authors with expertise often develop facility or preference for a subgroup of methods and may find it difficult to identify one set of criteria that would stretch across methods and methodologies—even those drawn together under umbrella or generic terminology. As examples, Bryant, who authored Chapter 8 on The Grounded Theory Method, and Rogers, author of Chapter 6 on Critical Discourse Analysis, both speak to the reader about the ways in which they narrow their approaches to mean a very specific set of methods, as indicated by capitalized letters. Both authors offer accompanying quality criteria rather than a loosely defined laundry list of criteria that can be applied to all studies that invoke the labels "grounded theory" or "discourse analysis." We chose not to include multiple chapters on these and other methodologies that have expansive usages in social science research. Instead, we encouraged chapter authors to explain the diversity of perspectives within their fields at key junctures in chapter, engaging the issue of quality in context. Along this same vein, we entrust readers with the task, albeit an intellectually enjoyable one, of reading author's positions recognizing that they sometimes speak from positions of authority for their methodologies (as Clandinin and Caine do in Chapter 12 on Narrative Inquiry) while at other times they speak to reviewers more directly (as Trainor does in Chapter 9 on Interview Research). In the former, criteria must be inferred, in the latter they are stated more directly.

The elasticity of qualitative methodologies fosters the very diversity of which we speak. Differing epistemological and ontological perspectives steer and are steered by researchers as they make decisions about methods. Two researchers simultaneously employing ethnographic methods on similar topics, for example, may, and commonly do, vary widely in their views of truth and of knowledge. Thus, each (re)presents divergent designs, interpretations, and implications of their work. The challenge for the chapter authors was to identify reviewing criteria that captured quality without excluding research by virtue of innovation, creativity, or researcher flexibility. We asked chapter authors to be explicit about their epistemological and ontological positions to underscore the importance of philosophical alignment in methodological decision making.

To accomplish these goals that seemed to, at times, make conflicting demands on chapter authors' attention to quality, we developed a chapter framework that fosters a complex discussion of quality and its controversies in qualitative research, multiple conceptualizations of quality, and explicitness in claims about value. Each chapter is framed around select terms, a discussion of methodological diversity, indicators of quality, additional resources, counter-perspectives, and author reflections on philosophy and positionality. We hope that this volume expands and complicates quality indicators while simultaneously providing reviewer guidance.

Identifying Vocabulary

The author-identified *Select Terms* across chapters not only demonstrates that there is a wide range of terms whose meanings and usages are centrally important to differing methods, but also that common terms may have shades of meaning or play differing roles of importance across discussions of methods. For example, Stoecker and Brydon-Miller (Chapter 3) define participation as a central term in action research, one that indicates full involvement of research participants as contributors to design, implementation, interpretation, and dissemination of research. While Kendall and Thangaraj (Chapter 7, Ethnography) also define participants as individuals who may share the responsibilities of research, they present a range of roles that researchers and participants may fulfill and they emphasize the distinctions between the two groups of people by defining them separately.

Acknowledging Diversity

A glance across the discussions of *Diversities in Perspective, Context, and Form* introduces another juncture for authors to acknowledge and illustrate to reviewers that quality indicators in qualitative research are not inflexible, and nor are they inscrutable. Here we asked authors to address issues of flexibility, variation, critique, and innovation that are integral to the qualitative endeavor of interest. This section serves to remind reviewers that no set of qualitative touchstones can be applied blindly or routinely. In Chapter 6, Rogers distinguishes Critical Discourse Analysis from other discourse analysis methods by contextualizing diverse perspectives about quality. Here she identifies a specific approach within a family of approaches and delineates how one approach within a constellation of methodologies coexists or relates to others in the same family. Reviewers who see this distinction may react happily if the paper they are reviewing matches the target of the chapter author's discussion, or unhappily if the paper is a member of the larger family of approaches, the latter case possibly requiring more inferences. In other examples, Bryant, who in Chapter 8 provides a historical perspective of The Grounded Theory Method, or Kendall and Thangaraj, who in Chapter 7 tether diversity to disciplinary roots across fields of ethnographic research, focus their lenses on diversity more broadly and further afield than reviewers might anticipate. Exploring yet another variegation Compton-Lilly (Chapter 5, Case Study) emphasizes ways in which epistemological differences lead experts to draw divergent conclusions about quality criteria within a fairly circumspect set of methods. Mertens (Chapter 10, Mixed Methods) also places import on epistemology, adding axiology, ontology, and methodology as ways to sort out diverse expectations about value and quality. We believe that reviewers will come away with a deeper knowledge of the breadth of qualitative approaches and the extent to which such diversity challenges reviewers to accept multiple approaches to identifying valuable research. This subsection, however, is not the focus of the chapters, merely a springboard from which authors frame existing divergent approaches and their underlying beliefs.

Selecting Criteria for Quality

For the aforementioned reasons, one of the greatest challenges for many of the contributors to this volume seemed to be to make declarative statements about quality. Many qualitative researchers do approach their work from an interpretive stance and are quite comfortable with thinking about quality indicators intuitively. To codify quality by suggesting a set of strictly applicable rules that can be routinely applied is neither our desire as editors, nor is it a priority for experts within the fields of qualitative research. At the same time, the identification of what we call *Qualitative Touchstones*, the foci of each chapter, are parameters for criteria for estimating, if not evaluating, the quality of qualitative research. As Clandinin and Caine (Chapter 12, Narrative Inquiry) and Kendall and Thangaraj (Chapter 7, Ethnography) assert in their respective subsections on qualitative touchstones, absolute claims about quality are simply not useful in methodologies that rely so heavily on relationships among people (i.e., researchers and participants) to jointly interpret and construct knowledge. As Stoecker and Brydon-Miller point out in Chapter 3 (Action Research), interpretation and relationships are not solely concerns of researchers who implement qualitative research projects; communities of participants and communities of consumers of research must also consider its value.

The internal framework of *Qualitative Touchstones* in many of the chapters generally follows the key stages of research design, implementation, and dissemination (e.g., sampling, data collection, analysis, and representation), but this was not suggested by us as editors. In fact, several authors avoid this common schema, demonstrating creativity as a characteristic of qualitative research. For example, Janesick (Chapter 11, Oral History, Life History, and Biography) extends the metaphor of dance as research, a comparison for which she is well known, to establish overarching qualitative touchstones such as "balance" that are not conceivably compartmentalized to any one stage of research. Such creativity may, we hope, defy facile application of a dichotomous good/bad list of quality indicators. We ask readers to embrace such variation and artistic interpretations by chapter authors, and to interpret for themselves what priorities for quality such discussions reveal about a particular method or methodology. As we and other chapter authors acknowledge throughout the volume, expanding researchers' and reviewers' notions of quality is in keeping with the flexibility within qualitative approaches, the variation across qualitative methods and methodologies, the opportunities for iteration and critique, and the innovative turns that constantly evolve qualitative application.

Throughout the discussion of the touchstones, chapter authors continue to remind reviewers of the range of approaches and their connections to and from axiology, ontology, epistemology, and methodology. Embedded in discussions of quality, chapter authors reach consensus on one key point: congruous ties between the philosophical threads underlie quality in representation in publications or other shared works. Moreover, as Stoecker and Brydon-Miller (Chapter 3, Action Research) astutely point out, this is not a unique feature of qualitative research. Mertens (Chapter 10, Mixed Methods) concurs and explicitly recommends that reviewers of mixed methods studies will likely need to consider postpositivist and constructivist quality criteria in tandem. In doing so, the chapters underscore that the estimation of quality in a field of inquiry with extensively divergent views should center on the harmony and compatibility of beliefs and actions relative to the research endeavor. Kendall and Tangaraj (Chapter 7, Ethnography), Rogers (Chapter 6, Critical Discourse Analysis), and most other authors identify or locate congruency as an agreement between the researcher and the design, implementation, and dissemination decisions and disclosures. Others in this volume point to another angle on congruency: that is, agreement between the reviewer's epistemology and ontology, in particular, and those (re)presented in the work under scrutiny. For example, see Trainor (Chapter 9, Interview Research), Bryant (Chapter 8, The Grounded Theory Method), and Stoecker and Brydon-Miller (Chapter 3, Action Research). In cases of incompatibility or discontinuity on this level, where a reviewer does not accept the researchers' truth claims or views of the nature of reality to the point that such a disparity makes a fair evaluation of a text impossible, reviewers are advised to decline the invitation to review.

Other claims about quality run through these multiple and many-faceted discussions of qualitative touchstones. One claim is that the evaluation of the relational aspects of qualitative research, and how researchers demonstrate reflexivity about relational and positional aspects of inquiry, is of primary concern in the evaluation of quality. Poulos (Chapter 4, Autoethnography) sketches out ways in which reflexivity is a linchpin quality indicator, without which other criteria dissipate. Kendall and Thangaraj (Chapter 7, Ethnography) and Janesick (Chapter 11, Oral History, Life History, and Biography) both focus on ways that researchers should demonstrate ethical treatment of participants as an indicator of quality.

The second claim is a consistent claim that the significance of findings or the "*so what?*" that often culminates in the results section of traditional scholarly papers is prioritized over the exact, detailed, or replicable justification for the tools used to design, implement, and analyze collected data. As Bryant says in Chapter 8, The Grounded Theory Method, the "value of the outcomes" rather than "methodological purity" is of utmost concern to many qualitative researchers.

The notion of purity is continuously problematized throughout the volume, In Poetics and Performance (Chapter 14), Prendergast and Belliveau explore arts-based criteria that link to methods-based qualitative touchstones and assert that reviewers who judge the quality of poetic and performative research must include aesthetic criteria. On the other hand, Stoecker and Brydon-Miller (Chapter 3) acknowledge that action research may be rigorous by some standards, but accomplish little action, thus failing to meet their expectations for quality.

Maintaining Open-endedness Criteria

Beyond the identification of qualitative touchstones, we asked chapter authors to explicitly acknowledge the relevance of diversity and perspective in three additional chapter subsections. First, in *Further Reading*, we wanted authors to include annotated references, highlighting key works that provide further guidance and multiple perspectives from the field. We wanted to increase reviewers' awareness of other views and approaches, and to provide information about related resources. In addition, as Bryant (Chapter 8, The Grounded Theory Method) explains, relative to divergent views in grounded theory approaches, citations that lump together incompatible source references may be a clue to reviewers that the author of the submitted paper, proposal, artifact, etc., may not grasp a sophisticated understanding of an approach or methodology.

Second, we asked authors to specifically identify scholarship that represented distinct perspectives than those represented in the chapter they authored. This section, usually addressed herein as an additional annotated reference, was one more way for authors to acknowledge the reality of manifold conceptualizations of quality characteristic of qualitative research. The purpose of the *Counterpoint Perspectives* subsection was to further extend or broaden the frame of the touchstones presented. There is variation in these sections across the chapters. Compton-Lilly (Chapter 5, Case Studies) introduces related methodologies such as single-subject research and Clandinin and Caine (Chapter 12, Narrative Inquiry) pair this section with further readings. As editors, we observed that this section introduced yet another challenge—qualifying assertions about qualitative touchstones by describing what they are not.

Finally, in the subsections entitled, *Author's Reflection on Quality*, we provided space for researchers to explicitly contextualize their perspective and provide relevant details regarding their trajectories that have contributed to their interpretive philosophy, tradition, and technique. Authors were asked to respond to this prompt: How does your presentation of qualitative touchstones in this chapter reflect your life and work as a scholar? For us, these sections were both informative and interesting. We were able to get a glimpse of how authors make sense of their understanding of quality and how they identify their personal philosophies and the journeys they have taken during their development as researchers.

How to Use this Guide

We have purposefully avoided creating a series of checklists to be routinely applied in an effort to calculate the overall value of a qualitative research. In our view, such a checklist is impossible to create without violating the fundamental and characteristic aspects of all qualitative methodologies: research for the purpose of producing knowledge is an interpretive and/or constructive act with the researcher soundly positioned at the center of such endeavors. We would argue that this is true of quantitative methods as well, but that is another story. For this volume, it has been our goal to provide touchstones, a word that implies a basis for quality criteria for qualitative research, and a forum for the discussion of tolerance of variability. Nor do we espouse our approach as legitimization of "anything goes."

Important to note is that these chapters are not intended to serve as "how to" discussions. Many authors note that some methodological discussions, such as deep discussions of epistemology or ontology, are beyond the scope of these chapters. Still, reviewers, upon reading the chapters in their entirety, should be able to associate touchstones with perspective and consensus within the context of qualitative social science research. As a group of authors, we have intentionally avoided lists of "must haves" or "deal breakers." Instead, we have attempted to provide a cogent and deep discussion about quality that will guide reviewers to make fair and critical analyses of research.

Note

1. We constructed this fictitious meeting by piecing together our initial conversations with each other and our colleagues, and weaving in the verbatim comments (indicated here in italics) from our proposal's blind review to illustrate the dissonance reflected in the field of qualitative research about the development of this reviewer's guide.

References

Brantlinger, E. A., Klingner, J. K., & Richardson, V. (2005). Importance of experimental as well as empirical qualitative studies in special education. *Mental Retardation, 43*(2), 92–119.

Caelli, K., Ray, L., & Mill, J. (2003). "Clear as mud": Toward greater clarity in generic qualitative research. *International Journal of Qualitative Methods, 2*(2), 1–9.

Ceglowski, D., Bacigalupa, C., & Peck, E. (2011). Aced out: Censorship of qualitative research in the age of "scientifically based research." *Qualitative Inquiry, 17*(8), 679–686. doi: 10.1177/1077800411415497.

Chatterjui, M. (2008). Synthesizing evidence from impact evaluations in education to inform action. *Educational Researcher, 37*(1), 23–26.

Chesebro, J. W. & Borisoff, D. J. (2007). What makes qualitative research qualitative? *Qualitative Research Reports in Communication, 8*(1), 3–14. doi: 10.1080/17459430701617846.

Denzin, N. K. (2008). The new paradigm dialogs and qualitative inquiry. *International Journal of Qualitative Studies in Education, 24*(4), 315–325. doi: 10.1080/09518390802136995.

Denzin, N. K. & Lincoln, Y. S. (Eds.). (2000). *Handbook of Qualitative Research (2nd ed.).* Thousand Oaks, CA: Sage.

Denzin, N. K., Lincoln, Y. S., & Giardina, M. D. (2006). Disciplining qualitative research. *International Journal of Qualitative Studies in Education, 19*(6), 769–782.

Eisenhart, M. & Towne, L. (2003). Contestation and change in national policy on "scientifically-based" education research. *Educational Researcher, 32*(7), 31–38.

Freeman, M., deMarrais, K., Preissle, J., Roulston, K., & St. Pierre, E. i. (2007). Standards of evidence in qualitative research: An incitement to discourse. *Educational Researcher, 36*(1), 25–32.

Lather, P. (2004). Scientific research in education: A critical perspective. *British Educational Research Journal, 30*(6), 760–773. doi: 10.1080/0141192042000279486.

Lather, P. (2006). Paradigm proliferation as a good thing to think with: Teaching research in education as a wild profusion. *International Journal of Qualitative Studies in Education, 19*(1), 35–57.

Lincoln, Y. S. (1995). Emerging criteria for quality in qualitative interpretive research. *Qualitative Inquiry, 1*(3), 275–289.

Lincoln, Y. S. & Guba, E. G. (1986). But is it rigorous? Trustworthiness and authenticity in naturalistic evaluation. *New Directions for Program Evaluation, 30*, 73–84.

Morrow, S. L. (2005). Quality and trustworthiness in qualitative research in counseling psychology. *Journal of Counseling Psychology, 52*(2), 250–260.

Morse, J. M., Barrett, M., Mayan, M., Olsen, K., & Spiers, J. (2002). Verification strategies for establishing reliability and validity in qualitative research. *International Journal of Qualitative Methods, 1*(2), 13–22.

Sandelowski, M. (1993). Rigor or rigor mortis: The problem of rigor in qualitative research revisited. *Advances in Nursing Science, 16*(2), 1–8.

Thorne, S. E. (1991). Methodological orthodoxy in qualitative nursing research: Analysis of the issues. *Qualitative Health Research, 1*(2), 178–199. doi: 10.1177/104973239100100203.

Tracy, S. J. (2010). Qualitative quality: Eight "big tent" qualitative criteria for excellent qualitative research. *Qualitative Inquiry, 16*(10), 837–851. doi: 10.1177/1077800410383121.

2

Standing at the Corner of Epistemology Ave, Theoretical Trail, Methodology Blvd, and Methods Street

The Intersections of Qualitative Research

Elizabeth Graue and Anne Karabon

> In a qualitative research class I teach I have had an assignment that asks students to do a visual representation of the landscape of qualitative research. I've seen an array of intriguing and innovative formats—a solar system, game boards, a script for a play. One project that has stuck with me across the years is a city map, divided into sections by epistemology. Superimposed on the sections are streets named by methodology and methods. Displayed in this way, you can see how research studies are multiply determined, simultaneously representing ways of knowing, ways of thinking about knowledge generation, and methods of generating data. It is this idea that animates this chapter.
>
> (Beth)

With qualitative research, judging quality is complex. It is not just a matter of checking that methods are appropriately implemented. Epistemology, or the theory of knowing, gets thrown in the mix. Elements of method are defined in relation to methodology but, more importantly, in the context of specific conceptions of how we come to know. For example, *a case* conceptualized within *case study* might be seen as a sample that represents the population or intrinsically interesting in its uniqueness (Stake, 1995). To spice things up even further, the theoretical framework used orients researchers in particular ways so that certain methods are preferred. All these things come together in design and, consequently, in quality judgments.

Just as the above assignment rendered a variety of products, how the information was known, how it was thought about, and how it was completed was dependent on the student's understanding. There was no single right way to display understanding, so assessment was based on the quality of demonstrating the interplay among the components of qualitative research.

The contingent nature of quality, which marks all elements of qualitative research, is the topic of this chapter. We will play with what we see as key concepts in reviewing across traditions, mapping their meaning within specific notions of knowing and doing.

Select Terms

Language both reflects and shapes knowing.

The language of qualitative research reflects its heritage, at times derivative of its quantitative neighbors and at other times explicitly speaking against its reality-making structures. Extending the geographic metaphor used in the beginning, the language and terms used in research could be seen as dialects shaped by location. Sometimes dialects are unique in a context of geographic isolation; other times they are mashups of languages like Creole. The terms we identify as relevant in this section reflect our travels in the land of qualitative inquiry.[1]

Various definitions of qualitative research:

By the term qualitative research we mean any kind of research that produces findings not arrived at by means of statistical procedures or other means of quantification.

(Strauss & Corbin, 1990, p. 17)

[Qualitative research] seeks to understand phenomena via induction; to emphasize process, values, context, and interpretation in the construction of meaning and concepts; and to report in narrative form.

(Goodwin & Goodwin, 1996, p. 19)

Qualitative Research is open and supple, and one of its strengths is that it incorporates philosophies, theories, and research designs and methods as diverse as postpositivist multimethods approaches and postmodernist social critiques.

(Freeman et al., 2007, p. 25)

Qualitative researchers stress the socially constructed nature of reality, the intimate relationship between the researcher and what is studied, and the situational constraints that shape inquiry.

(Denzin & Lincoln, 2000, p. 10)

What is qualitative research? The answer to this seemingly simple question often depends on who, when, how, and why you ask. We agree with Denzin & Lincoln, who state that depending on the social science employing it, that it is surrounded by "a complex, interconnected family of terms, concepts, and assumptions" (2005, p. 2). Qualitative research represents efforts to describe, sometimes, scientifically, other times artistically; to understand, sometimes inductively, sometimes deductively; and always to challenge, by looking closely at something and learning through particularity.

Considering the complexity and difficulty in defining qualitative research in itself, we will explore some of the key terms that serve as coordinates as we map qualitative research.

At every point in our research—in our observing, our interpreting, our reporting, and everything else we do as researchers—we inject a host of assumptions. These are assumptions about human knowledge and assumptions about realities encountered in our human world. Such assumptions shape for us the meaning of research questions, the purposiveness of research methodologies, and the interpretability of research findings.

(Crotty, 1998, p. 17)

Epistemology: As qualitative research is about understanding, a key element is *epistemology*, formally known as a theory of knowledge. Issues of epistemology deal with the basic question of *how we know*. Is knowing merely recording a stable existing reality, is it negotiated through interaction, or is it located within discourses? Epistemology describes *how we know*. Depending on the cartographer, the terrain of epistemology has different coordinates. As an example, we will use those provided by Michael Crotty: objectivism, constructionism, and subjectivism.

- *Objectivism* is the view that truth and meaning reside in entities that are independent of consciousness and experience (Crotty, 1998). Objects have meaning outside of human interactions or cultural impacts (Kamberelis & Dimitriadis, 2005). In an objectivist world, a chair is a chair due to its inherent chairiness. For objectivists, observations must reflect the stable characteristics of a thing—they are more or less a measurement of the object's appearance.

- *Constructionsim* refers to the construction of knowledge through active interaction with environments, emphasizing the purposeful production of knowledge. The pursuit of truth is not the goal. Rather constructionists interpret the meanings created through social life. It is emergent and less specific in direction at onset yet moves to seek a naturalistic or personalized orientation.
- *Subjectivism* holds that meaning is imposed by a subject independent of the object (Crotty, 1998). From this perspective, reality is made and does not exist outside of that making. Individual, personal experience is the source of factual knowledge and understanding of the world. All knowledge is personal knowledge and reflects beliefs and experiences that vary from person to person.

Theoretical framework is a lens or way of looking at something. Theoretical frameworks are a way to explain, bringing together assumptions about a particular topic and showing how they are enacted in practice. Theoretical frameworks are ways of thinking, evolved in particular locations that allow shared understandings. Theoretical frameworks, as sensemaking tools, shape the types of methodologies and methods used in research. They are used as foundations to make sense of the methodology and guide the action of the research through a set of beliefs or paradigms (Creswell, 2007; Lincoln & Guba, 2000). Theoretical frameworks are *how we think* in research. Common theoretical frameworks that are discussed in qualitative research include postpositivism, Marxism, postmodernism, feminism, critical theory, and poststructuralism.

Methodology is often referred to as an "approach" and is the context of specific conceptions of how we come to know. It is the description and action plan that researchers create when designing their work. It is the justification for choosing certain methods. Methodologies should not restrict the research, but should rather frame and guide the work (Hammersley, 1992). Methodology is more than tools—it is the shared meanings *around using* the methods. Methodology is *how we do research*, a unifying conception of all aspects of inquiry. Commonly employed methodologies include phenomonology, ethnography, and action research. This book is organized around diverse methodologies.

Method is the well-defined procedures used to generate[2] and analyze data (Crotty, 1998). This is the action of the research, the *how*, in data collection and examination. Methods are the *what we do* in research; the action of the research project. The type(s) of methods chosen for research are generally based on participants, location, and time. Deep consideration is also given to the three previously defined components that structure *how* data are generated and later *how* the data are analyzed and represented. The methods are universal in the composition of practice yet are different when employed in a particular paradigm (Denzin & Lincoln, 2000). Types of qualitative methods include interviews, observations, surveys, open coding, document collection, or focus groups.

Diversities in Perspective, Context, and Form

Qualitative research is characterized by its diversity on just about every dimension you might consider. This diversity is so pronounced that some people have argued that qualitative is not a very clear descriptor (Kamberelis & Dimitriadis, 2005). It is ironic that researchers who work to understand categories and meanings seem so ill at ease with defining their practice. In fact, we often worry that all that holds the qualitative community together is its notion of being nonquantitative. In this section, we explore the variance in qualitative methodologies, working to understand how the notion of intersections serves to support more complex understanding of qualitative research.

When an editor of a journal assigns a reviewer to a manuscript, there is typically a type of matchmaking on perceived expertise. What constitutes expertise? This is where the diversity of qualitative research is most keenly felt and most distinctly different from quantitative research.

Lest we think that the current political context is unique in its wariness of qualitative research, it would be good to realize that this is the second time that the value of qualitative research has been questioned, especially in education. Twenty-five years ago, one of the major journals in education research, *American Educational Research Journal*, contained a statement from an editor "it is meant to signify to the discipline that manuscripts based on qualitative research are being welcomed by AERJ editors" (Smith, 1987, p. 173). Smith took as her task identifying, for skeptical researchers, the community that uses qualitative methods and suggesting criteria for reviewing. She labeled this a daunting task:

> The body of work labeled qualitative is richly variegated and its theories of methods diverse to the point of disorderliness. Qualitative research is vexed by the problem of different labels . . . the field has grown out of diverse disciplines (anthropology, sociology, psychology). Qualitative research is further divided by different views of the nature of reality (whether there is a world of social objects and forces separate from the observer's perception of them), of object fields judged to be appropriate for study (from whole institutions or communities to brief encounters), of beliefs about the merits of different research methods and ways of representing findings, and of criteria of judging studies. These divisions have created socially bounded territories, acrimonious exchanges among adherents, and institutionalized schools of thought.
>
> (p. 173)

It is with recognition that qualitative research is definitely a multidimensional entity that has multiple sources and histories and that it evolves to respond to diverse purposes that we look at the issues of perspectives, context, and forms.

Perspectives

How we know, epistemology, and how we look, theoretical frameworks, shape what counts as data, design, analysis, and presentation. As a result, the elements that are least likely to be discussed in a manuscript are also the ones that are most likely to have strong effects on judging quality. Let us look at an example. A researcher is interested in looking at the kindergarten readiness. That general topic will not tell you much about what a good study would look like. How that topic is translated into a research question is *through* both epistemology and theoretical frameworks. One researcher might decide to look at whether the age of kindergarten entry shapes success in school. Another researcher might choose to explore how communities have different conceptions of kindergarten readiness. Furthermore a third might examine the discourses about readiness that circulate in a district's curriculum and assessment materials and the perspectives of the kindergarten teachers. All researchers are studying readiness and they could be doing the work in the same school but the assumptions that they use to design their work, the data they collect, and the way they present their findings could be completely different. Judging the quality of the work is even more complex if you take into account the way that the researcher conceptualizes the notion of readiness. Depending on the theoretical framework used, readiness might be viewed through a lens of risk and resilience, social constructionism, or feminism. As a result, the methodology and methods used shift depending on the perspective taken on the topic.

Context

The context of interest might be thought of as how the research question and study are staged. What is in the foreground? What is in the background? How much context is needed to understand the meaning of a particular issue? Using the example of readiness, whether the design would need to consider local history, demographic characteristics, or power is dependent on the theoretical framework employed. Do we think of context as something to be controlled across cases or is it seen as something that constitutes the case? In looking at readiness, one project could make the age of the student the major focus while another might look at socioeconomic status and attendant cultural practices as key, and the third could examine how the portrayal of the ready child serves to normalize who is ready for kindergarten. What we are arguing is that context situates knowing in particular ways and must be considered in evaluations of quality. Reviewers must consider how the level of context or the amount of surrounding detail supplied in a manuscript informs an author's argument. The assertions are bounded by the context.

Form

The form of a research report can be taken as given, addressing issues agreed upon by professional groups. For example, APA format outlines the parts of a manuscript as: Title, Abstract, Introduction, Method, Results, Discussion, References, and Appendices. Each element has an agreed-upon form and authors learn what goes into each component. This approach to writing makes it clear what the researcher did and what happened as a result. The scientifically derived results are what should shine in this type of manuscript as it is the most important outcome of the study. All aspects of the report are presumed to represent directly data collected by the author.

In contrast, other forms of writing can be used to communicate research results. Starting with the interpretive turn in anthropology (Rabinow & Sullivan, 1979), researchers have used narrative forms created in the literary community to represent issues, experiences, and ideas that are too complex for a traditional research text. For example, Beth uses fictionalized vignettes (Erickson, 1986; Graue & Walsh, 1998) in her work to present ideas that she might not have observed directly but that represent issues that have been recounted by participants or that can stand for ideas derived from other data sources. The vignette in the Introduction is an example of this approach, using reviewer feedback on the prospectus submitted to Routledge. Others have used drama (e.g., Saldana, 2003), poetry, and performance (e.g., Predergast & Belliveau, this volume) to represent the knowledge generated in research.

Decisions about form are related to epistemological perspectives that underlie the work. For those who choose what might be seen as alternative forms (using standard APA form as mainstream), it is the form itself that provides another dimension to analysis. In writing vignettes or poetry, the researcher–author may come to understand nuances in the analysis unavailable before. Further, readers are thought to be actively engaged by these texts in ways that promote deeper recognition of the ideas presented in the manuscript and personal interpretation of what is being suggested.

Qualitative Touchstones

Alignment is a critical element in judging the quality of research and all of our touchstones speak about alignment of different elements. This focus on alignment is founded on the value placed on coherence. For some this might be seen as a modernist fixation—there are probably worse things than being modernist.

1. All elements of the research process should be aligned so that the assumptions and ways of knowing are compatible

Problems of misalignment are probably the most common issues seen with novice researchers. For example, someone might say that she is doing a feminist narrative study of what causes girls to drop out of advanced science courses in high school. Further she argues that she is doing this study from a subjectivist perspective. The data will involve analysis of lab books from advanced biology, chemistry, and physics courses. Do all of these things go together? Not so well. While feminism is a reasonable theoretical framework for a study related to gender equity issues, the focus on cause would be very unlikely from a subjectivist position. Further, relegating data collection to analysis of lab books is not well designed for narrative as it locates participants as subjects without interaction with the researchers.

It should probably be a given that alignment involves the appropriate use of any element. Defining what is appropriate is a key task of both the author and the reviewer. In the previous example, one of the issues is with the methodology narrative. The lack of attention to the storied lives of participants makes narrative a poor tool for this study. Analysis of lab books could be done in other research types.

2. Authors clearly label relevant traditions

Reviewing should not be a guessing game. Given the combinations and permutations of epistemology, theoretical framework, methodology, and methods possible in qualitative research, researchers should specifically name the tools used in their work to allow readers to assess their alignment. Reviewers should find enough description of each research element to assess their specific combination in a study. That said, we find that authors rarely explicitly label epistemology as it is much like asking a fish to describe water—epistemology is such an all-encompassing element that it remains tacit rather than explicit. For this reason, we do not expect to see information about epistemology in a research text. We do, however, look for markers of epistemology, like theoretical framework or methodology cohere implicitly. In the readiness example given earlier, if an author says she studied how different communities viewed readiness for kindergarten, a reviewer could infer that this is not an objectivist study. This inference would be sensible particularly if the work entailed case studies of how teachers and families constructed local meanings of readiness.

A reviewer and/or reader of qualitative research considers, as a complete package, these markers used in the designing, collecting, analyzing, and the presenting of the work. The audience considers how these separate pieces contribute to not only the production of the research but also the interplay between them as they cohere to create a final piece. Given the complexity of potential combinations of epistemology, theoretical framework, methodology, and method, reviewers' and authors' perspectives rarely match 100 percent so it is important for authors to position work in relation to relevant pieces from their methodological field.

3. The criteria for quality must be aligned with the researcher's practices

In the scholarly game of rocks, paper, scissors, who wins when conflicts ensue between researcher and reviewer around epistemology or theoretical frameworks? Taking the rule of alignment as primary in decision making, the reviewer should judge a piece of research from within the researcher's frame of reference rather than her own. Weighing quality as a reviewer should be less of a critique of the research in general and more of a critique of the alignment of theoretical framework and methodology, the author's representation and the generalizability of the data and the contributions the topic has to a particular field. Much easier said than done! This is often like a political argument. Reviewers should understand their own viewpoints while being able to listen to and evaluate the opposing perspective based on the quality of support provided.

4. The written form chosen for communicating research should align with other elements

Writing is too often an afterthought, something taken for granted after the important work has occurred in the field and at the desk (Kuntz, 2010). From this perspective, writing is a given, with standard forms and unquestionable constructions. We would suggest that writing, instead, is a step in the chain of inquiry that exemplifies the authors' assumptions and practices (Richardson, 1990). For example, the *APA Manual 2001*, which guides much of the writing in social science, has the following advice for writers:

> You can achieve clear communication which is the prime objective of scientific reporting, by presenting ideas in an orderly manner and by expressing yourself smoothly and precisely. By developing ideas clearly and logically and leading readers smoothly from thought to thought, you make the task of reading an agreeable one.
>
> (p. 31)

Who could disagree with this? Well, it is something that is contested on the basis of epistemology. The idea of clear communication, order, smoothness, and precision implies a unitary realism that is characteristic of objectivism. It ignores the value that variation, disruption, and ambiguity can have for increasing understanding. Many readers would prefer not to be led by the author but want to have a more active role as they read research, just as one uses a map as a guide yet has their own experiences on their journey.

In thinking about alignment of written form, reviewers should recognize that reading research is a dialogic act, one that involves both the reader and the text. Understanding is created in the interaction. This is not to say that anything goes—bad writing does not help a reader understand the world or herself. Is bad writing like pornography—we know it when we see it? We would prefer a different metaphor, one that does not infer potentially illegal acts. The style of writing used is epistemologically contingent—related to ideas about how we come to know. Ultimately, the written form should enable new ways of knowing. It is in part an aesthetic judgment that is made through the interaction of the text and the reader.

5. Reviewers are thoughtful about how standards constrain knowledge and how they support its generation in new contexts

In many ways we see this touchstone as the coordinate that closes the circle in this discussion. When an author is smarting from a tough review, awareness of the social construction of standards and the degree to which they police knowledge generation can be a soothing balm. It can also be a cheap excuse for not carefully considering the advice of a colleague. The key is to be reflexive about how author and reviewer choices are socially arbitrary but real, representing assumptions about how the world works and how knowledge is generated in the academy. Standards are held by communities because individuals and groups agree to them through professional socialization. Sometimes the standards are designed to *standardize* actions like writing and reading so that the content is easy to process. Other times the standards result in maintaining the status relationships in a community. In revolutionary situations, the only way to change thinking is to change the agreed-upon social rules that guide interaction (Kuhn, 1962). In research, this was the itch that qualitative research scratched, opening up new types of questions with new methods of inquiry (Denzin & Lincoln, 1994).

This is all to say that reviewers of qualitative research could do well to take up the practices that prompted so many of us to go into the field: to listen and read carefully the author's perspective in a written account of research. Telling a different story, in a different format, asking different questions, using different expectations are not necessarily aberrant. They can, instead, be exactly what is needed to bring to light new experiences, new practices, and new meanings. Avoiding confirmatory near-sightedness, standards should support the reader to walk through the door to experience something new rather than reflect only the practices of the reviewer.

Further Reading

Bryman, A. (1984). The debate about quantitative and qualitative research: A question of method or epistemology? *British Journal of Sociology*, 35(1), 75–92. Retrieved from www.jstor.org/stable/10.2307/590553.
Outlines the debates about the similarities and differences between qualitative and quantitative research, with a focus on philosophical foundations. Points to the clustering of arguments around epistemological and technical issues and the confusion between the two. Argues that there is not a 1:1 relationship between methodology and technique in qualitative research.

Crotty, M. (1998). *Social Foundations of Qualitative Research*. Thousand Oaks, CA: Sage Publications.
In this text, Crotty provides a framework of methodologies intended to be used by both research students and already practicing researchers. A brief overview of the four elements (epistemology, theoretical framework, methodologies, and methods) leads to a description of the structure of qualitative research. He offers an abbreviated history on each methodology to provide a starting point for novice or curious social researchers.

Graue, M. E. (1998). Writing as context. In M. E. Graue & D. J. Walsh (Eds.), *Studying Children in Context*. Thousand Oaks, CA: Sage Publications.
Part of a book on studying children, this chapter takes writing as an active part of the research project. It follows this process through data analysis presented earlier in the book and illustrates different approaches to representation.

Guba, E. G. & Lincoln, Y. S. (1994). Competing paradigms in qualitative research. In N. K. Denzin & Y. S. Lincoln (Eds.), *Handbook of Qualitative Research* (Vol. 2, pp. 163–194). Thousand Oaks, CA: Sage Publications.
A chapter that appeared in the first volume of the handbook, Guba and Lincoln describe and contrast four paradigms in relation to ontology, epistemology, and methodology: positivism, postpositivism, critical theory and other ideological perspectives, and constructionism. They critique a focus on quantification and define the notion of paradigm.

Schwandt, T. A. (2000). Three epistemological stances for qualitative inquiry: Interpretivism, hermeneutics, and social constructionism. In N. K. Denzin & Y. S. Lincoln (Eds.), *Handbook of Qualitative Research*. Thousand Oaks, CA: Sage Publications.
Published in the second handbook, Schwandt parses the terrain of qualitative research by epistemology, which he defines as interpretivism, hermeneutics, and social construction. This analysis provides the reader with a sense of the philosophical underpinnings of each perspective, its history, and implications for inquiry.

Counterpoint Perspectives

At this point in the chapter, we are seeing the whole argument as counterpoints. There is one point that is worth exploring in more depth here. The suggestion that coherence is a vital aspect of quality is in conversation with two distinctly different ideas in qualitative research. The first addresses the idea that we can/cannot mix qualitative and quantitative methods or elements from different epistemological perspectives. Strict constructionists argue that we cannot mix perspectives as they are epistemologically conflicted. That would imply an incoherent design and, as a result, incoherent research (see Mertens, this volume).

The second comes at the issue of coherence from a different perspective. For those who value epistemological conflict, the disequilibrium produced when perspectives are mixed prompts new ways of knowing (Crotty, 1998). The hybrid of these seemingly different ways of knowing come together to add complexity in how individuals and groups experience and make sense of the world. Instead of polarizing qualitative and quantitative approaches, researchers should make decisions on what elements come together cohesively to best fit a research question (Ercikan & Roth, 2006). It is a jolt of the new that shakes up assumptions that allows the reader a fresh look at the world.

Author's Reflections on Quality

[C]ertain voices are being kept out of the conversation, especially voices that traditionally have been marginalized in and by the field of educational research. The peer review process often functions as a gatekeeper, weeding out groups that have yet to learn or refuse to conform to prevailing assumptions about what makes research "high quality," as well as groups that critique the mainstream—or, more precisely, that indirectly critique the perspectives and practices of the reviewer.

(Kumashiro, 2005, p. 285)

As we toiled over this chapter, the general idea for its form and message was sketchy at best, and we did the only thing we could do—we wrote to understand. It was not until we were reminded of the piece quoted above that we realized what we meant the chapter to be. It is our attempt to wrestle with a topic that moves notions of quality in qualitative research beyond the merely technical and to highlight its conflicted nature. Its multidimensional history, values, practices, and purposes make every value judgment contingent on multiple entities and parties. It is this piece that makes the map metaphor so helpful. Furthermore in this virtual age, the mapping cannot be simply two-dimensional—we might be able to position things with a GPS—or we will have to wait until technology develops sufficiently to represent the complexity of qualitative research.

Using a mapping system guides one in an unfamiliar location to a final destination, sometimes known and other times it may be different once traveling begins. Authors of qualitative research must utilize the classical elements of each individual component and intermix them to create a path toward the final destination. The reviewer's job is to determine whether or not the path was the best choice, not always the most direct and whether the intersection where the paths meet is an intentionally sound place.

But the contingent nature of qualitative research is not what draws us to this work. Instead, it is the chance, often remote, to bring experiences that might otherwise be ignored to the attention of those who have the power to change things.

Research communities are gated communities, and so are their playgrounds. Although the community is slowly being integrated, the reliance on particular rules in judging scholarship and, therefore, scholars, limits who can play. The drive to open the research community is based on the recognition that as a social practice, research reflects the values and characteristics of its social actors and, therefore, the power relations in which they are embedded.

(Graue, 2006, p. 37)

Reviewers should always consider the cost–benefit ratio between standards of research quality and potential for new knowledge. Standards should not be used to keep authors out of the research discourse. Instead, standards should be used to support diverse forms of communication among diverse scholars. Rather than asking "What will be lost if this piece of work is published?" we have taken to asking "What will be lost if this piece is NOT published?" Approaching every manuscript looking for its assets and writing reviews from the perspectives of strengths makes reviewing a pedagogical rather than punitive activity.

Notes

1. We recognize the limits of using this map metaphor. Our recognition is an example of our belief that language both reflects and shapes knowing. In using this metaphor, we intend to assist the reader in making sense of the components of qualitative research.
2. How one thinks about data is shaped by epistemology. For objectivists, researchers collect data. For constructionists and subjectivists, data are generated.

References

American Psychological Association. (2001). *Publication Manual of the American Psychological Association (5th ed.).* Washington, DC: American Psychological Association.

Bryman, A. (1984). The debate about quantitative and qualitative research: A question of method or epistemology? *British Journal of Sociology, 35*(1), 75–92. Retrieved from www.jstor.org/stable/10.2307/590553.

Creswell, J. W. (2007). *Qualitative Inquiry and Research Design: Choosing five approaches (2nd ed.).* Thousand Oaks, CA: SAGE.

Crotty, M. (1998). *The Foundations of Social Research: Meaning and perspective in the research process.* Thousand Oaks, CA: SAGE.

Denzin, N. K. & Lincoln, Y. S. (1994). *Handbook of Qualitative Research (2nd ed.).* Thousand Oaks, CA: SAGE.

Denzin, N. K. & Lincoln, Y. S. (2000). *The Sage Handbook of Qualitative Research (5th ed.).* Thousand Oaks, CA: SAGE.

Ercikan, K. & Roth, W. M. (2006). What good is polarizing research into qualitative and quantitative? *Educational Researcher, 35*(5), 14–23.

Erickson, F. (1986). Qualitative methods on research on teaching. In M. Wittrock (Ed.), *Handbook of Research on Teaching* (3rd ed., pp. 119–161). Washington, DC: American Educational Research Association.

Freeman, M., deMarrais, K., Preissle, J., Roulston, K., & St. Pierre, E. (2007). Standards of evidence in qualitative research: An incitement to discourse. *Educational Researcher, 36*(1), 25–32.

Hammersley, M. (1992). *What's Wrong with Ethnography?: Methodological exploration.* New York: Routledge.

Goodwin, W. L. & Goodwin, L. D. (1996). *Understanding Quantitative and Qualitative Research in Early Childhood Education.* New York: Teachers College Press.

Graue, B. (2006). The transformative power of reviewing. *Educational Researcher, 35*(9), 36–41.

Graue, M. E. & Grant, C. (2002). Questions, calls and conversations for researchers in teacher education. *Journal of Teacher Education, 53*(3), 268–272.

Graue, M. E. & Walsh, D. J. (1998). *Studying Children in Context.* Thousand Oaks, CA: SAGE.

Guba, E. G. & Lincoln, Y. S. (1994). Competing paradigms in qualitative research. In N. K. Denzin & Y. S. Lincoln (Eds.), *Handbook of Qualitative Research* (Vol. 2, pp. 163–194). Thousand Oaks, CA: SAGE.

Kamberelis, G. & Dimitriadis, G. (2005). *Qualitative Inquiry: Approaches to language and literacy research.* New York: Teachers College Press.

Kuhn, T. (1962). *The Structure of Scientific Revolutions.* Chicago: University of Chicago Press.

Kumashiro, K. K. (2005). Peer-review process for journal-article publication. *Harvard Educational Review, 75*(3), 257–286.

Kuntz, A. M. (2010). Representing representation. *International Journal of Qualitative Studies in Education, 23*(4), 423–433.

Lincoln, Y. S. & Guba, E. G. (2000). Paradigmatic controversies, contradictions, and emerging influences. In N. K. Denzin & Y. S. Lincoln (Eds.), *Handbook of Qualitative Research* (2nd ed., pp. 163–188). Thousand Oaks, CA: SAGE.

Rabinow, P. & Sullivan, W. (1979). The interpretive turn: Emergence of an approach. In P. Rabinow & W. Sullivan (Eds.), *Interpretive Social Science* (pp. 1–21). Los Angeles, CA: University of California Press.

Richardson, L. (1990). *Writing Strategies: Reaching diverse audiences.* Thousand Oaks, CA: SAGE.

Saldaña, J. (2003). Dramatizing data: A primer. *Qualitative Inquiry, 9*(2), 218–236. doi:10.1177/1077800402250932.

Schwandt, T. A. (2000). Three epistemological stances for qualitative inquiry: Interpretivism, hermeneutics, and social constructionism. In N. K. Denzin & Y. S. Lincoln (Eds.), *Handbook of Qualitative Research.* Thousand Oaks, CA: SAGE.

Smith, M. (1987). Publishing qualitative research. *American Educational Research Journal, 24*(2), 173. Sage Publications. Retrieved from http://aer.sagepub.com/content/24/2/173.full.pdf.

Stake, R. (1995). *The Art of Case Study Research.* Thousand Oaks, CA: SAGE.

Strauss, A. & Corbin, J. (1990). *Basics of Qualitative Research: Grounded theory procedures and techniques.* Newbury Park, CA: SAGE.

3
Action Research

Randy Stoecker and Mary Brydon-Miller

Action research is just one term that describes the collaboration of professional researchers with groups or organizations attempting to understand or produce change in a real-life context. Other terms used to describe the same form of research are community-based research (Strand et al., 2003), community-based participatory research (Israel, Eng, Schulz, & Parker, 2005; Minkler & Wallerstein, 2003), participatory research (Gaventa, 1988; Park, Brydon-Miller, Hall, & Jackson, 1993; Tandon, 2008), participatory action research (Fals-Borda & Rahman, 1991), classroom-based or educational action research, practitioner inquiry (Cochran-Smith & Lytle, 2009; Noffke & Somekh, 2009), arts-based action research (Brydon-Miller, Antal, Friedman, & Gayá Wicks, 2011), appreciative inquiry (Cooperrider, Whitney, & Stavros, 2003; Ludema & Fry, 2008; Reed, 2007), and feminist action research (Brydon-Miller, Maguire, & McIntyre, 2004; Maguire, 1987; Reid & Frisby, 2008).

Action research is often associated with applied research. What distinguishes the two, however, is that applied research can still be done solely by researchers acting in isolation from the people who will use the results or be impacted by them. In contrast, action research engages those people as much as possible at every stage of the research process. So, while action research is not a specifically qualitative method (indeed, it is not a method at all, but a methodological framework within which various quantitative and qualitative methods can be used), it follows a qualitative logic. That is, the research is conducted in relationship between the researcher and the people of a community, group, or organization focused on some real-life issue that the research will be used to address. Even when a survey or other more quantitative instrument is being used in action research, the design, implementation, and analysis are done collaboratively. Qualitative touchstones, then, focus more on the broader processes of research design, implementation, and application, than on a singular research method.

Select Terms

Participation refers to the process by which those people who will use or be impacted by the research are involved in its design and conduct. Following Arnstein's (1969) oft-cited ladder of citizen participation, we emphasize the full involvement of people in shaping the entire research process from selection of the research question through the use of research findings to bring about change, not token participation where people are limited to only agreeing with the researcher's agenda.

Action involves the integration of the research with an explicit action agenda throughout the process. The action agenda arizes from a community problem or concern that a group wants to solve, and incorporates the desire to use the research process itself to build relationships. In any event, the research is designed from the start with a specific purpose in mind of how the results of the work will be used by the group or organization. The role that the researcher will play and the ways in which the researcher will use the results are also included in the discussion with the group or organization from the start of the process.

Community or constituency is an important concept in action research, since so much of it occurs in various community contexts. We emphasize communities of place in the sense that they constitute a unit of action. Neighborhoods are the quintessential community of place, but even identity communities (such as a gay or lesbian community) that span neighborhoods are often still connected in community action across that larger space. A group whose members have shared experiences or face similar challenges, such as people receiving welfare payments, may not be organized into a community but could be, and these groups may be more appropriately termed a constituency. In some cases, the term stakeholder is used when there is no intention of organizing constituency members into longer term action. Stakeholders might also represent different perspectives or interests and may reflect different levels of power in relation to the issues that need to be taken into consideration in conducting the action research project.

Community covenantal ethics provides a new framework for understanding the ethical foundations for action research. Distinct from strict Christian definitions of the term, in action research covenantal ethics refers to research practices based on an understanding of "the unconditional responsibility and the ethical demand to act in the best interest of our fellow human beings" (Hilsen, 2006, p. 28) and guided by "the acknowledgement of human interdependency, the cogeneration of knowledge, and the development of fairer power relations" (Brydon-Miller, 2009, p. 247).

Epistemology is the study of what knowledge is and how we come to acquire it. The epistemology underlying action research emphasizes how knowledge is acquired in relationship, mutual inter-subjectivity, and through action to create change. This is in direct contrast to positivist epistemology, which sees relationship and intersubjectivity as the primary contaminants of knowledge.

Methodology is the study of specific methods, which also involves the creation of frameworks to guide the implementation of specific research methods. In this sense, action research is most accurately described as a methodology, since it guides the use of a wide variety of quantitative and qualitative research methods from surveys to focus groups and beyond.

Method is a specific data collection procedure such as an interview, a survey, a document analysis, or others. All methods are implemented through a methodology that is informed by or reflects an epistemology.

Diversities in Perspective, Context, and Form

Action research and its associated practices have diverse origins. In the United States, the term action research itself is most often associated with social psychologist Kurt Lewin (1946; 1948). In Lewin's approach, the action researcher was very much in control of the research design and implementation processes. Lewin was heavily involved in workplace management studies, and action research came to represent a conservative, less participatory approach when associated with his legacy (Stoecker, 2003). However, more recently, the term action research has been associated with highly participatory approaches (Stringer, 1999). The term participatory research, in contrast, reflects Rajesh Tandon's (2008) work with the Society for Participatory Research in Asia (PRIA), which is highly collaborative and based in a more system-critical perspective. John Gaventa's work, particularly during his time with the Highlander Research and Education Center, is also associated with both the term and the perspective (Park, Brydon-Miller, Hall, & Jackson, 1993). On the other hand, William Foote Whyte's (1990) work, for which he used the label participatory action research, much more resembled Lewin's more conservative practice. Moreover in public health, the increasingly popular term community-based participatory research is used for everything from clinician-directed interventions to community-controlled change processes (Community–Campus Partnerships for Health, 2007; Sullivan et al., 2001). Overall, we see the practice trending toward more constituency participation, but there is also continuing diffusion of related practices that use the language of participation without granting constituency members real control over the research process.

We will define action research as a methodology whose methods are created, carried out, and applied in collaboration with the community or constituency that the research concerns; and that is designed to support an action agenda drawn up by that community or constituency. This definition tends toward those practices that have their origins more in the global south, such as that done by Rajesh Tandon (2008) or Paulo Freire (1974).

In addition to this more community-focused approach to action research are forms of first-person action research (Chandler & Torbert, 2003), classroom-based action research (Noffke & Somekh, 2009), and practitioner inquiry (Cochran-Smith & Lytle, 2009) that often focus on providing individual practitioners with strategies for critically examining and improving their own practice. These forms of inquiry can be very powerful tools for critical self-reflection and the development of more effective professional practices. Moreover while they are generally less participatory in nature, there is often a strong collaborative component among practitioners working together and supporting one another's efforts to improve practice. As we will discuss below, practices such as translational research, increasingly popular in medical fields but lacking a participation component, or knowledge transfer, popular in Extension circles but again lacking a participation component, are even further from our preferred definition.

It is important to understand that, as a *methodology*, forms of action research diverge around much more than participation and action. They also diverge around methods. Action research can include anything from carefully controlled "objective" quantitative measurements of pollutants and epidemiological statistics (Merrifield, 1993), on the one hand, to collections of indigenous systems of knowledge (Kildea, Barclay, Wardaguga, & Dawumal, 2009), on the other. The methods of action research are eclectic, determined by the issue or problem the research is attempting to address and the skills and resources of the participants.

A couple of examples can illustrate the diversity of research methods used in action research projects. In a recent project with Community Shares of Wisconsin (CSW), Catherine Willis and Randy Stoecker designed a research project with the staff and board of CSW to better understand the fundraising impacts of their unique bloc recruitment strategy. CSW is similar to the United Way in that it raises funds through workplace giving campaigns. However, CSW is governed by its member organizations—primarily social action groups—rather than a board of elites and focuses on social change. Furthermore instead of adding a new group or two each year, they add a large number of groups (one to two dozen) every six or so years. They wanted to know how this "bloc recruitment" strategy impacted workplace fundraising and their member groups. So over a period of months the researchers and CSW representatives met to develop a multimethod research design that included surveys of donors, interviews with member organization representatives, interviews with workplace campaign coordinators, and a sophisticated statistical analysis of all the donations coming into CSW across more than a decade. CSW has been using the research results in organizing their workplace campaigns and orienting new member organizations (Willis, Anders, & Stoecker, 2011).

In another example, Dadit Hidayat and Randy Stoecker worked with The Natural Step Monona (TNSM), a sustainability organization in the village of Monona, Wisconsin. Here again, the researchers met with TNSM over a period of months to develop a community survey that would both inform Monona residents of TNSM's activities and also learn about resident attitudes toward sustainable living. The researchers engaged a capstone class of 12 students in working with a group of 14 residents to distribute surveys to nearly 3,100 households door to door that they could fill out on the Internet or on paper. The results of the survey were then presented at a community event attended by about 50 residents who developed ideas for community action. TNSM is now planning a campaign around water preservation and conservation as a result of the research (Stoecker, 2011).

Many action research methods were initially developed by individual researchers or teams in response to local demands that have later been more widely adopted by researchers for use in other contexts. For example, photovoice, the use of photography and text created by community participants to explore specific issues often with a view toward influencing public policy, was first developed by Caroline Wang in her work on the health concerns of women in rural China (1999; Wang & Burris, 1994; Wang, Burris, & Xiang, 1996). This method has since been used in work with Guatemalan community health workers (Lykes, 2001; McIntyre & Lykes, 2004); in classrooms (Meyer et al., 2004); and in a variety of other settings and has been adapted to electronic media in the form of digital storytelling (Frey & Cross, 2011). In addition to photography, a variety of arts-based action research methods have been developed that involve the use of music (Flicker et al., 2008), puppetry and textile arts (Clover, 2011), and participatory theater (Boal, 1985; Guhatakurta, 2008, Tofteng & Husted, 2011). In each case, the method was developed to encourage broader participation and engagement by community participants and to generate new forms of knowledge and understanding through the arts.

The qualitative epistemology of action research has produced other methods that are mostly specific to the methodology, in addition to the broader frameworks such as photovoice noted above. One such method is collaborative interviewing, where role distinctions between interviewer and interviewee are intermingled as interviewees actually influence and guide their own interviews (El-Dinary et al., 1994; Laslett & Rapoport, 1975). Another is respondent validation or member checking, where the researcher asks the individuals who provided raw data, usually in the form of interviews, to review and authorize the use of that data in the research (Bloor, 1978; Bradshaw, 2001; Bryman, n.d; Buchbinder, 2011).

What makes an action research methodology qualitative is its epistemological underpinnings. In contrast to positivist epistemologies grounded in the principle that knowledge is best obtained through minimizing the relationship between the researcher and the researched, action research is based on the conviction that knowledge is best obtained through relationship. The positivist administering a quantitative survey, for example, would make sure that the research "subject" knew as little as possible about the person administering the survey, based on the assumption that the greatest barrier to getting accurate data is personal feelings. The action researcher, in contrast, would usually work as hard as possible to build relationships with those people answering the survey, based on the assumption that the greatest barrier to getting accurate information is trust. Furthermore, indeed, a lack of trust in the research relationship can produce inaccurate or incomplete data (Oakley, 1981). In most cases, the action researcher would have developed the survey itself collaboratively with the constituency members to assure that it reflected the interests and issues facing the community partners in the research. Accuracy is only part of the issue, however. As important to action researchers is the ethical demand that knowledge creation is a democratic process and that the results of the process be available to participants to promote positive social change (Brydon-Miller, 2009).

Building upon this notion of the ethics and action research, and attached to this qualitative epistemology is a set of ethical guidelines antithetical to a quantitative epistemology. Community covenantal ethics offers a set of principles that go far beyond the Belmont Report's (The National Commission for the Protection of Human Subjects of Biomedical and Behavioral Research, 1978) limited moral scope, which focused on the conventional research ethics triad of autonomy, beneficence, and justice. In practice, these involve respecting the subjects' right to retain control over their involvement in research, designing research to minimize risks to subjects, and not selecting subjects just because they can be easily coerced or conned into taking part in the study. To these principles community covenantal ethics adds a set of relational standards for research to meet. As noted earlier, these include "the acknowledgement of human interdependency, the cogeneration of knowledge, and the development of fairer power relations" (Brydon-Miller, 2009, p. 247; see also Hilsen, 2006). Applying such principles in action research requires a relationship between the researcher and the researched that ultimately breaks down the distinction between the two and engages them together in a collaborative project (Brydon-Miller, 2008). Such principles are anathema in the context of the supposed "gold standard" randomized trial world of positivism in which the existence of such relationships is most often viewed as a form of contamination rather than as a positive and important contribution to the research process.

Action research has not received a serious hearing by the still positivist-dominated social sciences, leading to it and its practitioners more often being dismissed than carefully critiqued. Critiques of the methodology have mostly arisen among practitioners in the field. Such critiques have focused on the questions of participation and action that are the two supposed hallmarks of the methodology. Some research has shown that much of the practice done in the name of action research (or the other labels) is neither very participatory nor well integrated with action (Stoecker, 2009), and that neither participation nor outcomes are systematically documented and established (Viswanathan et al., 2004). Some have also questioned the use of some methods specific to action research, such as respondent validation—a process in which research subjects have a chance to critique the researcher's work as part of the research process. Critics question whether asking people who occupy positions of economic or political power to review research could lead to censorship (Bradshaw, 2001). This willingness to engage in internal question and critique allows action researchers to challenge their own assumptions and practices, thereby improving practice.

Qualitative Touchstones

The quality criteria that are most relevant in reviewing manuscripts using an action research methodology involve both theory and practice, as well as both process and outcomes. The leading journal in the field, *Action Research* (2008), identifies seven specific criteria for reviewers assessing submissions. We use these standards as a foundation for our touchstones, along with criteria regarding research ethics that we add to this list:

1. Articulation of objectives

The clear articulation of objectives is a criterion common to all forms of research, but in an action research project the objectives reflect not only the researcher's goals, but also the specific community or organization concerns the research is designed to address and the local outcomes they have identified related to these issues. The success of the research is determined in part by its effectiveness in responding to these more practical change initiatives. Reviewers might consider whether the description of research objectives reflects both the stated goals of the community partners regarding the issues they have identified as important in achieving positive change and the researcher's interest in creating meaningful new understandings of the issues to contribute to future research and practice.

One question that is frequently raised by researchers new to action research relates to the question of responsibility and ownership of the research objectives. Is it legitimate, they ask, for me to have a question in mind or a topic I would like to investigate together with my community partners? Action research is in most cases collaboration between academic researchers and community partners (we say in most cases because in some cases communities conduct their own research without the support of academic partners). For the process to be successful, both parties must have the opportunity to contribute to the process of crafting the research questions to be addressed and to articulating specific objectives for the research. So it is quite appropriate for the academic researchers to approach community partners with a general sense of the direction they would like to investigate together. However, they must also be prepared to change direction or to adjust their expectations if their community partners identify a different set of priorities. Telling the story of the process in a publication involves documenting these changes in direction.

As one example, there is currently a great deal of concern regarding the issue of childhood obesity and the related health issue of increased rates of Type II diabetes among children and youth. But while this is certainly a serious issue, when community-based participatory researchers (Burklow & Mills, 2009) at Harmony Garden—a girls' health and wellness program focusing on low-income neighborhoods in Cincinnati, Ohio—asked community residents what they believed to be the major health issues facing girls in their community, they listed violence, teenage pregnancy, and sexually transmitted diseases as the most critical concerns. Responding to this input from the community, the researchers at the organization shifted their focus to address these issues. At the same time, the knowledge and expertise of the researchers regarding the potential health impact of childhood obesity also became a part of the general conversation among the community participants, and together with antiviolence programs they initiated a neighborhood walking program designed to increase physical activity among residents. This negotiation of objectives is a common aspect of action research and should be reflected in the manuscript.

2. Partnership and participation

Action research, even when it employs quantitative methods, shares with most forms of qualitative research a focus on process and relationships that distinguishes this methodology from more conventional forms of quantitative research. Action research goes beyond simply acknowledging the importance of relationships between researchers and research participants to consider the quality of relationships among all of the participants in the process and the impact that the research has on the broader community. Another aspect of action research that distinguishes it from other approaches is its attention to power and privilege in the research process and relationships. Given these foci, an assessment of the extent and nature of the relationships between the researcher and the community, and among research participants, is an important consideration for reviewers. Researchers should be prepared to provide a detailed description of the ways in which these relationships have been created and sustained. A discussion of the breadth of participation is an important component of this description. Who has participated in the research? How did the researcher identify, recruit, train, and engage these communities and individual participants? What mechanisms did the researcher put in place to allow full participation by these community members?

Thus, the discussion of who participates in the research, and how, is quite different than it is in other forms of research. Genuine partnership demands that participants are respected for the knowledge and expertise they bring to the process and that they are afforded decision-making authority to guide the research. Issues of power within communities and among various stakeholder groups are also important concerns. The language of stakeholder engagement is sometimes used to mask internal hierarchies that privilege some members of the community over others. An example here is Campbell's (2003) description of attempts to involve a broad range of community participants in the development of HIV/AIDS prevention programs in South Africa. In an attempt to address the problem, researchers and health officials brought together local officials, trade union representatives, international funders, and members of local grassroots organizations including sex workers. But, as Campbell notes in her analysis of the process, "again and again, the Summertown experience highlighted the way in which the deceptive neutrality of the term 'stakeholder' may serve to mask very real differences in the power that different local interest groups had to influence the course of the Project" (p. 181).

Acknowledging power dynamics within communities, and between communities and researchers, in open dialog with participants and developing strategies to ensure that all participants have the opportunity to contribute their knowledge and expertise to a project is a critical component of action research. Recent efforts to create local community advisory boards empowered to determine whether or not researchers will be allowed to conduct studies in local communities emphasize the importance of community sovereignty and have been an important development in the effort to balance power between academic researchers and local communities. Action researchers need to carefully discuss the power dynamics in the research setting and how they affected participation and the overall research process, including the involvement of community members in various forms of co-authorship (Greenwood, Brydon-Miller, & Shafer, 2006). In evaluating the success of authors' efforts to effectively reflect these complex dynamics, reviewers should assess the extent to which all participants in the process have contributed to the research and how their voices are reflected in the final document. Where the goals of full participation are not fully achieved, researchers should provide an explanation of how local circumstances have affected the process of participation.

3. Contribution to action research theory/practice

As noted above, action research is designed to meet two sets of objectives. The first is to address local concerns and to create positive change in communities. But at the same time, if the work is to be meaningful as a form of research, it must be effective in helping other communities to deepen their understanding of similar issues and develop their own strategies for dealing with them. This demands that the knowledge generated through the action research process be communicated in a clear and comprehensible manner to other researchers and other communities. While positivist standards for generalizing research focus on an ability to replicate findings exactly, action research emphasizes the transferability of knowledge based on the ways in which other researchers and other communities might adapt and apply the methods and the resulting knowledge to their own situations.

It is also important that action research contributes to a deeper understanding of theory as well as informing practice. Action researchers draw on a variety of theoretical frameworks including feminist, postcolonial, Critical Race Theory, critical theory, and critical pedagogy. In addition to articulating a clear theoretical stance, authors should discuss how their work and the results of their research relate to their theoretical framework and speak to the current literature in the field. The tendency to overlook the importance of articulating a theoretical position and relating the work to theory is a frequent shortcoming of action research manuscripts and something reviewers might encourage authors to pay greater attention to in writing their work up for publication in academic journals.

4. Methods and process

The process of carrying out action research is a learning opportunity for both participants and readers of action research, so a full accounting of how the project was conducted is an important component of an action research manuscript. Action researchers should develop a focused, concise description of the research process where they describe specific methods and link them to the broader action research literature. At the same time, this is not simply a "how-I-spent-my-summer-vacation" style research narrative. Given the collaborative nature of most forms of action research, there may in fact be multiple stories reflecting inconsistent experiences and interpretations of the participants.

The aim is not necessarily to resolve these discrepancies but rather to explore their origins and to demonstrate how the tensions that do exist might be used in a positive and productive manner to further the aims of the project. Reviewers should assess the extent to which these different interpretations are represented, understanding that there may be conflicting points of view.

Telling the whole story, providing a strong theoretical framework, and seeking to explore the significance of the work also means avoiding the tendency found in many fields to engage in "salami research" in which the emphasis is on submitting work based upon the "least publishable unit"—a strategy for increasing the researcher's overall number of publications by offering only the minimum amount of data that will still be considered publishable by reviewers without attention to providing a fully realized description of the research process. An action research project may be composed of a number of research projects and multiple action strategies that cannot be easily or usefully sliced up. Action research accounts may, as a result, be somewhat longer than average research manuscripts. So rather than focus on an arbitrary word count requirement, reviewers might seek to determine whether the length-to-contribution ratio is reasonable.

Similarly to many forms of qualitative research, some issues that are considered critical in discussions of quantitative research are not automatically relevant in action research. While sample size clearly influences the extent to which the results of specific quantitative methods are useful in an overall action research project, the appropriate number of participants in that larger action research process is determined more by the nature of the issues themselves and the identification of those individuals most likely to be interested in participating in the process. Action research is not based on a hypothesis testing model so it is not appropriate for researchers to state a null and alternative hypothesis. Rather, a clear problem statement and discussion of objectives, as outlined above, provides the reader with an understanding of the direction of the research.

The writing style of action research reflects the theory and method of the work. Manuscripts reporting the results of quantitative research are generally written in the third person, emphasizing the notion that such work is supposed to be objective and value-neutral (not that any form of research actually is). Action research, on the other hand, is explicitly engaged and its practitioners most often write in first person singular or plural, emphasizing the relationships and personal engagement that are the core of the research process.

As noted earlier, action research is a methodology and an ethical stance related to knowledge generation and dissemination that incorporates a variety of data collection methods that may be both qualitative and quantitative in nature. But, as noted earlier, action researchers have also developed a range of methods designed specifically for the unique characteristics of the action research context and process, many of which are highly interactive and engage participants in more creative and collaborative ways. Arts-based action research methods might include the use of photography (Wang, 1999), participatory theater, and other forms of visual and performance arts (Boal, 1985; Guhatakurta, 2008; Tofteng & Husted, 2011) so reviewers need to be open to what they might consider unorthodox methods. The important criteria here are the relationships developed between the researcher and the community, the nature of the knowledge generated, and the actionability of the research.

5. Actionability

Action research is predicated on the notion that we learn by doing—that to understand how change takes place you must take part in the process. While the ability to compare experimental and control groups is an important consideration in most forms of quantitative research, in action research the best way to judge the outcome is in terms of actionability. That is, the value of action research is determined by the extent to which the process has resulted in substantive change in a specific community, and the potential transferability of that knowledge to other settings and other researchers.

Thus, actionability is a central measure of action research. This is not to say that a useful action research article depends on the success of our efforts to achieve positive social change. As we all know, some of the most valuable learning experiences come from the challenges we confront and action researchers should not be afraid to acknowledge when things have gone wrong. The important point is to critically examine the process and to share these insights with other researchers in the hope of improving practice. This willingness to expose the problems encountered in the research process is a powerful tool in action research (Arieli, Friedman, & Agbaria, 2009; Boser, 2006; Stoecker, 1997). Such a level of self-reflection and self-critique is not always found in qualitative research, nor in quantitative research where the tendency is to report only statistically significant findings, even though as we all know, this biases our understanding and can lead to serious mistakes in determining the importance of the research and its implications for future studies.

Most important to the task of reporting on actionability is presenting the outcomes of the overall project. What changed as a result of the project, for individuals, groups, organizations, communities, and even larger entities? Why did changes occur? This information needs to be presented in enough detail, with particular attention to the context of the project, so that reviewers can assess the specific impacts of the research process on the participants and the community.

6. Reflexivity

The researcher's own knowledge and experience are important components of the action research process and the interpretation of the outcomes, so it is important that authors include a description of their own position vis-à-vis the community and the issues being examined. This often takes the form of a short reflexive description of the author's background and relationships with the community. In many cases the researcher's experience is very different from that of the community partners in terms of race, gender, income, education levels, and many other factors that contribute to greater power and privilege for the researcher. It is important that researchers remain mindful of these differences and not presume to understand the experience of those whose life stories differ radically from their own. This requires humility and open-mindedness, qualities that should be reflected in the way in which authors present the research process and outcomes.

Some forms of action research, including first-person action research, studies based on the teacher-as-researcher model, and other practitioner inquiry models, focus solely upon the researcher's own experience, in much the same way as autoethnography, but with an explicit intent to use this process to improve practice. In evaluating this type of research for possible publication the same questions of actionability and transferability of knowledge are important. To what extent has the author managed to use the process to improve practice and will readers be able to apply the knowledge generated through the process to improve their own practice or to better understand the nature of the issues under investigation?

7. Research ethics within an action research framework

Because action research is an explicitly political practice focused on creating positive social change, the ethical implications of the work are especially important and researchers should assess the ethics of the entire research process from the initial development of the research question and creation of community partnerships through the development of strategies to disseminate the results of the research and apply them toward addressing critical community concerns. Action research is based on a respect for the knowledge and experience of all participants, on the importance of democratic processes of decision making, and on "the pursuit of practical solutions to issues of pressing concern to people, and more generally the flourishing of individual persons and their communities" (Reason & Bradbury, 2008, p. 4). Authors should articulate how their work reflects these values and include a discussion of the ethical challenges they faced in conducting the research and how they worked with community partners to address these concerns. One particularly compelling example of this kind of ethical reflection is Lundy and McGovern's discussion of a process of community "truth-telling" and postconflict transition in the North of Ireland (2006). As these authors note, "delving into the personal and collective memories of a community that has experienced the traumatic impact of conflict over three decades raises acute questions over the potential costs and benefits that such sensitive research will bring in its wake" (p. 62). Their honest reflection on the challenges and real pain involved in the process for the community members with whom they worked underscores the idea that risk avoidance is often not the most ethical approach to conducting research that seeks to address social injustice and community problems.

8. Significance

The overall significance of an action research manuscript is a combination of these factors. Reviewers will want to take into consideration the audience for the publication and their background in reading action research. If the readership is largely unfamiliar with the theory and practice of a particular action research project, a more detailed discussion of the process might be appropriate. Otherwise, the most important criterion is that the manuscript provides a clear and well-documented description of the project and a balanced assessment of the outcomes achieved. Ideally, this means evaluating what community changes resulted from the project and how (Stoecker, 2005). The work should provide opportunities for the voices of participants to be heard and should reflect honestly on any challenges encountered in the process of carrying out the project. Admission and analysis of challenges, in contrast to the self-congratulatory rhetoric that is too common in most such papers, along with the presence of community voices, will be indicators of that honest reflection. Finally, the manuscript should capture the spirit and values that underlie action research, the curiosity, engagement, commitment, caring, and concern for genuine problem solving and practical impact that are the hallmarks of this form of research.

Further Reading

Action researchers represent a diverse set of disciplinary locations, organizational and community settings, and theoretical foundations. Our selection of recommendations for further reading is an attempt to reflect this diversity.

Coghlan, D. & Brannick, T. (2010). *Doing Action Research in Your Own Organization* (3rd ed.). Los Angeles, CA: SAGE Publications.
Focusing on the practice of insider action research, this concise, highly readable book provides a clear introduction for those interested in applying the principles of action research to improving practice within their own organizations. The step-by-step description of this form of action research is accompanied by a set of exercises designed to guide the reader through the process and provide a framework for evaluating their project, which includes a critical examination of the context of the work, the quality of relationships, the quality of the action research process, and the outcomes, reflecting the same criteria outlined above. As the authors note, "telling the story, making sense of it and applying a rigorous methodology to that sense making are directed toward the generation of useful knowledge which must produce outcomes which are of value to others" (p. 151).

Freire, P. (1974). *Education for Critical Consciousness*. New York: Continuum.
While not Freire's most famous book, this is perhaps the work that best elucidates the idea of conscientization—the process of integrating consciousness, knowledge, and action. It also contains the essay Extension or Communication that critiques knowledge transfer approaches to working with communities from the standpoint of the more empowering participatory approaches used by forms of action research like the popular education approach he popularized.

Greenwood, D. J. & Levin, M. (2006). *Introduction to Action Research: Social Research for Social Change*. Thousand Oaks, CA: SAGE Publications.

First published in 1998, this volume provides an especially helpful introduction to the history and practice of action research as a strategy for achieving positive social change. Drawing on their own work in Norway and Spain, along with examples from a variety of other action research traditions, the authors examine the underlying principles and values that inform the practice of action research and offer a thoughtful, critical analysis of the ways in which action research is practiced and taught.

Horton, M. & Freire, P. (1990). *We Make the Road by Walking: Conversations on Education and Social Change*. Philadelphia, PA: Temple University Press.

This book is based on a series of conversations between Myles Horton, one of the founders of the Highlander Research and Education Center in Tennessee, and Paulo Freire, the Brazilian educator, philosopher, and author of many important works including *Pedagogy of the Oppressed*. This book captures a thoughtful and warm conversation between two friends about the issues they both care most deeply about—education, democratic approaches to achieving positive change, and social justice.

Minkler, M. & Wallerstein, N. (Eds.) (2003). *Community-based Participatory Research for Health*. San Francisco, CA: Jossey-Bass.

and

Israel, B. A., Eng, E., Schulz, A. J., & Parker, E. A. (Eds.) (2005). *Methods in Community-based Participatory Research for Health*. San Francisco, CA: Jossey-Bass.

These two companion volumes provide a wonderful introduction to the theory, practice, and challenges of community-based participatory research, the form of action research most often associated with work in the area of community-based health promotion. The first volume focuses on defining the field and on presenting the range of issues and approaches created and adapted by researchers using this methodology while the second volume focuses more specifically on providing examples of the vast array of methods that might be used to conduct research related to improving health outcomes, addressing inequities in medical care, improving treatment, and creating more effective public policy related to health and wellness.

Noffke, S. & Somekh, B. (Eds.) (2009). *The SAGE Handbook of Educational Action Research*. Los Angeles, CA: SAGE Publications.

This edited volume draws together work in educational action research from a diverse set of contributors focusing on all aspects of theory and practice from professional development strategies to the broader political implications of the work. While the book incorporates a wide variety of perspectives on the practice of action research in schools and community-based educational settings, there is a common focus on understanding the political nature of education and its importance in furthering the development of democratic processes and our ability to work together to address pressing social issues.

Reason, P. & Bradbury, H. (Eds.) (2008). *The SAGE Handbook of Action Research: Participative Inquiry and Practice (2nd ed.)*. Los Angeles, CA: SAGE Publications.

This second edition includes forty-nine chapters covering the history and theoretical foundations of action research as well as discussions of the multiple practices which fall under the broad action research umbrella, exemplars of how action research is actually practiced, and descriptions of specific methods and skills that inform the practice of action research. This volume also represents the global nature of action research with a broad range of international contributors.

Stoecker, R. (2005). *Research Methods for Community Change: A Project-based Approach*. Thousand Oaks, CA: SAGE Publications.

Soon to be in a second edition, this book shows how research can serve community change processes through four steps. In the first stage, diagnostic research helps the community understand the causes and extent of a community issue. Prescriptive research then helps the community understand the strengths and weaknesses of alternative ways to address the issue. The third stage, implementation, involves the community actually putting their chosen alternative into practice, but may also involve research if the intervention is community theater or other media forms that require further community knowledge in its production. The final stage is evaluation to track the effects of the intervention.

Strand, K., Marullo, S., Cutforth, N., Stoecker, R., & Donohue, P. (2003). *Community-based Research and Higher Education: Principles and Practices.* San Francisco, CA: Jossey-Bass.

This book focuses on the practice of community-based research or CBR (similar to CBPR but more likely to involve students and used more commonly in the liberal arts disciplines) from a higher education perspective. The book reviews the methodological principles behind CBR, the pedagogical principles behind doing CBR with students, and the higher education administrative structures supporting CBR. It then explores practical ways of implementing those principles in communities and in classrooms.

Stringer, E. (1999). *Action Research (2nd ed.).* Thousand Oaks, CA: SAGE Publications.

Some of the best approaches to action research have been heavily influenced by indigenous communities. This book explores the lessons coming out of the author's experiences working with Aboriginal communities in Australia. Among its strengths are its attention to the power and relationship issues between researchers and communities and its sensitivity to the processes involved in managing those issues.

Counterpoint Perspectives

There are many practices out there that use the labels of action research, community-based research, community-based participatory research, or others. But a number of them do not practice either the principles of participation or action that we emphasize. One practice, heavily favored by university extension programs, is knowledge transfer. In knowledge transfer, researchers choose research problems designed around practical problems faced by practitioners, such as agricultural research addressing problems attributed to farmers. The researchers then conduct the study and give the practitioners solutions based on the researchers' knowledge and biases. This is in contrast to a process that emphasizes constituency participation from the very start in defining the problem and the characteristics of desired solutions, and developing the capacity in practitioners to integrate research and action (Freire, 1974; Ison & Russell, 2007). Translational research is a similar practice in medicine, where the practitioners of interest are physicians but the problems are medical issues faced by their patients and other members of the community. The common denominator, however, is that the research is designed and controlled by professional researchers and then given to practitioners to apply to a human population or to livestock or food crops (Woolf, 2008).

Authors' Reflections on Quality

We are two of the many academics who have come to the practice of action research through a search for meaning that we did not find in traditional academic research. We are, it is true, drawn to action research because of its qualitative logic, but for us that logic also challenges the empiricist and objectivist assumptions that underpin even most qualitative research. For us, it is not the richness of the data that is of the highest value, but the richness of the relationship and, ultimately, the dismantling of the researcher–researched dichotomy and the elimination of the colonizing practice of "othering" people that we value in action research. Perhaps we could even say that the relationships that form the foundation of action research are the fullest flowering of qualitative logic. Moreover outside of, and perhaps even opposed to, the qualitative logic of the research component of action research is the importance to us that the research be directly useful. Methodological fetishism asserts the value of one method over another regardless of context. Methodological pragmatism asserts the importance of designing the research to serve the project—in our case the social change project—whether at the organizational, community, societal, or even global level.

It is difficult to arrive at such a risky professional identity without worldview-shattering experiences. For Randy, those experiences began in graduate school. Interestingly enough, it was in the midst of taking a qualitative research methods course, where the assignment was to do an interview and submit the interview notes for a grade. I decided the assignment was a good excuse to interview someone from my local neighborhood organization so I could find out why most of the houses in my Minneapolis neighborhood were undergoing foundation to roof renovation. When I approached my interview subject, however, he called me on the carpet for being just another exploitive student, taking up his time and not giving anything back to the community. He made me promise to give him a copy of what I wrote. When I dutifully returned a couple of weeks later I was full of angst and asked the question that would forever alter my career: "Is there anything else I can do?" Tim Mungavan, then the community organizer/architect for the West Bank Project Area Committee, gave a wry smile and suggested I clean up a hallway that was blocked by boxes of "junk." Of course, he knew what I would actually find were boxes of documents that told the story of why all that housing was getting rehabbed. When I finished cleaning up that hallway, I had all my dissertation just the way I wanted it and an unbreakable relationship with the Cedar-Riverside neighborhood (Stoecker, 1994). That was in 1985. Last week I talked to Tim on the phone about helping to provide some content for their website. It's now 2011.

If I learned about the importance of participation in the research process from the people of Cedar-Riverside, I learned about the importance of action from the people of Toledo, Ohio. This time the role model was Dave Beckwith, a long-time community organizer. He actually attended my lecture when I interviewed for my first academic job at the University of Toledo, and asked the hardest questions. When I arrived as a new academic in the fall of 1988, he called me up barely two weeks into the semester and suggested we meet. When we sat down to lunch, he handed me a sheet of paper listing all the research projects that community-based groups in Toledo wanted done, demanding to know how many I could get started on right away. I thankfully negotiated him down to one project—an assessment of the local nonprofit neighborhood development organizations. It was horribly depressing research—few if any of the groups were accomplishing much at that time. But he turned those negative findings into a community event that built a new neighborhood-based development coalition and guided a subsequent action research project by me that the coalition used to bring two million dollars into the city to support those same organizations (Stoecker & Beckwith, 1992). Today you can drive the streets of those neighborhoods and see the many blocks of new and rehabbed housing built because of those funds.

Now for Mary's reflection. Although Randy and I have known each other for years, I was not familiar with his story of coming to action research and was struck by how similar it is to my own. I shouldn't be surprised. When Davydd Greenwood, Pat Maguire, and I put together the article "Why Action Research?" (2003) for the inaugural issue of the journal *Action Research* we queried all of the members of the editorial board to find out why they had chosen to become action researchers. For many of us this experience was similar to that of Bob Dick who said, "the research methods I knew well didn't fit my new situation. Either I found something else or I abandoned research altogether" (p. 13).

My own worldview-shattering moment also came in a graduate-school research methods class—in my case in a discussion of the use of deception in psychological research. While the professor and other students in the course seemed satisfied with the justification that deception was necessary because otherwise subjects would not tell the truth, I could simply not accept the idea that it was okay to lie to people. In exasperation I finally just said, "If you ask people questions that matter to them, they'll tell you the truth." I still believe that.

This came at about the same time that I was wrestling with the problem of finding a way to bring together my life as a scholar with my life as an activist—both absolutely essential components of how I understand not just my professional stance, but really fundamental aspects of my identity. I couldn't accept what I was being told by my advisors—that to be a scholar I must abandon my activism—that passion and commitment could not drive a quest for knowledge. Actionability and reflexivity—partnership and participation along with a contribution to theory and practice—the quality touchstones that define action research, also make possible this integration of academic rigor and a commitment to social justice. After more than twenty-five years, I honestly can't imagine working in any other way.

For us, then, the question of quality in relation to action research is quite complicated. First, quality needs to be determined in two contradictory contexts. What is quality in a community or organizational context may not be considered quality in a positivist-dominated academic context. What is important in a community context is whether the research supports the ability of local groups to develop power/knowledge (Foucault, 1980; 1975)—that is, to develop knowledge that can help them build their own power, and that can then produce new knowledge and further build their power, and so on—so they can engage in effective action. It is possible that, in such contexts, quick and dirty research may be as useful as highly sophisticated research with normed and verified measures following all the dictates of empiricist science. In addition, much action research consists of very basic research that tells stories or counts occurrences that groups can use to inform action, rather than data collections that purport to resolve esoteric disputes that are popular with academics but useless from a practical standpoint. Consequently, a substantial amount of highly useful action research would never stand a chance in most academic journals and would instead be relegated to the few specialist journals that might publish stories of academic–community engagement or trade publications interested in real-life stories.

And it is not necessarily the case that research designed to meet academic demands for arbitrary standards of so-called scientific rigor could also meet standards for quality action research. The costs, in terms of time and money to do such research, could easily implode groups with few resources and short deadlines. Academic demands to address theoretical questions, rather than only practical ones, or to get enough data to support academic publications, could so suppress participation as to render the research unusable at best, and undoable and alienating at worst, in some community contexts.

So it is important to understand that the first challenge to assessing the quality of action research, from an academic standpoint, is the need to have the research meet the quality standards of a participatory action standpoint. When such projects can withstand that initial test, the second test is whether they are generating research findings that can meet academic definitions of quality. There are many cases where researchers can publish the research findings, derived from academically sound methods, and simply omit the discussion of the action research methodology. Of course, such closeted "passing" does not always feel comfortable and rewarding.

Coming out of the closet, for action researchers, also requires challenging the peer-review process. Anonymous peer review, based on the same positivist epistemology as the randomized trial, is held up as a gold standard of knowledge production. But the evidence is mixed, at best, on whether double-blind peer review does anything to assure quality knowledge (Affi, 2006; Campanario, 2009; Jefferson et al., 2008; Shatz, 2004). What happens if we apply the principles of covenantal ethics described earlier in this chapter to the relationships between authors and reviewers? As a reader of this volume, you have already demonstrated your commitment to improving the review process. It is our hope that this kind of caring can be extended to our authors to help them improve their work through a supportive collegial relationship rather than an anonymous distanced one. So our final recommendation is intended not only to those reviewing action research manuscripts, but to all reviewers, and that is to see our task as one of creating a community of scholars dedicated to deepening our practice and helping one another to become more thoughtful, more engaged, and more committed to each other and the communities around us.

References

Action Research Journal. (2008). Quality Criteria for Action Research Journal. Retrieved July 31, 2011 from www.uk.sagepub.com/repository/binaries/doc/Final_Quality_Criteria_for_ARJ_Oct2008.doc.

Afifi, M. Reviewing the "Letter-to-editor" section in the Bulletin of the World Health Organization, 2000–2004. *Bulletin of the World Health Organization*. Retrieved July 29, 2011 from www.who.int/bulletin/bulletin_board/84/letters/en/index.html.

Arieli, D., Friedman, V. J., & Agbaria, K. (2009). The paradox of participation in action research. *Action Research, 7*(3), 263–290.

Arnstein, S. R. (1969). A ladder of citizen participation. *JAIP, 35*, 216–224.

Bloor, M. (1978). On the analysis of observational data: A discussion of the worth and uses of inductive techniques and respondent validation. *Sociology, 12*, 545–552.

Boal, A. (1985). *Theatre of the Oppressed*. London: Pluto.

Boser, S. (2006). Ethics and power in community–campus partnerships for research. *Action Research, 4*(1), 9–21.

Bradshaw, M. (2001). Contracts and member checks in qualitative research in human geography: Reason for caution? *Area, 33*, 202–211.

Brydon-Miller, M. (2009). Covenantal ethics and action research: Exploring a common foundation for social research. In D. M. Mertens & P. E. Ginsberg (Eds.), *The Handbook of Social Research Ethics* (pp. 243–258). Los Angeles, CA: SAGE.

Brydon-Miller, M. (2008). Ethics and action research: Deepening our commitment to principles of social justice and redefining system of democratic practice. In P. Reason & H. Bradbury (Eds.), *The SAGE Handbook of Action Research: Participative Inquiry and Practice* (2nd ed., pp. 199–210). Los Angeles, CA: SAGE.

Brydon-Miller, M., Antal, A. B., Friedman, V., & Gayá Wicks, P. (2011). The changing landscape of arts and action research. *Action Research, 9*(1), 3–11.

Brydon-Miller, M., Maguire, P., & McIntyre, A. (Eds.). (2004). *Traveling Companions: Feminism, Teaching, and Action Research*. Wesport, CT: Praeger.

Bryman, A. E. (n.d.) Member Validation. Retrieved July 29, 2011 from www.referenceworld.com/sage/socialscience/mem_valid.pdf.

Buchbinder, E. (2011). Beyond checking: Experiences of the validation interview. *Qualitative Social Work, 10*, 106–122.

Burklow, K. A. & Mills, L. C. (2009). Giving voice to underserved and culturally diverse groups using community-based participatory research. *The Open Medical Education Journal, 2*, 75–79.

Campanario, J. M. (2009). Rejecting and resisting Nobel class discoveries: Accounts by Nobel Laureates. *Scientometrics, 81*, 549–565.

Campbell, C. (2003). *Letting Them Die: Why HIV/AIDS Prevention Programmes Fail*. Bloomington, IN: Indiana University Press.

Chandler, D. & Torbert, W. (2003). Transforming inquiry and action: Interweaving 27 flavors of action research. *Action Research, 1*(2), 133–152.

Clover, D. (2011). Successes and challenges of feminist arts-based participatory methodologies with homeless/street-involved women in Victoria. *Action Research, 9*(1), 12–26.

Cochran-Smith, M. & Lytle, S. (2009). *Inquiry as Stance: Practitioner Research for the Next Generation*. New York: Teachers College Press.

Coghlan, D. & Brannick, T. (2010). *Doing Action Research in your Own Organization (3rd ed.)*. Los Angeles, CA: SAGE.

Community–Campus Partnerships for Health. (2007). Achieving the Promise of Authentic Community-Higher Education Partnerships: Community Partners Speak Out! Seattle, WA: Community–Campus Partnerships for Health. Retrieved July 29, 2011 from http://depts.washington.edu/ccph/pdf_files/CPSReport_final1.15.08.pdf.

Cooperrider, D. L., Whitney, D., & Stavros, J. M. (2003). *The Appreciative Inquiry Handbook*. Bedford, OH: Lakeshore Communications.

El-Dinary, P. B., Pressley, M., Coy-Ogan, L., Schuder, T., & Strategies Instruction Teachers. (1994). The Teaching Practices of Transactional-Strategies-Instruction Teachers as Revealed Through Collaborative Interviewing. National Reading Research Center, Reading Research Report No. 23. Retrieved July 29, 2011 from http://eric.ed.gov/ERICWebPortal/contentdelivery/servlet/ERICServlet?accno=ED378555.

Fals-Borda, O. & Rahman, M. A. (Eds.). (1991). *Action and Knowledge: Breaking the Monopoly with Participatory Action-Research*. New York: Apex Press.

Flicker, S., Maley, O., Ridgley, A., Biscope, S., Lombardo, C., & Skinner, H. A. (2008). e-PAR: Using technology and participatory action research to engage youth in health promotion. *Action Research, 6*(3), 285–303.

Foucault, M. (1975). *Discipline and Unish: The Birth of the Prison*. New York: Random House.

Foucault, M. (1980). *Power/Knowledge: Selected Interviews & Other Writings 1972–1977*. Edited by Colin Gordon. New York: Pantheon Books.

Freire, P. (1974). *Education for Critical Consciousness*. New York: Continuum.

Frey, A. F. & Cross, C. (2011). Overcoming poor youth stigmatization and invisibility through art: A participatory action research experience in Greater Buenos Aires. *Action Research, 9*(1), 65–82.

Gaventa, J. (1988). Participatory research in North America. *Convergence, 21*, 9–28.

Greenwood, D., Brydon-Miller, M., & Shafer, C. (2006). Intellectual property and action research. *Action Research, 3*(1), 81–95.

Greenwood, D. J. & Levin, M. (2006). *Introduction to Action Research: Social Research for Social Change.* Thousand Oaks, CA: SAGE.

Guhatakurta, M. (2008). Theatre in participatory action research: Experiences from Bangladesh. In P. Reason & H. Bradbury (Eds.), *The SAGE Handbook of Action Research: Participative Inquiry and Practice* (pp. 510–521). Los Angeles, CA: SAGE.

Hilsen, A. I. (2006). And they shall be known by their deeds: Ethics and politics in action research. *Action Research, 4*(1), 23–36.

Horton, M. & Freire, P. (1990). *We Make the Road by Walking: Conversations on Education and Social Change.* Philadelphia, PA: Temple University Press.

Ison, R. & Russell, D. (Eds.). (2007). *Agricultural Extension and Rural Development: Breaking out of Knowledge Transfer Traditions.* Cambridge, UK: Cambridge University Press.

Israel, B. A., Eng, E., Schulz, A. J., & Parker, E. A. (Eds.). (2005). *Methods in Community-Based Participatory Research for Health.* San Francisco, CA: Jossey-Bass.

Jefferson, T., Rudin, M., Brodney Folse, S., & Davidoff, F. (2008). Editorial peer review for improving the quality of reports of biomedical studies (Review). The Cochrane Collaboration.

Kildea, S., Barclay, L., Wardaguga, M., & Dawumal, M. (2009). Participative research in a remote Australian Aboriginal setting. *Action Research, 7*(2), 143–163.

Laslett, B. & Rapoport, R. (1975). Collaborative interviewing and interactive research. *Journal of Marriage and the Family, 34,* 968–977.

Lewin, K. (1948). Resolving social conflicts: Selected papers on group dynamics. Edited by G. W. Lewin. New York: Harper & Row.

Lewin, K. (1946). Action research and minority problems. *Journal of Social Issues, 2*(4), 34–46.

Ludema, J. D. & Fry, R. E. (2008). The practice of appreciative inquiry. In P. Reason & H. Bradbury (Eds.), *The SAGE Handbook of Action Research: Participative Inquiry and Practice* (2nd ed., pp. 280–296). Los Angeles, CA: SAGE.

Lundy, P. & McGovern, M. (2006). The ethics of silence: Action research, community "truth-telling" and post-conflict transition in the North of Ireland. *Action Research, 4*(1), 49–64.

Lykes, M. B. (2001). Activist participatory research and the arts with rural Mayan women: Interculturality and situated meaning making. In D. L. Tolman & M. Brydon-Miller (Eds.), *From Subjects to Subjectivities: A Handbook of Interpretive and Participatory Methods* (pp. 183–199). New York: New York University Press.

McIntyre, A. & Lykes, M. B. (2004). Weaving words and pictures in/through feminist participatory action research. In M. Brydon-Miller, P. Maguire, & A. McIntyre (Eds.), *Traveling Companions: Feminism, Teaching, and Action Research* (pp. 57–77). Westport, CT: Praeger.

Maguire, P. (1987). *Doing Participatory Research: A Feminist Approach.* Amherst, MA: The Center for International Education, University of Massachusetts.

Merrifield, J. (1993). Putting scientists in their place: Participatory research in environmental and occupational health. In P. Park, M. Brydon-Miller, B. Hall, & T. Jackson (Eds.), *Voices of Change: Participatory Research in the United States and Canada* (pp. 65–85). Westport, CT: Bergin & Garvey.

Meyer, H., Hamilton, B., Kroeger, S., Stewart, S., & Brydon-Miller, M. (2004). The unexpected journey: Renewing our commitment to students through educational action research. *Educational Action Research, 12*(4), 557–573.

Minkler, M. & Wallerstein, N. (Eds.). (2003). *Community-Based Participatory Research for Health.* San Francisco, CA: Jossey-Bass.

The National Commission for the Protection of Human Subjects of Biomedical and Behavioral Research (1978). The Belmont Report: Ethical Principles and Guidelines for the Protection of Human Subjects of Research. Retrieved March 8, 2011 from http://videocast.nih.gov/pdf/ohrp_belmont_report.pdf.

Noffke, S. & Somekh, B. (Eds.). (2009). *The SAGE Handbook of Educational Action Research.* Los Angeles, CA: SAGE.

Oakley, A. (1981). Interviewing women: A contradiction in terms. In H. Roberts (Ed.), *Doing Feminist Research* (pp. 30–61). London: Routledge and Kegan Paul.

Park, P., Brydon-Miller, M., Hall, B., & Jackson, T. (Eds.). (1993). *Voices of Change: Participatory Research in the United States and Canada.* Westport, CT: Bergin and Garvey.

Reason, P. & Bradbury, H. (Eds.). (2008). *The SAGE Handbook of Action Research: Participative Inquiry and Practice* (2nd ed.). Los Angeles, CA: SAGE.

Reed, J. (2007). *Appreciative Inquiry: Research for Change.* Thousand Oaks, CA: SAGE.

Reid, C. & Frisby, W. (2008). Continuing the journey: Articulating dimensions of feminist participatory action research (FPAR). In P. Reason & H. Bradbury (Eds.), *The SAGE Handbook of Action Research: Participative Inquiry and Practice* (2nd ed., pp. 93–105). Los Angeles, CA: SAGE.

Shatz, D. (2004). *Peer Review: A Critical Inquiry.* Lanham, MD: Rowman and Littlefield.

Stoecker, R. (2011). Results of the UW capstone Monona sustainability survey. Retrieved July 29, 2011 from www.tnsmonona.org/results-of-the-uw-capstone-monona-sustainability-survey/.

Stoecker, R. (2009). Are we talking the walk of community-based research? *Action Research, 7*(4), 385–404.

Stoecker, R. (2005). *Research Methods for Community Change: A Project-based Approach.* Thousand Oaks, CA: SAGE.

Stoecker, R. (2003). Community-based research: From theory to practice and back again. *Michigan Journal of Community Service Learning, 9,* 35–46.

Stoecker, R. (1997). The imperfect practice of collaborative research: The Working Group on neighborhoods in Toledo, Ohio. In P. Nyden, A. Figert, M. Shibley, & D. Burrows (Eds.), *Building Community: Social Science in Action.* Thousand Oaks, CA: Pine Forge Press.

Stoecker, R. (1994). *Defending Community: The Struggle for Alternative Redevelopment in Cedar-Riverside*. Philadelphia, PA: Temple University Press.

Stoecker, R. & Beckwith, D. (1992). Advancing Toledo's neighborhood movement through participatory action research: Integrating activist and academic approaches. *The Clinical Sociology Review, 10*, 198–213.

Strand, K., Marullo, S., Cutforth, N., Stoecker, S., & Donohue, P. (2003). *Community-Based Research and Higher Education: Principles and Practices*. San Francisco, CA: Jossey-Bass.

Stringer, R. (1999). *Action Research (2nd ed.)*. Thousand Oaks, CA: SAGE.

Sullivan, M., Kone, A., Senturia, K. D., Chrisman, N. J., Ciske, S. J., & Krieger, J. W. (2001). Researcher and researched-community perspectives: Toward bridging the gap. *Health Education and Behavior, 28*, 130–149.

Tandon, R. (2008). *Participatory Research: Revisiting their Roots*. New Delhi: Mosaic Books.

Tofteng, D. & Husted, M. (2011). Theatre and action research: How drama can empower action research processes in the field of unemployment. *Action Research, 9*(1), 27–41.

Viswanathan, M., Ammerman, A., Eng, E., Gartlehner, G., Lohr, K. N., Griffith, D., Rhodes, S., Samuel-Hodge, C., Maty, S., Lux, L., Webb, L., Sutton, S. F., Swinson, T., Jackman, A., & Whitener, L. (2004). Community-based participatory research: Assessing the evidence. Evidence Report/Technology Assessment No. 99. RTI–University of North Carolina Evidence-based Practice Center. Retrieved July 29, 2011 from www.ahrq.gov/downloads/pub/evidence/pdf/cbpr/cbpr.pdf.

Wang, C. (1999). Photovoice: A participatory action research strategy applied to women's health. *Journal of Women's Health, 8*(2), 185–192.

Wang, C. & Burris, M. (1994). Empowerment through photonovella: Portraits of participation. *Health Education Quarterly, 21*(2), 171–186.

Wang, C., Burris, M., & Xiang, Y. P. (1996). Chinese village women as visual anthropologists: A participatory approach to reaching policymakers. *Social Science and Medicine, 42*(10), 1391–1400.

Willis, C., Anders, C., & Stoecker, R. (2011). When the community leads. In P. Nyden, L. Hossfeld, & G. Nyden (Eds.), *Public Sociology: Research, Action, and Change*. Thousand Oaks, CA: SAGE.

Whyte, W. F. (1990). *Participatory Action Research*. Thousand Oaks, CA: SAGE.

Woolf, S. H. (2008). The meaning of translational research and why it matters. *JAMA, 299*, 211–213.

4

Autoethnography

Christopher N. Poulos

Ethnography began, simply, as an attempt to study, mostly through careful observation, various people and the cultures they inhabit, and "write up" an "objective" account of the ethnographer's observations.[1] But over time, early anthropological field workers began to realize that constructing "realistic" or "scientific" research reports, grounded in researcher "objectivity"—and thus separating the researcher's personal impressions, reactions, emotions, and responses from "data" collected— was harder than it seemed. Indeed, perhaps it was impossible. They were, after all, *human*, and thus became *involved* in the human communities they studied. As time went on and researchers became entrenched in communities, it became more and more difficult—and less and less desirable—to separate self and personal experience from the "data" drawn out of the lifeworld under study (Crawford, 1996; Denzin, 1997; Geertz, 1973; Goodall, 1994, 2000; Philipsen, 1992; Van Maanen, 1988).

But it wasn't just the difficulty of detaching from the lives of research "subjects" that drove the evolution of ethnographic writing toward personal narrative and autoethnography. Researchers began to understand that crucial data—researcher knowledge, personal insight, everyday communication, involvement in an unfolding story, emotional response, and participation in various forms of daily praxis—was missing from their reports. Besides, researchers were never fully separate or detached from the groups or individuals being researched. They were *involved*. These were not "mere observers;" they were *participants* in the scene being studied. As such, they contributed to—indeed, sometimes shaped—events, conversations, actions, and struggles taking place in the world. A researcher, it turns out, is no mere "fly on the wall," unnoticed by the humans in the surround. Much like the insight of the "observer effect" in quantum mechanics, the presence of the ethnographer is intricately entwined in the reality under study. In fact, participants in the scene *respond* to the presence of the observer (and the observer, in turn, responds to them), thus blending, as humans do, action and interaction.

So ethnographers began to experiment with different sorts of texts, attempting to evoke deeper, richer, more textured representations of their subjects of study. In "Deep Play: Notes on the Balinese Cockfight," Clifford Geertz (1973/2005) begins with what John Van Maanen (1988) later came to call a "confessional tale," in which he probes and explores his own participation in the scene (in this case, cockfighting culture in Bali), as well as his own emotional and intellectual responses to the events taking place, and how his engagement in the scene is, in many ways, grounded in the responsiveness (or, to be more precise, the assiduous pretense of a *lack* of such responsiveness) of the participants to his presence.

In "Deep Play," Geertz not only demonstrates the practice of "thick description"—evocative writing that draws the reader into the scene—he also implicates himself as an important player in the events that take place. Moreover the revelation comes not only from his own insight, but also from the insights and actions of the other knowledgeable agents who participate in the scene. His presence has been *noticed*, and adapted to. Moreover, as he explores the implications of this revelation, he begins to evoke, in the written text, the emotions he felt, as well as the interpretive and analytical thoughts that came to him in response to the scene.

And so, as Denzin and Lincoln (2000) show, by the 1980s, the so-called "crisis of representation" in qualitative inquiry was in full swing: "The erosion of classic norms in anthropology (objectivism, complicity with colonialism, social life structured by fixed rituals and customs, ethnographies as monuments to a culture) was complete" (p. 18). No more would the researcher be effaced from the process of research. The ethnographer was *involved* in the scene, fully immersed—a pattern-seeker, perhaps, an interpreter, to be sure—but, more to the point, a *participant* in the lifeworld.

Meanwhile, as Rabinow and Sullivan (1979) note, the social sciences were moving beyond positivist approaches, moving into the so-called "interpretive turn." As Charles Taylor (1987) points out, "there is no such thing as the structure of meanings for him (man) independently of his interpretation of them" (p. 46). In other words, since all inquiry is from a particular point of view, it is subject to a multiplicity of interpretations. There is no "neutral" or "objective" stance from which to view human social phenomena.

As the 1990s came into view, the "autoethnographic turn" in qualitative inquiry began to build steam. The work of Bochner & Ellis (1992), Ellis (1995, 1999), Ellis & Bochner (1991, 1996), and Goodall (1994, 1996) in communication studies, and Behar (1997) in anthropology began to break new ground, centering the ethnographer as a vital, engaged, vulnerable, open, emotional, and creative constructor of texts about the human condition. Furthermore this "new ethnography" (Goodall, 2000) clearly, directly, and unswervingly began to center the experience of the researcher as a crucial locus of research. The "ethnographic I" (Ellis, 2004) was itself now a subject of deep study.

Autoethnographies—or ethnographies of self—are made possible by the insight that the ethnographer is, in fact, a pivotal player in the world being studied. But autoethnography goes further (perhaps deeper) into treating personal experience as important data than the early "confessional" and "impressionist" tales catalogued and described by Van Maanen (1988). Autoethnography takes the ethnographic lens and turns it directly inward, focusing conscious and careful attention on the emotional–volitional experiences, responses, and impressions of the ethnographic researcher, while ever looking outward as well, into the world *as inhabited and experienced* by the author of the text. Indeed, autoethnography engages the ethnographer as an *author* in every sense of that word.[2]

Select Terms

Autoethnography: Carolyn Ellis, a pioneer in "emotional sociology" and autoethnography, offers an excellent working definition of autoethnography. In her groundbreaking autoethnographic novel, *The Ethnographic I*, Ellis (2004) defines autoethnography as "research, writing, story, and method that connect the autobiographical and personal to the cultural, social, and political" (p. xix). Later extending this definition, Ellis and her colleagues write: "Autoethnography is an approach to research and writing that seeks to describe and systematically analyze personal experience in order to understand cultural experience" (Ellis, Adams, & Bochner, 2011, p. 1).

Confessional tale: Van Maanen (1988) offers a catalog of various sorts of ethnographic tales; among these is the confessional tale. Confessional tales, in their original iterations among field ethnographers, were offered as support and context for realist tales. The idea was that "laying bare" some of the methods, approaches, impressions, and even sentiments of the ethnographer would offer a complementary text or context for the more traditional realist tale, inserting a *person* (as opposed to a merely detached observer) into the mix. The confessional tale offers an account of the author and his or her actions, practices, point of view, and understanding of the situation at hand. The purpose was to render a more "natural" account that offered up some good context for the more analytical parts of the text.

Ethnography: Drawn from the Greek root words "*ethnos*" (people) and "*grapho*" (to write), ethnography is, quite literally, "writing about people." Originally, ethnographers studied exotic cultures, but the practices of ethnographic participant-observation have spread throughout the social sciences and humanities. Ethnographers study people-in-action, and often use methods of participant observation, interviews, and other interactive means of gathering data, while writing field notes, journals, and other texts, in the attempt to shape observations into coherent narratives that describe, engage, evoke, analyze, and interpret the actions of those under study. The ethnographer's aim is to develop deeper understandings of social and cultural patterns, practices, and actions, and to communicate those understandings via compelling written texts.

Evocative writing seeks to evoke the emotion, feeling, tone, and sense of the scene or of life experiences as felt by the author. The autoethnographer uses evocative writing to develop a story that draws the reader deeply into the lifeworld of the author, with the intent of moving or transforming the reader, and/or transforming the situation being written about. Evocative writing is personal, vivid, engaging, powerful, and moving to read.

Field notes: Traditional ethnographers use field notes to record observations, interviews, encounters, impressions, and insights as they occur in the field.[3] Autoethnographers use field notes, journals, and other devices to record and construct observations, impressions, insights, emotional responses, text fragments, poems, interviews, encounters, struggles, and epiphanies in advance of—or in concert with—the construction of the primary autoethnographic text. Today's autoethnographers also employ blogging, social networks, and recording devices as they develop the "rough drafts" for later, more complete or polished texts.

Impressionist tale: In contrast to the realist tale's attempt to offer an "objective" view of reality, the impressionist tale draws its conventions from phenomenology, poststructural theory, postmodern-ism, and feminist theory. The impressionist tale attempts to present a multivocal, multiperspectival view of the culture or scene being studied; one that is clearly responsive and responsible to the natives (i.e., implicating ethics). As Van Maanen (1988) explains, "The idea is to draw an audience into an unfamiliar story world and allow it, as far as possible, to see, hear, and feel as the fieldworker saw, heard, and felt (p. 103)," but also to leave, rather than a certain knowledge, more of an *impression* of what is going on. Knowledge, in this impressionist view, is often fragmented, contradictory, tenuous, and local. Theoretical questions may well be left unresolved and unresolvable, but this is not seen as problematic.

New ethnography is Goodall's (2000) catchall term for all the various emerging forms of ethnographic writing emerging on the scene early in this century (and late in the last), including autoethnography, performance ethnography, impressionist ethnography, poetic ethnographies, personal narrative ethnographies, and so on.

Personal narrative/Narrative ethnography: These are ethnographic texts, rendered as stories that focus primarily on ethnographic description, analysis, and interpretation of the actions of others, but that also incorporate the experiences and responses of the ethnographer. The narrative presented may intersect in intriguing ways with the ethnographer's analysis/interpretation of practices, patterns, processes, etc.

Realist tale: In traditional field ethnography, especially in the early days, ethnographers attempted to offer an "accurate and complete" representation of the culture or group or phenomenon being studied. The narrative is seen as a mirror that reflects the reality of what is being observed. The observer is detached and objective. The story that unfolds certainly has authorial power, but the voice and the perspective of the ethnographer are put into the background in favor of an attempt to be "realistic" in all portrayals in the text (Van Maanen, 1988).

Reflexivity and reflexive ethnographies focus attention on changes or transformations that take place in the life and orientation of the researcher, largely as a result of doing fieldwork. Reflexive/narrative ethnographies focus investigation at least in part on the transformative process/experience of ethnographic work. Conscious recognition of the transformation is implied by this built-in reflexivity, though it may come either suddenly or gradually, and may not always make its way into the text (though a reviewer may well want to call for such acknowledgment). Reflexivity is an active attempt to be aware of one's placement in relation to the world and the text, but like all human phenomena, it may be limited in its power.

"Thick" description: In his book, *The Interpretation of Culture*, Clifford Geertz (1973) offers a clear and compelling case for the ethnographer not as mere observer of exotic others, but as a *describer of his participation and thinking* in the context of studying others; he inscribes the action in the scene, and in so doing, he is not merely trying to "capture" what is going on in the world, he is also seeking to "capture" his own impressions *in situ*.[4] The tool of "thick description," a concept for which he attributes credit to Gilbert Ryle, offers the opportunity to show this involvement through deeply engaged, highly descriptive, and interpretive writing—an attempt to evoke and invoke the layered realities of the social situation being interpreted. "Thick description" not only involves observations of what is going on "out there" but also what is going on "in here"—in the observer, in the thinker doing the observing, in the writer who inscribes culture onto the page. Thus, thick description is description that engages all the senses and thoughts and impressions and insights of the observer.

Diversities in Perspective, Context, and Form

Pioneers in the new narrative ethnographies and other alternative, intuitively driven qualitative research methodologies, including William Braud, Rosemarie Anderson, Norman Denzin, Yvonna Lincoln, Laurel Richardson, Bud Goodall, Art Bochner, Carolyn Ellis, Thomas Frentz, Janice Hocker Rushing, Nick Trujillo, and Ron Pelias, to name but a few, have pushed back the boundaries of human social research. They write texts that are grounded in imagination and mystery and concrete emotional experience, rather than certainty, explanation, and detached observation—texts about experiences of our humanness, experiences that are unique rather than replicable, and that show human social reality in all its complexity, seeking to open pathways to possibility rather than offer clear and certain answers to research questions.

This writing seeks to engage a broader audience, including not just the discipline within which it is written, but also other disciplines, our students, and even (maybe especially) communities outside the academy. It seeks to be accessible, engaging, clarifying, and open-ended. The tradition of qualitative inquiry of this sort, of course, has a long history, and its parameters and conventions are broadly accepted (even celebrated) in several fields of study (Braud & Anderson, 1998; Bochner, 2001; Denzin, 1997; Denzin & Lincoln, 2000, 2001; Garfinkel, 1967; Geertz, 1973/2005; Goodall, 1994, 1996, 2000; Richardson, 2000b; Turner, 1969; Turner & Bruner, 1986; Van Maanen, 1988). The new narrative turn, of which autoethnography is one vibrant stream, is simply an extension and expansion of this long history—the next moment in the evolution of qualitative research.

As this evolutionary trend has unfolded, beginning in the mid-1980s and early 1990s, the "new ethnographers" (Goodall, 2000) have taken up the exploration of the *interior* depths of the social world via evocative writing as a primary research methodology. Ellis' (1991) pioneering work in "emotional sociology" opened the door for the many layers of memory, story, and emotional evocation that the autoethnographic voice allows, in ways that other modes of research do not. Work by Ellis and Bochner (1991) on the experience of abortion, and later work by Ellis (1995) on death and loss paved the way for emerging autoethnographers to explore their own inner "secret lives" as eating-disordered adults (Tillmann-Healy, 1996; Tillmann, 2009), survivors of sexual abuse (Fox, 1996), disoriented children of "mentally retarded" parents (Ronai, 1996), members of gangs (Towns, 2007), gays struggling with coming out of the "closet" (Adams, 2011), and recovering members of secretive families (Poulos, 2009), to name but a few.

"Confessional tales" and "impressionist tales" (van Maanen, 1988)—and their later auto-ethnographic extensions—have become an important locus of the literature on the connections between the lived interior experiences of authors and the social worlds they inhabit (Ellis, 2004). The intuitive, imagined, and lived experience of the ethnographer has become an accepted— if not expected—form of textual response to the world. The "new ethnographies" take many forms.

Layered accounts set the author's experience alongside, or in conversational layers with, the data, various forms of abstract or grounded analysis, relevant literature, and so on. This form of ethnographic text emphasizes and frames the research process as a source of questions, and employs poetic writing, vignettes, reflexive writing, multiple voices, and introspection (Ellis, 1991) to call the reader into doing and writing research. The authors of layered accounts consider evocative, concrete texts to be at least as important as abstract analyses (Ronai, 1996).

Performance texts/performance ethnographies: In the 1980s and 1990s, Dwight Conquergood (1989, 2002), Norman Denzin (1997), and others began developing a branch of ethnography that centered performance and the political nature of the practices of the ethnographer as objects of study, and advocated for methodological dialogism from the point of encounter to the practices of research reporting. Performance studies, performance ethnography, and performance texts center the human performance ("doing" life, "doing" culture, "doing" gender, and so on) as direct objects/subjects of inquiry. Furthermore the *process* (performance) of defining the performance itself becomes a practice in performance studies.

Poetry/poetic autoethnography involves the use of poetry as a way to evoke and invoke deeper, spirited layers of the human condition (Boylorn, 2006, 2009; Denton, 2011). As an alternative form of exposition, poetry is a tool and a mode of exploration and expression in many of the "new ethnographies" being written these days.

Community autoethnographies use the personal experiences of researchers collaborating with members of a community (as coauthors and coresearchers) to examine, evoke, illuminate, and illustrate how a community engages, manifests, or deals with the social/cultural issues it confronts. Community autoethnographies, therefore, often center on community building and community transformation/intervention (Ellis, Adams, & Bochner, 2011).

Co-constructed narratives "illustrate the meanings of relational experiences, particularly how people collaboratively cope with the ambiguities, uncertainties, and contradictions of being friends, family, and/or intimate partners" (Ellis, Adams, & Bochner, 2011, p. 7). Co-constructed narratives attempt to show the joint authorship and collaboration that is implicit in relationships. Co-constructed research projects and the narratives produced in these contexts are written dialogically/responsively as a way to show and build the collaborative–dialogic nature of the relationship and the project. Excellent examples of co-constructed narratives include the work of Bochner & Ellis (1992) and Vande Berg & Trujillo (2008).

Personal narrative (auto)ethnographies offer stories about authors who view themselves as central phenomena among other human phenomena. The aim is to write compelling, evocative *stories that focus directly on their own everyday lives among others, including their academic, research, and personal lives* (e.g., Berry, 2007; Goodall, 2006; Pelias, 2004, 2011; Poulos, 2009; Tillmann-Healy, 2001; Tillmann, 2009). Personal narratives can be controversial in that they may or may not offer analysis or connections to scholarly literature, depending on the intent of the piece and the author (Ellis, Adams, & Bochner, 2011). These are stories of the self in some sort of interaction with a cultural, social, or relational context. The narrative offers the author a chance to craft a compelling tale of human social reality, and to reflect on these intersections or interactions.

Qualitative Touchstones

Reviewers will quickly recognize that this I-driven, self-aware ethnographic writing is different from other forms of traditional academic writing. Autoethnography relies heavily upon the sorts of conventions and writing devices that animate fiction and creative nonfiction writing. It begins by situating characters (including the author) in time, space, and action. As Daniel Taylor (1996) puts it, "A story is the telling of the significant actions of characters over time" (p. 15). Plot, dialogue, temporal flow, spatial description, character development, metaphor—all of these animate autoethnographic writing. Several key questions that might orient the reader/reviewer of an autoethnographic text might include:

- Am I, as a reader, drawn into the story?
- Is the tale compelling?
- Am I moved, affected emotionally, or changed by the text?

Beyond these "overview" questions, several touchstones might help to orient the reviewer toward an authentic and careful, responsive reading of an autoethnography:

1. The experience of the ethnographer is central to the construction of the text. The auto-ethnographer embraces subjectivity as a vital mover of human social action. "Data collection" prominently focuses on introspection and writing about the personal experience of the researcher

In more traditional "realist tales" (Van Maanen, 1988) and analytic ethnographies (Philipsen, 1992) the focus is on coming to understand cultures and cultural practices from a detached, analytical stance. The epistemological commitments of these ethnographic works are more objectivist in origin, emphasizing researcher detachment, observation, and analysis over participation, performance, and interpretation. Texts are thus crafted as "reports" of "findings," with the author's experience, and his or her personal reactions to and within the scene, effaced from the writing as much as possible.

But in autoethnography, the researcher's experience is treated as the primary connective tissue that makes a full, rich, textured, and holistic account of the lifeworld inhabited by the researcher possible. The emphasis is on active participation, performance, praxis, and reflexivity. Thus, autoethnographers attempt to transform our ways of seeing, approaching, conceiving, and developing research from a "what's happening over there" approach into a practice of crafting performative and evocative texts "from within" life. These practices stem from an epistemology that sees and engages knowledge as active, engaged imaginative *praxis* (action, performance, accomplishment) rather than as *object* or a *product* of observation. Autoethnographers seek knowing-in-action, rather than knowledge-as-acquisition.

Thus, autoethnography proceeds by a logic different from the methodologies followed by traditional social scientists. Autoethnographers do not proceed via a hypothesis–test–conclusion mode, a linear–causal predictive view of reality, or a positivist or neopositivist paradigm grounded in prediction, control, and analysis. Rather than seeking validity, reliability, objectivity, prediction, and generalizability, autoethnography seeks heuristic (instructive) value, reflexivity, intersubjectivity, resonance, and consistency. Autoethnography does not seek to generate data, test predictions, control outcomes, or draw out generalizations or explanations of social phenomena. Rather, it seeks to embrace, and possibly make storied sense of—or at least *move through, into, or with*—human experience and the mystery that animates human life (Goodall, 1996, 2000; Marcel, 1960). Autoethnography focuses on exploring, evoking, and interpreting the author's emotional, volitional, intellectual, spiritual, interpretive, and imaginative response(s) to the lifeworld. It also eschews the broadly drawn generalizations of more "objective" approaches, and favors instead consistency between text and theoretical commitments, and textual integrity, reflexivity, and heuristic value. Mutual author–reader understanding—resonance between evoked "truths" of the text and the reader's own life experiences—is a primary aim of autoethnography.

2. Autoethnography is not "merely" the rendering of the author's experience, however; it also seeks to link the personal to the larger cultural, social, political, and academic world-matrix in which the autoethnographer participates

The autoethnographer is called to explore his or her own emotional, reflective, and intellectual responses to life, and, at the same time, to reach beyond his/her own experience to make connections to the larger world (making sense of personal experience by linking it to the wider human social world).

Thus, autoethnography does not consist of "just" the musings, reflections, interpretations, and emotional reactions of the autoethnographer. Autoethnography also involves analysis of the connections between existing knowledge and the knowledge being produced in the text. Autoethnography proceeds from an assumption—and takes action toward building—the text as a dialogic entry into conversation with culture. The author is, of course, implicated as a knowledgeable agent constructing a worldview; that said, the autoethnographic text proceeds as a *dialogue* between the author and other knowledgeable agents with varying worldviews, and seeks to tie the author's worldview, in significant and compelling ways, to the larger world he/she inhabits.

In my own work (Poulos, 2008, 2009), I have tried to make this intersection of worldviews, encountered and extended via dialogue between the autoethnographer and his/her interlocutors, clear and explicit. In *Accidental Ethnography* (2009), for example, I often address the reader directly, urging him/her to work toward coming to grips with the power of this kind of writing-as-inquiry. In *Accidental Dialogue* (2008), I offer an exemplar of a reflexive dialogue about dialogue that unfolded between me and the reviewers and editor of the text, showing how the text reaches beyond my own inner world into the larger world of the academic and practical study (and practice) of dialogue itself. In their dialogically constructed (auto)ethnographic tale of their courtship, life together, cancer diagnosis, and, eventually, the death of Leah Vande Berg, Vande Berg and Trujillo (2008) speak poignantly into the pain of the experience of cancer and death, both with each other and with the larger community of support they reach out to, and that reaches toward them. In the end, both texts are "spoken" in dialogue with readers, who respond in varying ways to the invitation to dialogue, making connections to their own experiences and worldviews, and then speaking into the broader dialogue that is the literature of autoethnography.

3. Autoethnographic writing is aimed at crafting evocative, compelling, emotionally, and intellectually rich tales that draw the reader into the lifeworld of the researcher. The autoethnographer writes in such a way as to achieve aesthetic/literary merit, using the conventions of the creative writer to achieve this goal

This practice is the alternative writing format produced by autoethnographers, in contrast to more traditional qualitative research reporting formats.

A key focus of the autoethnographer is on the engagement and craft of writing as a central process of discovery. In other words, autoethnography treats writing itself as a method of inquiry (Richardson, 2000a, 2000b). The result of this active, engaged process of research-as-writing is the richly textured, evocative, reflexive, and intersubjective tale of human lived experience. In other words, autoethnographers write as active, engaged members of their human communities, rather than as detached scientific observers. As Ellis, Bochner, and Adams (2011) point out, "This approach challenges canonical ways of doing research and representing others and treats research as a political, socially-just and socially-conscious act. A researcher uses tenets of autobiography and ethnography to do and write autoethnography. Thus, as a method, autoethnography is both process and product" (p. 1).

Autoethnography begins as writing *from within* the experience, allowing theory and analysis, if necessary or appropriate, to flow from the story, rather than the other way around. The first step is for the author to claim experience *as one's own*. Next, the autoethnographer is called to bring that personal experience into resonance with the experiences of the reader. So, autoethnographers attempt to write compelling, evocative stories that *draw the reader into* their worlds, and also tie that experience to a larger social, cultural, or political matrix.

The mantra of autoethnographers is simple (though not necessarily *easy*): "*Show*, don't tell!" Autoethnographers work to reveal and to demonstrate, to evoke and to show, how their experience unfolds in this complex human lifeworld we all inhabit. To accomplish this, in practice, the autoethnographer applies the conventions of personal narrative (memoir, autobiography), novelistic, and creative nonfiction writing, adopting literary devices to craft evocative and compelling tales that capture and evoke, with resonance and depth, the deeper emotional–volitional layers of human lived experience. The conventions of the novel—plot and action, characterization, scene setting, thick description, dialogue, and emotion—are emphasized, and are used, methodologically, to draw the reader into a story that attempts to render a richly textured picture of human social reality.

Along the way, autoethnographers do make the broader social–cultural–political connections, commentaries, and critiques; this is not mere "navel gazing" (Pelias, 2004), nor is an autoethnography "merely" my story of what I experience (Ellis, Adams, & Bochner, 2011). Rather, it is my attempt, as an author, to engage my deeper knowledge of my lifeworld, and to bring it directly to bear upon—and into dialogue with—the experience of readers, critics, and other interlocutors.

Questions that may be asked of the work include: Does this work succeed esthetically? Does the text invite interpretive responses? Is the text artistically shaped, satisfying, complex, and engaging?

4. Autoethnography proceeds from an assumption that moving or changing/transforming both author and reader (emotionally, intellectually, actively) is a primary aim of research. Thus, autoethnography can be evaluated from an interrogation of how, and to what extent, this movement or transformation is accomplished. The autoethnographer attempts to write in such a way as to achieve very real impact on the reader

"When researchers do autoethnography, they retrospectively and selectively write about epiphanies that stem from, or are made possible by, being part of a culture and/or by possessing a particular cultural identity" (Ellis, Adams, & Bochner, 2011, p. 4). The point of engaging such epiphanies in research is to connect personal experience and story to our larger, shared, communal experience and story. Such writing of and through epiphanies (moments of transformation in thinking, emotion, and approaches to living) requires attention both to the aesthetic merits and to the substance of the intellectual contributions of the research. Thus, in evaluating autoethnographic works as contributions to our shared literature about human social life, it may be useful to adopt, adapt, and extend criteria that Richardson (2000a) offers for all ethnography. The *end product of autoethnographic research* is a rich, substantive, aesthetic, reflexive, and impactful piece of written work.

Autoethnographies may also prove to be *therapeutic*, for both writer and reader. The Greek root *therapeutikós* means "curative" or "restorative." In his *Poetics*, Aristotle outlines the ways in which a tragic work may be *cathartic* (Greek *kátharsis*—a cleansing), or allow or invoke purging, discharging, or relieving of emotions. Because autoethnographic texts are emotionally evocative, they may well allow such a therapeutic–cartharctic curing or cleansing to take place, though that is not their only aim. Certainly, therapeutic shifts or transformations may occur.

Thus, these questions arise as ways to begin to evaluate impact: Does the reader feel moved (emotionally) or called into the emotional world of the author? Does the writing generate new questions? Does it move the reader to read further, or to write/respond, or to try new research practices? Does the text call the reader to action? Does the writing evoke (draw forth, call up, summon) memory, feeling, or passion? Is the text vividly rendered in such a way that the reader feels or connects to the world being represented? Does this text embody a fleshed out, embodied sense of lived experience? Does it seem "true"—a credible account of a cultural, social, individual, or communal sense of the "real"? Does the text resonate with the reader's experience? As an autoethnographer, my end is to craft and produce work for readers who can and will respond affirmatively to these queries.

5. The autoethnographer writes with "heart" as well as "head"

Does the writer's *heart* infuse the work? Does the writing offer a window into the author's soul? Is this writing that, as Ruth Behar (1997) puts it, "breaks your heart?" Is the author a vulnerable participant-observer? Further, is the intellect of the author (and of the reader) engaged in trenchant or insightful analysis and interpretation of the connections between personal experience and the broader intellectual, social, cultural, and political world inhabited by the autoethnographer?

6. Autoethnographies are grounded in a theory of knowledge (epistemology) that is reflexive, praxis-driven (i.e., grounded in and driven by action, performance, accomplishment), and built out of phrônesis (practical–moral wisdom; ethical knowing)

The knowledge invoked and accomplished in these texts is socially constructed, collaboratively built, and ethically concerned meaning-making in action. As such, the aim is not to generalize to all cases, but rather to draw knowledge out as situated, contextual, social, and personal. It draws on what John Shotter (1993) calls "knowing from within"—a kind of knowledge about how to proceed with the business of living among humans (including communicative knowledge).

7. Autoethnography proceeds as an interpretive process

Drawing from the insights of an interpretive (hermeneutic) paradigm rather than a scientific, critical, or rhetorical paradigm, autoethnography owes its intellectual roots more to the work of phenomenologists such as Gadamer (1975), who assert that we can reach the truth only by understanding (even mastering) and interpreting our experience, than it does to any social scientific tradition. In the tradition of hermeneutic phenomenology, experience and knowledge are not fixed, stable categories; rather, they are ongoing interpretive constructions. Autoethnographers enter their texts into a dialogue about what human experience might *mean*, rather than as a claim to universal knowledge. Because of autoethnography's intensity of personal revelation, and the focus on reflexive, introspective *interpretation*, it is, to say the least, a controversial approach. But it is unabashedly *not* scientific in the traditional sense of that word.

Further Reading

Behar, R. (1997). *The Vulnerable Observer: Anthropology That Breaks Your Heart.* New York: Beacon Press.
Behar challenges traditional theories and approaches to ethnographic anthropological research, offering a personal approach in which the line between observer and observed is not so easily drawn. Ethnographic observers are not merely visible in this approach, but *vulnerable* in ways that get them closer to their subjects, thus fleshing out our knowledge with *heart*. Behar famously writes, "I say that anthropology that doesn't break your heart just isn't worth doing anymore" (p. 177). That statement alone makes this one worth reading.

Bochner, A. & Ellis, C. (Eds.) (2002). *Ethnographically Speaking: Autoethnography, Literature & Esthetics.* Walnut Creek, CA: AltaMira Press.
This collection of works by diverse ethnographers is a showcase of intriguing approaches and unique voices. It is compelling reading, and serves beautifully as a set of models in diversity of approaches to the art of writing ethnography.

Crawford, L. (1996). Personal ethnography. *Communication Monographs,* 63: June, 158–170.
This article shows, with great clarity, how—and why—one ethnographer decided to make the "turn" toward what he calls "personal ethnography." It offers a cogent rationale for moving beyond traditional "fieldwork" into new, more personal, "auto" approaches that engage, involve, acknowledge, and invite the subjectivity of the researcher into the text.

Ellis, C. (1995). *Final Negotiations: A Story of Love, Loss, and Chronic Illness.* Philadelphia, PA: Temple University Press.
This painful, evocative text chronicles the slow and grinding death by emphysema of Ellis' former professor and life partner, and the toll the illness took on their relationship. It is probably the first book-length autoethnography published. This pioneering work deals directly with end-of-life issues, loss, grief, and communication problems evocatively, vividly, painstakingly, and magnificently.

Ellis, C. (2004). *The Ethnographic I: A Methodological Novel about Autoethnography.* Walnut Creek, CA: AltaMira Press.
This autoethnographic novel demonstrates the craft of autoethnography by chronicling Ellis' teaching of a graduate autoethnography seminar. The author crafts the book as a way to show how autoethnography is done, and how autoethnographers must grapple with important issues of the writing craft, and face ethical, logistical, and practical concerns in their research and writing. Issues, concerns, problems, and breakthroughs that come up as students craft their own autoethnographic work are shown via in-class dialogues, meetings with the professor, and various encounters (in writing and in speech) between students, professors, and research participants.

Ellis, C. (2009). *Revision: Autoethnographic Reflections on Life and Work*. Walnut Creek, CA: Left Coast Press.

In this evocative book, Ellis takes a "meta-autoethnographic" approach to stories she has previously written—stories about love and loss and growing up in a small town—layering new interpretations, reflections, insights, and revisions onto the original texts. In this way, she explores the capacity of autoethnographers to revisit, revise, and reenvision their previous work in compelling and meaningful ways.

Ellis, C. & Bochner, A. (Eds.) (1996). *Composing Ethnography: Alternative Forms of Qualitative Writing*. Walnut Creek, CA: AltaMira Press.

This collection of compelling ethnographic texts focuses the writers' and the readers' attention on the art of composition in ethnography. It is an excellent beginning text for readers and students of ethnography who want to explore a variety of styles and forms of ethnographic texts.

Ellis, C., Adams, T., & Bochner, A. (2011). Autoethnography: An overview. *Forum: Qualitative Social Research*. 12:1, Art. 10, January, pp. 1–18.

This is an excellent article for anyone who is interested in learning about the history, the practice, and the variations of autoethnographic writing. It offers an overview of the history of autoethnography; the process of "doing" autoethnography; the writing as a product; the potentials, pitfalls, and concerns of autoethnographers; the forms and approaches to autoethnography; issues of reliability, generalizability, and validity; and various critiques of and responses to autoethnography.

Goodall, H. L., Jr. (2000). *Writing the New Ethnography*. Walnut Creek, CA: AltaMira Press.

Once called "the little red Bible" by Art Bochner at a meeting of the National Communication Association, this book offers a fine mix of the author's wisdom and practical advice, gained from many years of crafting compelling, evocative narratives of his own. Goodall shows how an ethnographer can convert field notes and journal entries into intriguing narratives, how to "find the story in words," and how to develop ideas into important "new ethnographies." The book's title, as well as its content, pays homage to the growing range of textual forms employed by ethnographers, but it also goes further, by advocating that ethnographers locate their "ethnographic imaginations" and find their unique voices in and through the process and craft of *writing*.

Goodall, H. L., Jr. (2008). *Writing Qualitative Inquiry: Self, Stories, and Academic Life*. Walnut Creek, CA: Left Coast Press.

This book extends Goodall's *Writing the New Ethnography* across various genres of qualitative writing. Goodall offers a practical text that speaks into the contested and political nature of qualitative inquiry and writing. His approach to crafting narratives for qualitative audiences offers cogent insight into the structure and development of compelling narratives. This is an excellent handbook for anyone who wants to engage in narrative writing in human social research, or even in creative nonfiction, fiction, autobiography, memoir, or other forms of personal narrative.

Pelias, R. (2004). *A Methodology of the Heart: Evoking Academic and Daily Life*. Walnut Creek, CA: AltaMira Press.

This performative text explores the contours of life in today's academy, as well as relationships in everyday life. It is an excellent exemplar of poetic, evocative, dramatic writing, and it is highly recommended as a way to introduce graduate students to the life of an academic.

Pelias, R. (2011). *Leanings: A Poetics of Personal Relations*. Walnut Creek, CA: Left Coast Press.

This stirring, evocative collection of stories, poems, and essays explores and evokes the contours and the mysteries of close personal relationships. The book serves well as both a text for courses in communication and as an exemplar of exquisitely crafted autoethnography. Pelias writes with heart, while speaking to the head, balancing the goals of autoethnographic inquiry beautifully.

Poulos, C. (2009). *Accidental Ethnography: An Inquiry into Family Secrecy*. Walnut Creek, CA: Left Coast Press.

This evocative book is designed to accomplish three things: (1) Teach, by showing and by coaxing (through exercises and challenges) the craft of "accidental ethnography" (a blending of autoethnographic and personal narrative approaches to writing ethnographies about "accidental" moments of discovery in everyday life); (2) Explore the dark contours of family secrecy as an exemplar case of the kind of (inter)personal phenomenon an autoethnographer might find him/herself writing about; and (3) Expose to the light of day the problematic nature of the communication conundrums and ethical dilemmas that arise from confronting secrecy via autoethnographic exploration and writing.

Tillmann-Healy, L. (2001). *Between Gay and Straight: Understanding Friendship across Sexual Orientation*. Walnut Creek, CA: Alta Mira Press.

Tillmann-Healy captures, in vivid narrative ethnographic prose, the intrigues and the challenges of initiating, developing, and maintaining friendships across sexual orientation. Presented as a series of narratives about her friendship with members of a gay male softball team, the book offers compelling insight into friendship, friendship as an ethnographic method, and friendship that transcends difference. The book is an excellent example of narrative ethnography, and will interest anyone who wants to explore friendship, difference, ethnography, equality, and trust.

Van Maanen, J. (1988). *Tales of the Field: On Writing Ethnography*. Chicago, IL: University of Chicago Press.

In this now-classic book, Van Maanen approaches the craft of writing ethnography by examining and showing various forms of ethnographic texts and their purposes. He pays particular attention to three paradigmatic cases: the realist tale, the confessional tale, and the impressionist tale. This book is a must-read for any new ethnographer who wants to get a sense of the rich history, purpose, and craft of ethnographic writing.

Vande Berg, L. & Trujillo, N. (2008). *Cancer and Death: A Love Story in Two Voices*. New York: Hampton Press.

This powerful book offers a dialogic, participatory coauthored autoethnographic text about the slow death by ovarian cancer of communication scholar Leah Vande Berg, and the impact it had on her relationship with fellow communication scholar and husband, Nick Trujillo. The text offers a poignant, evocative look at the contours of love, pain, loss, and transcendence through co-construction of illness narratives and conversations about the meanings of life and death.

Counterpoint Perspectives

As autoethnography is a relatively new form of scholarship, it has yet to develop many subaltern or counterpoint perspectives from within the ranks of autoethnographers. Generally, critiques and alternative perspectives have come from those who practice *other* forms of scholarship, but no really substantive alternative approaches have been offered from within the practitioners of autoethnography. That said, many ethnographers are what Denzin and Lincoln (2000) refer to as *bricoleurs*—researchers who employ a wide range of methodologies to achieve their research goals, among them, auto-ethnography, performance, and more traditional field ethnography. Choices about employment of these methodologies are made based upon the subject and purpose of a given study.

Philipsen, G. (1992). *Speaking Culturally: Explorations in Social Communication*. Albany, NY: State University of New York.

Philipsen, G. (1997). "A Theory of Speech Codes." In G. Philipsen and Terrance A. Albrecht (Eds.), *Developing Communication Theories*. Albany, NY: State University of New York Press, 119–156.

For a thoroughly systematic and analytical approach to ethnography, Gerry Philipsen's work is unmatched in quality, integrity, and clarity of exposition and execution. Philipsen proceeds from an "ethnography of speaking" paradigm, originally developed by Dell Hymes (1974), in which the ethnographer attempts to observe and decode the cultural meanings of linguistic/communicative actions of members of so-called "speech communities." The emphasis here is on analytical understanding of social interaction via application of a careful, rigorously structured theoretical model. The work sees theorizing about cultural codes as the main end product of ethnographic study and analysis. Thus, it stands out as a distinct approach from the autoethnographic approaches outlined here, as it attempts to develop a more objective/analytical stance toward the phenomena under study (which are seen as events of cultural codes), and does not emphasize or centralize the role of the observer or the emotional tone of encounters or stories.

Gingrich-Philbrook, C. (2005). "Autoethnography's Family Values: Easy Access to Compulsory Experiences." *Text and Performance Quarterly* 25: 4297–4314.

Gingrich-Philbrook's essay offers both an appreciation of autoethnography, and, at the same time, a suspicion of autoethnography as a legitimate form of scholarship. Gingrich-Philbrook points to a double bind between the epistemic and aesthetic demands of autoethnography and autoethnographic performance. He attempts to critically engage this double bind by questioning the privileging of transparency (as opposed to indeterminacy or some other possibility) in autoethnography.

Author's Reflection on Quality

The "qualitative touchstones" presented here reflect deep commitments about how to approach human social research. In my own practice, I see no distinction between my "life" and my "research." I am, fundamentally, a living, breathing, inquiring, searching and researching, participating human being. As such, I am, quite naturally, called to live autoethnography. As Art Bochner once famously said at a meeting of the National Communication Association, in response to a query about what ethnography is: "It's not a method; it's a *way of life*."[5] Autoethnography is, indeed, a way of life.

Autoethnography is about embracing the simple truth that any researcher is, in fact, an active, participating human being in an active, co-involved human world. As such, the autoethnographer has much insight, experience, knowledge, and emotion to share in the context of a research praxis that is, quite simply, a way of life—an approach to research that celebrates the whole experience of living and practicing social research. A primary insight of autoethnography is that effacing the researcher's involvement in fieldwork and the construction of texts leaves out vital data from the research. Many autoethnographers would argue that objectivity among humans is neither possible nor desirable, and that beginning to practice an honest, straightforward, and even brazenly "I"-driven research practice (Ellis, 2004; Mitra, 2011) is, as Robert Coles (1989) puts it, merely answering "the call of stories."

We humans are, at our very core, storytellers and story-consumers—Walter Fisher's (1987) *homo narrans*. As Bochner (2001) brilliantly argues, perhaps we ought to just embrace our storytelling as a vital methodology of human social research:

> We can call on stories to make theoretical abstractions, or we can hear stories as a call to be vigilant to the cross-currents of life's contingencies. When we say with a story, refusing the impulse to abstract, reacting from the source of our own experience and feelings, we respect the story and the human life it represents, and we enter into a personal contact with questions of virtue, of what it means to live well and do the right thing.
>
> (p. 132)

In my own work, the justifications for writing autoethnography have been more simply drawn, and more personal in origin. There is, really, no better way to get at the questions, concerns, dilemmas, emotions, epiphanies, and strange encounters that have constituted my life. An objective, theoretical, analytical, detached, or scientific stance is simply not sufficient to get at the kinds of narrative truths I have sought in my work.

To put it another way, autoethnography "speaks" to me in ways that other research methodologies do not. This is true both as author and as reader. Autoethnography speaks deeply *into* me—and through me—almost at a cellular level. It pulses in my veins, it infuses my heart, and it forces my fingers to fly across keyboards.

It all began, for me, as a response to a shattering event in our world: 9/11. As I stood before my university classroom of 170 students that morning, announcing this unspeakable news, I knew, in a flash—a flash as quick as the toppling of buildings and the destruction of lives that had just taken place—that I simply had to write about this life-changing situation. I could not *not* write about it. But the text that emerged was not a standard academic "scholarly" text. It was an autoethnography of the events that unfolded during that week, and the feelings and fears and losses and changes we all collectively endured. It was about pain, it was about uncertainty, it was about loss, it was about transformation.

And, thus, my life was changed. Since the day after 9/11, I have only written autoethnographically. I have felt—and answered—the call of stories. Furthermore my work (and the work of my colleagues in autoethnography) demonstrates that, for some matters—particularly matters of the human heart—there is simply no better way of getting at the heart of the matter at hand.

In the end, autoethnography and other narrative and performative approaches find themselves on a different sort of footing from other methods and texts of human social research. Coherently evaluating the quality of an autoethnographic text depends on the reviewer's ability to look with an eye toward narrative truth and storied resonance, and with a sense of wonder at being *moved* by the text.

Notes

1. Ethnography: Drawn from the roots "*ethnos*" (people) and "*grapho*" (writing)—i.e., writing about people.
2. That is, the author is not only the writer, but also, in this case, the creator, the originator, the first-person narrator, and the energy behind the text. The autoethnographer is a maker of narratives that compel the reader to enter the world of the author. As Franz Kafka (1973) put it, "Writing means revealing oneself to excess." The autoethnographer reveals him/herself, and the emotional, intellectual, imaginative, and social contours of the lifeworld of which he/she is an active, engaged inhabitant.
3. See Goodall, 2000, for a full treatment of the uses and variations on field notes.
4. This is especially highlighted in his first chapter (aptly titled *Thick description: Toward an interpretive theory of culture*). In the chapter titled *Deep play: Notes on the Balinese cockfight*, he demonstrates the use of "thick description" in ethnographic writing.
5. This claim has been immortalized in song by the mythic virtual rock band *The Ethnogs*. See: www.hu.mtu.edu/~pjsotiri/preconference/The_Ethnogs.html and http://theethnogs.blogspot.com/.

References

Adams, T. E. (2011). *Narrating the Closet: An Autoethnography of Same-sex Attraction*. Walnut Creek, CA: Left Coast Press.

Behar, R. (1997). *The Vulnerable Observer*. New York: Beacon Press.

Berry, K. (2007). Embracing the catastrophe: Gay body seeks acceptance. *Qualitative Inquiry, 13*(2), 259–281.

Bochner, A. (2001). Narrative's virtues. *Qualitative Inquiry, 7*, 131–157.

Bochner, A. & Ellis, C. (1992). Personal narrative as a social approach to interpersonal communication. *Communication Theory, 2*(2), 165–172.

Bochner, A. & Ellis, C. (Eds.). (2002). *Ethnographically Speaking: Autoethnography, Literature & Aesthetics*. Walnut Creek, CA: AltaMira Press.

Boylorn, R. M. (2006). E Pluribus Unum (Out of Many, One). *Qualitative Inquiry, 12*(4), 651–680.

Boylorn, R. M. (2009). Southern black women: Their lived realities. *Theses and Dissertations*. Paper 1869. http://scholarcommons.usf.edu/etd/1869.

Braud, W. & Anderson, R. (1998). *Transpersonal Research Methods for the Social Sciences: Honoring Human Experience*. Thousand Oaks, CA: Sage.

Coles, R. (1989). *The Call of Stories: Teaching and the Moral Imagination*. Boston, MA: Houghton Mifflin Company.

Conquergood, D. (1989). *I am a Shaman: A Hmong Life Story with Ethnographic Commentary*. Chicago, IL: Center for Urban and Regional Affairs.

Conquergood, D. (2002). Performance studies: Interventions and radical research. *The Drama Review*, 46, 145–153.

Crawford, L. (1996). Personal ethnography. *Communication Monographs*, 63, 158–170.

Denton, D. (2011). Betrayals of gravity: The flight of the Phoenix. *Qualitative Inquiry*, 17(1), 85–92.

Denzin, N. K. (1997). *Interpretive Ethnography: Ethnographic Practices for the 21st Century*. Thousand Oaks, CA: Sage.

Denzin, N. K. (2001). *Interpretive Interactionism*. Thousand Oaks, CA: Sage.

Denzin, N. K. & Lincoln, Y. S. (2000). The discipline and practice of qualitative research. In N. K. Denzin & Y. S. Lincoln (Eds.). *Handbook of Qualitative Research* (2nd ed.). Thousand Oaks, CA: Sage.

Denzin N. K. & Lincoln, Y. S. (Eds.). (2001). *The American Tradition in Qualitative Research*. Thousand Oaks, CA: Sage.

Ellis, C. (1991). Emotional sociology. *Studies in Symbolic Interaction*, 12, 123–145.

Ellis, C. (1995). *Final Negotiations: A Story of Love, Loss, and Chronic Illness*. Philadelphia, PA: Temple University Press.

Ellis, C. (1999). He(art)ful autoethnography. *Qualitative Health Research*, 9, 653–667.

Ellis, C. (2000). Creating criteria: An ethnographic short story. *Qualitative Inquiry*, 6, 273–277.

Ellis, C. (2001). With mother/with child: A true story. *Qualitative Inquiry*, 7, 598–616.

Ellis, C. (2002a). Shattered lives: Making sense of September 11 and its aftermath. *Journal of Contemporary Ethnography*, 31(4), 375–410.

Ellis, C. (2002b). Take no chances. *Qualitative Inquiry*, 8, 42–47.

Ellis, C. (2004). *The Ethnographic I: A Methodological Novel about Autoethnography*. Walnut Creek, CA: AltaMira Press.

Ellis, C. (2007). Telling secrets, revealing lives: Relational ethics in research with intimate others. *Qualitative Inquiry*, 13, 3–29.

Ellis, C. (2009). *Revision: Autoethnographic Reflections on Life and Work*. Walnut Creek, CA: Left Coast Press.

Ellis, C. & Bochner, A. (1991). Telling and performing personal stories: The constraints of choice in abortion. In C. Ellis & M. Flaherty (Eds.), *Investigating Subjectivity: Research on Lived Experience* (pp. 79–101). Thousand Oaks, CA: Sage.

Ellis, C. & Bochner, A. (Eds.). (1996). *Composing Ethnography: Alternative Forms of Qualitative Writing*. Walnut Creek, CA: AltaMira Press.

Ellis, C., Adams, T., & Bochner, A. (2011). Autoethnography: An overview. *Forum: Qualitative Social Research*, 12(1), 1–18.

Fisher, W. (1987). *Human Communication as Narration: Toward a Philosophy of Reason, Value, and Action*. Columbia, SC: University of South Carolina Press.

Fox, K. (1996). Silent voices: A subversive reading of child sexual abuse. In C. Ellis & A. Bochner (Eds.), *Composing Ethnography: Alternative Forms of Qualitative Writing*. Walnut Creek, CA: AltaMira Press.

Gadamer, H. G. (1975). *Truth and Method*. (J. Weinsheimer & D. G. Marshall, Trans.). New York: Continuum Books.

Garfinkel, H. (1967). *Studies in Ethnomethodology*. Cambridge, UK: Polity Press.

Geertz, C. (2005/1973). Deep play: Notes on the Balinese cockfight. *Daedalus*, 134, 56–86. [Reprinted from: Geerz, C. (1973). *The Interpretation of Culture*. New York: Basic Books.]

Geertz, C. (1973). *The Interpretation of Culture*. New York: Basic Books.

Gingrich-Philbrook, C. (2005). Autoethnography's family values: Easy access to compulsory experiences. *Text and Performance Quarterly*, 25, 4297–4314.

Goodall, H. L., Jr. (1994). *Casing a Promised Land: The Autobiography of an Organizational Detective as Cultural Ethnographer*. Carbondale, IL: Southern Illinois University Press.

Goodall, H. L., Jr. (1996). *Divine Signs: Connecting Spirit to Community*. Carbondale, IL: Southern Illinois University Press.

Goodall, H. L., Jr. (2000). *Writing the New Ethnography*. Walnut Creek, CA: AltaMira Press.

Goodall, H. L., Jr. (2008). *Writing Qualitative Inquiry: Self, Stories, and Academic Life*. Walnut Creek, CA: Left Coast Press.

Hymes, D. (1974). *Foundations of Sociolinguistics: An Ethnographic Approach*. Philadelphia, PA: University of Pennsylvania Press.

Kafka, F. (1973). *Letters to Felice*. (J. Stern & E. Duckworth, Trans.). New York: Schocken Books.

Marcel, G. (1960). *The Mystery of Being*. Chicago, IL: Regnery-Gateway.

Mitra, R. (2010). Doing ethnography, being an ethnographer: The autoethnographic research process and I. *Journal of Research Practice*, 6(1), 1–21.

Pelias, R. (2004). *A Methodology of the Heart: Evoking Academic and Daily Life*. Walnut Creek, CA: AltaMira Press.

Pelias, R. (2011). *Leanings: A Poetics of Personal Relations*. Walnut Creek, CA: Left Coast Press.

Philipsen, G. (1992). *Speaking Culturally: Explorations in Social Communication*. Albany, NY: SUNY Press.

Philipsen, G. (1997). A theory of speech codes. In G. Philipsen & T. A. Albrecht (Eds.), *Developing Communication Theories* (pp. 119–156). Albany, NY: SUNY Press.

Poulos, C. (2008). Accidental dialogue: The search for dialogic moments in everyday life. *Communication Theory*, 18(1), 117–138.

Poulos, C. (2009). *Accidental Ethnography: An Inquiry into Family Secrecy*. Walnut Creek, CA: Left Coast Press.

Rabinow, P. & Sullivan, W. (1979). The interpretive turn: Emergence of an approach. In P. Rabinow & W. Sullivan (Eds.), *Interpretive Social Science*. Los Angeles, CA: University of California Press.

Richardson, L. (2000a). Evaluating ethnography. *Qualitative Inquiry, 6*, 253–255.

Richardson, L. (2000b). Writing: A method of inquiry. In N. K. Denzin & Y. S. Lincoln (Eds.), *Handbook of Qualitative Research*. Thousand Oaks, CA: Sage.

Ronai, C. R. (1996). My mother is mentally retarded. In C. Ellis & A. Bochner (Eds.), *Composing Ethnography: Alternative Forms of Qualitative Writing*. Walnut Creek, CA: AltaMira Press.

Shotter, J. (1993). *Conversational Realities: Constructing Life through Language*. Thousand Oaks, CA: Sage.

Taylor, C. (1987). Interpretation and the sciences of man. In P. Rabinow & W. Sullivan (Eds.), *Interpretive Social Science*. Los Angeles, CA: University of California Press.

Taylor, D. (1996). *Tell Me a Story: The Life-shaping Power of our Stories*. St. Paul, MN: Bog Walk Press.

Tillmann-Healy, L. (1996). A secret life in a culture of thinness: Reflections on body, food and bulimia. In C. Ellis & A. Bochner (Eds.), *Composing Ethnography: Alternative Forms of Qualitative Writing*. Walnut Creek, CA: AltaMira Press.

Tillmann-Healy, L. (2001). *Between Gay and Straight: Understanding Friendship across Sexual Orientation*. Walnut Creek, CA: AltaMira Press.

Tillmann-Healy, L. (2003). Friendship as method. *Qualitative Inquiry, 9*(5), 729–749.

Tillmann, L. (2009). Body and bulimia revisited: Reflections on "A Secret Life." *Journal of Applied Communication Research, 37*(1), 98–112.

Towns, A. (2007). *Rosez 4 a Gun: Da demonz of a Young Black Male*. New York: iUniverse.

Turner, V. (1969). *The Ritual Process: Structure and Anti-structure*. Chicago, IL: Aldine Publishing.

Turner, V. & Bruner, E. (Eds.). (1986). *The Anthropology of Experience*. Urbana, IL: University of Illinois Press.

Van Maanen, J. (1988). *Tales of the Field: On Writing Ethnography*. Chicago, IL: University of Chicago Press.

Vande Berg, L. & Trujillo, N. (2008). *Cancer and Death: A Love Story in Two Voices*. New York: Hampton Press.

5

Case Studies

Catherine Compton-Lilly

Case studies are like birds. If someone randomly uttered the word "bird," most of us would think of a prototypical bird—small, nests in trees, eats worms—despite the fact that we all know there are a huge range of birds from humming birds to ostriches. Case studies are much the same. When someone references a case study, we generally think of a detailed analysis of one person and his/her experiences even though we know that there are many types of case studies. Stake (1978) reported that the "object (target) of a social inquiry is seldom an individual person or enterprise. Unfortunately, it is such single objects that are usually thought of as 'cases'" (p. 7). This is a challenge I face as I write a chapter that provides researchers and reviewers with information that will be helpful in judging the quality of case studies. Case studies can be large or small, qualitative or quantitative, individual or collective, involve long or short timeframes and multiple physical locations, draw upon a range of epistemological assumptions, and serve a variety of purposes. While in this chapter I focus only on qualitative case studies, a range of possibilities exist.

I open the chapter by defining the term case study and some of the vocabulary associated with the methodology. I then review a sampling of types of case study in order to capture the range and the diversity of the "species." A set of qualitative touchstones—criteria that are associated with successful and valued case studies—is presented. Next, suggestions for further reading, including a discussion of perspectives that are not discussed in the chapter, are shared. Finally, I close the chapter with my own reflections and insights as case study researcher.

Select Terms

Case study is the study of the particularity and complexity of a single case, coming to understand its activity within important circumstances.

(Stake, 1995, p. xi)

Case studies are rich empirical descriptions of particular instances that are typically based on a variety of data sources.

(Eisenhardt & Graebner, 2007)

A case study is a study based upon evidence of a case in progress. This involves the gathering of evidence, its criticism, and its interpretation.

(Stenhouse, 1978, p. 31)

Case studies are constructed, not found, as researchers make decisions about how to angle their vision on places overflowing with potential stories of human experience.

(Dyson & Genishi, 2005, p. 2)

As the above descriptions suggest, there is no single definition of case study. While these definitions highlight different roles for researchers—understanding activity (Stake, 1995), crafting "empirical descriptions" (Eisenhardt & Graebner, 2007), critiquing and interpreting evidence (Stenhouse, 1978), and constructing cases—all definitions share an emphasis on making sense of localized experiences by focusing on a "case" or the "particular." In addition, researchers can approach cases from various epistemological locations. Thus cases cannot be defined by what the researcher does or believes. Merriam (1998) argues that it is the boundedness of the object of study that best differentiates the case study from other forms of qualitative research.

Merriam (1998) was concerned that the term case study has not been used "precisely" (p. 43) and has often been a "catchall for studies that are clearly not experimental, survey, or historical" (p. 43). He argues that the term "case" can refer to the object of study, the methodology, or a final written product (Merriam, 1988). For example, Stake contends that case study is not a methodology; to Stake (1995), the term case study denotes the boundedness of the research focus. Merriam explains that "the *process* of conducting a case study is conflated with both the unit of analysis (the case) and the product of this type of investigation" (1998, p. 27). Yin (2009), and others, distinguish among case study, ethnography, and grounded theory reminding the scholarly community that these techniques are not mutually exclusive; many researchers draw on these methodologies while retaining their work's essences as case studies.

Creswell (1998) advocates using a case study methodology to study entities with clear boundaries. In contrast, Merriam (1998) argues that case studies are particularly suited for "situations in which it is impossible to separate the phenomenon's variables from their context" (p. 29). As ironic as it may seem, both of these claims are valid. As Luck, Jackson, and Usher (2006) report, while it may be difficult to distinguish the case from the context, it is "important that the boundaries of the case are readily distinguishable from event, behaviour or actions that are outside the boundaries of the case" (p. 104).

Although Stake maintains, "we use ordinary language and narratives to describe the case" (Stake, 1995, p. 134), there is a specialized vocabulary that surrounds case study research. In the appendix of Creswell's book (1997) on qualitative methodology, he identified and defined twenty-two different terms and phrases related to case study. In the following section, I highlight a sampling of terms that are key to the definition and implementation of case study methodology.

Case boundaries: A case has been described as a "bounded system," "a specific, complex, functioning thing" (Stake, 1995, p. 2) that entails boundaries that determine what is included and what is excluded (Barone, 2000). Stake (1995) explains that "not everything is a case" (p. 2). The construct of case boundaries distinguishes the case from everything that is not the case. Thus a case study of a particular child would include the child and other people, events, policies, and institutions that affect that child. While the construct of boundedness helps researchers to frame the scope of their project, researchers often cite a tension between a case as bounded and a case as contextualized within larger structures and institutions. Dyson and Genishi (2005) note that while it helps to "place boundaries around spaces and times of interest, so that we can identify 'the case'" (Dyson & Genishi, 2005, p. 43) "every 'something' exists within a context, which defines the case and teaches us about the 'something small'" (Dyson & Genishi, 2005, p. 43). Thus relevant aspects of context can be contested. The construct of boundedness is related to Yin's discussion of "unit of analysis" (Yin, 2003, p. 30). As he notes the unit of analysis—the individual, group, setting, classroom, event, or entity that is the focus of a case study—can be revisited and redefined during the course of a study (Yin, 2003). Thus, exemplary case study researchers will successfully negotiate between two potentially conflicting aspects. The boundaries of their case will be clearly defined, while the case itself will be richly contextualized within multiple contexts (e.g., social, political, cultural, and institutional).

Intrinsic case study: An intrinsic case study focuses on a person, place, program, policy, institution, or other bounded case for the purpose of learning about that particular entity (Stake, 1995). Rather than exploring a general issue or problem, intrinsic case studies are chosen for their unique qualities and focus on what is interesting within a particular case. Useful and informative intrinsic case studies are in part contingent on the identification of compelling cases that highlight unique situations, challenges, or opportunities. Crafting a useful and informative intrinsic case study is partly contingent on the identification of a compelling case that highlights unique situations, challenges, or opportunities. Learning about unique cases should reveal possibilities, name challenges, or highlight caveats that can inform the ways researchers think about unique as well as typical cases.

Instrumental case study: When researchers wish to examine an issue or idea that affects many people in many places, he/she may conduct an instrumental case study (Stake, 1995). An instrumental case study is designed to "provide insight into an issue or to redress a generalization. The case is of secondary interest, it plays a supportive role, and it facilitates our understanding of something else" (Stake, 2000, p. 437). Thus rather than the case study focusing on a particular teacher and her teaching, an instrumental case study might focus on a particular policy and how that policy affected teaching in a particular site. The focus of an instrumental case study is chosen based on its usefulness in illustrating an issue. The power of instrumental case studies rests in not only the selection of generally compelling issues, but also in the ability of researchers to connect local actors and practices to general policies and the ways those policies act on people and influence communities.

Collective case study: Due to their interest in particular issues, instrumental case study researchers often focus on more than one person and/or site. A collective case study focuses on the ways a defined issue is enacted and experienced in more than one context (Stake, 1995, p. 4). Barone (2000) notes that collective case studies can be controversial in that the focus on multiple cases generally results in the loss of detail and richness that can be documented and reported. However, collective case studies are often compelling to researchers and scholars who are interested in understanding how different people experience particular situations and how issues might affect practices across sites. Exemplary collective case studies should meet two criteria. First, it must be clear that the issue of interest to the researcher is sufficiently similar across cases. Second, the unique situations and contexts for each case must be highlighted allowing the audience to extrapolate how general policies play out in both comparable and unique ways. As with the case boundaries discussed above, designing and presenting a compelling collective case study requires negotiating boundaries—in this case establishing similarities across cases while highlighting the unique contextual considerations of each case.

Diversities in Perspective, Context, and Form

Case studies are both a well-established genre for scholars to learn about issues in local fields and a controversial methodology. Case studies have a long history; as Stoecker (1991) suspects, they may be the earliest method of systematic investigation. Case studies have historically been used in medicine, law, psychology, and political science (Creswell, 1998). For example, Anderson's and Meier-Hedde's report (2001) on historical case studies documenting early cases of dyslexia date back to

1676. Likewise, much of Piaget's work can be described as involving case studies of children. Hamil and Fotin (1991) trace the history of contemporary case studies to the fields of anthropology and sociology, noting the significant contributions made by members of the Chicago School. Some scholars argue that case study methods were popular throughout the first half of the twentieth century perhaps due to the lack of other methodological procedures (Hamil & Fotin, 1991). However, people have attributed the decrease in the number of case study projects between the 1950s and the 1970s to the "rise of probability sampling, statistics, survey methods, and computer analysis" (Stoecker, 1991, p. 90). As he reports, "the case study was relegated to the status of a cute, but relatively useless, sociological practice"(Stoecker, 1991, p. 90). These critiques generally focused on the problems of bias and generalizability. One response to these critiques was for some researchers to attempt to "inject greater scientific rigour into the case study" (p. 92) through discussions of internal and external validity in order to meet "the standards set by quantitative scientific sociology" (p. 92). Scholars, such as Yin (2009), argue that well-constructed case studies can play an essential role in theory development and in the identification of cause/effect patterns.

Dyson and Genishi (2005) maintain that it is the "messy complexity of human experience that leads researchers to case studies in the qualitative or interpretative tradition" (p. 3). Qualitative case study researchers referenced by Dyson and Genishi recognize, accept, and expect that similar phenomena will look and sound different in different cultural and social contexts as will the meanings people make of these experiences (Dyson & Genishi, 2005). Thus case study can be a means to investigate the local with the understanding that multiple local contexts can collectively inform general understandings.

Dyson and Genishi argue for an explicitly descriptive, local, and phenomonological approach to case study research. As they explain, "Given this emphasis on meaning perspectives and contexts, the aims of qualitative research are not compatible with efforts to identify the 'scientifically proven' teaching methods that will cure children of language and literacy ills and ensure all a healthy literacy future in school" (Dyson & Genishi, 2005, p. 11). Their version of case study challenges simple models that assume that "teaching methods are causal" (Dyson & Genishi, 2005, p. 11).

However, the epistemological premises in the work of the qualitative literacy case study scholars cited above are not representative of the full scope of case study research. While these studies attend to variations in literacy practices based on culture and community, the privileging of particular literacy practices within schools, and the interpretative, and perhaps subjective role of the researcher, not all case studies reflect these premises. In particular, the work of Yin (2009) draws on a different epistemological foundation. Unlike Dyson and Genishi (2005), Yin argues "theory development prior to the collection of any case study data is an essential step in doing case studies" (p. 36).

Yin's (2009) clearly delineated approach identifies "five components of a research design" for case study (p. 27), recommends the use of a "case study protocol" (pp. 80–81), and recommends "five analytic techniques" (p. 136) that case study researchers might adopt. These analytical procedures involve procedures such as pattern matching in which researchers identify predicted patterns based on prior research that they compare with the "empirically based patterns" (p. 136) in their own work, explanation building, which involves identifying a "presumed set of causal links" that explain how or why something happened (p. 141), and logic models that stipulate "a complex chain of events" that are "staged in repeated cause-effect-cause-effect patterns, whereby a dependent variable (event) at an earlier stage becomes the independent variable (causal event) for the next stage" (p. 149). Both Yin's (2009) language (e.g., "causal links," "prediction," and "independent/dependent variables") and the analytic processes he describes are grounded in epistemological assumptions that highlight the systematic nature of the world, the predictability of outcomes, and the role of the researcher in uncovering theories that are assumedly scientific and true. Yin's (2009) approach to case study differs greatly from approaches, such as Dyson's and Genishi's (2005), which highlight variation among literacy practices, the socially constructed notion of school literacy attainment, and the constructive and interpretative role of the researcher.

While case studies are generally recognized as best for addressing "how" and "why" questions (Barone, 2000; Eisenhardt & Graebner, 2007; Yin, 2009), the specific goals identified by researchers are varied. Merriam (1998) describes the goal as depicting the essence or basic structure on an experience. Dyson and Genishi (2005) describe the end goal of case study research as understanding "how the phenomenon matters from the perspectives of participants in the case" (p. 81). They note that case study researchers "aim to construct interpretations of other people's interpretations—of other people's 'real worlds'" (p. 18). Case studies can also be: tools for critiquing existing practices; attempts to represent and examine typical situations; opportunities to explore extreme or unique situations; forums for revealing novel aspects or interpretations of familiar experiences, and can lead to the construction of longitudinal accounts, holistic interpretations, or explorations of how local lives are embedded in larger institutions and contexts.

Despite the range of epistemological premises and purposes that underlies case study research, some scholars have attempted to identify elements and criteria for high-quality case studies. Stake offers a "critique checklist for a case study report" (Stake, 1995, p. 131) and provides his readers with an annotated case study to illustrate various aspects of case study writing and presentation (Stake, 1995) that include advice related to writing and style, argument construction, the presentation of data, and the report format. Taking a very different approach, Yin (2009) offers a set of general criteria for judging research design; he identifies construct validity, internal validity, external validity, and reliability as critical elements. Yin describes the importance of multiple sources of evidence, a linear chain of evidence, and participants reviewing research findings as important, while Merriam (1998) highlights the length of time spent in the field and attention to ethical issues. Barone (2000) argues that exemplar case studies involve "rigorous data collection and analysis that most often included multiple observations, interviews and artifacts" (p. 21).

Rather than contributing to this long and varied list of elements and criteria, in the following section I identify a set of shared characteristics or touchstones that are reflected in many excellent case studies. It is critical to note that many well-crafted case studies will not present all these characteristics. Some may feature several dimensions while others may include only a few. Still others will include dimensions that are not included on this list. However, the characteristics described below are generally recognized as contributing to high-quality case studies.

Qualitative Touchstones

1. Case studies are complex

Barone (2000) maintains that case studies are particularly effective when researchers are studying complex phenomenon (Barone, 2000; Stake, 1995). While a given case, perhaps a person, may present as a defined entity, all people are contextualized within particular relationships, social networks, communities, and institutions that in turn are defined by traditions, cultures, beliefs, and policies. Thus understanding the case requires the researcher to attend to the complexities involved while simultaneously making decisions about which complexities matter to a particular case.

The complexity of cases has two critical effects. First, this complexity highlights nuance and variation. By conducting cases within a general population, there is an inherent recognition that individual and collective cases are worthy of analysis and that variation exists within populations. Researchers who aspire to craft essentializing theories, premises, or constructs based on case studies that can be universally applied to groups of people are intrinsically flawed.

Second, the complexity of cases warrants the use of multiple sources of data. While considering multiple sources of data does not ensure the validity of a study, it is one means of triangulation and addressing the ethical obligations that qualitative researchers have "to minimize misrepresentation and misunderstanding" (Stake, 1995, p. 109). Triangulation in case study research can involve multiple sources of data, observations and interpretations of multiple researchers who bring various theoretical background to the research site and to the data, the use of multiple methodologies, and the incorporation of member checking practices in which participants are invited to review and analyze the results of the study.

2. Case studies are evolving

Because case studies occur across time, things happen to people and within the contexts that are studied. Thus researchers are constantly grappling with and must be responsive to the possibility of change. As Dyson and Genishi (2005) argue, working within particular contexts always involves fluid meanings that are constituted by and through ongoing social activities. Time, space, people, and activity are never static and case study researchers must be open to documenting change and inconsistency as well as the ways people's interpretations of their worlds are contextualized within multiple spaces and reflect multiple discourses. Effective case study researchers will recognize patterns of change and stasis across time by noting the duration of their studies, shifts in perspectives and practices, and changes in participants' situations and resources.

Not only can case studies be recognized as moving and shifting targets, but the research process is also evolving as the researcher becomes increasingly familiar with the researcher site, the participants, and the issues that are presented in the case. Stake (1995) describes the researcher moving from a focus on etic issues, those brought to the case by the researcher, toward emic issues raised by participants and reflecting the perspectives and experiences of participants. Parlett and Hamilton (1976) describe "progressive focusing" as the need to change a research design when early questions are not working and new issues become apparent to the researcher. While the design of a research project must always depend on the questions asked, the questions cannot be allowed to constrain the design (Dyson & Genishi, 2005). The challenge for case study researchers is to design a study "loosely but not too loosely" (Dyson & Genishi, 2005, p. 59) allowing researchers to adjust the study's design to the particulars of the local context. As Stake (2000) argues, "one cannot know at the onset what the issues, the perceptions, the theory will be" (p. 441). Rather than trying to craft cases to support initial assumptions and theories, sensitive and grounded case study researchers will shift their foci and confront the shortcomings of their original premises. Changes might be made in terms of the data collected, the analytical processes used, and even the questions asked; when these changes are made, case study researchers should clearly describe what was changed and why.

3. Case studies are contextualized

Cresswell (1998) identifies the careful description of the research context as a hallmark of case study research. Likewise, Yin (1981) explained that all case study researchers "must cope with the essential problem that because the context is part of the study, there will always be too many 'variables' for the number of observations to be made, this making standard experimental and survey design irrelevant" (Yin, 1981, p. 59). Context is both a hallmark of case study research and a challenge for case study researchers. In fact, Stake (1995) invites case study researchers to "develop *vicarious experiences*" (p. 63, italics in the original) for their audiences that provide a sense of "being there" (p. 63). Geertz (1973) explained that this "thick description" includes not only detailed description of the context but also the local perceptions of participants and recognition of their phenomenological understandings. As Merriam (1998) argued, the rich descriptions available in case studies entail a "sense of immediacy" (p. 243) relative to the experiences of participants.

Notably, these claims present great hurdles for case study researchers—requiring strong writing skills and the presentation of carefully selected details that convey the essence of the context without losing sight of more general arguments and issues. At the same time, attempts to capture and write other people's worlds harbor significant dangers. As many qualitative researchers have warned, all researchers bring their own assumptions, values, biases, and perspectives to their work. Thus the renderings that we produce are always partially our own and never simple descriptions of what we witness. Well-crafted descriptions carry the danger of deluding readers into focusing on issues that are more constructed than present, accept readings that do not honor the complexity of the situation, and/or sample contexts and issues from a small range of perspectives. Reflexivity on the part of the researcher—a willingness to reveal one's own situatedness—is essential so that readers recognize the potential contingencies and limits that accompany the analyses and the words that they read. Thus developing "vicarious experiences" and constructing "thick descriptions" must be accompanied by honest and often humbling researcher reflexivity.

Descriptions of context must also recognize how cases are situated within larger contexts. Erickson (1986) reported that interpretative researchers—including those who conduct case studies— are obligated to "combine close analysis of fine details of behavior and meaning in everyday social interactions with analysis of the wider societal context" (Erickson, 1986, p. 120). To Dyson and Genishi (2005) this involves "historical, economic and cultural forces that intersect in any local space" (p. 8). As they maintain, everyday events carry epistemological value and in schools this valuing is based on commonly accepted understanding about what counts, what is considered natural, when is someone assumed to be mature, and what is right or pleasing. These meanings are related to identity and ideologies that reflect both individual and collective understanding of the world. As Stake (1978) argues "case studies may be epistemologically in harmony with the reader's experience and thus to that person a natural basis for generalization" (p. 5). Thus high-quality case studies require not only expertly crafted descriptions of contextual factors but may also require a willingness to challenge existing epistemological, ideological, and generally accepted assumptions that limit the ways case study data are interpreted and explained. Case studies not only exist within contexts, but also have the potential to talk back to contextualized understandings by presenting counter narratives that challenge commonly accepted premises and assumptions.

4. Case studies complicate notions of generalization

The construct of generalization can be a contentious issue for case study researchers. Several researchers have proposed various conceptualizations of generalization. Stake (1995) differentiates between "petite generalizations" (p. 7)—"generalizations about a case or a few cases in a particular situation," and "grand generalizations" (p. 7) that involved accepted understandings of how things work that can be "modified" by case study research (p. 7). As he explains, "The real business of case study is particularization, not generalization" (p. 8) and while case study researchers are rarely "trying to generalize to other cases, still some comparison to other cases is inevitable" (Stake, 1995, p. 134).

Yin (2009) takes a different approach to generalization. He argues that case studies are generalizable in relation to theoretical propositions rather than to individuals or particular populations. He argues that the goal of a case study is not to "enumerate frequencies" (p. 15)—the propensity of particular events and outcomes—but to "expand and generalize theories" (p. 15). "Analytic generalization" occurs when "a previously developed theory is used as a template with which to compare the empirical results of the case study" (p. 38).

Consternation has existed over the generalizability of case study findings. For example, in 1978, Stenhouse argued that cumulations of case study findings conducted in the past can be the basis for generalizations that can inform educational practice and policy. "Retrospective generalizations are attempts to map the range of experience, rather than to perceive within that range the operation of laws in the scientific sense" (Stenhouse, 1978, p. 22). While arguing that even outcomes based on quantitative patterns across time are not entirely predictable, Stenhouse argued for the "utilisation of history in the present and future works, through the refinement of judgment, not the refinement of prediction" (p. 22). That same year, Stake (1978) highlighted the power of "naturalistic generalizations" that "derive from the tacit knowledge of how things are, how people feel about them, and how things are likely to be later or in other places with which this person is familiar" (p. 6).

Stake and Trumbull (1982) distinguished between formal or propositional generalizations that are supported by scientific experiments and explicitly stated, often by people of authority and naturalistic generalizations. While they recognize that individual case studies are not a strong basis for making propositional generalizations, they argue that other, more personal, and often unarticulated, naturalistic generalizations are possible. These naturalistic generalizations are based on direct testimony, rich description, and other phenomological data, and are constructed in conjunction with people's existing knowledge of other cases and other related research.

Dyson and Genishi (2005) maintain that scholars may generalize information from case studies in "private, personal ways, modifying, extending, or adding to their generalized understandings of how the world works" (Dyson & Genishi, 2005, p. 115). They continue, "By understanding the particulars of its social enactment, the case can be compared to the particulars of other situations. In this way, "truths" or assumptions can be extended, modified, or complicated" (Dyson & Genishi, 2005, p. 116). Stake (2000) makes a similar point; "meanings aggregate or attenuate. Associations become relationships, relationships become theory . . . Generalization can be an unconscious process for both researcher and reader" (p. 442).

In summary, many recognize that forms of generalizability are possible with case study research, however, as Stake (2000) reminds us, "damage occurs when the commitment to generalize or to theorize runs so strong that the researcher's attention is drawn away from features important for understanding the case itself" (p. 439). Well-argued case studies will neither argue for or against generalizability, but will identify the types of information and insights that extend beyond a particular case. The findings from some case studies might be cautiously generalizable to local populations or communities that share similar situations, challenges, and resources. These generalizations should be tested locally and adapted as needed providing educators with hints about what might matter in local communities rather than formulas for action. In other cases, the methods used to learn about communities, classrooms, families, and/or children might be generalizable in the sense that the similar research methods may elicit valuable insights and information in vastly different contexts. For example, methodologies that seek themes and insights through grounded data analysis might result in very different findings in different communities while the methods used to access and identify those findings might be remarkably similar.

5. Case studies are often methodological hybrids

Like some bird-like creatures of mythology, including the Sphinx, a winged lion with a woman's head, and Pegasus the winged horse, case studies often employ multiple identities. While case studies are generally categorized as case studies based on the bounded nature of the research, they often involve various methodologies and analytical processes (Hamil & Fortin, 1991) and can often be cross-categorized as interview studies, grounded theory studies, ethnographies, historical narratives, narrative studies, biographical research, or a number of other methodologies. Merriam (1998) notes that this variety extends to the types of data that might be collected:

> Unlike experimental, survey, or historical research, case study does not claim any particular methods for data collection or data analysis. Any and all methods of gathering data, from testing to interviewing, can be used in a case study, although certain techniques reused more often than others.
> (Merriam, 1998, p. 28)

With few exceptions (e.g., Yin, 2009), guides to case study research do not identify particular methodologies or analytic procedures.

This flexibility, which characterizes case study research, is also apparent in the various roles that can be ascribed to case study researchers. Case study researchers play multiple roles in the research process contingent on the questions they ask, the data they collect, and the purposes they espouse. Stake (1995) notes that case study researchers can act as teachers, advocates, evaluators, biographers, or interpreters. In addition, case study researchers often develop highly personal relationships with participants. Stake explains that "Persons studied are studied in depth. Researchers are encouraged to include their own personal perspectives in the interpretation. The way the case and the researcher interact is presumed unique and not necessarily reproducible for other cases and researchers" (Stake, 1995, p. 135). This personal role and its proximity to the field and to participants is similarly recognized by Dyson and Genishi (2005), "Researchers' data gathering, analysis, and indeed, eventual write-up of others' experiences are mediated by their own lives" (p. 81).

Because so many methods and roles are available to case study researchers, it is critical that case study researchers are explicit about the roles they play, the positionings they assume, and the methods they use. Experts, writing about case studies, may not identify particular methods for collecting and analyzing data. Thus it is essential that case study researchers provide these details about their research so that readers have a clear sense of how researchers approach and understand the cases they present.

Further Reading

Dyson, A. H. & Genishi, C. (2005). *On the Case: Approaches to Language and Literacy Research*. New York: Teachers College Press.

Dyson and Genishi (2005) explore in detail "what it means to be 'on the case' in language and literacy studies" (p. 1). After introducing case studies and exploring a few theoretical and methodological issues, they present a hypothetical research example that is woven through the book to illustrate various issues and complexities related to case study research. This highly readable text is an excellent start for novice researchers interested in delving into case studies related to literacy and language.

Merriam, S. B. (1998). *Qualitative Research and Case Study Applications in Education*. San Francisco, CA: Jossey-Bass.

A revision and an expansion of an earlier version of this text, titled *Case Study Research in Education: A Qualitative Approach* (Merriam, 1988), the revised version addresses qualitative research generally and situates case study within this larger body of work. Of the eleven chapters, three are dedicated specifically to case study issues. This book is ideal for the researcher who is intent on doing qualitative research but is questioning whether case study is the most appropriate method.

Stake, R. E. (2006). *Multiple Case Study Analysis*. New York: Guilford Press.

In *Multiple Case Study Analysis*, Stake (2006) builds on his prior work with case study to explore the complications that accompany looking across multiple cases. He describes the *quintain* as the "collective target" being studied. As he notes, "For the proverbial blind men describing the elephant, the elephant is the quintain" (p. 6). The book leads the reader through three alternative processes of data analysis depending on the degree of contextualization desired and the amount of data collected. As he notes, a balance must be achieved between the focus on local cases and the interest in collective themes based on the researcher's purposes and the scope of the project. To illustrate various issues related to multiple case study analysis, Stake presents three cases from a project focused on international implementation of an early childhood education program.

Yin, R. K. (2009). *Case Study Research: Design and Methods*, 4th edition. Los Angeles, CA: Sage Publications. As noted above, Yin (2009) takes an approach to case study that is epistemologically different from the other scholars noted above. His approach highlights theory building and presents a vision of case study as a scientific venture. Any novice researcher planning to use this book is well advised to take a close look at the analytical processes that are recommended and to consider whether these processes are consonant with the questions being asked and the epistemological assumptions that the researcher brings. This is an excellent text for researchers who are interested in conducting case studies that are logically compelling and theoretically grounded.

Counterpoint Perspectives

Qualitative case study research can also be defined in terms of what it is not (Merriam, 1998). In this section, I briefly comment on case-based work that does not entail qualitative case study and was not addressed in this chapter. I invite readers to draw on the descriptions referenced below to gain a richer sense of these methodologies. As reviewers we must recognize that the divergent purposes implicit in these studies warrant different criteria for evaluation and review. While each of these approaches deals with small numbers of participants that can be described as "cases," adequate reviewing of these studies would require specialized knowledge of particular methods and the criteria that are specific to the types of questions asked and the methods used.

Theory Building from Cases

Eisenhardt, K. M. & Graebner, M. E. (2007). Theory building from cases: Opportunities and
  challenges. *Academy of Management Journal*, 50(1), pp. 25–32.
Theory building from cases involves drawing on one or more cases to develop theoretical constructs grounded in empirical data. Eisenhardt and Graebner (2007) describe it as "one of the best (if not the best) of the bridges from rich qualitative evidence to mainstream deductive research. Its emphasis on developing constructs, measures, and testable theories make inductive case research consistent with the emphasis on testable theory within mainstream deductive research" (Eisenhardt & Graebner, 2007, p. 25). Inherent in the focus on theory building across cases or in dimensions of cases is the loss of detailed contextual framing. The focus on theory building reveals a set of epistemological assumptions that differ from those brought by qualitative case study researchers who aspire to describe local contexts, the ways participants make sense of those contexts, and the events that occur within them.

Instructional Case Studies or Teaching Cases

Shulman, J. H. (2002). Happy accidents: Cases as opportunities for teacher learning. Paper presented
  at the American Educational Research Association Conference, New Orleans, Louisiana.
Shulman, J. H., Whittaker, A., & Lew, M. (2002). *Using Assessments to Teach for Understanding: A
  Casebook for Educators*. New York: Teachers College Press.
Instructional or teaching cases are "compelling narratives, situated in an event or series of events that unfold over time" (Shulman, 2002, p. 3) and are used for instruction, staff development, and/or consultation. For example, Shulman, Whittaker, and Lew (2002) present a set of case studies focused on issues related to student assessment practices. Teaching cases are described as "candid, dramatic, highly readable accounts of teaching events or a series of events. They offer a problem-based snapshot of an on-the-job dilemma" (p. xi). Shulman, Whittaker, and Lew (2002) argue that reading various cases related to a particular issue can help teachers to effectively frame problems, explore multiple perspectives, identify crucial factors, recognize potential risks and benefits, identify and plan possible solutions, and eventually generate new theories and principles for future work.

However, Shulman and her colleagues (2002) maintain that the benefits of teaching cases extend beyond the reading and discussion of exiting cases. They argue that teachers benefit from collaborative case writing experiences and propose a process for working with teachers as they identify potential cases, write initial drafts, discuss drafts with colleagues, and collaboratively refine these drafts. They describe this as an "iterative set of writing activities with collective feedback after each event over a period of several months" (Shulman, 2002, p. 4). Once final drafts are complete they are field-tested with a new group of teachers and final changes are made prior to publication. As they explain, these cases provide a "way of capturing veteran teachers' knowledge" (p. 127) in texts that involve problem-centered plots that unfold over time within complex and realistic contexts as well as the thoughts and reflections of experienced teachers. The writing process provides teachers with time to reflect on their practices, opportunities to question their assumptions, increased understanding, and empowerment that highlights situated learning, and collaborative opportunities to connect theory with practice.

Author's Reflections on Quality

Just as when people see an ostrich, or a chicken, or a penguin, they know that it is a bird, when people read my work they generally identify my research as involving individual or collective case studies. Of the researchers described above, I am avowedly most drawn to the descriptions of case study from Dyson and Genishi (2005). In fact, it was when I read the work of Anne Haas Dyson that I first entertained the possibility of becoming a researcher. The stories she told of classrooms were real, compelling, and thought-provoking. I agree that case studies are constructed and recognize the multiple subjectivities that converge in the cases that I envision and write. I believe that case studies are complex, evolving, and contextualized. I argue for generalization of ideas, insights, considerations, and approaches rather than findings or truths. It is generalization in "private, personal ways" (Dyson & Genishi, 2005) that I believe has contributed to my knowledge as a researcher and as an educator. While I appreciate the perspectives of scholars, including Yin (2009), who advocate for case studies that systematically refine theories and scientifically examine relationships, perhaps it is my eighteen years of classroom teaching that attracted me to narrative and grounded accounts that feature the voices of children and the challenges faced by teachers.

My own version of case study has been an "odd-bird" in the field. In particular, I am attracted to longitudinal qualitative case studies—investigations of people and their experiences that continue over years and sometimes a decade or more (Compton-Lilly, 2003, 2007, 2012). I am interested in not only how people make sense of their past experiences, which would involve life history research, but also how they understood schooling and literacy as they lived it and how stories emerged and evolved over time. I worry that we have not done enough to document the cumulative and evolving experiences of children—especially children from communities that have been underserved in school. Thus, I work to conduct case studies that involve collecting parallel types of data across long periods of time (e.g., a self-portrait in crayon at age 6 and a Facebook page at age 16), allowing researchers to note both change and consistency as well as providing the participants with opportunities to reflect on prior selves. For me, the case is the bounded family as they span time together—the children moving through school and into early adulthood, the parents moving from raising young children to raising adolescents, and the contextual changes (e.g., institutional, economic, and social) that situate their trajectories.

References

Anderson, P. L. & Meier-Hedde, R. (2001). Early case reports of dyslexia in the United States and Europe. *Journal of Learning Disabilities, 34*(1), 9–21.

Barone, D. (2000). Case study research. In N. K. Duke & M. M. Mallette (Eds.), *Literacy Research Methodologies* (pp. 7–27). New York: Guilford Press.

Compton-Lilly, C. (2003). *Reading Families: The Literate Lives of Urban Children*. New York: Teachers College Press.

Compton-Lilly, C. (2007). *Rereading Families: The Literate Lives of Urban Children, Four Years Later*. New York: Teachers College Press.

Compton-Lilly, C. (2012). *Reading Time in Middle School*. New York: Teachers College Press.

Creswell, J. W. (1997). *Qualitative Inquiry and Research Design: Choosing among Five Traditions*. Thousand Oaks, CA: Sage.

Dyson, A. H. & Genishi, C. (2005). *On the Case: Approaches to Language and Literacy Research*. New York: Teachers College Press.

Eisenhardt, K. M. & Graebner, M. E. (2007). Theory building from cases: Opportunities and challenges. *Academy of Management Journal, 50*(1), 25–32.

Erickson, F. (1986). Qualitative methods on research on teaching. In M. Wittrock (Ed.), *Handbook of Research on Teaching* (3rd ed., pp. 119–161). Washington, DC: American Educational Research Association.

Geertz, C. (1973). *The Interpretation of Cultures*. New York: Basic Books.

Hamil, G. & Fotin, S. D. D. (1991). *Case Study Methods*. Newbury Park, NJ: Sage.

Luck, L., Jackson, D., & Usher, K. (2006). Case study: A bridge across the paradigms. *Nursing Inquiry, 13*(2), 103–109.

Merriam, S. B. (1988). *Case Study Research in Education: A Qualitative Approach*. San Francisco, CA: Jossey-Bass.

Merriam, S. B. (1998). *Qualitative Research and Case Study Applications in Education, Revised and Expanded from Case Study Research*. San Francisco, CA: Jossey-Bass.

Parlett, M. & Hamilton, D. (1976). Evaluation as illumination: A new approach to the study of innovative programmes. In G. Glass (Ed.), *Evaluation Studies Review Annual, 1,* 140–157. Thousand Oaks, CA: Sage.

Shulman, J. H. (2002). Happy accidents: Cases as opportunities for teacher learning. Paper presented at the American Educational Research Association Conference. New Orleans, Louisiana.

Shulman, J. H., Whittaker, A., & Lew, M. (2002). *Using Assessments to Teach for Understanding: A Casebook for Educators*. New York: Teachers College Press.

Stake, R. E. (1978). The case study method in social inquiry. *Educational Researcher, 7*(2), 5–8.

Stake, R. E. (1995). *The Art of Case Study Research*. Thousand Oaks, CA: Sage.

Stake, R. E. (2000). Case studies. In N. K. Denzin & Y. S. Denzin (Eds.), *Handbook of Qualitative Research (2nd ed.)* (pp. 435–454). Thousand Oaks, CA: Sage.

Stake, R. E. (2006). *Multiple Case Study Analysis*. New York: Guilford Press.

Stake, R. E. & Trumbull, D. (1982). Naturalistic generalizations. *Review Journal of Philosophy and Social Science, 7*(1), 1–12.

Stenhouse, L. (1978). Case study and case records: Towards a contemporary history of education. *British Educational Research Journal, 4*(2), 21–39.

Stoecker, R. (1991). Evaluating and rethinking the case study. *Sociological Review, 39,* 88–112.

Yin, R. K. (1981). The case study crisis: Some answers. *Administrative Science Quarterly, 26*(1), 58–65.

Yin, R. K. (2003). *Applications of Case Study Research (2nd ed.)*. Los Angeles, CA: Sage.

Yin, R. K. (2009). *Case Study Research: Design and Methods (4th ed.)*. Los Angeles, CA: Sage.

6

Critical Discourse Analysis

Rebecca Rogers

Discourse analysis has become a popular set of theories and methods used to investigate questions in the social sciences. Indeed, dozens of journals are devoted to discourse studies and an increasing number of conferences and courses have sprung up in the past decade. Because the field is wide and the space for this chapter is short, I focus on only one variety of discourse analysis—those that have been termed critically oriented forms of discourse analysis (Blommaert, 2005; Gee, 2010; Rogers, 2004/2011). Gee (2004/2011) makes the distinction between "critical discourse analysis" and "Critical Discourse Analysis." The former, cda (with small letters), refers to a variety of approaches that may include action-oriented discourse analysis, narrative analysis, rhetorical analysis, public consultative discourse analysis, ethnographic analyses, nexus analysis, and others whose central concern are issues of power, domination/liberation, and ideology. "CDA" (with capital letters) refers to those who associate their work with the theories and methods of Norman Fairclough, Ruth Wodak, Teun van Dijk, and Theo van Leeuwen. Both are concerned with power and privilege and the relationships between discourse and social structure.

The emergence of critical discourse analysis as a serious field of inquiry raises questions about how the quality of such inquiry might be evaluated. Reviewers might sensitize themselves to the common criticisms in the field. These can serve as a point of departure in conducting and reviewing scholarship. Some of the common critiques are:

- political and social ideologies are read onto data rather than revealed through the data (Widdowson, 1998);
- there is an unequal balance between social theory and method (van Dijk, 2000);
- analyses often lack close textual or linguistic analysis (Antaki, Billig, Edwards, & Potter, 2003);
- analysis tends to be decontextualized (Blommaert, 2001);
- there is an overemphasis on domination and oppression versus liberation and freedom (Luke, 2004; Martin, 2004);
- there has been little attention to learning and the nonlinguistic aspects of interaction such as emotions and activity (Rogers, 2004/2011).

One way to address such critiques is through attention to the criteria by which we evaluate scholarship in the field. In this chapter, I highlight touchstones that can be used to evaluate both the process and product of critically oriented discourse analysis. Many of these insights come from reviews that I have either written or received over the years, a review of literature (Rogers et al., 2005), and research I have conducted on how people learn discourse analysis (Rogers, 2011).

The language of criteria for critical discourse studies is under development (and sometimes debated) in the research community. It should be noted that there is no uniform set of tools attributed to critically oriented forms of discourse analysis and the criteria of acceptability varies journal by journal depending on the aims and goals of the editor and the editorial board. Thus, this review not only provides a summary of what seems to be agreed upon, but also leaves room for those criteria that are being established. It should be noted that there is a great deal of overlap between discourse analysis and other qualitative traditions.[1] Rather than review criteria addressed elsewhere in this volume, I have focused on those areas specific to critical discourse studies and, in some cases, when a touchstone is more general have adapted it to be relevant to critical discourse studies.

The chapter is structured with qualitative touchstones that move in a sequential manner from the beginning to the end of a research article. This structure might provide a guide for reviewers as they think about evaluating the merits of a study. At the heart of this chapter is the assumption that reviews should be educative, constructive, and offer feedback, guidance, and new ways of thinking about research. Throughout, I reference exemplars of studies within each touchstone so that reviewers and authors might have specific examples for further examination.

Select Terms

Critical discourse studies refers to an interdisciplinary network of scholarship. Van Dijk champions the term critical discourse studies instead of critical discourse analysis because the latter implies an emphasis on methods and lacks theoretical commitments.

Critical discourse analysis refers to approaches in a wide net of discourse analyses that explore power, domination, liberation, and privilege. There are many analytic approaches that fall under this umbrella including: positive discourse analysis, action-oriented discourse analysis, nexus analysis, multimodal discourse analysis, and so on. These approaches can also be termed critically oriented approaches to discourse analysis.

Critical Discourse Analysis refers to a set of approaches that are most often linked to what are commonly referred to as the founders of critical discourse analysis—Norman Fairclough, Ruth Wodak, Teun van Dijk, and Theo van Leeuwen.

Qualitative Touchstones

1. The unit of analysis is explicitly addressed and is congruent with the research question and the analytic procedures

Units of analysis are the primary entity that the discourse analyst chooses to analyze. The unit includes both *what* is under examination (e.g., interaction) and *how* it is being examined (by turns or by clauses, for example). Reviewers should expect to see a conceptual and procedural description of the unit of analysis. Conceptually, the unit helps the reviewer understand the frame and boundaries of the analysis. Procedurally, an explanation of the unit of analysis is crucial in evaluating the thoroughness of the analysis and the congruence between the research questions and the findings.

Because discourse includes spoken, written, and signed communication, there is wide array of possible foci for analysis including artifacts, events, and contexts. Texts might include fieldnotes, transcripts of interviews, video-recordings of meetings, and printed artifacts such as reports, policy documents, newspapers, books, manuals, curricular documents, emails, photos, and other visual evidence. Often, in articles, analysts will include *what* they are looking at (e.g., texts, events, and interactions) but not *how* they are looking at it. The how are the specific entities that frame the analysis (e.g., lines, eye gaze, stanzas, lexical items, and turns). Analysts may choose the clause as Rogers & Mosley (2008) do in their work, the idealized line (e.g., Medina, 2010), the stanza (e.g., Juzwik, 2006; López-Bonilla & Englander, 2010), gaze (e.g., Wohlwend, 2011), episode (e.g., Lee & Majors, 2003), or another unit deemed as suitable for answering the research question. Reviewers might prompt scholars with the question: *What is the focus or unit of analysis and why?*

2. The theory of language is congruent with the paradigmatic line of inquiry and the analysis

Most scholars engaged in critically oriented forms of discourse analysis will assume the following about language—language is historical, socially and culturally situated, and embedded with ideology and is dialectical (Fairclough & Wodak, 1997). In a review of critical discourse analysis in education, Rogers et al. (2005) discovered that only 33percent of the articles reviewed discussed their theory of language. We concluded this was troublesome because language is the object of study. It should be kept in mind that some theories of discourse will be more familiar to many readers and thus analysts may choose to not discuss the theory in detail. Sociocultural theories of discourse, for example, are more familiar than say, multiethnic theories of discourse. However, authors should spend at least a paragraph or two discussing their theoretical commitments around discourse. An in-depth treatment of the theoretical commitments around discourses—taken in combination with the methodology and findings of the study—can lead to new theoretical insights. Detailed treatment of discourse theories can be found in the work of Chouilaraki (1996) and Medina (2010).

Reviewers can assess the congruence of the researcher's theoretical commitments through a closer examination of the researcher's language choices. Does the researcher discuss discourse as dialectical but then discuss how social institutions shape educational discourses but not how those same institutions are shaped by discourses? Do they attempt to study representations and learning around multicultural education but fail to engage with multiethnic theories of discourse? These choices signal to reviewers a possible incongruence between the stated theoretical commitments and how these commitments are brought to life in their research. In essence, the reviewers—sensitized to the workings of discourse in/and social life—are conducting a discourse analysis of the article itself.

3. Transcription procedures are transparent

Transcripts—a record of what is communicated—are a major data source for discourse analysts. Transcripts include verbal and multimodal records of communication (Norris, 2002). Transcription is the process by which the research record is constructed. Initially it might seem that the act of transcription is devoid of any interpretation. Yet, it soon becomes apparent that when a researcher hits the pause button on the recorder, what one chooses to transcribe first, the layout of the page, and a myriad of other decisions all correspond to the content of the record and our subsequent meaning-making process. This is particularly the case when transcribing video data because the construction of a multimodal transcript demands that researchers attend to the multiple ways in which meanings are being made. What does it mean, for example, to first transcribe the verbal interactions and then attend to the gestures? Should still images be placed before or after the verbal transcript? The same questions and concerns apply when researchers ask others to transcribe video or audio recordings. A transcriptionist may provide the researcher with what I would refer to as a draft of a transcript but the researcher still spends ample time with the transcript—checking for semantic accuracy and segmenting the record into manageable units for further analysis.

Many scholars agree that transcription is an interpretive act (Green, Franquiz, & Dixon, 1997; Ochs, 1999). It is a recursive process of listening, writing, and re-listening. As such, the transcript is a resource for meaning making rather than a definitive record of reality. As reviewers evaluate a manuscript, they should look carefully at the assumptions the researcher makes about the act of transcription and how they represent their transcripts.

Reviewers should evaluate the level of detail in the transcript against the research questions being asked. Do their questions warrant a close linguistic analysis? If so, the reviewer should expect to see a fairly detailed description and representation of transcriptions. Does their research question focus on broad representations through institutional discourses? In this case, the reviewer might expect to see a historical and ethnographic description of discourses and not a detailed transcription.

If the researcher is engaged with the study of discourse at the interactional level, researchers should include, at a minimum, a description of their transcription process; acknowledging how the record was constructed. Beyond that, reviewers can expect to find a continuum of detail, depending on the question under study. On the one end, they might find a simple notation system that explains the symbols in the transcript and a simple turn-by-turn representation of a participant's dialogue or conversation represented speaker by speaker. On the other end of the continuum, researchers might include a detailed explanation of their decision making in the transcription process, including the mechanics and representation of the transcript. The mechanics of the transcript include aspects such as: the researcher's choice in transcribing verbals and/or nonverbals and decisions around segmentation and turn taking. Issues of representation include areas such as: the presentation of the transcript on the page; the vertical or horizontal layout; consecutive versus alternating line numbers; time codes; and the placement of the designation of the speakers on the page. If decisions about the transcription process are not transparent, reviewers might ask questions about either the mechanics or the representation of the transcript. Here is a sample of questions reviewers might ask:

> *What defines a turn in your transcript? Are there other ways of defining a turn?*
>
> *What are other features of the interaction that were present but not transcribed? What is your relationship to the data? In what way does that matter?*
>
> *What has been privileged in your transcript? Left out?*
>
> *How do your choices impact what is represented and what sense can be made, what questions can be asked and answered about this data?*

Reviewers should note that more attention paid to the transcript in the text is an issue of space and this limits the amount of contextual detail, frame, and/or discussion that the researcher might include. These trade-offs should be taken into account when reviewing a manuscript.

4. Treatment of context should be explicit

The question of context is a provocative theoretical and methodological issue for discourse studies and one that often arises in reviews. One of the big questions that arises in discussions around context is: How much of the context—beyond the here and now of the interaction—is important or necessary to understand the interaction? Critically oriented forms of discourse analysis tend to pay attention to the macro-context—the societal and institutional as well as the grammatical resources that make up a text, event, or social practice, which, in turn, is connected to the macro-context. Conversation analysts believe, on the other hand, that all that is relevant is the "here and now" of the interaction, not what came before or after it. This group of scholars argues that CDA does not attend closely enough to the linguistic resources that constitute interactions but instead focus on how macro-relations are mapped onto micro-interactions (Widdowson, 1998). Another, related issue, is that critically oriented forms of discourse analysis have been critiqued as being "out of context"; that is, interpretations are drawn from relatively small amounts of text which are analyzed outside the context of their production, consumption, distribution, and reproduction and interpretations are often read onto the data with findings being predetermined. This is an issue worthy of reviewers' consideration.

Researchers engaged with critically oriented forms of discourse analysis in the field of education have tended to counter this criticism because a great deal of the scholarship is set within ethnographic contexts (Rogers et al., 2005). As Blommaert (2005) says, "analysis should not start . . . as soon as people open their mouths. It should have started long before that" (p. 67). Yet, the question of context is a fertile one for the field. Part of the richness is due to the idea that certain aspects of context exist and others are being created through every interaction. Gee (2004/2011) refers to this dilemma as the "frame problem" and describes it this way:

> Any aspect of context can affect the meaning of an utterance. Context, however, is indefinitely large, ranging from local matters like the positioning of bodies and eye gaze, through people's beliefs to historical, institutional, and cultural settings. No matter how much of the context we have considered in offering an interpretation of an utterance, there is always the possibility of considering other and additional aspects of the context, and these new considerations may interpret how we interpret the utterance. Where do we cut off consideration of context? How can we be sure any interpretation is right if considering further aspects of the context might well change that interpretation?
>
> (p. 27)

Reviewers might ask questions thinking about the multiple and intertwined levels of contexts (e.g. Bloome et al., 2008). Productive questions that can be asked of analysts include: *Can you offer a descriptive analysis of the discourse practices under study (e.g., word counts, amount of time that speakers are speaking, and gender break down of speakers)? What other contextual details about the particular moment of the cultural scene under analysis might help the reader understand this analysis? How does this social practice relate to other events and institutions? What is the history of the interaction—including the production, circulation, and consumption of this particular discourse practice? How do the multiple contexts affect each other?*

It should be kept in mind that scholars in the field think differently about the issue of context. van Dijk (2008), for example, views context as mental models that mediate the relationship between discourse processes and social structure. van Leeuwen (2008), on the other hand, believes the concept of context creates a false hierarchy between texts and contexts whereas texts are privileged and contexts are seen as superfluous. Thus, he prefers the term "social practice" instead of context. Blommaert (2005), drawing on ethnographic approaches to discourse analysis, foregrounds text trajectories and an awareness that every text is contextualized through its production, reproduction, circulation, and consumption. This cycle, in turn, involves changes in contexts. Knowledge of this diversity of approaches around the issue of context can help reviewers support and extend the kind of approach to context that analysts are providing in a manuscript. Regardless of the approach, reviewers can prompt authors for contextualization throughout the article—in the literature review, design of the study and methods, and in representing their findings. This, in turn, can help develop the concept in the field.

5. There is no one method of discourse analysis

Sometimes authors claim to call on the "tools" or "methods" of discourse analysis. I find this problematic as a reviewer. There is no uniform set of tools attributed to discourse analysis and the criteria of acceptability seem to vary journal by journal depending on the aims and goals of the editor and the editorial board. Critical discourse studies are a broad subfield in discourse studies with many different approaches. Thus, scholars should carefully locate their approach within a tradition—social semiotics (Kress, 2009, 2011), public consultative discourse analysis (Scollon, 2010), discourse-historical approaches (Wodak & Meyer, 2001), ethnographic approaches (Blommaert, 2005; Collins, 2001; Martín Rojo, 2010; Rogers, 2003, 2011), systemic functional linguistics (Schleppegrell, 2004), and so forth and their treatment and explanation of discourse and methods should follow the analytic standards set forth in this tradition. These standards are reviewed in numerous books and handbooks and cannot be covered here. However, reviewers should know to consult the appropriate reference for standards depending on the tradition that the scholar indentifies with.

The other problem I encounter as a reviewer is when the researcher fails to consider discourse analysis as both method and theory, instead, most often, treating discourse analysis strictly as a methodology. Identifying discourse analysis as both theory and method leads to a more robust treatment of the question under study and, I believe, can lead to greater insights in the field more generally. An example: Someone submits a paper that focuses on the construction of race in discussion groups in a high school English classroom. The researcher identifies their approach to discourse analysis in the tradition of James Gee and describes how they approached their analysis of the interactions through Gee's (2010) seven building tasks. Their theoretical framework provides a few brief references to sociocultural theory. As a reviewer I wonder: Why haven't they included scholarship from Critical Race Theory or whiteness studies? Similarly, Gee's framework can and does make sense to draw on with the questions they are asking but are they aware of the traditions of discourse studies that have attended to race and ethnicity (e.g., van Dijk and Wodak)? Ideally, reviewers can prompt researchers to align and develop their theoretical framework alongside of their methodology seeking coherence between theory and method.

6. Issues of sampling and overgeneralization are addressed

As is the tradition in qualitative research, sampling is the representation of individuals and subsets making up the population group from which results can be generalized or transferred (Creswell, 1998; Le Compte & Preissle, 1993). Critically oriented forms of discourse analysis do not attempt to generalize findings but to be transferable—that is, the findings in one area may yield insights or ring true in another, similar area (Lincoln & Guba, 1985). However, how to achieve transferability from study results is also dependent on the nature of data needed for the particular study as well as the research design. The challenge for critical discourse analysts lies in the assumption that every interaction is, in a Bakhtinian sense, unique and therein lies the fiction of true transferability. However, in more general terms, the potential of discourse analysis lies in its ability to find how any social practice is remade anew and, at the same time, is imbued with history and tradition.

There are a range of sampling procedures that analysts draw on, including theory based sampling, snowball sampling, politically important cases, purposeful sampling, and convenience sampling. Reviewers should expect to understand the purpose and goal of the texts or social practices subject to analysis; that is, the researcher should identify which sampling procedure they used and why. Beyond this, sampling might be framed as part of the original research design or come from within a data set after the study has been conducted, either approach can be inductive or deductive.

Drawing a sample as part of the original research design can be seen in the work of Hays (2000), Bloome & Power-Carter (2001), Woodside-Jiron (2011), and Pini (2011). This approach is more often found in studies that are grounded in analysis of a large corpus of written texts. In these cases, reviewers might want to ask: *What texts or practices were chosen for analysis and why? What are the limitations and biases in their sampling? Has the researcher stayed within their sample in drawing conclusions? Have they explained the parameters of sampling with detail?*

Drawing a sample from an existing data set is often seen within studies that combine ethnography and discourse analysis (see, for example, Chouilaraki, 1996; Green & Inés Heras, 2010; Lee & Majors, 2003). In cases where scholars define a sample within the data set, reviewers might want to ask: *How does this kind of interaction represent the totality of interactions? Was this an anomalous or typical kind of interaction?* Either is fine but it is important for researchers to identify the typicality of the interaction so reviewers can get a sense of their purpose and goal of studying this interaction.

A researcher might be interested in an interaction precisely because it is anomalous or in other cases, a researcher might be interested in the sort of social practice that is common place or naturalized—say, for instance, sharing time in a primary grade classroom (Michaels, 1981) or a discussion among teachers in a professional development setting (Lewis & Ketter, 2010). In these more deductive approaches, the researcher wants to understand and unpack the typicality through a close analysis of the discursive contours of the social practice.

Discourse analysts need to be careful not to overstate the transferability of their findings. This often appears as statements that certain discursive features represent, for example, "*the* discourse of special education" with failure to acknowledge that discourses are complex and contradictory. As a reviewer, I often caution researchers against the fiction of conducting an exhaustive analysis and urge them to look for counter examples, surprises, and to consider if their claims are trustworthy. As Burman (2004) writes, "rather than formulating a monovocal account, good discursive analyses acknowledge the multiple and contested character of the interplay of discourses by showing how different discursive representations are built to interact with and ward off others" (p. 7).

7. Reflexivity should be addressed

In our review (Rogers et al., 2005), we learned that much of the scholarship in educational research that drew on CDA included a researcher role section where the researcher reflects on her or his involvement, background, or participation in the research—a move that is common in qualitative research. However, the majority of scholarship did not move from reflection to reflexivity. Bucholtz (2001) defined reflexivity as a process whereby "the analyst's choices at every step in the research process are visible as a part of the discourse investigation and critique does not stop with social processes, whether macro-level or micro-level, but rather extends to the analysis itself" (p. 166). Reflexivity within a CDA framework arises from a concern about the stabilization of knowledge claims and the slipperiness of language itself. That is, researchers are part of the discursive practices they seek to study (Chouilaraki & Fairclough, 1999). Reflexivity is especially important in educational research where researchers have a long history of participation within the institutions and contexts that they study. A hallmark indicator of reflexivity is when researchers take their analytic frame and turn it on themselves as researchers and participants in the study.

Aside from considering whether reflexivity exists and the kind of reflexivity, reviewers might also consider the intention of reflexivity. Reflexive intentions may vary from building rigor in the research to questioning the epistemological and ontological foundations of the knowledge claims that can be made (Alvesson & Skoldberg, 2000). Building rigor in the research process through reflexivity is akin to traditional claims of validity, which often safeguard researchers from a truly self-reflexive paradigm. This may be considered problematic within a critical framework, given that the epistemological moorings reject the view of an objective and neutral science. On the other hand, researchers may turn the analytic framework back on themselves to analyze how their participation in the research contributed to the reproduction or disruption of power relations. Regardless of the intention, some portion of the methodology should be spent discussing the researcher's positionality vis-à-vis the discourse under examination.

When thinking about the level and intention of reflexivity in an article, reviewers might also pay attention to the kind of language choices that researchers use when describing their methods. Do they discuss "applying" a methodology (versus using the methodology as a tool)? The difference is whether the researcher takes responsibility for the analysis or attributes the analysis to an abstract framework. When researchers refer to the analysis as a tool, they are positioning themselves as the instrument of meaning making versus applying the method. Often these language choices signal subtle commitments that reviewers can probe researchers to think more deeply about (Rogers, 2011).

8. Analysis should be transparent

There are as many different approaches to analysis within critical discourse analysis as there are problems to be studied. In general, the view of methods is that one finds a research topic, applies a set of theoretical frames (or lets the frames emerge from the data), and then selects appropriate methods, depending on the questions being asked and the theories being used. Some analysts draw on extensive ethnographic fieldwork; others collect large corpuses of texts from historical archives, websites, or news sources. As a reviewer, I expect the analytic procedures to be explained in detail.

One question that has yet to be resolved in the field is the extent to which being systematic in the methodology is an indicator of more rigorous research. Especially with critically oriented varieties of discourse analysis, there may be the guise of scientism, which masks a critical paradigm. Certainly, reviewers will encounter articles with close linguistic analysis and others that focus more on societal and institutional discourses. The methods that one chooses should be commensurate with the research questions being asked. What is important is that the analyst defines discourse, offers adequate methodological detail, and there is congruence across the paper. Reviewers might keep in mind the advice from Norman Fairclough who stated, "you may not be doing much textual analysis but at least maybe you should be aware that whether you do or not is an issue" (Fairclough, 2011). Reviewers can remind authors of these tensions and ask them to consider them in their discussion. In what follows, I address two issues that routinely crop up in articles I review— underanalysis and attention paid to isolated features or cases.

Attention to "what" is said and "how" it is said. Analysis should include investigation of both *what* is said and *how* it is said/written. The "what" of the analysis includes the themes/content. The "how" of the analysis includes the linguistic choices that the writer/speaker makes, which tells us as much about the meaning of their discourse. Often times, researchers only include a summary of the themes. This might take the appearance of large text excerpts—from an interview or newspaper source, for instance—embedded within the text without much attention to the way in which the linguistic features of the text build meanings. This is part of an inductive approach and may prepare a researcher for discourse analysis but is not discourse analysis. In these cases, reviewers might prompt researchers for more analysis.

Patterns, not Isolated Features or Instances. Discourse analysis uncovers patterns in the rhetorical and discursive strategies that a speaker/writer uses. Too often when I review articles, I see a sampling of linguistic features—verbs or pronouns—for instance, and I wonder: Why these and not other discursive resources? Antaki, Billig, Edwards, & Potter (2003) refer to this type of underanalysis as "feature spotting." I do not see feature spotting as reason to reject an article but it may suggest the need for more analysis and significant revisions. In my own research of how students learn to become discourse analysts (Rogers, 2011), I have found that feature spotting helps analysts build conceptual leverage and connect their findings to the larger field of study. Thus, when reviewers spot feature spotting in an article, they can prompt the researcher to use their initial findings as a way of connecting with other research that has been done in the field—thus expanding the scope, and potentially the significance of the study. For instance, a study that focuses on pronouns might connect with other research in their content area where pronouns are the unit of analysis.

With the infinite array of discursive features that might be relevant in any interaction, our task as reviewers is to critically evaluate the discursive features included (and excluded) in the analysis. If, for example, the researcher is asking about social identities evoked during a sharing time discussion, prosody in speech may be just as relevant to the research question as lexical choices (e.g., Michaels, 1983). Inclusion and exclusion criteria of discursive features should be clear.

A related issue is that sometimes analysts get so deeply into their analysis that they forget the importance of framing their argument in a way that others in the field will care about. This is something reviewers can remind them about. This issue is discussed in more depth in the section on representation.

9. Issues of representation are considered

Thus far, I have addressed touchstones that focus on the process of conducting discourse analysis. However, reviewers are also concerned with judging the quality of the product of inquiry. The question reviewers can ask is: *What is the quality of the narrative presented?* When done properly, the reader does not feel lost in minutiae but always has a sense of the whole. How to balance the whole and the detail of linguistic analysis is a difficult task for writers. Part of the difficulty in representing discourse analysis is in finding ways to understand and portray the complexity of linguistic moves, while at the same time, portray the complexity of the ongoing story. It is important that reviewers have a sense of the overall argument of the research; that is, how this research both speaks to the field and contributes to it. In particular, when reviewing research, I find the following craft moves particularly helpful: summary of the overall findings; a balance between the micro- and macro-; connections to existing research. I will address each in turn.

First, because discourse analysis attends to both linguistic and social structures, it can be difficult for the analyst to present the "big picture" while also attending to the small details of analysis. Providing a summary at the beginning of the findings (or interpretations) section that outlines the key interpretations and how the findings will flow is crucial to guide the reviewer through the article. The reviewer wants to know what to expect and how the author has chosen to represent the findings of their analysis. See Juzwik (2006, pp. 502–503) for an excellent example of such an overview.

Second, balancing the micro- and macro- in the representations/findings section can be a challenge for even the experienced analyst and yet it is absolutely critical for a cohesive article. One of the common problems that I encounter as I review studies is that excerpts are provided from interviews or other texts and they are brief and decontextualized. Often, authors do not provide information about how the excerpts of talk or text are connected to the data set as a whole. Sometimes, the author summarizes the excerpts without real analysis or providing additional context from the study. Presenting fragments of texts leaves readers with unanswered questions about the contextualization of the texts. Discourse analysis should attend to "text trajectories" (Blommaert, 2005, p. 11) or what occurred before and after the interaction. Balancing textual analysis and context, however, is not an easy feat, especially when space is at a premium as it always is in writing for academic journals. The reader needs to get a sense of the context—through rich descriptions—to get a sense of the text trajectory of the text under investigation.

The third issue to consider in the representation of discourse analysis is the question of: *So what?* Reviewers want to know how this analysis connects and contributes to the existing field. When I review an article, I often look at how the author connects their findings to other research and demonstrates the ways that the current analysis pushes the field forward.

Finally, reviewers need to feel comfortable that the interpretations offered seem reasonable given the data shared. They might encourage the author to provide counter-interpretations or extend an invitation to her readers to generate such alternative readings.

10. Discourse analysis should extend existing knowledge

When at the conclusion of an article, reviewers might ask: *Is this research likely to inspire additional research? Does the researcher explore new conceptual or theoretical ground or address issues of long concern to educational researchers in new ways?* In the discussion section, researchers should indicate how their research has contributed to the field and what additional research might be conducted in the future.

One critique of discourse analysis, particularly the critically oriented types, is that analysts use their discourse analysis to simply prove a preexisting point. That is, that they have an overt political and social agenda and their discourse analysis exists to further this agenda. In some writing it looks as if the author is taking sides (or distancing themselves) with the speaker (Antaki, Billig, Edwards,

& Potter, 2003). In these cases, there is generally an overemphasis on theory at the expense of deep textual analysis. Excerpts are chosen that exemplify this position taking. This might take the appearance of the author extracting isolated quotes to demonstrate a salient theme. Sometimes the analysis, indeed, results in patterns that reinforce what is known about power and ideology. However, it is important for researchers to be open to their theories being challenged. Researchers and reviewers can deliberately look for counter-examples and challenges to the theories used. If, for example, a researcher's findings suggest that a participant used a particular voice (say, active voice) and tense (say, future tense) consistently (signaling a kind of identity), the reviewer might wonder about cases where the participant spoke in a passive voice. How did the researcher deal with discrepant cases?

Another, related concern is that analysts do not spend enough time considering the scholarship that has been conducted and discussing how their research adds to this database. Reviewers can spot this weakness in the literature review when researchers use long strings of citations to support a point. Or, related, we see a series of citations that are grouped together but the researcher fails to distinguish between studies. This is a signal that the researcher has not conducted a close reading of the existing literature and, therefore, it is unlikely that they will be offering insights that will add to key issues in the field.

Related, discourse analysis can contribute to theory building. Discourse analysis is both theory and method. Too often, the theoretical groundings of discourse analysis get short-changed and there is an overemphasis on methods. When approached as a set of theories and methods, discourse analysis holds the potential to crack open new ways of theorizing about social practices. Researchers can contribute to theory building through improved methods, providing insights into current theories or providing data that may be useful to theory development. Reviewers might ask: *Does the research extend the boundaries of relevant theories?*

Critically oriented forms of discourse analysis conducted within educational contexts and/or by educational researchers have contributed a great deal to the field of discourse studies more generally (Rogers et al., 2005). Some of these contributions include: bringing CDA into ethnographic contexts, attention to diversity, power, and learning (Rex et al., 2010), and a focus on interactional analyses versus written texts. Reviewers might keep these contributions in mind and search for ways that they can extend scholars to deepen their insights in each of these areas.

11. Commitment to advocacy and social change should be considered

Critical forms of discourse analysis address social problems. At the heart of such scholarship, regardless of how explicit this is in writing, is a commitment to equity and justice (Rex et al., 2010). A provocative issue for those engaged with a critically oriented form of discourse analysis is how their research promotes or leads to justice, advocacy, and social change. This touchstone is a relatively new consideration—one with much potential for development. To begin, we need to consider how do researchers identify advocacy and social change within their research? Next, how might we evaluate such approaches as reviewers?

Reviewers might consider the following kinds of social change stemming from critically oriented discourse analysis: reading texts differently, framing questions in terms of liberation versus domination, social action stemming from findings, or social action included as part of the research design. I will discuss each one in turn.

Reading (and Writing) Texts Differently

While CDA might not provide answers to problems it often enables one to understand the ideological roots of an issue by offering not only a description and interpretation of the problem but an explanation as well. This conceptualization of social change focuses on the affects an analysis and set of findings/interpretations has on the reader. CDA can encourage people to read texts differently through its close attention to the naturalization of ideology. It could be argued that if scholarship helps others in the field realize their own conceptual shortcomings and encourages people to think differently about social problems, this is a form of social change.

Another way in which scholars may promote social change is through making explicit attempts to reference scholars of color and international scholars. This, too, asks people to read and write differently. North-Atlantic perspectives and scholars have dominated the field of critical discourse analysis, and more attention needs to be paid to the good work happening around the world. If scholars do not include references to scholars of color, reviewers might prompt them to do so. This, in turn, asks that reviewers consciously educate themselves about the diversity of scholars within critical discourse analysis—extending their own boundaries—which, in turn, might have a ripple effect in their own work and beyond.

Positive Discourse Analysis

It has been argued that critical discourse analysis has, for too long, studied how oppression is discursively constructed. By way of contrast, a number of scholars are calling for a focus on productive uses of power (Janks, 2005; Luke, 2004; Macgilchrist, 2007; Martin, 2004; Scollon & Scollon, 2004; Mosley & Rogers, 2011). Luke (2004) points out the potential for what he calls "reconstructive" versions of discourse analysis that focus on how liberation, solidarity, and community are constructed. Martin (2004) refers to this approach as "positive discourse analysis," which can provide a complementary focus on "how people get together and make room for themselves in the world—in ways that redistribute power without necessarily struggling against it" (p. 183).

Social Action from the Findings

In our review of the literature (Rogers et al., 2005), we found that very few articles moved toward emancipatory action with the results of their analyses. We concluded "the lack of action in the studies is surprising given that many of the authors defined CDA in terms of liberatory goals and aims" (pp. 386–387). There are, however, examples where researchers designed actions based on the findings of their analyses. Price (2009), for example, examined the discourses surrounding conferences and how they represent people with disabilities. She argued that conferences are among the least accessible spaces that people with disabilities encounter since they combine routine inaccessibility of public spaces with conference participants' lack of familiarity with the space. She asked: How does each conference document imagine the disabled conference participant? She analyzed the verbal and visual choices made in the documents produced by eight professional organizations that explain its policy on accessibility surrounding the academic conference. The results of the discourse analysis led Price to pose questions intended for professional organizations to consider in light of their policies on accessibility. One of the outcomes of this study was that the Conference on College Composition and Communication began looking more seriously at its policy statements. The article itself was only one part of a larger effort, but this past year there have been some concrete positive outcomes—including the organization's decision to institute a permanent position called the "Accessibility Coordinator" for each annual conference and to fund an ADA audit of each annual conference site.

Reviewers might prompt researchers to think about the following question:

What are the implications for the educational practices that are being studied, the methodologies for doing so, and the educational designs that might result?

Too often research stays within the narrow confines of the academy. Individual researchers might do a better job of distributing their research to local communities and work alongside them to read, reflect, and act on the research.

Action as Part of Research Design

Other scholars might choose to incorporate action into their research design as a form of participatory research. This kind of commitment to advocacy and social action can most often be seen in teacher research studies that utilize CDA (e.g., Schaenen, 2010). Action as a part of the research design is the explicit goal of public consultative discourse analysis (PCDA). According to Scollon (2010), PCDA "is oriented toward bringing discourse analysis in any relevant form into the process of making public policy" (p. 7). PCDA seeks to put the analysis to work in the policy-making process, making the results of the discourse analysis immediately relevant to the context, actors, and actions.

With each of these approaches to advocacy and social change, reviewers might prompt scholars to include criteria for evaluating such efforts in their article. The role of advocacy and social change in discourse analysis is a provocative issue for discourse analysis and one that deserves further attention.

Further Reading

The following texts represent a survey of some of the approaches within critically oriented approaches to discourse analysis. Most of them provide analytic standards and conceptualizations of quality expected within their tradition.

Blommaert, J. (2005). *Discourse*. New York: Cambridge University Press.
This book provides an introduction to critically oriented perspectives in discourse analysis. Blommaert draws on a wide range of people and perspectives in discourse studies and is organized around central themes and tensions in the field (e.g., text and context, and choice and determination). A key feature of this text is its global perspective.

Bloome, D., Carter, S. P., Christian, B. M., & Madrid, S. (2008). *On Discourse Analysis in Classrooms: Approaches to Language and Literacy Research* (An NCRLL volume). New York: Teachers College Press.
This book provides an introductory discussion of discourse analysis of language and literacy events in classrooms. The authors introduce approaches to discourse analysis to researchers new to the process and prepare researchers to appropriate questions and to think about pathways of discourse analysis.

Fairclough, N. (2001). *Language and Power*. New York: Longman.
This is a touchstone text in critical discourse analysis, written by one of the "founders" of the contemporary critical discourse studies movement. *Language and Power* reviews central theories—discourse, intertextuality, power, ideology, and then describes the "steps" (vis-à-vis orders of discourse) of conducting critical discourse analyses.

Gee, J. P. (2010). *An Introduction to Discourse Analysis: Theory and Method*. New York: Routledge.
This book is a theoretical handbook for discourse analysts building on theories of language-in-use. Gee draws on data to illustrate an analytic framework that he refers to as "seven building tasks." A synthesis of key conceptual work in discourse studies is included.

Kress, G. & van Leeuwen, T. (2001). *Multimodal Discourse: The Modes and Media of Contemporary Communication*. New York: Oxford University Press.
This is a seminal text in the field of multimodal studies. Drawing on work in systemic functional linguistics and social semiotics, Kress and van Leeuwen outline a framework for the grammar of visual design. This includes attention to the ways in which communicative modes (gesture, image, speech, writing, gaze) work together to create meanings. Drawn together by the theory of the "motivated sign," the text works nicely with other texts in critical discourse analysis. The book is rich with theory and examples of multimodal discourse analysis.

Norris, S. (2004). *Analyzing Multimodal Interaction: A Methodological Framework*. New York: Routledge.
Analyzing Multimodal Interaction is one of the few books that show, in detail, how to carry out multimodal discourse analysis. Norris introduces key concepts such as modal density, embodied and disembodied modes,

multimodal transcripts, and levels of awareness. Particularly useful are the guiding questions at the beginning of the chapters as well as the sample "assignments" at the end, which ask the reader to try out what has been explained in the chapter. The examples provided in the book are general social interactions, not specific to educational settings.

Rogers, R. (2011). (Ed). *An Introduction to Critical Discourse Analysis in Education* (second edition). New York: Routledge.

This book introduces key concepts and issues in critical discourse analysis and situates these within the field of educational research. The book invites readers to consider the theories and methods of three major traditions in critical discourse studies—discourse analysis, critical discourse analysis, and multimodal discourse analysis— through the empirical work of leading scholars in the field. Beyond providing a useful overview, it contextualizes critical discourse analysis in a wide range of learning environments and identifies how critically oriented forms of discourse analysis can shed new insights on learning and social change. There is a companion website designed to extend inquiry and dialogue beyond the chapters in the book. The website includes: chapter extensions, videos with leaders in CDS, bibliographies, and resources for teaching CDA.

Scollon, R. (2010). *Analyzing Public Discourse: Discourse Analysis in the Making of Public Policy*. London: Routledge.

In this book, Scollon describes public consultative discourse analysis (PCDA) as "oriented toward bringing discourse analysis in any relevant form into the process of making public policy" (p. 7). PCDA seeks to put the analysis to work in the policy-making process, making the results of the discourse analysis immediately relevant to the context, actors, and actions. This book describes the theoretical and methodological potential of this approach through vivid case study data.

Wodak, R. & Meyer, M. (2001). *Methods of Critical Discourse Analysis*. London: Sage.

This book provides an overview of the main approaches to critical discourse analysis as represented through the work of key people in each area. Each approach is introduced, both the theory and examples of methods. Each chapter contains a reflection section and a further reading section. The examples in this book are broadly located in the economy, media, government, but not in educational settings.

General Approach to Discourse Studies

Resources prepared by Teun A. van Dijk
  www.discourses.org/

Counterpoint Perspectives

To extend the touchstone related to transcription, I offer three Internet resources that offer different theories and methods of transcription. Through these resources, readers can explore the affordances and constraints of different approaches to transcribing communication.

Schegloff's Transcription Tutorial

Rooted in the tradition of conversation analysis, Emanuel Schegloff created an online transcription tutorial. The tutorial includes language samples and a guide for analysts to explore transcription notation systems. The core of this set of notational convention was first developed by Gail Jefferson and is commonly drawn on in discourse studies.
  www.sscnet.ucla.edu/soc/faculty/schegloff/TranscriptionProject/index.html

Resources for the Representation of Linguistic Interaction

"Transcription in Action: Resources for the Representation of Linguistic Interaction" is a resource from University of California, Santa Barbara that includes several helpful links, PDFs, and other materials.
  www.linguistics.ucsb.edu/projects/transcription/representing

Sigrid Norris's Website

This website provides resources for multimodal research, generally, and the design of multimodal transcripts, specifically. Norris includes video data and examples of multimodal transcripts. Drawing on social semiotics, Norris includes many resources for those interested in understanding multimodal interaction.

www.sigridnorris.com/transcription.htm

Author's Reflections on Quality

I recently wrote a paper that examined how an elected school board in St. Louis (of which I am a member) advocated for a policy change using Scollon's (2010) framework of public consultative discourse analysis. Data sources consisted of public records (e.g., agendas, media reports, transcripts of public hearings, and reports). In the spirit of PCDA, I did not simply analyze these texts and associated discourses but used the ongoing analyses to intervene in public policy. Three of the board's interventions were the focus of the paper.

I submitted this article to a well-known interdisciplinary journal in discourse studies. The article was not sent out for review. Instead, I received a short note from the editor saying that he found the subject of the research very interesting but the linguistic analysis was not systematic enough for this journal and that I should send it to an education journal. This comment caused me to reflect on the status of critical discourse analysis in education, generally, and about my scholarship, more specifically.

What does it mean to be systematic in a critically oriented discourse analysis? The editor's comments suggest that education journals that include discourse analysis studies privilege content over discursive analysis and perhaps the studies lack rigor in their treatment of the discursive. This perception may reflect the status of discourse analysis studies fifteen years ago but it does not hold true today. It could be argued that earlier, many studies referenced Gee's (2010) theory of discourse/Discourse but carried out little detailed analysis. However, as discourse analysis has become more common in education, there is a growing number of scholars conducting critically oriented discourse analysis in education and, thus, the pool of reviewers has broadened and deepened. Likewise, editors of journals are more familiar with the theories and methods and are able to call on qualified reviewers—reviewers who have background education in discourse analysis and have conducted discourse analyses themselves. As a result, we have seen the quality of analyses increase as well.[2] Indeed, throughout this chapter I have pointed to journals in education where exemplary studies have been published (e.g., *Reading Research Quarterly, Teachers College Press, Linguistics & Education, Anthropology & Education,* to name a few). But perhaps the editor's comment reflects a broader perception about the status of discourse analysis in education and it is up to scholars and reviewers to change it.

As I hope I have pointed out in this chapter, the very concept of being "systematic" in one's analysis is open for debate. In the article I sent out for review, I was detailed in my description of the methodology of PCDA and how the school board used this theory/method in our work shaping public policy. I understand the editor's comments to mean the inclusion of a detailed linguistic analysis. The analysis we engaged in as board members was intentionally designed to intervene in the ongoing creation of public policy and often included broad strokes versus close linguistic analysis because of our awareness of the audiences we needed to address. However, I was careful to offer this as a disclaimer and point out what I saw as the significance of the article—that is, being a case study of public consultative discourse analysis within education. The review from the editor served as a reminder to me that understandings of key concepts in discourse studies vary journal by journal. I share these reflections to underscore a point that I believe is important about reviews: every review contains seeds of important points and offers the potential to stimulate growth and reflection.

Conclusion

My aim throughout this chapter has been to make visible the sorts of touchstones that reviewers might consider as they think through research submitted for publication. Critical discourse analysis is an interdisciplinary subfield, and it is helpful if reviewers understand the complexity of critical discourse studies (the range of issues and tensions, etc.), have a background in a particular approach to discourse analysis (e.g., narrative analysis and historical approaches), and are familiar with the discipline in which the study is focused. It is important that reviewers consider not only the methodological and theoretical sophistication but also the potential the study has for offering new insights to the field of study. My hope is that these touchstones offer reviewers a guide that, in turn, will help extend the theory and practice of critically oriented forms of discourse analysis. Through their reviews, reviewers should encourage a creative union of theories and methods that generate new insights and research questions. This kind of review can keep the field alive with self-reflection and new insights.

Notes

1. It should be noted that quantitative analyses are carried out within a critical discourse studies tradition. However, the focus in this chapter is on the qualitative tradition.
2. It should also be noted that because the field of critical discourse analysis continues to diversify, it is important that scholars who submit articles calling on a particular kind of discourse analysis—say, nexus analysis, or multimodal discourse analysis—get their scholarship reviewed by someone who has some familiarity with the approach. It is important to evaluate the study based on knowledge of the purpose and goals of a particular approach.

References

Alvesson, M. & Skoldberg, K. (2000). *Reflexive Methodology: New vistas for qualitative researchers.* London: Sage.

Antaki, C., Billig, M. G., Edwards, D., & Potter, J. A. (2003). Discourse Analysis means doing analysis: A critique of six analytical shortcomings. *Discourse Analysis On-Line, 1.* Retrieved from www.shu.ac.uk/daol/articles/v1/n1/a1/antaki2002002-paper.html October, 2008.

Blommaert, J. (2001). Context is/as critique. *Critique of Anthropology, 21*(1), 13–32.

Blommaert, J. (2005). *Discourse: A critical introduction.* Cambridge, UK: Cambridge University Press.

Bloome, D. & Power Carter, S. (2001). Lists in reading education reform. *Theory into Practice, 40*(3), 150–157.

Bloome, D., Power Carter, S., Morton, B., Madrid, S., Otto, S., Shuart-Faris, N., & Smith, M. (2008). *Discourse Analysis in Classrooms: Approaches to language and literacy research.* New York: Teachers College Press.

Bucholtz, M. (2001). Reflexivity and critique in discourse analysis. *Critique of Anthropology, 21*(1), 165–183.

Burman, E. (2004). Discourse analysis means analyzing discourse. Some comments on Antaki, Billig, Edwards, & Potter's "Discourse analysis means doing discourse analysis: A critique of six analytic shortcomings." *Discourse Analysis Online.* Retrieved from http://extra.shu.ac.uk/daol/ October 10, 2008.

Chouliaraki, L. (1996). Regulative practices in a "progressivist" classroom: "Good habits" as a "disciplinary technology." *Language and Education, 10*(2/3), 103–118.

Chouliaraki, L. & Fairclough, N. (1999). *Discourse in Late Modernity: Rethinking critical discourse analysis.* Edinburgh, Scotland: Edinburgh University Press.

Collins, J. (2001). Selling the market: Educational standards, discourse and social inequality. *Critique of Anthropology, 21,* 143–163.

Creswell, J. (1998). *Qualitative Inquiry and Research Design: Choosing among five traditions.* London, New Delhi, Thousand Oaks, CA: Sage.

Fairclough, N. (2011). Interview with Norman Fairclough. In Companion Website to R. Rogers (Ed.), *An Introduction to Critical Discourse Analysis in Education* (2nd ed.). New York: Routledge. http://cw.routledge.com/textbooks/9780415874298.

Fairclough, N. & Wodak, R. (1997). Critical discourse analysis. In T. van Dijk (Ed.), *Discourse as Social Interaction* (pp. 258–284). London: Sage.

Gee, J. (2004/2011). Discourse analysis: What makes it critical? In R. Rogers (Ed.), *An Introduction to Critical Discourse Analysis in Education* (2nd ed., pp. 23–45). New York: Routledge.

Gee, J. P. (2010). *An Introduction to Discourse Analysis: Theory and method.* New York: Routledge.

Green, J. & Inés Heras, A. (2010). Identities in shifting educational policy contexts: The consequences of moving from two languages, one community to English only. In G. López-Bonilla & K. Englander (Eds.), *Discourses and Identities in Contexts of Educational Change: Contributions from the United States and Mexico* (pp. 155–194). New York: Peter Lang Press.

Green, J., Franquiz, M., & Dixon, C. (1997). The myth of the objective transcript: Transcribing as a situated act. *TESOL Quarterly*, *31*(1), 172–176.

Hays, J. (2000). Anguished laments: A critical discourse analysis of education, representation and development of the San of Botswana. *Journal of the African Activist Association*, *28*(3), 23–41.

Janks, H. (2005). Deconstruction and reconstruction: Diversity as a productive resource. *Discourse*, *26*(1), 31–44.

Juzwik, M. (2006). Performing curriculum: Building ethos through narratives in pedagogical discourse. *Teachers College Record*, *108*(4), 489–528.

Kress, G. (2009). *Multimodality: A social semiotic approach to contemporary communication*. New York: Routledge.

Kress, G. (2011). Discourse analysis in education: A multimodal social semiotic approach. In R. Rogers (Ed.), *An Introduction to Critical Discourse Analysis in Education* (2nd ed., pp. 205–226). New York: Routledge.

Le Compte, M. & Preissle, J. (1993): *Ethnography and Qualitative Design in Educational Research*. London: Academic Press.

Lee, C. & Majors, Y. (2003). "Heading up the street": Localised opportunities for shared constructions of knowledge. *Pedagogy, Culture and Knowledge*, *11*(1), 49–67.

Lewis, C. & Ketter, J. (2010). Learning as social interaction: Interdiscursivity in a teacher and researcher study group. In R. Rogers (Ed.), *An Introduction to Critical Discourse Analysis in Education* (2nd ed., pp. 128–153). New York: Routledge.

Lincoln, Y. & Guba, E. (1985). *Naturalistic Inquiry*. Newbury Park, CA: Sage.

López-Bonilla, G. & Englander, K. (Eds.). (2010). *Discourses and Identities in Contexts of Educational Change: Contributions from the United States and Mexico*. New York: Peter Lang Press.

Luke, A. (2004). Notes on the future of critical discourse studies. *Critical Discourse Studies*, *1*(1).

Macgilchrist, F. (2007). Positive discourse analysis: Contesting dominant discourses by reframing issues. *Critical Approaches to Discourse Analysis*, *1*(1), 74–94.

Martin, J. (2004). Positive discourse analysis: Solidarity and change. *Revista Canaria de Estudios Ingleses*, *49*, 179–200.

Martín Rojo, L. (2010). *Constructing Inequality in Multilingual Classrooms*. Berlin, Germany: De Gruyter Mouton.

Medina, C. (2010). "Reading across communities" in biliteracy practices: Examining translocal discourses and cultural flows in literature discussions. *Reading Research Quarterly*, *45*(1), 40–60.

Michaels, S. (1981). "Sharing time": Children's narrative styles and differential access to literacy. *Language in Society*, *10*, 423–442.

Mosley, M. & Rogers, R. (2011). Inhabiting the "tragic gap": Preservice teachers practicing racial literacy. *Teaching Education*, *22*(3), 303–324.

Norris, S. (2002). The implications of visual research for discourse analysis: Transcription beyond language. *Visual Communication*, *1*(1), 97–121.

Ochs, E. (1999). Transcription as theory. In A. Jaworski & N. Coupland (Eds.), *The Discourse Reader* (pp. 167–182). New York: Routledge.

Pini, M. (2011). The discourses of educational management organizations: A political design. In R. Rogers (Ed.), *An Introduction to Critical Discourse Analysis in Education* (2nd ed., pp. 267–291). New York: Routledge.

Price, M. (2009). Access imagined: The construction of disability in conference policy documents. *Disabilities Studies Quarterly*, *29*(1). Accessed at www.dsq-sds.org/article/view/174/174 on October 10, 2009.

Rex, L., Bunn, M., Davila, B., Dickinson, H., Carpenter-Ford, A., Gerben, C., McBee-Orzulak, M., & Thompson, H. (2010). A review of discourse analysis in literacy research: Equitable access. *Reading Research Quarterly*, *45*(1), 94–115.

Rogers, R. (Ed.). (2011/2004). *An Introduction to Critical Discourse Analysis in Education* (2nd ed.). New York: Routledge.

Rogers, R. (2011). Becoming discourse analysts: Constructing meanings and identities. *Critical Inquiry in Language Studies*, *8*(1).

Rogers, R. (2003). *A Critical Discourse Analysis of Family Literacy Practices: Power in and out of print*. Mahwah, NJ: Lawrence Erlbaum Associates.

Rogers, R. & Mosley, M. (2008). A critical discourse analysis of racial literacy in teacher education. *Linguistics and Education*, *19*, 107–131.

Rogers, R., Berkes, E., Mosley, M., Hui, D., & O-Garro, G. (2005). A critical review of critical discourse analysis. *Review of Research in Education*, *75*(3), 365–416.

Schaenen, I. (2010). Genre means: A critical discourse analysis of fourth grade talk about genre. *Critical Inquiry into Language Studies*, *7*(1), 28–53.

Schleppegrell, M. (2004). *The Language of Schooling: A functional linguistics perspective*. Mahwah, NJ: Lawrence Erlbaum Associates.

Scollon, R. (2010). *Analyzing Public Discourse: Discourse analysis in the making of public policy*. London: Routledge.

Scollon, R. & Wong Scollon, S. (2004). *Nexus Analysis: Discourse and the emerging Internet*. New York: Routledge.

van Dijk, T. A. (2000). *Critical discourse analysis*. Retrieved from www.discourse-in-society.org/OldArticles/The%20reality%20of%20racism.pdf on March 6, 2003.

van Dijk, T. (2008). *Discourse in Context: A sociocognitive approach*. Cambridge, UK: Cambridge University Press.

van Leeuwen, T. (2008). *Discourse and Practice: New tools for critical discourse analysis*. Cambridge, UK: Cambridge University Press.

Widdowson, H. (1998). The theory and practice of critical discourse analysis. *Applied Linguistics*, *19*(1), 136–151.

Wodak, R. & Meyer, M. (2001). *Methods of Critical Discourse Analysis*. London: Sage.

Wohlwend, K. (2011). Mapping modes in children's play and design: An action-oriented approach to critical multimodal analysis. In R. Rogers (Ed.), *An Introduction to Critical Discourse Analysis in Education* (2nd ed., pp. 242–266). New York: Routledge.

Woodside-Jiron, H. (2011). Language, power and participation: Using critical discourse analysis to make sense of public policy. In R. Rogers (Ed.), *An Introduction to Critical Discourse Analysis in Education* (2nd ed., pp. 154–182). New York: Routledge.

7

Ethnography

Nancy Kendall and Miriam Thangaraj

Ethnography is often equated with qualitative, case study, or fieldwork-based research. Atkinson and Hammersley (2007) note that ethnography has taken on so many meanings and usages that it may sometimes appear to be synonymous with qualitative inquiry. Indeed, Erickson (1986) lumps ethnographic, naturalistic, interpretive, grounded, phenomenological, subjective, and participant observational research methods all within the same "family."

The use of the term "ethnography" to describe a broad range of qualitative research approaches and studies may simply reflect ethnographers' eclectic use of methods (including interviews, observations, focus and other group discussions, and document analysis) commonly employed in diverse qualitative research traditions. Ethnography, however, may be more clearly delineated from other qualitative approaches by its historic development in anthropology, its conventional aim to understand cultural patterns in "emic" terms (Agar, 1996), and its common use of participant observation as the central research method. Ethnography as written product embodies many aspects of ethnographic methodology.

Judging the quality of ethnographic work can be tricky for at least three reasons. First, good qualitative research may be sometimes called ethnography (when it presents fine-grained and detailed accounts of an unfamiliar setting, for instance), but it may not reflect an engagement with issues, such as reflexivity, expected of researchers working within the ethnographic tradition.[1] Second, anthropological history and traditions have shaped an understanding that the written ethnography is an integral part of *doing* the research and not just its product, and that doing research and writing ethnographies are best learned inductively by reading other ethnographies. The result of this history was that, for many years, judging an ethnography depended on judging the qualities of the ethnographer and the persuasiveness of their story; judgments of ethnographic quality were thus highly individualized and disciplinarily bounded. Though we discuss a number of more recent efforts to develop criteria to judge the quality of ethnographies, this history continues to shape judgments of ethnographic qualities in various genres and disciplines. Finally, and perhaps most pressing for reviewers today, is the further complexity resulting from the expanded diversity of ethnographic disciplines, fields, epistemologies, ideologies, and theoretical lenses over the past century; and the explosion of analytic and presentational approaches over the past forty years.

Our three-point list above appears to suggest that a good reviewer of ethnography has, on the one hand, a deep and balanced appreciation of particular disciplinary approaches and histories and,

on the other hand, a broad understanding of multiple fields and their analytic approaches. We suggest, more pragmatically, the need for reviewers to make contingent judgments about the quality of any ethnographic work. These judgments, we will argue, are best anchored in reviewer reflexivity (keeping aware of and accounting for their own disciplinary lenses and limitations) and in reviewers attending closely to the alignments among how authors frame their research goals, epistemologies, theories, data sources, positionality, and presentational aesthetics.

We add a caveat for reviewers: the space allowed, particularly within article-length ethnographic work, for "meta" authorial notes on intent, goals, epistemology, and research processes may be limited, adding to the difficulty of the review process. We are hopeful that the list of touchstones we offer will nevertheless serve as a useful guide for the reviewer.

Select Terms

Ethnography: The term "ethnography" is used to describe both a research process and the products of this research. Tedlock (2003) describes ethnography as "combin[ing] research design, fieldwork, and various methods of inquiry to produce historically, politically, and personally situated accounts, descriptions, interpretations, and representations of human lives" (p. 165). This definition speaks to the interrelatedness of ethnographic methods, analysis, and representation, and is broad enough to cover the variety of theoretical and disciplinary orientations represented in ethnographic genres.

Across disciplines, fields, and purposes, ethnography is perhaps distinguished by the centrality of ethnographer–research participant relationships in the research process, and the aim of understanding cultural variation of/and human universalities. The aims of ethnographic research may be broad, such as to generate theory about cultural patterns and shared human practices through cross-cultural study (for example, the range of genders and gender relations acknowledged in the world, or the ways humans categorize and mark social distinctions). Or the aims may be more specific and aimed at solving a particular "problem" or exploring a prespecified question. In such cases, ethnographic insight may be set to the task of making better schools, machines, organizational routines, social policies, or shopping malls and public spaces. In either case, ethnographic methods are particularly useful in identifying emergent themes—often even new research questions in the course of research; and the discovery of the apparently counterfactual often identifies the most widely known and successful ethnographies.

The key elements of ethnography are:

- ethnographic "fieldwork" ("the empirical scrutiny of social situations in vivo," according to Holstein & Gubrium, 2008);
- "participant observation" (the primary research tool of ethnographic fieldwork, involving continuous and "reflexive" engagement (see Davies (1999) for a partial review of "reflexivity") with research participants, often in their local languages (Hammersley & Atkinson, 2007; Marcus, 1998), and often for an extended period of time; sometimes described, in shorthand, as observing what people say, what they do, and what they say they do);
- the process of analyzing fieldwork engagements and writing ethnography (which includes maintaining "fieldnotes" and writing analytic memos during fieldwork [see Emerson, Fretz, & Shaw (2011) for one of the most prescribed social science texts on fieldnotes; or the attempt by Clifford (1990) or Jackson (1990) to unpack fieldnotes] and more or less formal strategies for coding, analysis, and representational modes).

Ethnographer/Investigator/Researcher/Co-researcher: The person(s) engaged in ethnographic research; historically, a professionalized position held by "outsiders" who were attempting to understand a culture through the careful study of "insiders," their ideas, beliefs, actions, relations, and environment. Ethnographers are their own research tools, learning by actively experiencing fieldwork alongside their research subjects. Unlike other social science research methods, as LeCompte and Schensul (2010) point out, ethnographers do not enter "controlled environments"; they enter often unfamiliar settings as "invited guests," needing to develop intimate involvements in their fieldwork sites. Their ability to build rapport and trust with research subjects—whether by speaking the same language, spending sufficient time and resources for a "deep" enough ethnography, or developing a keen ethical sense—and their ability to appropriately situate field experiences within methodological and analytic traditions, qualifies their ethnographic research output.

Unlike the "Lone Ranger" role of the early twentieth-century Western anthropologist on his (or her)[2] "Solitary Quest" (Salzman McGill, 1989), the latter half of the twentieth century has seen greater diversity in the roles and characteristics of ethnographers, and greater acknowledgment of the significant contributions of "key informants." (See, for example, Narayan's (1997) collaboration with local villager Urmila*ji* on a book of Himalayan folktales, or Elyachar's (2005) discussion of the contribution of Essam, her translator, to the ethnography.) Consequently, a wide range of terms—researcher, co-researcher, collaborator, apprentice—are used to reflect the (perceived or desired) intersubjective, co-constructed, and cooperative nature of much ethnographic research.

Collaborative ethnographic endeavors, recognized as a useful and ethically progressive research method (Rappaport, 2008), have also grown in number, type, and stature. Such approaches include comparative work across multiple fieldwork sites (for example, the Six Cultures Project on childrearing and development, under the Whitings' leadership in 1954–1956); teams of social scientists working together in a single site on a preformulated set of research questions (often popular in policy evaluation projects; see Erickson & Stull, 1998); or ethnographer and "informants" working together closely (see, for example, the forthcoming special issue of the journal *Collaborative Anthropologies* that includes ethnographies co-authored by researchers and indigenous activists in Latin America).

In short, over the past sixty years, the recognition that the ethnographer is never "solitary" is increasingly embodied in ethnographic practices. Similarly, the ethnographer is no longer characteristically White and Western; the "natives [have been] gazing and talking back," as ethnographers from the "third world" or minority communities, working as cultural "insiders" within their own populations, have published ethnographic work in increasing numbers (Jacobs-Huey, 2002; Medicine, 2001; see Narayan (1993) for her influential piece problematizing the "native" in the native anthropologist).

In this context, it is appropriate to remind the reviewer that no account of ethnography can afford to ignore its problematic and complex relationship with imperial and colonial government (see Lewis, 1973), again evident in the U.S. military's Human Terrain System (see Sider, 2009). This history continues to inform the relationship among ethnographers, research participants, and governments. Whether as a means of observation and control of the "native other," or as the means of generating professional knowledge to advance imperialistic projects, or in efforts to "voice" indigenous people in struggles against neocolonialism, ethnographers cannot claim the role of "objective outsider." Power, as discourse and practice (as Asad (1991) notes with respect to European colonialism), has always been part of the reality ethnographers seek to understand, and of the research that they do.

The past four decades have witnessed new ethnographic genres—including critical, feminist, and postmodern—that have trained their lens precisely on the power relations that produce

ethnographic knowledge. Arguing for transformations in relations of power and authority in fieldwork, these genres have fueled a general shift from "participant observation to the observation of participation" (Tedlock, 1991), which decenters the ethnographer and emphasizes the relational, dialogic/polyphonic, intersubjective character of ethnographic research. Reviewers are right, therefore, to expect ethnographers to account for their relational, research, and narrative choices in their writing.

Informants/Key informants/Participants/Co-researchers/Consultants: Historically, informants *were* the subject of study of ethnographers, literally informing the ethnographer about their world with as much detail and accuracy as possible. As mentioned above, as ethnographic pursuits have become more politically and epistemologically conscious, the relations between research participants and researchers have been problematized—in terms of social structural and power differences, in psychological, emotional, or sexual terms, and in terms of structuring access to other research participants (Abu-Lughod, 2008; Lassiter, 2005; Wolcott, 2002). Participant/researcher relations have also become an object of study and of theorizing about the sociocultural and political projects of ethnography itself. These shifts have been accompanied by a greater consideration of the ethics of and expectations from researcher–co-researcher relations (e.g., Lassiter, 2005; Davies, 1999; Busier et al., 1997).

Reviewers should evaluate the author's engagement with the issue of participant/researcher relationships in an article; if this engagement is not direct, then the terms used by the researcher should align with the epistemological, theoretical, analytic, and narrative approaches adopted. Also, reviewers might attend particularly to the use of the term "key informant," which is increasingly popular, but often misused, in research protocols and articles. A "key informant" is a critical collaborator (or, as Lassiter (1998) would have it, consultant), helping to shape the research and often the analysis and writing of an ethnography. The shape and scope of such relationships should be clearly explicated in written products. Using the term "key informant" to refer to a person who has participated only briefly in the ethnographic process (for example, one in-depth interview) likely signals a lack of understanding on the author's part of ethnographic research conventions and terms.

Field/Fieldwork: Ethnography *is* the genre of fieldwork. The defining feature of anthropological enquiry—and a rite of passage for anthropologists—fieldwork was historically regarded as systematic, intimate, long-term, detailed, and contextualized data collection through immersion of an "outsider" in a "non-literate" society (Hammersley & Atkinson, 2007).

With the new opportunities and challenges presented by travel and communication technologies, the end of colonialism and the Cold War (and related demise of state funding for multiyear fieldwork projects), the onslaught of globalization forces and resultant calls for new forms of ethnography to examine their effects, and the increasing diversity of ethnographic genres, there remain few straightforward assumptions about "field" and "fieldwork." No longer can the reviewer evaluate ethnographic work using the gold standard of one to two years of fieldwork, or assume that the field is "there," geographically bounded, and restricted to homogeneous small-scale societies (Gupta & Ferguson, 1997). Fieldwork may be conducted for a year or may span an academic career (e.g., Dehyle, 2009); it may involve short bursts of time as part of a research team or a translocal comparative project; it may be virtual (Wittel, 2000); or it may involve an individual or a team conducting "multi-site ethnographies" (Hannerz, 2003; Marcus, 1995), with shorter periods of time in a range of sites (e.g., Escobar, 2008). It may be an "ethnography of connection," tracking the global movement of people, capital, or information across locations and levels (e.g., Hart, 2002; Khosravi, 2011; Tsing, 2005), or it may be situated in a "global ethnoscape" of transnational cultural flows (Appadurai, 1991) or a "global assemblage" (Ong & Collier, 2005).

The traditional ethnographic expectation of long-term fieldwork located in a single site—resulting in part from pragmatic considerations of long distances and lengthy voyages (for example, the landmark "armchair"-busting Cambridge Expedition of 1898 to the Torres Strait Islands (Haddon, 1890; Rivers, 1910)) and perhaps even more from the serendipitous stranding of Malinowski on the Trobriand Islands during the First World War (leading to the establishment of the rigorous fieldwork methods of the British structural–functionalist school)—has crumbled under the realities of academic life, the shrinking of fieldwork funding sources, and the need to engage ethnographically with flows, connections, and disjunctures across space and time. Ethnographers (and reviewers) may have to be content with twelve months or less of fieldwork, and fieldwork that may have many different (and differently constituted) "fields." Time in the field, in and of itself, is no assurance of quality ethnography, but it is expected that the ethnographer will conduct fieldwork of a duration that enables him/her to learn sufficiently about the field setting, from the perspectives of research participants. Optimum periods of fieldwork may vary with the "cycle of activity" of interest; the ethnographer's skill, sensitivity, training, research questions, and field settings; and the contractual agreements or funding modalities under which research is conducted (Wolcott 2005, 1987).

While the diversity of fields and fieldwork resources has resulted in innovation, it also makes developing clear and comprehensive guidelines for assessing the quality of ethnographic research more difficult; a generic rule of thumb for reviewers, drawing on Hammersley and Atkinson (2007), is that the more exploratory the nature of the ethnographic inquiry the greater the expectation that research design with be open ended and emergent, and the greater the likelihood that fieldwork will take a "considerable amount of time. . . . often over the course of a year or more" (pp. 3–5). In contrast, when the ethnographer is familiar with a particular context, place, or problem (having worked on or in it for a long time previously, for instance), or when ethnography is responding to less-open-ended questions, the length of fieldwork may be significantly shorter than a year. For example, in fields like information systems where ethnographic questions are often more directed, exemplary, "long-term" ethnographic research may take only eight months (Myers, 1999).

Thus, we suggest that reviewers: (1) attend to how field definitions and fieldwork duration align with the goals and design of the ethnographic project, and (2) consider the field and disciplinary conventions in the ethnographic traditions upon which the researcher draws (see, for instance, Jeffery & Troman (2004) for examples of different forms of "ethnographic time" in educational ethnography, Visconti (2010) for a categorization of business ethnographies as "limited," "mildly extended," and "extended," or Wittel (2000) for a consideration of the practical implications of doing multisite ethnography, including on length of fieldwork).

To give a concrete example, when Kendall (2012) conducted ethnographic research to examine how federal abstinence-only education policies shaped (1) students' daily experiences of sex and sexuality in high schools, and (2) school–community relations, the effort took over two years of multisite fieldwork across five states in the United States. The project required an intimate grasp of the texture of everyday life in schools (acquired through participation and observation in classrooms and school activities, and interviews with students and school personnel) and an appreciation of the mutual expectations of the community and the school (culled from participant observation and interviews with parents, teachers, officials, and community leaders). These in turn had to be situated with respect to policy analyses spanning multiple social levels. Were Kendall to claim these goals could have been achieved through a six-month ethnographic study, the reviewer would be justified in raising red flags about the appropriateness of her ethnographic time for the breadth, exploratory nature, and multisitedness of her questions.

Participant observation, as a research tool, embodies the core methodological stances of ethnography. It involves the ethnographer trying to make sense of research subjects' daily realities, the use of ethnographers themselves as research instruments, and the centrality of ongoing, situated engagement between ethnographer and research participants. Participant observation thus expresses a fundamental epistemological claim that there are no "'external" positions from which to study the social world. The ethnographer is not a detached observer: the ethnographer is always and ever a part of the social scene, the field of study. At the same time, the ethnographer is always also recording the experiences in which she/he is a participant observer—typically in the form of "fieldnotes"—and in so doing, narrating and shaping research data and the field of study.

In most cases, research subjects are aware of the ethnographer's presence as a participant observer and typically serve as gatekeepers of research (though see, for example, Goffman (1961) for an example of covert participant observation). Given the intense and intersubjective nature of participant observation—perhaps more so than any other qualitative research method—ethnography requires researchers to engage in a careful and reflexive examination of their roles, positions, and identities in the field. As a result, ethnographers have often led the way in identifying, analyzing, critiquing, and engaging with issues of subjectivity, reflexivity, and ethics in the social sciences (e.g., Davies, 1999; Blackman, 2007). How they do so varies significantly, however, because of the different epistemological weight attributed to these issues within diverse traditions. For example, engagement with the issue of subjectivity ranges from acknowledging and "managing" one's subjectivity (e.g., Peshkin, 1993), to calling for a move away from "comfortable" engagement with conceptions of subjectivities that are fixed or nonrelational (e.g., Pillow, 2003; Heshusius, 1994).

It is now *de rigeur* for ethnographers to address issues of subjectivity, reflexivity, and ethics in ethnographies, so a lack of engagement should be noted and evaluated by reviewers with the caveat that journal editors may have little patience for extensive discussion of these matters. The touchstones below discuss potential reviewer criteria for considering these issues.

Diversities in Perspective, Context, and Form

While many scholars hold that there are no exclusive claims to ethnographic methods—"the methods belong to all of us," Bernard (2006, p. xviii) insists—it may be instructive to begin our discussion of ethnography with respect to the discipline in which it originated—anthropology—and its preoccupation with the Other. As Radcliffe-Brown (1952), one of the founders of British social anthropology described it: "a meeting of teachers from Oxford, Cambridge and London was held [in 1909] to discuss the terminology of our subject. We agreed to use 'ethnography' as the term for descriptive accounts of non-literate peoples."

The advent of ethnography as the professionalized, systematic, and scientific study of non-Western (and particularly nonliterate) cultures is traced to Franz Boas and Bronislaw Malinowski in the 1910s and 1920s (Hammersley & Atkinson, 2007). Under their influence, ethnographic fieldwork became the touchstone of anthropology. From the start, fieldwork was as much a method as an epistemological stance: the proper conditions for ethnographic work were to live "right among the natives" (Malinowski, 1984 [1922]), because it was the best means of developing "scientific descriptions" and foregrounding "the native's point of view." The goal, in Boas' day, of "getting it down and getting it right, in the natives' own languages," often in exhaustive and exhausting detail remains part of the mental maps of ethnographers today (Bernard, 2006, p. 470).

Nonetheless, these rather positivistic goals have been critiqued (Hymes, 1969; Kuper, 1988; Davies, 1999) and have changed over time as ethnographers have incorporated a range of epistemological approaches, representational forms, and distinct disciplinary interests. Sample the diversity in the labels and descriptors attached to ethnography:

- "educational" (e.g., Lacey, 1970; Pollock, 2004; Spindler & Spindler, 2000), "health" (e.g., Farmer, 2005; Friedson, 1996; Scheper-Hughes, 1993; Wendland, 2010), or "legal" (e.g., Merry, 1990; Moore, 1986; Rosen, 1989) ethnographies are distinguished by their attachment to specific fields;

- "realist," (e.g., Evans-Pritchard, 1968 [1940]; Malinowski, 1984 [1922]) "interpretivist," (e.g., Geertz, 1973; Turner, 1967); "critical" (Anyon, 1997; Carspecken, 1991; Escobar, 1995; Ferguson, 1990); "subaltern" (Behar, 1994; Gold & Gujar, 2002) or "reflexive" ethnographies (e.g., Briggs, 1970; Khosravi, 2011; Rabinow, 1977; Rosaldo, 1999) foreground their epistemology;
- "Marxist" (e.g., Burawoy, 2009; Donham, 1999; Willis, 1977), "feminist" (e.g., Aretxaga, 1997; Bell, 1983; Mahmood, 2005) or "Foucaultian" ethnographies (e.g., Ferguson & Gupta, 2002; Li, 2007; Ong, 2006) reflect theoretical frames of critique;
- while "narrative" (Marvasti, 2003; Narayan, 1989; Thomas & Znaniecki, 1927), "visual" (e.g., Bateson & Mead, 1942; Heider, 1976; Pink, 2001), "digital" (e.g., Coleman, 2009; Coover, 2005; Wesch, 2009), or "microethnography" (Bloome et al., 2005; Goodwin & Goodwin, 1992; LeBaron & Streeck, 1997; see Mehan (1998) for a review in education) describe specific bundles of ethnographic representational practices and analytic techniques and technologies.

(In additon, see Hammersley & Atkinson, 2007; Myers, 1999; Genzuk, 1999; Guba & Lincoln, 1994; and Van Maanen, 1988 for different approaches to categorizing ethnographic traditions.)

Qualitative social scientists such as Denzin (1997) hold that theory, writing, and ethnography are inseparable and that the concepts researchers "think with" are as much procedural as they are theoretical—that is, ethnography is a way of doing research, as well as a way of making sense of the world. Indeed, as ethnography has proliferated across disciplines and fields, distinct types and subgenres of ethnographies have been produced, each embodying a "way of looking" that reflects particular epistemologies employed in the service of area-, field-, and discipline-specific concerns. For instance, sociology, another discipline that has a long association with ethnography, brought "the field" home and turned the ethnographic gaze to the "civic Other" through community studies and urban ethnography (Vidich & Lyman, 1994).

Ethnography also has over half a century's association with educational fields (see Spindler & Spindler, 2000 for an overview of much of this history, and Carspecken & Walford, 2001 for a discussion of critical ethnography in education); and a significant history as a widely used research approach in the medical fields (see Bloor (2001) for an overview of the ethnography of health and medicine; see Charmaz and Olsen (1997) for a comprehensive account of ethnographic research in medical sociology) and organizational studies (see Bate (1997) for a review). Moreover, reflecting the increasing professionalization of ethnography—the commercial use of ethnographic research to inform product development, marketing, and institutional practices—it has increasingly become popular in the business world, with unique ethical challenges and understandings of what constitutes a useful and successful ethnography (see, for example, Radka (2007) and Lombardi (2009)).

Keeping in mind that ethnography has been successfully cross-pollinated in a wide range of other disciplines and fields, the methodological landscape of ethnography seems ever more crowded and bewildering: How does one review an ethnography without being privy to the specialized bodies of knowledge and methodological traditions that constitute a genre? One answer might be that reviewers can look for alignment between research methods and the ethnographer's stated methodological positions, but we would agree with social researchers, such as Seale (1999), who suggest that the use of particular methods does not necessarily proclaim a prior epistemological commitment. For instance, the use of triangulation strategies does not, in itself, signal a positivistic ethnography—it may be used with equal facility in a postmodern ethnography to demonstrate multivocality.

In reviewing ethnographic research, then, we suggest that the reviewer might ask two less specific, more pragmatic questions to guide their evaluation:

1. Is the project ethnographic, "involving direct and sustained social contact with agents and of richly writing up the encounter, respecting, recording, representing at least partly in its own terms the irreducibility of human experience"? (Willis & Trondman, 2000 p. 394).
2. If so, are the ethnographer's toolkit and the uses to which she/he puts those tools successfully explained and rationalized in the particular terms of the project at hand? Is the choice of field(s), funding sources and research intent, fieldwork methods (including time conducting research and languages used), engagement with research participants, and analytic and representational strategies (and participant input into these) internally consistent, rationalized, and clearly addressed?

The touchstones below address what we feel are the key criteria for answering the two questions above. There are many lists of criteria—many "criteriologies" (Schwandt, 1996)—for evaluating the quality of ethnographic and qualitative inquiry. While we have drawn on some of them (for instance, Denzin & Lincoln, 2002; Guba & Lincoln, 2005; Seale, 2002; Tong et al., 2007; Tracy, 2010; Bochner, 2000; Richardson, 2000; Schwandt, 1996; Howe & Eisenhart, 1990), our criteria, terminology, and inflections are informed by our own ethnographic research experiences, our disciplinary affiliations with anthropology, and our broadly critical constructivist approach to ethnography. Thus, although we would argue that each of the touchstones described below should be addressed in any ethnographic account, they will and should be addressed in different ways across genres.

Qualitative Touchstones

The touchstones we picked engage the core concerns of ethnography considered in its fullness: as a methodology, as a set of research and analytic procedures and relations, and as a representational form. Each touchstone speaks to diversity in ethnographic genres and to multiple research stages and processes, from selecting questions and research sites, to designing (and continuously redesigning) data collection approaches, to analysis, and writing.[3] We urge reviewers to examine whether and how an ethnographer's methodological choices align across the individual touchstones; we have provided citations for and examples of how the touchstones have been successfully addressed by authors working from diverse genres.

The touchstones are:

1. Persuasiveness/credibility/believability/trustworthiness
2. The Ethnographic Warrant/significant contribution/worthiness
3. Reflexivity/subjectivity
4. Ethics
5. Analytic rigor/resonance/coherence
6. Aesthetics and representation

Very broadly, we conceptualized the touchstones as applying to the three sets of ethnographic relations that shape any ethnographic project, irrespective of genre or particular methods used:

1. Relations with academic/field/disciplinary traditions and knowledge (ethnographic warrant/ substantive contribution, believability/credibility/persuasiveness, analytic rigor)
2. Relations among ethnographers and research participants (reflexivity, ethics, believability/ credibility/persuasiveness, analytic rigor)
3. Relations with the reader (ethnographic warrant, aesthetic merit, believability/credibility/ persuasiveness)

We see the reviewer as making contingent, project-based judgments about each touchstone, with a keen awareness of how each touchstone informs and aligns with the others across the ethnographic project. If this sounds vague, it is with reason! In the first instance, it accommodates the prolific and productive use of ethnography to address the concerns of an ever-expanding range of epistemological, disciplinary, and topical fields, without also generating a parallel proliferation of ethnographic criteriologies. A "big tent" approach to qualitative research that celebrates a diversity of ethnographic objects and a plurality of research paradigms (Denzin, 2008) is, as Tracy (2010) notes, best served by criteria that address the end results of good ethnographies (e.g., credibility) rather than stipulating the methodological means that characterize such work (e.g., the extensive use of direct quotes, or great detail about textual data management).

Finally, in our experience, journals and journal editors are not always interested in what they view as "methodological detail." As Briggs (1986) eloquently puts it, "Collecting data is viewed as an intrinsically sound, if not necessarily glamorous, pursuit. The realm of pure theory is exciting and important, even if empirically minded skeptics are likely to dismiss one's efforts as vapid. But methodology loses on both counts, being generally regarded as both mundane and unimportant" (p. xiii). Indeed, we have been asked to remove detail about methods and methodology from articles reporting the "results" of ethnographic research in academic journals. Consequently, we and numerous ethnographer colleagues have found ourselves using a positivistic shorthand—number of participants interviewed or number of hours spent observing—to describe our research, even though these numbers signify little in terms of our research or roles as ethnographers and, in fact, may be inconsistent with our methodological and ethical objectives.

Given how integral writing is to the ethnographic craft and given the methodological imperatives for detailed narratives and thick description (Geertz, 1973), ethnography, perhaps more than other kinds of qualitative research, is particularly susceptible to rules that journals have about word limits and data presentation formats. In fact, the brief journal article format itself is viewed as suspect among some ethnographers for being too short to provide the evidence—in terms of both results and methods—necessary to lay out and support an argument. Often then, in the interests of a deeper engagement with data, ethnographers may be forced to make short shrift of their "disclosure of process." Hence, we encourage reviewers, whether at an institutional review board or at a journal with tighter word limits, to apply our touchstones in light of the constraints imposed by the publication or certification process.

1. Persuasiveness/credibility/believability/trustworthiness

Our engagement with reviewing ethnographic research begins and ends with our response to the story being told: Do we find it persuasive and trustworthy? And does it work to deepen or shift the way we understand the world around us? We suggest that any representation of ethnographic research must "make words fly" (Glesne & Peshkin, 1992). Some (e.g., Eisner, 1998) would argue that the veracity of the story (or the notion of veracity itself) matters not at all—what matters is the extent to which the story speaks powerfully and persuasively to our understanding of a situation, a group, a problem, an institution, an event. While we do not hold this position on research and evidence, we acknowledge that what is felt to be a believable and persuasive account is dependent on disciplinary, field, and epistemological traditions and on the readers' own engagement with the account.

In quantitative traditions, the truthfulness of research accounts is typically constructed in terms of validity, reliability, and generalizability. In qualitative research, different truth-claims have characterized different "moments" in the ethnographic tradition (Denzin & Lincoln, 2005): from claims based on the researcher's integrity, to those based on how tightly woven the fabric of argument is, to those that privileged "scientific," "objective" fieldwork data or the experiential, empiricist "being there-ness" of the researcher, to more recent approaches that have problematized and deconstructed truth-claims by centering the political, theoretical, and epistemological commitments of the ethnographer.

As a result, different ethnographic genres make different claims to evidence and persuasiveness. A positivist ethnography might base its truth-claims on greater descriptive detail and the completeness of its categorization schemes (e.g., Boas, 1940), while a poststructuralist tale might aim to persuade through a fragmented, multivocal narrative (e.g., Lowe, 2006) or an ethnographic fiction (e.g., Hecht, 2006). In each of these genres, there are diverse expectations regarding the use of extended direct quotes, field notes, analytic memos, photographs, and other types of information to substantiate claims.

We suggest that the reviewer may be best served by a broad consideration of what makes an account powerful and useful, in light of the ethnographer's stance and ethnography's fundamental purposes of making (other) social realities accessible, intelligible, and analytically meaningful to the reader. A reviewer of a more positivist or traditional constructivist ethnography might ask:

> To what extent do the findings match the evidence and are they convincing? When the author is arguing evidentially, is the evidence marshaled rigorously and opened up for external audit? Are the researcher's interpretations plausible and justified? Can readers see what the researcher saw even if they disagree with the conclusions drawn by the researcher?
>
> (Finlay, 2006, p. 13)

Or:

> Are the truth-claims made by the ethnographer plausible, given what we know about a particular situation? Is the author's core argument supported by detailed and persuasive evidence that brings the reader into contact with a new way of understanding some aspect of the world? Are different types of claims effectively supported by ethnographic data (such that, for instance, theoretical contributions warrant greater evidential support compared to descriptive contributions)?
>
> (Hammersley, 1992)

In contrast, a review of a more subjectivist ethnography might include questions such as: "Does this text embody a fleshed out, embodied sense of lived-experience? Does it have aesthetic merit?" (Richardson, 2000).

These criteria point to the importance of: (1) the author's presentation of sufficient evidence to convince the reader of their analysis (see also Touchstone 5), (2) sufficient engagement with existing literatures to situate the research within existing disciplinary or epistemological traditions, and (3) sufficient engagement with readers' commonsense notions of how the world operates (even if only to disrupt these commonsense assumptions).

Reviewers can and should make determinations of ethnographic persuasiveness by (1) drawing on their own experiences and knowledge of the broader social concerns the ethnography deals with, (2) evaluating the extent to which the ethnography's core arguments are warranted by the evidence presented, and (3) paying attention to their own response to the ethnography (and the experiences and potential biases that shape this response).

Ethnographic analyses are powerful because they "take into account all of the complexities that present themselves in a study and. . . . deal with patterns that are not easily explained" (Guba, 1981). The best ethnographies are therefore often category-busting and "displace" readers, opening them up to new understandings of their own lives, and enabling them to grasp the deep and unexpected levels of the daily life of another. For example, Herdt's (1981) ethnography on "Sambian" sexual cultures examines how the process of masculinization shapes male and female sexual behavior in Papua New Guinea. Herdt carefully details how boys move through three sexual phases in order to become an adult. Boys first provide oral sex to young men (thus strengthening themselves by receiving semen), then as young men receive oral sex from boys, and then marry and transition to heterosexual behavior. Young men's first heterosexual encounters are of providing oral sex to prepubescent wives, mirroring their initial sexual encounters as unmarried boys.

Herdt's account of Sambian sexual and gender practices challenged accepted Western categories of sexual identity, gender roles and relations, and norms of childhood and sexuality, and opened new windows to ongoing debates about sexuality in the United States. It provided persuasive and extensive evidence of multiple ways of making sense of sexuality and sexual identity, and their links to gender relations. It also generated backlash from people who held that sexual identity was genetic, and from those who felt that the book validated child sexual abuse. A reviewer of this piece would, therefore, have sought to evaluate whether and how Herdt presented "enough" evidence to substantiate his claims about Sambian practices and their contextualized meanings and consequences; how his data and claims engaged existing Papuan, regional, and global literatures on sexuality, gender, and childhood; and what visceral responses the story provoked in the reviewer (and how these responses were shaped by the reviewer's personal beliefs and mores, and the author's narrative devices).

Ethnography also holds up a mirror to the participants themselves (Turner, 2007), and therefore recent ethnographic genres often expect systematic reflection on the engagement between and among ethnographers and research participants during the research and/or writing process. For example, "member checks" may be seen as a key means of establishing the credibility of ethnographic data, by allowing participants to contest the researcher-writer's explanations (Creswell, 1998; Lincoln & Guba, 1985). It is generally expected in this tradition that differences will be openly discussed and examined, laying bare for the reader some of the complexities of "writing other people's lives" (Josselson, 1996).

In critical ethnographic traditions, a careful explication of research participants' involvement in multiple stages of the ethnographic process, and the potential effects of this engagement, is expected (Carspecken, 1996; see Deyhle (2009) for an example). In collaborative ethnographic traditions, the co-analytic and co-authorial roles of participants must be addressed (Lassiter, 2005). Furthermore in poststructural traditions, the notion of a member check may itself be problematic because of its assumption of verification and lack of recognition of how ethnography "writes" its own worlds (see, e.g., St. Pierre, 1999).

2. The ethnographic warrant/significant contribution/worthiness

Katz (1997) identifies the need to establish a "warrant" for ethnography as a unique methodological challenge. Faced with, on the one hand, a methodological silence on issues of proof (in terms of the quantitative tradition of reliability, representativeness, or replicability), and, on the other, the silences resulting from readers' and funding agencies' desire for compelling resolutions to controversial issues, ethnographers are pushed to respond to the "so what" or "who cares" question. As Katz has it, ethnographers, and social ethnographers who work in familiar places in particular, must establish the grounds to argue that there is a need for their study in the first place.

The warrant for ethnography was historically established by studying populations that were different—remote, isolated, socially deviant, or admired—and then comparing the cultural practices with those of the groups with which the (Western) ethnographer identified. For example, Mead's *Coming of Age in Samoa* (1928) has the subtitle: *A psychological study of primitive youth for Western civilization*, and she says of the purpose of the book: "I have tried to answer the question which sent me to Samoa: Are the disturbances which vex our adolescents due to the nature of adolescence itself or to the civilization? Under different conditions does adolescence present a different picture?" (foreword to the 1973 edition). This approach deconstructed the social framing that marked a group or people off as unique, but in the process sometimes served repressive purposes by exoticizing research populations or normalizing or sanitizing "them" as essentially similar to "us," but living in difficult or troubled circumstances.

As ethnographers struggled to transform the consequences of this type of ethnography of the "other," as they began to conduct more research in their "own" cultures and societies, as globalization further blurred these categories, and as ethnography was taken up by diverse fields for diverse purposes, the warrants for ethnographies also had to change. Katz suggests the following warrants for ethnography:

- the study of historically emergent social phenomena;
- the study of theoretically strategic sites that demonstrate everyday patterns of social life but in extreme form suitable for analysis;
- the processual study of policy research that problematizes the people types and place types that policies assume, and reveals situational contingencies;
- the need for narratives that fill out and reveal the complexity and logic of community life that is glossed over in social research that may narrowly abstract a single variable or issue.

Relatedly, Richardson suggests the following questions for examining the substantive contribution of a study: "Does this piece contribute to our understanding of social-life? Does the writer demonstrate a deeply grounded (if embedded) human-world understanding and perspective?" (Richardson, 2000, p. 254).

These questions emphasize the essential role of ethnography in deepening and problematizing our understanding of sociocultural phenomena, norms, and practices, while allowing for a broad range of approaches to achieving this goal. For example, Rasmussen (2003) describes the warrant for her poststructural and reflexive account of what happens when a group of Tuaregs with whom she has previously worked visit her in the United States:

Usually, anthropologists travel to what is called "the field site," often geographically remote from their home. What happens when longstanding informants/consultants/friends come from the field to the anthropologist, rather than vice versa? In this essay, I analyze a visit by Tuareg smith/artisans from the community where I conduct research in terms of recent efforts toward "siting" culture in transnational settings.

It has been correctly pointed out that the old concept of culture as unitary, neatly-bounded, and rooted in a single locality has limitations. Yet there is also the need to carefully deconstruct and critique these recent formulations of "global" and "moving" culture, and reassess their uses and limitations. Such concepts . . . are themselves rooted in our own cultural categories. There is still the need to foreground local responses to these processes, viewed from the other side of borderlands and meeting-grounds. How can anthropologists adequately convey local residents' responses to "moving" and global cultures, in terms which do not replicate our own categories?

(p. 8)

Reviewers will, of course, make personal judgments about what they view as the importance of particular topics and ways of participating in and making sense of the world; ethnographies that present new ways of understanding and analyzing a particular topic, drawing on "emic" standpoints, are often particularly valued in ethnographic traditions, while those that present evidence utilizing preexisting ("etic") frameworks might be viewed as a less significant contribution.

3. Reflexivity/subjectivity

As qualitative research has moved away from a positivistic orientation, the notion of "reflexivity" has become an increasingly important (and contested) tool in thinking about the politics, authority, methods, and purposes of ethnographic work. Broadly, reflexivity is awareness and acknowledgment of the personal, intersubjective, and social processes that shape research projects. To be reflexive as a researcher is to interrogate the interests, assumptions, and motivations (the subjectivity) one brings to the research; to be self-conscious about the shifting intersubjective dynamics and social and political relations that structure the relationship between the researcher and the research participants; and to situate the research with respect to the discourses and rhetoric that produce authoritative knowledge. In other words, reflexivity is an acknowledgment of epistemological and methodological commitments that mark the entire process of research, from the kinds of questions one asks, to how one asks, to an acknowledgment of one's own limitations, to the kinds and forms of academic and sociopolitical conversations in which one is engaged.

On the one hand, being reflexive has become rather *de rigueur* for qualitative researchers—as Finlay (2002) notes, "doing" reflexivity is a defining feature of qualitative research—to the extent that reflexivity is often marshaled to signal a truer or more authentic ethnographic account, in the process reinscribing a positivistic, authoritative discourse. On the other hand, Watson (1987) and Peshkin (1993) argue that ethnographers do not "do" reflexivity—reflexivity is simply an essential, inevitable property of all discourse and an inescapable feature of the human condition. In discussing subjectivity and reflexivity, ethnographers are simply attempting to limit its ability to undermine research and the researcher's authority. In turn, poststructural scholars, such as Pillow (2003) and Heshusius (1994), argue that this conception of subjectivity and reflexivity must itself be deconstructed, as it creates the comforting assumption—based on a flawed "alienated mode of consciousness that believes in the possibility of a regulated distance between self and other" (p. 15)—that subjectivity can be managed.

Davies (1999), while acknowledging postmodernist critiques of authorial voice and intention, rejects their "extreme pessimism," and suggests a pragmatic, realist compromise that positions research as a process of mediation between different constructions of reality. "Good" ethnography expresses a reality that is neither directly accessible only through native texts nor simply a reflection of the ethnographer's psyche (pp. 5, 6); reflexivity is a cooperative endeavor that encompasses the knowledge claims of both researchers and informants.

From this perspective, with which we have a great deal of sympathy, reviewers might evaluate an ethnographer's engagement with issues of reflexivity by considering questions such as:

- What counts as knowledge in the particular traditions in which the ethnographer situates her/himself?
- What does the researcher privilege as knowledge?
- What do research participants privilege as knowledge, and if this differs from the researcher's construction of knowledge, how are these reconciled?
- How—within what relations—is knowledge produced/constructed and represented?
- How does the ethnographer negotiate his/her relationships with research participants?
- How does the ethnographer negotiate her/his own subjectivity?
- Is it evident how these negotiations influenced data collection, analysis, and writing?

A number of ethnographies, including Wendland (2010), Deyhle (2009), Lather (1997), and Tyler (1987), provide exemplars for such engagement; Manias and Street (2001) provide an article-length example.

Reflexivity has not been without its critics, and the line between critical self-awareness and self-indulgent navel-gazing is slippery. Indeed, there are many social science journals that have little patience for discussions of reflexivity (Kendall, for instance, was asked to largely remove discussions about reflexivity from an article published in a generalist education journal). Nonetheless, the "reflexive" turn has also been tremendously productive. Anthropologists have drawn on postcolonial (see Said, 1978; Asad, 1973) and feminist critiques (Behar & Gordon, 1995) that seek to destabilize all claims to knowledge as situated, partial, and underpinned by relations of power (Marcus, 1998).

Aiming to reframe power balances between participants and researchers, reflexive ethnographies (see Crapanzano, 1980 for an exemplar) showcase new modes of knowing and kinds of knowledge, "other" voices, and experimentation with means of (re)presenting and writing.

As Lynch (2000) notes, the meanings and virtues of reflexivity are relative to particular theoretical and methodological commitments. Social science scholars have developed typologies of reflexivity that may help guide the review of diverse ethnographic traditions. Marcus (1994), for instance, identifies four styles of reflexivity: self-critique and personal quest; objective reflexivity as a methodological tool; reflexivity as "politics of location"; and experiential reflexivity as the practice of "positioning." Foley (2002) also lists four types of reflexivity: confessional, theoretical, textual, and deconstructive. Finlay's (2002) five variants—"maps" of reflexivity—are particularly useful in illustrating how any conceptualization of reflexivity reflects researchers' aims and focus.

1. "Introspection" draws on the researcher's own thinking, reflecting, and emoting as primary and experiential ethnographic data and, by moving beyond personal revelation, contributes to a deeper understanding of research subjects (see Abu-Lughod (1999) for an example).
2. "Intersubjective reflection" locates the researcher's individual subjectivity in ongoing research relations, focusing on the ongoing construction of inward and shared meanings in research interactions (the proliferation of "narratives of the self," for instance, see Gibb (2005) as an illustration).
3. "Mutual collaboration" stands for wide-ranging research methodologies that frame participants as co-researchers and co-ethnographers and vice versa (from "action research" to citing primary informants to co-authoring text to participant validation of data—see Deyhle (2009) as an example).
4. "Social critique" that situates ethnography within a strong theoretical framework about the social construction of power ("standpoint" ethnography of various critical genre; see Naples and Sachs (2000) as an example).
5. "Ironic deconstruction" that employs a self-consciousness about how researchers and participants are presenting themselves to each other and others (and is often discernible by a writing style that deliberately evokes the ironies and paradoxes of doing ethnography; see Jemielniak & Kostera, 2010 for an example and review of ironic deconstruction in institutional ethnography).

Reflexivity is also an epistemological and ethical concern. Tracy (2010) argues for viewing reflexivity as a fundamental aspect of research and its presentation: "Sincerity means that the research is marked by honesty and transparency about the researcher's biases, goals, and foibles as well as about how these played a role in the methods, joys, and mistakes of the research" (p. 841).

Faced with this variation in approaches to reflexivity, reviewers are encouraged to first determine whether the author has addressed key issues of reflexivity, and then to determine whether the author's discussion of reflexivity is aligned with her/his approach to other touchstones. Reviewers might ask, for example: Does the researcher attempt to be transparent about her/his biases and goals? Does the researcher discuss how his/her positionality and subjectivity influenced the research, and how these affected their relationships with research participants? Does the conception of knowledge construction that underlies their engagement with reflexivity align with their analytic approach and the choices they make about how to represent research participants?

Deyhle's (2009) book recounting twenty-five years of research with Navajo women offers one exemplar for thorough and aligned engagement with reflexivity, including a discussion of the positive and negative effects of her presence on research participants, her own positionality and its effects on the research, the roles that she played in the Navajo community during her research, the nature and feel of her relationships with research participants, and the effects of her deep engagement with participants in writing the book and in recognizing the limits of her voice and its relationship to the voices of participants.

4. Ethics

The central ethical concerns in evaluating ethnography relate to the ethnographer's relationships with and accountability to research participants. Of primary consideration are issues of harm—the protection of research participants from harm was the first and foremost purpose of the American Anthropological Association's original (1971) ethics code, and human subjects review processes largely patrol issues of harm. But issues of harm are complexly associated with issues of reciprocity—as Kent (1990) admits, the fieldworker typically comes uninvited, is bound to be intrusive, and while recognized and rewarded herself for her research, often offers little in return for the privilege of participating in her informants' lives.

Considerations of harm and reciprocity have been institutionalized in disciplinary ethics codes and human subjects review boards at universities; though these are also often required for publication in journals, neither is unproblematic. For one, the increasing professionalization of ethnography has in some cases subverted ethnographers' paramount responsibility to the researched with their accountability to funders, clients, and other stakeholders (Sluka & Robben, 2007). Institutional Review Boards (IRBs), as Bourgois (1991) points out, are more concerned with protecting universities and academic careers than with identifying and protecting the interests of the researched; their positivist assumptions of a detached observer preclude an activist approach or serious engagement with issues of reciprocity, and their notions of risk often preclude open ethnographic engagement about topics that are considered "dangerous" (e.g., sexuality, inequity, and political violence) and with those groups who are most marginalized in society (e.g., children and prisoners).

For example, Kendall, in her research on sexuality education in U.S. high schools, was only allowed to talk directly to students about their sex education experiences under extremely limited conditions, and was not allowed to ask students at any point about their sexual experiences, sexual identity, or experiences of sexual violence. Conducting research in which students could be seen but not heard raised significant ethical concerns for a critical ethnographer whose research was designed, in part, to provide space for students to "talk back" to policymakers. How Kendall weighed these concerns needed to be made transparent to the reader, as did the effects of this silencing on the capacity of the project to serve its original goals. This was possible in a book-length monograph (Kendall, 2012), but not in an article-length monograph (Kendall, 2008a).

Furthermore, the ethic of informed consent as interpreted by IRBs, or as an impression management strategy employed by the ethnographer, does not adequately address issues of unequal power relations and may in fact be a partial truth or even deception (Christians, 2005). For instance, as Fine (1993) points out, informed consent is often a fiction for ethnographers who "do not know what they looking for until they have found it" (p. 276).

According to Bourgois (1991), it would be dangerous and arrogant to assume definite answers to these ethical issues. Nevertheless, and though they have been problematized by postmodern scholars as naive and grounded in Western observational morality, the humanistic virtues of sympathy, openness, and honor continue to be touchstones of researcher–subject relations. For example, Fine (1993) identifies four common, potentially problematic, modes of presenting oneself and one's work as morally competent and trustworthy: the *candid ethnographer* is unobstrusive in his writing, claiming authority by "being there," and thus protects himself from readers' censure; the *chaste ethnographer* is engaged in a balancing act between preserving privacy and using intimate relations as ethnographic data; the *fair ethnographer* ignores personal motivations or keeps from her audience the sides she has taken during fieldwork; and the *literary ethnographer's* writing is so well fitted to her genre that it is inaccessible to those outside, or is so powerful that it obscures the lack of data, or is poetic enough that the reader is confused as to authorial intention.

Alternative notions of ethics and reciprocity have been offered, both from a perspective of engaged universalism that resists apolitical relativism, and from indigenous communities drawing on their own ethical codes. For example, Bishop (1998) lists five issues of power as criteria for evaluating (Maori) ethnographies: the extent to which research subjects themselves participate in the *initiation* of the study, reap the *benefits* of the research, are effectively *represented*, have the power to *legitimate* research, and hold researchers *accountable*. Some anthropologists have also called for a "compassionate turn" (Sluka & Robben, 2007) in ethnography; wearying of postmodernist critiques, Scheper-Hughes (1995), for instance, argues for "good enough ethnography" marked by empathy and compassion. Framed in terms that are almost theological, the ethnographer is ethically obligated to "witness" the social suffering (see Klienman, Das, & Lock, 1997) that results from political, economic, and institutional power.

Given that the potential ethical issues that might arise during a study are infinite, and given that processes of negotiating ethical engagement throughout fieldwork are often hidden in ethnographic texts, how do we judge the ethical engagement of the ethnographer? We concur with Finley (2006) that the most important criterion is that the researcher addresses their engagement with the sorts of ethical issues that logically arise from their epistemological and theoretical positionings. In our own research, for example, we attempt to voice the experiences of children identified as "vulnerable" by various institutions and adults (e.g., Kendall, 2008b). Since one of our aims is to destabilize assumptions about these children's lack of agency and resilience, we must ask ourselves whether our own writing silences these children or reinscribes the role of passive victim on children whose lives are much too complex to be so described. We must also constantly interrogate the roles we and our research participants are assuming in our interactions, and determine whether these interactions reconstitute relations of power and authority that silence participants. We concern ourselves with similar questions related to theoretical awareness and responsiveness to anthropological disciplinary traditions and bodies of educational knowledge, and transparency concerning the purposes and funding sources of the ethnography.

Again, we fall back on our strategy of situating the ethical interrogation of ethnographies in the context of the particular project under review. We would not expect every article to address all potential ethical issues; space will not allow such an engagement in most venues. Nonetheless, the ethical issues raised by researchers, description of how they addressed these issues, their transparency about research methods and resources, and how they present and represent the voices and experiences of research participants all provide evidence of an ethnographer's ethical engagement, and the lack of any such engagement should cause concern to a reviewer.

5. Analytic rigor/resonance/coherence

Analytic rigor, resonance, or coherence speaks to the rigor with which data were collected and the extent to which the ethnographer's engagement with data throughout the research process yield insightful, coherent, and significant analysis at the end. It is neither possible nor desirable for ethnographers to present all of the information that they gather. In the process of sifting and winnowing information, the ethnographer attempts to create an analytic tale about what they observed and experienced, rooted in a deep engagement with people's daily practices, in conversation with ongoing disciplinary, epistemological, or sectoral discussions, and that resonates with the reader. To create such a story, the ethnographer must provide enough, and the most appropriate, evidence to support their story to the reader (see also Touchstone 1).

In order to do this, the ethnographer must address ongoing questions about the data collection and analytic process. We recommend that the reviewer evaluate the ethnographer's approach by considering as a starting point the following questions:

- What did the ethnographer do to collect the information presented? Did she collect enough information, about the right topics, in the right places, and from the right people, to move analysis forward throughout the course of the research?
- How did the ethnographer think about and engage in analytic work, from the early stages of her/his research? For example, did she/he review field notes each evening in order to develop additional research questions or activities that might flesh out or undermine emerging analytic themes? Did she examine which themes were productive in generating discussion with participants? Did he talk to co-researchers (including research participants) about themes and ideas that were developing over the course of the research?
- How were co-researchers' responses integrated into the ongoing research and analysis? Did she engage in systematic counter hypothesis testing with her own data, or systematic interactions with co-researchers or colleagues that would have helped destabilize analytic assumptions?
- Did he track her own thinking about analysis—and track how this thinking affected the research design—systematically throughout the research process (e.g., through analytic memos)?

As the above list of questions suggests, there are many different data analysis processes. Often, authors will describe the data analysis process briefly, as steps taken after data collection. But data are transformed over the entire course of the research process, which is always and concomitantly an analytic process. Is this process clear to the reader, so that they can evaluate the ethnographer's analysis? Does the author make an "audit" of this process available to the reviewer?

There is a strong expectation in many ethnographic traditions that the ethnographer's initial research questions will be transformed as she/he gains a deeper understanding of contexts, participants, and topics through fieldwork (Hammersley & Atkinson, 2007). This narrative of change, often presented as a narrative of naïve discovery, in fact arises from the ongoing analytic process that constitutes fieldwork, right from this first moment. If the reader claims that such a change occurs, do they adequately explain why it occurred? Do they present sufficient evidence to support their claim that the questions that they later ask are better, or more important, or more comprehensible questions to research participants and readers alike?

When engaged in more focused analysis, often after the bulk of data collection for a particular written product has been completed, does the ethnographer engage in and describe a process of rigorous analysis, described by Tracy as: "marked by transparency regarding the process of sorting, choosing, and organizing the data" (Tracy, 2010, p. 841)? In sorting, choosing, and organizing the data for readers, does the ethnographer make the analysis resonate and cohere by providing both adequate primary data for the reader, and adequate commentary on these data? Or, as Atkinson (1990) describes, does the text adequately speak to the "interplay of concrete exemplification and discursive commentary"? (p. 103).

Despite what we view as the importance of analytic rigor and ethnographers' transparency about analytic processes, it is, in our experience, one of the touchstones least likely to be discussed in detail in articles. This is at least in part because of the significant "real estate" that it takes to discuss the recursivity of ethnographic practices over the course of a study. Sells et al. (1994) provide an example of an article that expends a significant amount of space on analytic approaches (from a traditional interpretivist perspective):

Ethnographic research that follows this theoretical framework is closely associated with Spradley's (1979, 1980) Developmental Research Sequence (DRS) model. The research design is cyclical and recursive. The researcher starts with a general problem or focus and begins with the initial collection of data from open-ended questions in interviews that are audiotaped and transcribed verbatim. In this study the general research question was "What are couple and therapist perceptions of reflecting team practice?" A detailed description of the interview and data analysis procedures from this study will be presented later in this section. From these transcripts, each sentence is analyzed through what is called a domain analysis to identify emergent themes and categories across interviews from different people in the same setting or culture (Spradley, 1979). In a domain analysis, long, complex sentences are broken down into shorter semantic relationships of meaning. A domain can be represented whenever someone makes a statement about something . . . From these semantic relationships, each interview and field note is analyzed using the systemic procedures of a domain analysis. For example, in this study a husband from one of the couple interviews stated, "I listen to them [the reflecting team] because I can't object, I'm forced to listen, and I have to digest it." Using a domain analysis, "forced to listen," "can't object," and "have to digest it" are all terms (included terms) that cause (semantic relationship of cause–effect) this couple to "listen to the reflecting team" (cover term). Therefore, the emerging domain for this group of sentences would be "causes of having the reflecting team." Constructing a list of domains like this one within each interview and set of field notes is a first step in capturing the underlying or latent meaning that therapists and couples use to interpret their experiences within a reflecting team context . . . Each of these domains is then grouped together in a tree diagram, table, or box diagram on a spreadsheet . . . A category system emerges based on themes and patterns across domains.

(p. 247)

Reviewers may, however, have little choice but to judge the rigor of the analytic process based only on the persuasiveness of the story told; indeed, this and the credibility of the individual ethnographer were for many decades the primary criteria for judging the quality of ethnographic analyses.

If this is the case in a manuscript under review, reviewers may benefit from paying particular attention to how the researcher describes the construction of analytic themes and to the evidence presented to support the themes. For example, if an article under review provides direct quotes from research participants, the reviewer may evaluate whether the author has engaged with the quote in a manner that the reviewer feels reflects a careful analytic engagement and that is aligned with the author's general epistemology (see McDermott & Varenne (1998) and Cornish & Ghosh (2007) for examples in education and health).

6. Representation and aesthetics

Concerns about "representation" in ethnographic work are rooted in epistemology. From (more or less) positivistic ethnographies aiming to be "authentic" descriptions by an omniscient author (e.g., ethnographies from the British structural–functional tradition, such as Evans-Pritchard's masterful accounts of the Nuer); to critical/reflexive perspectives on sociocultural realities that value transparency about the researcher's positionality with respect to his/her subjects (often described in the structural terms of class, race, and/or gender (see Stanley & Wise (1983, 1993) on feminist research); to the "literary" turn that focuses on the politics underpinning the "fixing" of personal fieldwork experiences as authoritative knowledge in the act of writing (Clifford, 1998); to postmodern ethnographies that eschew the "authentic" for the "evocative" (see Tyler, 1987 for an early exemplar); to collaborative (e.g., Lassiter, 2005) ethnographies that write with "the other"—each genre of ethnography, in more or less self-conscious ways, seeks to represent the authors' ethnographic practices in a manner consistent with their underlying aims, epistemology, ethics, and aesthetics.

In stylistic terms as well, different genres have developed distinct registers—from the magisterial singular authorial narrative of Malinowski writing about the Trobrianders, which submerges their individual voices and leaves out entirely his own personal anguish that his diaries capture so well (Malinowski, 1984 [1922]); to the "thick descriptions" of Geertz (1973) that, in describing "the Balinese"—with much wit and insight—assume that language is adequate to capturing and representing an entire cultural reality; to a highly reflexive, self-conscious, vulnerable, and personal ethnographic mode that undercuts authorial omnipotence (Robertson, 2002); to the dialogic, multivocal, and polyphonic accounts favored by postmodern ethnographers (Burawoy, 2000; Wolf, 1992; see Crapanzano (1980) or Mintz (1960) for earlier examples) that enlist the authorial presences of research participants to foreground the intersubjective nature of ethnography; to yet more recent and experimental forms of representation, including ethnographic fiction (Hecht, 2006; Narayan, 1999), as a means of "transporting the imagination" instead of reading an ethnography for its "realism"(Behar, 2007, p. 153).

What we want to signal to the reviewer by describing the diversity of (re)presentational forms in ethnography is that form is ideology. Thus, when Tsing (2005) writes in "ethnographic fragments" (p. 271) of the forests of Kalimantan, her patchwork presentational aesthetic reflects an epistemological stance against seamless generalization and a political commitment to interrupt dominant narratives. The jerkiness of her narrative deliberately seeks to disrupt and startle the reader, much as her project reveals the fragmented character of globalization. Tyler (1987) also emphasizes this experiential aspect of ethnography as a political/epistemological exercise, preferring a poetic aesthetic that, in a cooperative exercise between reader and writer, seeks to evoke possible worlds. (See Goodall (2000) for a discussion of whether such a mode of writing raises ethical questions about manipulating the vulnerabilities and emotions of readers.) Taussig (1991) invites readers to participate in his "surrealist" ethnography on shamanism, death, and healing, structuring it to follow the shape of a healing, with the readers as patients and the author as healer. Through this experience, the reader-as-colonizer is invited to experience the process by which the colonized can partially harness the "wildness" projected onto them by the colonizer. As Taussig explains it: "So it has been through the sweep of colonial history where the colonizers provided the colonized with the left-handed gift of the image of the wild man—a gift whose powers the colonizers would be blind to, were it not for the reciprocation of the colonized, bringing together in the dialogical imagination of colonization an image that wrests from civilization its demonic power" (p. 467).

In reviewing the representational and aesthetic merit of an ethnography, we hope to have encouraged the reviewer to be open to the aesthetic experience of an ethnography—not only as an end in itself, but also in terms of the work it does to further the research project and its goals. We take the position that there need be no complexity for complexity's sake, but that whether complex or startlingly direct, the aesthetic/affect of an ethnography should amplify its *raison d'etre*. Reviewers may therefore evaluate their response to an ethnography and its aesthetic as such, and also attend to the alignment between representational form, epistemological stances, and research goals.

Further Reading

On criteria for judging ethnography:

Finlay, L. (2006). "Rigour," "ethical integrity" or "artistry"? Reflexively reviewing criteria for evaluating qualitative research. *British Journal of Occupational Therapy* 69(7): 319–326.

Finlay's article lays out three criteria (rigor, ethical integrity, and artistry) that she argues could be used in place of traditional criteria (such as reliability, validity, and generalizability) to judge the quality of qualitative research. The piece is unique and helpful in Finlay's reflexive approach to describing the proposed criteria; the article's form provides an example of how ethnographers might engage theoretically, practically, and ethically in their work as researchers and reviewers.

Richardson, L. (2000). Evaluating ethnography. *Qualitative Inquiry* 6: 253.
Richardson argues that the most usable and useful criteria for evaluating ethnography combine the "scientific" and "artistic" lenses that have shaped ethnographic theory, research, and writing for the past century. She suggests five criteria that could be used to evaluate ethnographic monographs. She also discusses the implications of postmodernist traditions on representing ethnographic work.

Seale, C. (2002). Quality issues in qualitative inquiry. *Qualitative Social Work* 1(1): 97–110.
Seale argues that social theoretical traditions and research practices and techniques are too often felt to constrain one another. He presents a history of qualitative research "moments" and argues for a craft skill approach to research that reframes criteria commonly used to judge the quality of research. His review of others' criteria (such as Lincoln and Guba's and Hammersley's) may be particularly useful for reviewers.

Counterpoint Perspectives

The list of potential alternative perspectives to our description of ethnography and our choice of touchstones is vast. The readings below were selected to provide a sense of the breadth of alternatives—from authors who are writing from applied fields with little connection to a disciplinary approach to ethnography, to authors advocating for an understanding of qualitative inquiry and representation that emerges from the arts, with much less of a basis in the social sciences than that discussed above, or from more positivist traditions.

Lombardi's (2009) *The De-skilling of Labor: An Ethnographic Predicament* talks about business models of labor and how they are influencing the practice of ethnography. This piece speaks importantly to models of ethnographic labor that differ fundamentally from those on which we have focused herein, and raise a new set of issues related to ethics and a warrant for ethnography that are deserving of special attention because they are growing issues in ethnographic hiring practices.

Radka's (2007) *Enabling our Voices to be Heard* is a useful accompaniment to Lombardi's piece in thinking about the role of business models in and on ethnography. It is particularly useful in raising new concerns about the ethical uses to which ethnography is put. While anthropology as a discipline has struggled to understand its role in furthering colonialism, many would argue that the explosion of ethnographic research by and for corporations raises concerns about the complicity of this research in processes of global economic inequity.

Lincoln and Guba's (1985) *Naturalistic Enquiry* is an excellent resource on criteriology that is much more positivist in its inclinations than our own; it is also a foundational text for many later efforts to define criteria for evaluating qualitative, including ethnographic, work.

Eisner's (1998) *The Enlightened Eye* provides a useful counterpoint to more positivist accounts about what constitutes "data" and "research" in qualitative inquiry. Coming from a visual arts background, Eisner develops a research approach that he calls connoisseurship, modeled on artistic expertise, which draws on very different norms of research engagement and evidence than those of traditional ethnography. His arguments about aesthetic representation and fact versus fiction have also been quite influential in later discussions and debates about this topic.

The journal *Qualitative Inquiry* is an excellent resource for articles on aesthetics and representation in ethnography; most authors approach these questions from a more strongly poststructural frame than the one that we adopt in our own work. For example, Richardson's *Evaluating Ethnography* argues that ethnography should be judged through two lenses: arts and sciences. She presents an alternate set of touchstones for evaluating ethnography that draw from creative arts traditions. Richardson's five touchstones are: substantive contribution, aesthetic merit, reflexivity, impact, and expression of reality.

Authors' Reflections on Quality

We arrive at this chapter having learned our craft as ethnographers primarily through engagement with anthropologists. We each have research histories that span epistemic, theoretical, and topical foci, but have been lucky enough to work together on a cross-country ethnography of constructions of childhood and vulnerability in globally marginalized states and communities. We are both trained in the field of comparative and international development education, and our research examines issues of global educational policy practices across levels of social scale. That is, while rooted in particular places, events, and relationships, our work attempts to understand and analyze connections across social scales. Although grounded primarily in the discipline of anthropology, our work is colored by our desire to improve people's lives, and we therefore generally associate our work with critical modernist (e.g., Peet & Hartwick, 2009) and critical ethnographic (e.g., Carspecken & Walford, 2001) approaches to international development and education.

We are both privileged enough, in these days of limited resources, to be conducting multiyear ethnographies, which consist of extended periods of research punctuated by even more extended periods of absence from our subjects of study and co-researchers. We have developed long-term relationships in these settings, and our research has been and will be transformed by these relationships. We have also each conducted short-term consultancies in which we have utilized qualitative research methods, but in which we have been struck by how differently they function and how different they feel from our ethnographic work—and this experience has in turn affected what we think can and should constitute quality ethnography, versus other forms of qualitative inquiry.

Though we draw heavily from poststructural theories in our work, we do feel that there are more important stories and truths than others to be told, that these stories are connected to relations of power and authority that must themselves be analyzed (see, e.g., Denzin, 2000), and that telling these better stories takes careful and systematic looking. In other words, we feel that there is a "professionalized" ethnographic role to be filled by a researcher who has the time, training, and patience to spend a lot of energy trying to deeply understand something.

Our own research experiences and epistemic positions combine to determine how we make sense of quality ethnography. Our discussion of the history of ethnography and our selection of touchstones surely favors ethnographic approaches that consciously examine issues of power, authority, and inequity, and they tend to downplay the complexities of addressing these issues in both more positivist and more poststructual frameworks. They also favor extended fieldwork (though such fieldwork may occur in many different spaces) over shorter projects, as our own experiences convince us that no matter the researcher and the subject, ethnographers are always "professional strangers" (Agar, 1996)—that is, people attempting to make the familiar strange, and the strange familiar—and such work takes time and immersion in places, topics, problems, movements, and so forth.

Our thoughts on reviewing ethnography are also shaped by our personal experiences reviewing and writing ethnographies. We want to emphasize again that, in our experience, unless one is writing for an ethnography journal, there is often little space to address the complexities of ethnographic research described above. This is a loss to readers' understanding of the research, and to the authors' capacity to develop a deeply reflective, contextualized, and analytic account of their work. Reviewers can play a key role in encouraging ethnographers to include more of this information in their manuscripts, and in encouraging editors to allow this information to be included.

Notes

1. Admittedly, notions of "tradition" are contested and being constantly reworked as ethnographies are produced in new and diverse fields; while we attempt to signal this diversity, we have anchored much of this piece in the anthropological

and sociological traditions that have the longest engagement with ethnography, and that we are most familiar with in our own work.
2. Even in its formative years, anthropology was more welcoming of women than many other disciplines. See, for example, Mead and Bunzel (1960) on American anthropology and women's roles.
3. We do not mean to suggest that these are the only activities that occur when engaging in ethnography. For example, in our own work we have found our engagement with Institutional Review Boards to be complex and often to have a significant impact on research (re)design; yet in our experience, few articles or studies discuss these processes (c.f., Bledsoe et al., 2007).

References

Abu-Lughod, L. (1999). *Veiled Sentiments: Honor and poetry in a Bedouin society (2nd ed.).* Berkeley and Los Angeles, CA: University of California Press.

Abu-Lughod, L. (2008). *Writing Women's Worlds: Bedouin stories.* Berkeley and Los Angeles, CA: University of California Press.

Agar, M. H. (1996). *The Professional Stranger: An informal introduction to ethnography (2nd ed.).* San Diego, CA: Elsevier.

Anyon, J. (1997). *Ghetto Schooling: A political economy of urban educational reform.* New York: Teachers College Press.

Appadurai, A. (1991). Global ethnoscapes: Notes and queries for a transnational anthropology. In R. G. Fox (Ed.), *Interventions: Anthropologies of the present* (pp. 191–210). Santa Fe, CA: School of American Research.

Aretxaga, B. (1997). *Shattering Silence: Women, nationalism, and political subjectivity in Northern Ireland.* Princeton, NJ: Princeton University Press.

Asad, T. (1973). Introduction. In T. Asad (Ed.), *Anthropology and the Colonial Encounter.* New York: Humanities Press.

Asad, T. (1991). Afterword: From the history of colonial anthropology to the anthropology of Western hegemony. In G. Stocking (Ed.), *Colonial Situations: Essays on the contextualization of ethnographic knowledge.* Madison, WI: University of Wisconsin Press.

Atkinson, P. & Hammersley, M. (2007). *Ethnography: Principles in practice.* London and New York: Taylor & Francis.

Atkinson, P. (1990). *The Ethnographic Imagination: Textual constructions of reality.* London and New York: Routledge.

Bate, S. P. (1997). Whatever happened to organizational anthropology? A review of the field of organizational ethnography and anthropological studies. *Human Relations, 50*(9), 1147–1175.

Bateson, G. & Mead, M. (1942). *Balinese Character: A photographic analysis.* New York: The Academy of Sciences.

Behar, R. (1994). *Translated Woman: Crossing the border with Esperanza's story.* Boston, MA: Beacon Press.

Behar, R. (2007). Ethnography in a time of blurred genres. *Anthropology and Humanism, 32,* 145–155.

Behar, R. & Gordon, D. A. (Eds.). (1995). *Women Writing Culture.* Berkeley and Los Angeles, CA: University of California Press.

Bell, D. (1983). *Daughters of the Dreaming.* Melbourne: McPhee Gribble.

Bernard, R. H. (2006). *Research Methods in Anthropology: Qualitative and quantitative methods (4th ed.).* Lanham, MD: AltaMira Press.

Bishop, R. (1998). Freeing ourselves from neo-colonial domination in research: A Māori approach to creating knowledge. *International Journal of Qualitative Studies in Education, 11*(2), 199–219.

Blackman, S. J. (2007). Hidden ethnography: Crossing emotional borders in qualitative accounts of young people's lives. *Sociology, 41*(4), 699–716.

Bledsoe, C. H., Sherin, B., Galinsky, A., Headley, N., Heimer, C., Kjeldgaard, E., Lindgren, J., Miller, J., Roloff, M., & Uttal, D. (2007). Regulating creativity: Research and survival in the IRB iron cage. *Northwestern University Law Review, 101*(2), 593–642.

Bloome, D., Powers, C., Christian, M. M., Otto, S., & Shuart-Faris, N. (2005). *Discourse Analysis and the Study of Classroom Language and Literacy Events. A microethnographic perspective.* London: Lawrence Erlbaum Associates.

Bloor, M. (2001). The ethnography of health and medicine. In P. Atkinson, A. Coffey, S. Delamont, J. Lofland, & L. Lofland (Eds.), *Handbook of Ethnography* (pp. 177–187). Thousand Oaks, CA: Sage.

Boas, F. (1940). *Race, Language and Culture.* New York: Macmillan.

Bochner, A. (2000). Criteria against ourselves. *Qualitative Inquiry, 6*(20), 266–272.

Bohannan, P. (1957). *Justice and Judgment Among the Tiv.* London: Oxford University Press.

Bourgois, P. (1991). Confronting the ethics of ethnography: Lessons from fieldwork in Central America. In F. Harrison (Ed.), *De colonizing Anthropology: Moving further toward an anthropology for liberation* (pp. 110–126). Washington, DC: American Anthropological Association.

Briggs, C. L. (1986). *Learning How to Ask: A sociolinguistic appraisal of the role of the interview in social science research.* Cambridge: Cambridge University Press.

Briggs, J. L. (1970). *Never in Anger: Portrait of an Eskimo family.* Cambridge, MA: Harvard University Press.

Burawoy, M. (2000). *Global Ethnography: Forces, connections, and imaginations in a postmodern world.* Berkeley and Los Angeles, CA: University of California Press.

Burawoy, M. (2009). *The Extended Case Method: Four countries, four decades, four great transformations, and one theoretical tradition.* Berkeley and Los Angeles, CA: University of California Press.

Busier, H., Clark, K., Esch, R., Glesne, C., Pigeon, Y., & Tarule, J. (1997). Intimacy in research. *International Journal of Qualitative Studies in Education, 10*(2), 165–170.

Carspecken, P. F. & Walford, G. (Eds.). (2001). *Critical Ethnography and Education.* Amsterdam, New York, Oxford: JAI Press.

Carspecken, P. F. (1991). *Community Schooling and the Nature of Power: The battle for Croxteth comprehensive*. London and New York: Routledge.

Carspecken, P. F. (1996). *Critical Ethnography in Educational Research: A theoretical and practical guide*. London and New York: Routledge.

Charmaz, K. & Olsen, V. (1997). Ethnographic research in medical sociology. *Sociological Research and Methods*, 25, 452–494.

Christians, C. G. (2005). Ethics and politics in qualitative research. In N. K. Denzin & Y. S. Lincoln (Eds.), *Handbook of Qualitative Research* (3rd ed., pp. 139–164). Thousand Oaks, CA: Sage.

Clifford, J. (1990). Notes on fieldnotes. In R. Sanjek (Ed.), *Fieldnotes: The makings of anthropology* (pp. 47–70). Ithaca, NY: Cornell University Press.

Coleman, G. (2009). Code is speech: Legal tinkering, expertise, and protest among free and open source software developers. *Cultural Anthropology*, 24(3), 420–454.

Coover, R. (Director). (2005). The language of wine: An ethnography of work, wine and the senses [DVD]. LanguageOfWine.com

Cornish, F. & Ghosh, R. (2007). The necessary contradictions of "community-led" health promotion: A case study of HIV prevention in an Indian red light district. *Social Science and Medicine*, 64, 496–507.

Crapanzano, V. (1980). *Tuhami: Portrait of a Moroccan*. Chicago, IL: University of Chicago Press.

Creswell, J. W. (1998). *Qualitative Inquiry and Research Design: Choosing among five traditions*. Thousand Oaks, CA: Sage.

Davies, C. A. (1999). *Reflexive Ethnography: A guide to researching selves and others*. London: Routledge.

Denzin, N. K. (1997). *Interpretive Ethnography*. Thousand Oaks, CA: Sage.

Denzin, N. K. (2000). Interpretive Ethnography. *Zeitschrift für Erziehungswissenschaft*, 3(3), 401–409.

Denzin, N. K. (2008). The new paradigm dialogs and qualitative inquiry. *International Journal of Qualitative Studies in Education*, 21, 315–325.

Denzin, N. K. & Lincoln, Y. S. (1994). Introduction: Entering the field of qualitative research. In N. K. Denzin & Y. S. Lincoln (Eds.), *Handbook of Qualitative Research* (1st ed., pp. 1–18). Thousand Oaks, CA and London: Sage.

Denzin, N. K. & Lincoln, Y. S. (Eds.) (2002). *The Qualitative Inquiry Reader*. London and Thousand Oaks, CA: Sage.

Denzin, N. K. & Lincoln, Y. S. (2005). *The SAGE Handbook of Qualitative Inquiry (3rd ed.)*. London and Thousand Oaks, CA: Sage.

Deyhle, D. (2009). *Reflections in Place: Connected lives of Navajo women*. Tucson, AZ: University of Arizona Press.

Donham, D. L. (1999). *Marxist Modern: An ethnographic history of the Ethiopian revolution*. Berkeley and Los Angeles, CA: University of California Press.

Eisner, E. (1998). *The Enlightened Eye: Qualitative inquiry and the enhancement of educational practice*. New York: Macmillan.

Elyachar, J. E. (2005). *Markets of Dispossession: NGOs, economic development, and the state in Cairo*. Durham, NC: Duke University Press.

Emerson, R. L., Fretz, R. I., & Shaw, L. L. (2011). *Writing Ethnographic Fieldnotes*. Chicago, IL: University of Chicago Press.

Erickson, F. (1986). Qualitative methods in research on teaching. In M. C. Wittrock (Ed.), *The Handbook of Research on Teaching*. New York: Macmillan.

Erickson, K. & Stull, D. (1998). *Doing Team Ethnography: Warnings and advice*. Thousand Oaks, CA: Sage.

Escobar, A. (1995). *Encountering Development: The making and unmaking of the Third World*. Princeton, NJ: Princeton University Press.

Escobar, A. (2008). *Territories of Difference: Place, movements, life, redes*. Durham, NC: Duke University Press.

Evans-Pritchard, E. E. (1968 [1940]). *The Nuer*. Oxford: Clarendon Press.

Farmer, P. (2005). *Pathologies of Power: Health, human rights, and the new war on the poor*. Berkeley and Los Angeles, CA: University of California Press.

Ferguson, J. (1990). *The Anti-Politics Machine: "Development," depoliticization, and bureaucratic power in Lesotho*. Cambridge: Cambridge University Press.

Ferguson, J. & Gupta, A. (2002). Spatializing states: Toward an ethnography of neoliberal governmentality. *American Ethnologist*, 29, 981–1002.

Fine, G. A. (1993). Ten lies of ethnography: Moral dilemmas of field research. *Journal of Contemporary Ethnography*, 22(3), 267–294.

Finlay, L. (2002). Negotiating the swamp: The opportunity and challenge of reflexivity in research practice. *Qualitative Research*, 2(2), 209–230.

Finlay, L. (2006). "Rigour," "ethical integrity" or "artistry"? Reflexively reviewing criteria for evaluating qualitative research. *British Journal of Occupational Therapy*, 69(7), 319–326.

Foley, D. (2002). Critical ethnography: The reflexive turn. *Qualitative Studies in Education*, 15(4), 469–490.

Fox, R. G. (2000). Hearing where we're coming from—ethically and professionally. *Annals of the New York Academy of Sciences*, 925, 1–8.

Friedson, S. M. (1996). *Dancing Prophets: Musical experience in Tumbuka healing*. Chicago, IL: University of Chicago Press.

Geertz, C. (1973). *The Interpretation of Cultures*. New York: Basic Books.

Geertz, C. (1983). *Local Knowledge: Further essays in interpretive anthropology*. New York: Basic Books.

Geertz, C. (1988). *Works and Lives: The anthropologist as author*. Stanford, CA: Stanford University Press.

Genzuk, M. (1999). Tapping into community funds of knowledge. In *Effective Strategies for English Language Acquisition: A curriculum guide for the development of teachers, grades kindergarten through eight*. Los Angeles, CA: Los Angeles Annenberg Metropolitan Project/ARCO Foundation.

Gibb, C. (2005). An anthropologist undone. In A. Meneley & D. J. Young (Eds.), *Auto-ethnographies: The anthropology of academic practices* (pp. 216–228). Petersborough, Ontario: Broadway Press.

Glesne, C. & Peshkin, A. (1992). *Becoming Qualitative Researchers: An introduction*. White Plains, NY: Longman.

Glick Schiller, N. & Fouron, G. E. (2001). *Georges Woke Up Laughing: Long-distance nationalism and the search for home*. Durham, NC: Duke University Press.

Goffman, E. (1961). *Asylums: Essays on the social situations of mental patients and other inmates*. New York: Anchor books.

Gold, A. G. & Gujar, B. R. (2002). *In the Time of Trees and Sorrows: Nature, power, and memory in Rajasthan*. Durham, NC: Duke University Press.

Goodall, Jr., H. (2000). *Writing the New Ethnography*. Lanham, MD: AltaMira Press/Rowman & Littlefield.

Goodwin, C. & Goodwin, M. H. (1992). Context, activity, and participation. In P. Auer & A. DiLuzio (Eds.), *The Contextualization of Language* (pp. 77–100). Amsterdam: Benjamins B.V.

Guba, E. (1981). Criteria for assessing the trustworthiness of naturalistic inquiries, *Educational Communication and Technology Journal*, *29*(2), 75–91.

Guba, E. G. & Lincoln, Y. S. (1994). Competing paradigms in qualitative research. In N. K. Denzin & Y. S. Lincoln (Eds.), *Handbook of Qualitative Research* (1st ed., pp. 105–117). Thousand Oaks, CA: Sage.

Guba, E. G. & Lincoln, Y. S. (2005). Paradigmatic controversies, contradictions and emerging confluences. In N. Denzin & Y. S. Lincoln (Eds.), *The Sage Handbook of Qualitative Research* (Vol. 8, pp. 191–215). Thousand Oaks, CA: Sage.

Gupta, A. & Ferguson, J. (Eds.) (1997). *Anthropological Locations: Boundaries and grounds of a field science*. Berkeley and Los Angeles, CA: University of California Press.

Haddon, A. (1890). The ethnography of the western tribe of Torres Straits. *The Journal of the Anthropological Institute of Great Britain and Ireland*, *19*, 297–440.

Hammersley, M. (1992). *What's Wrong with Ethnography?—Methodological explorations*. London and New York: Routledge.

Hammersley, M. & Atkinson, P. (2007). *Ethnography: Principles in practice (3rd ed.)*. London and New York: Routledge.

Hannerz, U. (2003). Being there . . . and there . . . and there! Reflections on multisite ethnography. *Ethnography*, *4*(2), 201–216.

Hart, G. (2002). *Disabling Globalization: Places of power in post-apartheid South Africa*. Berkeley and Los Angeles, CA: University of California Press.

Hecht, T. (2006). *After Life: An ethnographic novel*. Durham, NC: Duke University Press.

Heider, K. G. (1976). *Ethnographic Film (1st ed.)*. Austin, TX: University of Texas Press.

Herdt, G. (1981). *Guardians of the Flutes: Idioms of masculinity*. New York: McGraw-Hill.

Heshusius, L. (1994). Freeing ourselves from objectivity: Managing subjectivity or turning toward a participatory mode of consciousness? *Educational Researcher*, *23*(3), 15–22.

Holstein, J. A. & Gubrium, J. F. (2008). Constructionist impulses in ethnographic fieldwork. In J. A. Holstein & J. F. Gubrium (Eds.), *Handbook of Constructionist Research* (pp. 373–395). New York: The Guilford Press.

Howe, K. & Eisenhart, M. (1990). Standards for qualitative (and quantitative) research: A prolegomenon. *Educational Researcher*, *19*(4), 2–9.

Hymes, D. (Ed.) (1969). *Reinventing Anthropology*. New York: Random House.

Jacobs-Huey, L. (2002). The natives are gazing and talking back: Reviewing the problematics of positionality, voice, and accountability among "native" anthropologists. *American Anthropologist*, *104*(3), 791–804.

Jackson, J. E. (1990). "Déjà Entendu"—the liminal qualities of anthropological fieldnotes. *Journal of Contemporary Ethnography*, *19*, 8–43.

Jeffery, B. & Troman, G. (2004). Time for ethnography. *British Educational Research Journal*, *30*(4), 535–548.

Jemielniak, D. & Kostera, M. (2010). Narratives of irony and failure in ethnographic work. *Canadian Journal of Administrative Sciences*, *27*(4), 335–347.

Josselson, R. (Ed.) (1996). *The Narrative Study of Lives*. Thousand Oaks, CA: Sage.

Katz, J. (1997). Ethnography's warrants. *Sociological Methods and Research*, *25*, 391–423.

Kendall, N. (2008a). Sexuality education in an abstinence-only era: A comparative case study of two U.S. states. *Sexuality Research and Social Policy*, *5*(2), 23–44.

Kendall, N. (2008b). "Vulnerability" in AIDS-affected states: Rethinking child rights, educational institutions, and development paradigms. *International Journal of Educational Development*, *28*, 365–383.

Kendall, N. (2012). *The Sex Education Debates*. Chicago, IL: University of Chicago Press.

Kent, L. L. (1990). Fieldwork that failed. In P. R. DeVita (Ed.), *The Naked Anthropologist: Tales from around the world*. Belmont, CA: Wadsworth.

Khosravi, S. (2011). *The "Illegal" Traveler: An auto-ethnography of borders*. Basingstoke: Palgrave Macmillan.

Klienman, A., Das, V., & Lock, M. (1997). *Social Suffering*. Berkeley and Los Angeles, CA: University of California Press.

Kuper, A. (1988). *The Invention of Primitive Society: Transformations of an illusion*. London and New York: Routledge.

Lacey, C. (1970). *Hightown Grammar: The school as a social system*. Manchester: Manchester University Press.

Lassiter, L. E. (1998). *The Power of Kiowa Song*. Tucson, AZ: University of Arizona Press.

Lassiter, L. E. (2005). *The Chicago Guide to Collaborative Ethnography*. Chicago, IL: University of Chicago Press.

Lather, P. (1997). Drawing the lines at angels: Working the ruins of feminist ethnography. *Qualitative Studies in Education*, *10*(3), 285–304.

LeBaron, C. & Streeck, J. (1997). Built space and the interactional framing of experience during a murder interrogation. *Human Studies*, *20*, 1–25.

LeCompte, M. D. & Schensul, J. J. (2010). *Designing & Conducting Ethnographic Research: An introduction*. Plymouth: Rowman AltaMira.

Lewis, D. (1973). Anthropology and colonialism. *Current Anthropology*, *14*(5), 581–602.

Li, T. (2007). *The Will to Improve: Governmentality, development, and the practice of politics*. Durham, NC: Duke University Press.

Lincoln, Y. S. & Guba, E. G. (1985). *Naturalistic Inquiry*. Thousand Oaks, CA: Sage.

Lombardi, G. (2009). The de-skilling of ethnographic labor: Signs of an emerging predicament. *EPIC*, 41–49.

Lowe, C. (2006). *Wild Profusion: Biodiversity conservation in an Indonesian archipelago*. Princeton, NJ: Princeton University Press.

Lynch, M. (2000). Against reflexivity as an academic virtue and source of privileged knowledge. *Theory, Culture, & Society*, *17*(3), 26–54.

McDermott, R. & Varenne, H. (1998). Adam, Adam, Adam, and Adam: The cultural construction of a learning disability. In H. Varenne & R. McDermott (Eds.), *Successful Failure: The school America builds*. Boulder, CO: Westview Press.

Mahmood, S. (2005). *Politics of Piety: The Islamic revival and the feminist subject*. Princeton, NJ: Princeton University Press.

Malinowski, B. (1984 [1922]). *Argonauts of the Western Pacific*. Prospect Heights, IL: Waveland Press.

Manias, E. & Street, A. (2001). Rethinking ethnography: Reconstructing nursing relationships. *Journal of Advanced Nursing*, *33*(2), 234–242.

Marcus, G. E. (1994). What comes (just) after "post": The case of ethnography. In N. K. Denzin & Y. S. Lincoln (Eds.), *Handbook of Qualitative Research* (1st ed., pp. 563–574). Thousand Oaks, CA: Sage.

Marcus, G. E. (1995). Ethnography in/of the world system: The emergence of multi-sited ethnography. *Annual Review of Anthropology*, *24*, 95–117.

Marcus, G. E. (1998). *Ethnography Through Thick and Thin*. Princeton, NJ: Princeton University Press.

Marvasti, A. (2003). *Being Homeless: Textual and narrative constructions*. Lanham, MD: Lexington Books.

Mead, M. (1973 [1928]). *Coming of Age in Samoa: A psychological study of primitive youth for Western civilization*. New York: William Morrow.

Mead, M. & Bunzel, R. L. (1960). *The Golden Age of American Anthropology*. New York: George Braziller.

Medicine, B. (2001). *Learning to be an Anthropologist and Remaining Native*, edited with S. E. Jacobs. Urbana, IL: University of Illinois.

Mehan, H. (1998). The study of social interaction in educational settings: Accomplishments and unresolved issues. *Human Development*, *41*(4), 245–269.

Merry, S. E. (1990). *Getting Justice and Getting Even: Legal consciousness among working-class Americans*. Chicago, IL: University of Chicago Press.

Mintz, S. W. (1960). *Worker in the Cane: A Puerto Rican life history*. New Haven, CT: Yale University Press.

Moore, S. F. (1986). *Social Facts and Fabrications: Customary law on Kilimanjaro, 1880–1980*. Cambridge: Cambridge University Press.

Myers, M. (1999). Investigating information systems with ethnographic research. *Communications of the Association for Information Systems*, *2*(23), 1–20.

Naples, N. A. & Sachs, C. (2000). Standpoint epistemology and the uses of self-reflection in feminist ethnography: Lessons for rural sociology. *Rural Sociology*, *65*(2), 194–214.

Narayan, K. (1989). *Storytellers, Saints, and Scoundrels: Folk narrative in Hindu religious teaching*. Philadelphia, PA: University of Pennsylvania Press.

Narayan, K. (1993). How native is a "native" anthropologist? *American Anthropologist*, *95*(3), 19–32.

Narayan, K. (1997). *Mondays on the Dark Night of the Moon: Himalayan foothill folktales in collaboration with Urmila Devi Sood*. Oxford: Oxford University Press.

Narayan, K. (1999). Ethnography and fiction: Where is the border? *Anthropology and Humanism*, *24*, 134–147.

Ong, A. (2006). *Neoliberalism as Exception: Mutations in citizenship and sovereignty*. Durham, NC: Duke University Press.

Ong, A. & Collier, S. (Eds.). (2005). *Global Assemblages: Technology, politics, and ethics as anthropological problems*. Malden, MA: Blackwell.

Peet, R. & Hartwick, E. (2009). *Theories of Development*. New York: Guilford Press.

Peshkin, A. (1993). The goodness of qualitative research. *Educational Researcher*, *22*(2), 23–29.

Pillow, W. S. (2003). Confession, catharsis or cure? Rethinking the uses of reflexivity as methodological power in qualitative research. *The International Journal of Qualitative Research in Education*, *16*(2), 175–196.

Pink, S. (2001). *Doing Visual Ethnography: Images, media and representation in research*. Thousand Oaks, CA: Sage.

Pollock, M. (2004). *Colormute: Race talk dilemmas in an American school*. Princeton, NJ: Princeton University Press.

Rabinow, P. (1977). *Reflections on Fieldwork in Morocco*. Berkeley and Los Angeles, CA: University of California Press.

Radcliffe-Brown, A. R. (1952). Historical note on British social anthropology. *American Anthropologist*, *54*, 275–277.

Radka, R. (2007). Enabling our voices to be heard. *EPIC*, 214–219.

Rappaport, J. (2008). Beyond participant observation: Collaborative ethnography as theoretical innovation. *Collaborative Anthropologies*, *1*, 1–31.

Rasmussen, S. (2003). When the field space comes to the home space: New constructions of ethnographic knowledge in a new African diaspora. *Anthropological Quarterly*, *76*(1), 7–32.

Richardson, L. (2000). Evaluating ethnography. *Qualitative Inquiry*, *6*(2), 253–255.

Rivers, W. (1910). The father's sister in Oceania. *Folk-Lore*, XXI, 42–59.

Robertson, J. (2002). Reflexivity redux: A pithy polemic on "positionality." *Anthropological Quarterly*, *75*(4), 785–792.

Rosaldo, R. (1999). *Culture and Truth: The remaking of social analysis (2nd ed.)*. Boston, MA: Beacon.

Rosen, L. (1989). *The Anthropology of Justice: The construction of social relations in a Muslim community*. Chicago, IL: University of Chicago Press.

Said, E. W. (1978). *Orientalism*. New York: Pantheon Books.

Salzman McGill, P. (1989). The lone stranger and the solitary quest. *Anthropology News*, *30*(5), 44.

Scheper-Hughes, N. (1993). *Death Without Weeping: The violence of everyday life in Brazil*. Berkeley and Los Angeles, CA: University of California Press.

Scheper-Hughes, N. (1995). The primacy of the ethical: Propositions for a militant anthropology. *Current Anthropology*, *36*(3), 409–420.

Schwandt, T. A. (1996). Farewell to criteriology. *Qualitative Inquiry, 2*(1), 58–72.

Seale, C. (1999). Quality in qualitative research. *Qualitative Inquiry, 5*(4), 465–478.

Seale, C. (2002). Quality issues in qualitative inquiry. *Qualitative Social Work, 1*(1), 97–110.

Sells, S. P., Smith, T. E., Coe, M. J., Yoshioka, M., & Robbins, J. (1994). An ethnography of couple and therapist experiences in reflecting team practices. *Journal of Marital and Family Therapy, 20*(3), 247–266.

Sider, G. M. (2009). Can anthropology ever be innocent? *Anthropology Now, 1*(1), 43–50.

Sluka, J. A. & Robben, A. C. G. (2007). Fieldwork in cultural anthropology: An introduction. In J. A. Sluka & A. C. G. Robben (Eds.), *Ethnographic Fieldwork: An anthropological reader* (pp. 29–32). Malden, MA: Blackwell.

Spindler, G. D. & Spindler, L. S. (2000). *Fifty Years of Anthropology and Education, 1950–2000: A Spindler anthology*. Mahwah, NJ: L. Erlbaum Associates.

Spradley, J. (1979). *The Ethnographic Interview*. Belmont, CA: Wadsworth Group/Thomas Learning.

St. Pierre, E. A. (1999). The work of response in ethnography. *Journal of Contemporary Ethnography, 28*(3), 266–287.

Stanley, L. & Wise, S. (1983). *Breaking Out: Feminist consciousness and feminist research*. London and New York: Routledge.

Stanley, L. & Wise, S. (1993). *Breaking Out Again: Feminist ontology and epistemology*. London and New York: Routledge.

Taussig, M. (1991). *Shamanism, Colonialism, and the Wild Man: A study in terror and healing*. Chicago, IL: University of Chicago Press.

Tedlock, B. (1991). From participant observation to the observation of participation: The emergence of narrative ethnography. *Journal of Anthropological Research, 47*(1), 69–94.

Tedlock, B. (2003). Ethnography and ethnographic representation. In N. Denzin & Y. S. Lincoln (Eds.), *Strategies of Qualitative Inquiry* (pp. 165–213). Thousand Oaks, CA: Sage.

Thomas, W. I. & Znaniecki, F. (1927). *The Polish Peasant in Europe and America*. New York: A. A. Knopf.

Tong, A., Sainsbury, P., & Craig, J. (2007). Consolidated criteria for reporting qualitative research (COREQ): A 32-item checklist for interviews and focus groups. *International Journal for Quality in Health Care, 19*(6), 349–357.

Tracy, S. (2010). Qualitative quality: Eight "big-tent" criteria for excellent qualitative research. *Qualitative Inquiry, 16*(10), 837–851.

Tsing, A. L. (2005). *Friction: Ethnography of global connection*. Princeton, NJ: Princeton University Press.

Turner, E. (2007). Introduction to the art of ethnography. *Anthropology and Humanism, 32*(2), 108–116.

Turner, V. W. (1967). *The Forest of Symbols: Aspects of Ndembu ritual*. Ithaca, NY: Cornell University Press.

Tyler, S. A. (1987). *The Unspeakable: Discourse, dialogue, and rhetoric in the postmodern world*. Madison, WI: University of Wisconsin Press.

Van Maanen, J. (1988). *Tales of the Field: On writing ethnography*. Chicago, IL: University of Chicago Press.

Vidich, A. J. & Lyman, S. M. (1994). Qualitative methods: Their history in sociology and anthropology. In N. K. Denzin & Y. S. Lincoln (Eds.), *Handbook of Qualitative Research* (1st ed., pp. 23–59). Thousand Oaks, CA: Sage.

Vincent, C. (1980). *Tuhami: Portrait of a Moroccan*. Chicago, IL: University of Chicago Press.

Visconti, L. (2010). Ethnographic case study (ECS): Abductive modeling of ethnography and improving the relevance in business marketing research. *Industrial Marketing Management, 39*, 25–39.

Watson, G. (1987). Make me reflexive, but not yet: Strategies for managing essential reflexivity in ethnographic discourse. *Journal of Anthropological Research, 43*(1), 29–41.

Wendland, C. L. (2010). *A Heart for the Work: Journeys through an African medical school*. Chicago, IL: University of Chicago Press.

Wesch, M. (2009). YouTube and you: Experiences of self-awareness in the context collapse of the recording webcam. *Explorations in Media Ecology, 8*(2), 19–34.

Willis, P. (1977). *Learning to Labor: How working-class kids get working-class jobs*. New York: Columbia University Press.

Willis, P. & Trondman, M. (2000). Manifesto for ethnography. *Ethnography, 1*, 5–16.

Wittel, A. (2000). Ethnography on the move: From field to net to internet. *Forum: Qualitative Social Research, 1*(1). Available online at: www.qualitative-research.net/index.php/fqs/article/viewArticle/1131/2517.

Wolcott, H. (1987). On ethnographic intent. In G. Spindler & L. Spindler (Eds.), *Interpretive Ethnography of Education* (pp. 37–57). Hillsdale, NJ: Lawrence Erlbaum Associates.

Wolcott, H. (2002). *Sneaky Kid and its Aftermath: Ethics and intimacy in fieldwork*. Lanham, MD: AltaMira Press.

Wolcott, H. (2005). *Art of Fieldwork (2nd ed.)*. Lanham, MD: AltaMira Press.

Wolcott, H. (2008). *Ethnography Lessons: A primer*. Walnut Creek, CA: Left Coast Press.

Wolf, M. (1992). *A Thrice-Told Tale: Feminism, postmodernism and ethnographic responsibility*. Stanford, CA: Stanford University Press.

8

The Grounded Theory Method

Antony Bryant

The grounded theory method (GTM) was introduced to the social science research community by Barney Glaser and Anselm Strauss in the mid-1960s; specifically in their now classic text *The Discovery of Grounded Theory* (Glaser & Strauss, 1967). The rationale for their methodological innovation was to break with the traditional model of research in the social sciences, which largely focused on the derivation and testing of hypotheses developed from the work of the grand theorists of the time. Glaser and Strauss drew stark contrasts between their approach—'grounded in the data'—and the more abstract, deductive ones promulgated in the social science academic communities, particularly those in the United States.

Kathy Charmaz and I, both separately and in concert (Charmaz, 2000, 2006, 2007, 2008; Bryant, 2002, 2003, 2009; Bryant & Charmaz, 2007a,b,c, 2012), have explained the background against which GTM emerged in the work of Glaser and Strauss, and how it then developed and diverged in the ensuing decades. Without going into this in further detail at this juncture, the key observation to be made for present purposes is that by the 1980s GTM had become far and away the most popular method in the general areas of the social and behavioural sciences—with several surveys indicating that the number of papers where GTM was specified as the prime method outnumbered all others put together (Titscher et al., 2000). Moreover, researchers using the method had produced award-winning and groundbreaking publications and research outcomes in the social sciences, health-care, and education in particular. This popularity, however, was contentious: Many papers claimed use of the method, but even a cursory reading of the paper itself indicated the paucity of such claims.

In an era when there is a near-universal expectation that any research proposal, report, or publication must specify and justify its methodological bases, GTM was an attractive option. In the name of GTM researchers could start on their research without clearly specified objectives, articulated research questions, or hypotheses. Moreover, they could side-step the literature review, and initiate interviews, and their subsequent analysis consisting of the derivation or extraction of *codes*—the description of which then constituted the research findings. This may appear as something of a crude and cruel caricature, but it does bear a significant semblance of truth. More importantly, something along these lines certainly chimes with many editors and reviewers who sometimes express severe reservations whenever a paper purporting to use GTM is submitted. Similarly for review boards where research proposals are presented for consideration.

GTM became victim of its own success, and in the process many people's understanding of the method has gone awry—leading in one direction to its widespread popularity and in another to the deep suspicion with which it is regarded. In keeping with the important rationale for this collection, what follows will focus on the ways in which the underlying misconceptions of both of the divergent paths can be remedied, so that the method is better understood by researchers as well as the gatekeepers of the journals, accreditations, and research funds. Readers looking for detailed elucidation of the method itself should refer to the items listed under Further Reading.

Select Terms

Reviewers are often perplexed at the terminology used within the context of GTM—in many cases terms that have one meaning outside the method are used with a different meaning within GTM. Thus the following selection is presented as an aide-memoire for reviewers—those looking for more definitive discussions should refer initially to Charmaz (2006), to the Glossary in *The Handbook of Grounded Theory* (hereafter referred to as 'the Handbook') (Bryant & Charmaz, 2007), and to the items listed in Further Reading.[1]

Categorizing is the process whereby a limited number of codes are selected on the basis of their significance and explanatory import. Moving from numerous codes to a restricted number of categories embodies a move from detailed findings to a more abstract and conceptually powerful level of analysis. Categories are then further explicated in terms of properties, contexts of operation, change, and interaction. 'Grounded theorists make their most significant theoretical categories into the concepts of their theory' (Charmaz, 2006).

Codes are produced throughout the research process; initially as proposed patterns or relationships between data—whether in the form of interview statements, observations, document segments, or similar materials. They eventually form the basis for more developed abstractions and categories, which themselves provide the basis for articulating grounded theories.

Coding is one of the key activities in GTM, as researchers seek to explicate and identify patterns and themes from their data. One of the key innovations introduced by Glaser and Strauss was the jettisoning of preconceived or predefined coding frameworks (common in quantitative and some qualitative research approaches), in favour of the admonition for researchers to develop their own codes as their research progressed. In this manner coding may well take the researcher into unforeseen areas and in unexpected directions. It should be noted that in far too many papers and proposals, researchers' use of GTM amounts to no more than somewhat incomplete or desultory forms of coding—i.e. breaking up interview transcripts into segments which are then subjected to nothing more than various forms of re-description. This has led to many GTM research findings being seen as simply re-stating the obvious; but on the other hand far too many research reports— both qualitative and quantitative—do exactly this; hence the epigrams about Popes and Catholicism, and bears and what they get up to in the woods!

Concept-indicator model refers to the outcome to be produced by researchers as they develop the constructs that encompass and account for relationships developed from gathering and interrogation of empirical data; thus the basis for each concept rests on some aspect of the 'empirical indications' (Charmaz, 2006). Hence concepts are 'grounded' in data.

Constant comparative method summarizes a key aspect of GTM; the constant iteration between data gathering and analysis. In effect, this iteration can be thought of as a spiral moving upward from concrete data toward more abstract concepts and theories. This process develops by comparing data with data, data with category, category with category, and category with concept. In this manner, higher level abstractions retain a link with the data in which they are grounded, as opposed to what Glaser has termed 'immaculate conceptualization'. 'If memos are the skeleton of the grounded theory method, use of the constant comparison is the full body' (Wiener, 2007).

Memos and memo-writing are key features of GTM, although in essence they can be seen to embody good practice for researchers in general. The act of memo-writing is pivotal in the iteration between data gathering and analysis: 'If data are the building blocks of the developing theory, memos are the mortar' (Stern, 2007). Memos can take the form of sets of notes on particular topics, incorporating 'slices of data' such as extracts or observations. In later stages they can be used to outline concepts and patterns; and taken together a set of memos can provide the basis for research papers and other outcomes.

Reasoning contrasts GTM with traditional research approaches; the latter using a predominantly *deductive* form of reasoning. Consequently, Glaser and Strauss characterized GTM as *inductive*. This is somewhat misleading; describing the form of reasoning involved as *abduction* is more apposite (see Reichertz, 2007 in Handbook). 'The skill of the grounded theorist is to abstract concepts by leaving the detail of the data behind, lifting the concepts above the data and integrating them into a theory that explains the latent social pattern underlying the behaviour in a substantive area' (Locke, 2001).

Substantive and formal grounded theory, when first articulated, will be a substantive one—i.e. firmly anchored in a substantive context such as patient care or implementation of new technologies. Later developments may transform such theories into formal ones, encompassing far wider domains and as such couched in more abstract and generic terms. 'By substantive theory we mean theory developed for a substantive or empirical area of sociological inquiry, such as patient care, geriatric life styles etc. . . . By formal theory we mean theory developed for a formal or conceptual area of sociological area such as status passage, stigma, deviant behavior, etc.' (Glaser & Strauss, 1967). 'Formal theories exacerbate the tension between our need to create rules of thumb to get things done and our postmodern awareness that the complexity of life can never be fairly captured in any theory' (Kearney, 2007).

Theoretical codes, coding families, coding paradigms represent various ways in which the founders of GTM, both in concert and then individually, have sought to offer guidance to researchers in their moves from amassing data to developing useful and insightful concepts. Glaser's discussion in *TS* offers the initial foundation for this, specifically the chapter on Theoretical Coding (Chapter 4). 'Without substantive codes, theoretical codes are empty abstractions. But substantive codes could be related without theoretical codes, but the result is usually confused, unclear theoretically, and/or typically connected by descriptive topics but going nowhere theoretically' (Glaser, 1998). Strauss and Corbin took this further, seeking to offer researchers more guidance in making these conceptual moves. They offered what they termed their 'coding paradigm', something to which Glaser took exception (see below). In his turn, Glaser put forward the idea of 'coding families', although he would argue that these operate in a completely different and distinctive manner, and are in no way equivalent to the Strauss–Corbin approach.

Theoretical sampling as opposed to random sampling is used in GTM to develop and enhance the categories that develop from initial and ensuing iterations between data gathering and analysis. As categories are developed they provide prompts for locating further sources of data—i.e. 'people, events, or information to illuminate and define the boundaries and relevance of the categories' (Charmaz, 2006). 'Theoretical sampling; that is, directing the data search to advance the developing theory' (Stern, 2007).

Theoretical saturation is the point beyond which further data centred on a specific category fails to reveal additional properties or theoretical insights relevant to the developing grounded theory.

Theoretical sensitivity refers to the skill needed in researching, whereby the researcher is able to 'see relevant data' and develop this, if necessary in further stages of analysis and data gathering, to develop theoretical concepts and grounded theories (see Kelle, 2007).

Diversities in Perspective, Context, and Form

Diversity is something that has manifested itself as a central feature of GTM—to some extent as a major distraction or irritant. In the years following the appearance of Glaser and Strauss' classic text, *Discovery of Grounded Theory* (1967), use of the method grew gradually, emanating from Strauss' base at University of California San Francisco [UCSF]. By the late 1970s, however, alumnae from the doctoral programme at UCSF had taken the ideas of GTM to a far wider audience, and there was a clamouring, particularly from the postgraduate community, for further and more accessible expositions of the method. *Discovery*, and the two other books by Glaser and Strauss (1965, 1968) that appeared around the same time, have been described as the 'best tutorial on grounded theory'; but in fact they were not really written to address novice researchers, rather they were aimed at those already imbued with 'traditional' modes of academic research. *Discovery* itself is really a manifesto for GTM, written as a challenge to the gate-keepers and grand instructors of the social science academies in the USA at the time. The other two books—*Awareness* (1965) and *Time* (1968)—are brilliant exemplars of the use of the method, but as such do not really bring the nuts-and-bolts of the method clearly to the attention of less informed readers (see the comments below in Further Reading).

Anselm Strauss in his teaching and lecturing in the United States and Europe (particularly Germany) became aware of the growing demand for further expositions of the method. He first responded in print with *Qualitative Analysis for Social Scientists* (1987), and then, together with Juliet Corbin, in *Basics of Qualitative Research: Grounded Theory Procedures and Techniques* (1990). In the first book he quoted at considerable and significant length from Glaser's *Theoretical Sensitivity* (1978), but in the second he and Corbin sought to offer a far more basic and accessible textbook-cum-manual for GTM. Glaser saw this as a significant divergence from GTM, even asking Strauss to withdraw the book (see Preface to Glaser, 1992); publishing his own rejoinder (1992), clearly distancing himself from Strauss.

Although Glaser claimed that Strauss had departed from GTM, angrily stating that the 'book is without conscience, bordering on immorality', in many respects the rapid growth in popularity of GTM can be dated from the publication of the book by Strauss and Corbin. Indeed, many publications citing use of the method make no mention of the disagreement between the two founders. Authors write about the method as if there is a simple continuity from *Discovery* to *Basics*. In many cases this may simply have been based on ignorance of Glaser's severe misgivings. In recent years, most authors do include some comments regarding the Glaser/Strauss controversy, but, perhaps understandably, take the issue no further.

Glaser's main point of contention was that his former collaborator had moved away from the model of 'emergence' that marked GTM as an innovative approach. For Glaser, GTM was a wholly inductive method; researchers gathering data from which grounded theories 'emerged'. Glaser described the approach offered by Strauss and Corbin as diametrically opposed to this, amounting to ways of 'forcing' the data in order to produce some theoretical outcome. At the time he labelled this 'forced, full, conceptual description'; in his more recent writings he often uses the term 'Qualitative Data Analysis' (QDA) as an umbrella term for forms of analysis that do not meet his criteria of what constitutes 'traditional' GTM.

Developments in the method were marked by this divergence in the 1990s, although Strauss did not respond in print to Glaser's criticism before his death in 1996. Glaser has continued to promote the method in his extensive publications, but there have been other developments emanating initially from students who studied with Strauss and Glaser at UCSF. In addition, Strauss had, and continues to have, a significant impact in the German-speaking world where his ideas and writings were highly influential, often couched explicitly in the context of his place in the tradition of pragmatism (see Bryant, 2009; also the chapters by Starr, 2007 and Strübing, 2007 in the Handbook).

During the 1990s there was a growing demand for researchers to outline their methodological rationale in proposals and subsequent publications and reports. This led to various issues arising with regard to GTM, whether of the Glaser or Strauss–Corbin variety. GTM, whether in the forms expressed by Glaser and Strauss in concert, or their later divergent statements, centred on 'data'. Yet the concept itself remained largely unexamined by both founding authors. In effect, this amounted to positivism by default, with the researcher given the fairly neutral role of data-gathering from which grounded theories would 'emerge'. This was somewhat ironic, since one of the key aspects of GTM was 'theoretical sensitivity'—something that remained a central term in Glaser's and Strauss' writings— and such sensitivity was clearly a skill that researchers need to develop and nurture in their *active* engagement with the research data. For some critics of the method the continued and unreflective use of GTM slogans or mantras such as 'the theory emerges from the data' (see Bryant & Charmaz, 2007b) was sufficient grounds for any claims for its use to be treated with suspicion or worse. But for others this issue could be addressed while retaining the power and rigour of the method itself.

The first person to publish widely on this aspect of the method was Kathy Charmaz, a member of the first cohort of doctoral students of Strauss and Glaser at UCSF. (Strauss was her thesis advisor.) The first edition of the *Handbook of Qualitative Research* had included a chapter on GTM by Strauss and Corbin, but the second edition, prepared and published after Strauss' death, included one by Charmaz in which she contrasted Glaser's 'objectivist' (i.e. positivist) account of GTM, with the 'constructivist' account that she has articulated in her many and various writings since the 1990s.

Soon after this (initially completely independently as a result of being woefully ignorant of the GTM literature beyond the early writings) I expressed similar ideas, albeit based on far less familiarity with the method itself (Bryant, 2003). In the ensuing years we have collaborated on several publications, notably the Handbook, and there is now a burgeoning of writers on GTM seeking to develop and enhance the method both by exemplifying its use across a growing range of contexts, practices, and disciplines and also in terms of exemplifying its bases and foundations. (The section on Further Reading gives some useful examples.)

One of the key outcomes of this constructivist account of GTM can be seen in the range of basic questions which a researcher should be prepared to pose at the outset of a research project. Glaser and Strauss' initial set encompassed the following high-level GTM questions:

- What is happening here? (Glaser, 1978)
- What is this data a study of? (Glaser, 1978, p. 57, Glaser & Strauss, 1967)
- What theoretical category does this datum indicate? (Glaser, 1978) (source 'What is Grounded Theory', PowerPoint presentation, Kathy Charmaz, 2008 http://eprints.ncrm. ac.uk/208/1/What_is_Grounded_Theory.ppt)

In her 2006 book Charmaz offers several further questions that develop a key aspect of GTM, but in a more specifically constructivist manner than is evident in Glaser's and Strauss' work. Thus she stresses that articulations of answers to the 'what is happening here?' question lead to consideration of 'basic social processes' and/or 'basic psychological processes'. Such consideration depends on the assessments and judgements made by the researcher(s) reflecting on the findings, and such reflection may encompass analysis of the data using further questions such as:

- From whose viewpoint is a given process fundamental?
- How do participants' actions construct (observed social processes)?
- Who exerts control over these processes?
- What meanings do different participants attribute to the process? (Charmaz, 2006, p. 20)

What might be seen by some as the flowering of the method is seen by others as its diminution and undermining—much as Glaser saw Strauss' efforts as a radical departure from their initial project. In the Handbook we described the current position as a 'family of methods', with some of our contributors pointing out that while families could be thought of as places of security and support, they could also be highly dysfunctional! Whatever one's views on this, the method has certainly matured, and those seeking to use it in their research cannot claim any lack of resources and sources of support and elucidation. Although there may still be some who regard GTM as founded on an 'epistemological fairy-tale' incorporating the magic of emergence, there is now a significant body of work to which researchers can turn for substantive support for incorporation of the method and its various techniques.

Perhaps in the long term, GTM will develop along lines similar to that of Action Research (AR), an orientation that now encompasses many varied and contending strands, but largely without the rancour that has characterized some of the methodological differences surrounding GTM. On the other hand, it should not be assumed that all is sweetness and light in other methodological realms: there is bitterness and controversy among users in many areas of both qualitative and quantitative methods.

Qualitative Touchstones

What follows in this section is intended to offer some guidelines for authors and reviewers/editors when confronted with GTM-based research papers and reports, regardless of which particular approach to GTM has been used, and also allowing for partial and innovative uses of the method.

1. Initiation and rationale

If the research was oriented around use of GTM from the start, then this should be confirmed from the outset of any discussion of method or approach. Moreover, readers should be informed that, as a consequence, the early stages may not necessarily have been informed or guided by specific hypotheses or even specific research questions—in practice, hypotheses may well be the outcome of GTM-based research. In such cases there should at least be discussion of the generic set of questions referred to in the previous section. Furthermore, and as a consequence, it is important that the rationale and impetus for the research should be clearly articulated and explained. This may be couched in generic terms, contextualized against wide-ranging issues or located in domains of specific practices. It may also be presented as emanating from the personal experience(s) of the researcher(s). Although such bases for research may cause reviewers some uneasiness, the critical issue is the extent to which the ensuing accounts move forward to coherent and rigorous analyses and constructs—as will be explained in ensuing sections. In some cases, however, this proves not to be the case, with much of what follows being simply a selection of anecdotes, partial observations, and vague descriptions of the context itself. These latter forms of reporting on purportedly GTM research have led to justified suspicions on the part of editors and reviewers when confronted with any account centred on GTM. The point, however, is to understand that persuasive and rigorous research can indeed emanate from highly personal experiences and motives, and that this is often a characteristic of insightful and informative GTM-based research. It is worth recalling that the initial GTM work on dying and hospitalization developed precisely as a result of the individual experiences of loss and bereavement on the part of both Barney Glaser and Anselm Strauss.

Some researchers will report that they did not use GTM from the outset, but rather decided, or were advised, to use it at later stages of their research. This change in direction is often motivated by researchers realizing that their data or findings do not actually work with their initial plans—for instance, they might have planned to use a quantitative approach, but their data proved to be far richer as a qualitative resource. Or they now recognize that their initial ideas or assumptions were ill-conceived, and it proved to be far more fruitful to develop using GTM. In these sorts of instances a strong and clear case will need to be presented for this change in direction, offering an explanation of how GTM was then used. Were earlier hypotheses or specific research questions jettisoned, or were they still used to guide the analysis and any later data gathering?

It may happen that researchers have gathered their data from several specific case studies before deciding that their planned forms of analysis will not work or provide a basis for persuasive or informative outcomes. Although going somewhat against the iterative spirit of GTM, the method can still prove effective in such contexts, with one of the cases being selected as a basis for initial coding and conceptual enhancement. This first-cut model then being applied to the other instances with a view to further conceptual enhancement or contrasting outcome.

These latter two applications of the method might seem to be at best forms of *GTM-lite*, but it is important to understand that any justification must emanate from and be judged by the value of the outcomes rather than from some criteria of methodological purity.

2. Use of literature

The role of the literature review has proved problematic for GTM research. Glaser has consistently maintained the view—initially expressed jointly by Glaser and Strauss in their early writings—that researchers should not access the literature central to their research until the later stages of their projects, i.e. after they have developed their models and concepts. The rationale for this being that the less they open themselves up to the influences of existing ideas the better.

In 1967 this might have been a justified concern, particularly since Glaser and Strauss were keen for researchers not to derive their ideas from the existing literature of the grand theorists, but with regard to current practices and expectations there are a number of problems with this strategy. First, there is the intellectual problem that researchers need to know if their initial concerns have been expressed by others, and if so, whether there is a body of work dealing with these matters. (See Weiner's discussion of this in the Handbook, 2007.) Moreover, researchers are often confronted with the necessity to gain institutional approval for their proposed work, and hence must demonstrate knowledge of the relevant literature and other sources.

For these reasons GTM researchers cannot wholly postpone the literature review, but they can adapt it to their chosen research strategy, provided it is done clearly and with coherent justification. For instance, it can be assumed that researchers will have a general idea of their research domain from the outset—even if this 'domain' is imprecise and generic in characterization at this point. In such cases the initial literature review can be limited to encompass only a small number of central concepts or issues, some of which have already been identified by applying high-level GTM questions of the sort outlined earlier.

As the research progresses, usually after some initial interviews or other forms of investigation, the nature of the research domain will become clearer or more specific even if in some instances it has veered away from its initial bases and presuppositions. In all cases, however, early analysis of the data should result in initial codes (see below) that can then be used to direct further reviews of appropriate literature and other sources. Whether this is taken up immediately, or left until a later stage of the research will vary from case to case.

The key is that assessors should not be too surprised if a GTM-based research proposal does not include a full literature review, instead offering an outline discussion with identification of likely sources and resources, and then including planning for a staged review interspersed with data gathering and analysis activities. Similarly editors and reviewers, as well as examiners of PhDs and other forms of research qualification, should not necessarily expect to see a single literature review in the final presentation; rather it may be presented in stages moving from an early overview of key topics, to an eventual comparison of the key GTM-based outcomes with the literature itself—with a significant part of the literature only being identified and scrutinized after the conceptual model has been fairly well developed. This is in contrast to what might be expected in other forms of research, but is perfectly understandable and justifiable from the GTM perspective. The onus, however, is on the researchers to clarify and justify this approach, assisting their readers in understanding the innovative procedures of GTM itself. Phyllis Stern alludes to this in her chapter in the Handbook (Stern, 2007).

3. Data collection and analysis

One of the key innovations of GTM is the iterative relationship between data gathering and analysis. Early data is gathered, often guided by the very high-level and generic GTM questions suggested by Glaser and Strauss, supplemented by Charmaz (see above). This is then immediately followed by initial analysis, the outcomes of which then guide further stages of data gathering. It has been assumed by many, both users of GTM and others, that the method is restricted to, or at the very least heavily slanted towards, open-ended face-to-face interviews, but this is not the case. As Glaser continually stresses—'All is data'. Anything can be treated as data for the purposes of a grounded theory study. In many GTM studies, people have used data from many sources—published accounts, literature, on-line sources, and so on, and they have also used quantitative data. The sub-title of *Discovery* is *Strategies for Qualitative Research*, but that does not mean that the procedures and techniques of the method cannot be applied to quantitative data. (Indeed it can and should be argued that all research using quantitative data involve various forms of interpretation and sets of assumptions. Using GTM can help bring such suppositions to the fore, rather than letting them slip by unheeded.)

The initial coding of data should be done without recourse to specific frameworks, hypotheses, or other sorts of precise or formally preconceived concepts. GTM was developed specifically as a reaction against research that derived hypotheses or specific research questions from existing theories or models. It also took the idea of coding and reversed the process whereby researchers developed and contrived coding frameworks *prior* to the investigative research itself—which was standard practice in a good deal of empirical social research at the time (1960s). One of Glaser's teachers at Columbia was Paul Lazarsfeld, a significant force in the development of American social science research. He had been one of the pioneers of large-scale social research, most notably the study of unemployment in Marienthal in Austria (1930s). This had used prepared coding frameworks, but in his later work Lazarsfeld explained that this was too prescriptive. Eventually, Glaser together with Strauss pioneered the approach of developing codes after the data gathering had been initiated.

In some cases researchers using GTM may outline a generic approach or topic which oriented their initial research, rather than simply leaving this open. But someone could not justifiably claim to be using GTM while also strictly implementing or adhering to a specified and formal coding approach prior to data collection.

On the other hand, as Dey has succinctly noted, 'an open mind does not mean an empty head'. Statements that imply or explicitly state that a researcher ignored or simply discounted all previous ideas or suppositions should be treated as the methodological fictions they undoubtedly are, and any research reports that make such claims should consequently be treated with some suspicion.

4. Sampling

The sampling endemic to GTM is termed theoretical sampling—as opposed to random sampling—with the researcher actively seeking out instances that might 'illuminate and define the boundaries and relevance of the categories' (Charmaz, 2006). Thus in Glaser and Strauss' early work, having studied one context in which people were involved in treatment of people with terminal illness, they then specifically focused on other contexts so that the initial ideas they had developed could be enriched, clarified, or challenged. Again the onus is on the researcher to offer a cogent rationale for using this approach in the project when presenting a proposal or a paper for publication.

So it is important to understand that in a GTM study the initial data gathering might have been performed within a specific context, but with a wide remit. This approach might sound somewhat inchoate and problematic, but in many instances it proves an effective starting point, offering researchers the possibility of fairly unconstrained investigation of the domain from the outset of their research. For instance, in Glaser and Strauss' initial work, they cast their net across the whole spectrum of people and actions in the hospital setting in which they began their research.

Once some initial data has been gathered, it can then be analyzed and configured using the technique of open coding. Unlike earlier forms of coding, which involved application of previously prepared coding structures to the data, grounded theory is based on close investigation of the data from which potential codes can be derived. It is important to stress that although this method does not start from a clear and specific research question it certainly does offer a series of more generic questions for the guidance of researchers. This involves asking questions such as the high-level ones referred to in an earlier section.

5. Codes and coding

This is a key aspect of GTM, and unfortunately it is often the only aspect demonstrated by researchers claiming to have used the method. Coding existed as a research activity prior to the appearance of GTM, but in these cases coding frameworks were developed before data gathering took place; being used to direct the process, rather than being an outcome of the research itself. This was particularly the case in quantitative methods where the results can then be tabulated and subjected to relevant statistical techniques.

In GTM initial data is gathered and then subjected to a preliminary analysis. The data in the form of text—perhaps verbatim transcripts of interviews, contemporaneous notes, or something similar—can be broken down into segments which can then be labelled and sorted. It is important that the labels used are closely linked to the data itself, rather than emanating from the researcher's prior knowledge or experience. Hence the issue of being wary about being too deeply immersed in existing literature. The strategy is for researchers to remain open to the data, being prepared to be surprised by one's findings and change one's orientation. The initial codes that are produced at this early stage are 'provisional, comparative, and grounded in the data' (Charmaz, 2006, p. 48). They are provisional because the researcher can expect to change, develop, or discard them as the research progresses through analysis, further sampling and later conceptualization. They are comparative because the initial level of analysis will encompass comparing incidents of the same order with a view to consideration of amalgamating these into something with more explanatory and conceptual power. They are grounded in the data because at this stage the codes themselves may be wholly or significantly expressed in terms used by those involved in the context under study, or the link between the researcher's codes and the data itself will be clear and persuasive.

Charmaz reiterates and reinforces Glaser's stress on coding with gerunds. Glaser outlines his arguments about this in TS (1978). Charmaz demonstrates the point in asking her readers to '[T]hink of the difference in imagery between the following gerunds and their noun forms: describing versus description, stating versus statement, and leading versus leader. We gain a strong sense of action and sequence with gerunds' (2006, p. 49). She then offers a 'code for coding' which every GTM researcher should use as a guide both in the research itself and in presenting an account of how they accomplished their coding; and a copy should also be on-hand for reviewers and editors.

Later stages of coding are more focused—hence the term 'focused coding', the results of which are 'more directed, selective, and conceptual than word-by-word, line-by-line, and incident-by-incident coding' (Charmaz, 2006 referring to Glaser, 1978). In some cases, these second order codes will be enriched forms of earlier ones, but they may also be newly devised codes that incorporate aspects of the initial ones. The process of moving from initial codes to more focused ones will involve further analysis and sampling by the researcher, and critically it also requires the researcher to select, revise, and discard earlier codes as well as even introducing new ones provided they can be shown to be grounded in the data. Any research publication reporting on a GTM-based project will need to explain and demonstrate the way in which focused codes were derived from initial ones. Charmaz offers some clear examples in her book as well as in her various writings. Again claims for the *emergence* of these codes from the data-cum-initial-codes must be taken as a sign of inadequate understanding of the researcher-led processes in operation.

Those using the Strauss–Corbin approach to GTM move from the activity of focused coding to one of axial coding. The aim of this form of coding is to bring together the different strands of ideas developed in earlier coding stages around the 'axis' of a category. In part, this can be accomplished by analysis of existing codes based around answering questions such as 'when, where, why, who, how, and with what consequences'. Although Glaser saw this as 'forcing' the data, it can be argued that Strauss and Corbin introduced this aspect or technique as a response to researchers who had tried to apply GTM but then found themselves overwhelmed by the range and extent of the codes their analysis generated. Charmaz offers a very useful overview and assessment of axial coding, clearly stating that she has 'not used axial coding according to Strauss and Corbin's formal procedures'. On the other hand there are many users of GTM who are guided by and incorporate the Strauss–Corbin model, producing useful and robust research findings. The main point at issue with regard to the submission of papers or reports to editors and reviewers is that there needs to be an explicit statement clearly indicating that this version of GTM has been employed. In many cases research reports incorporate the Strauss–Corbin approach as if it is simply a seamless continuation from the founding statements of the method, and reconcilable with Glaser's writings.

The final level of coding is termed 'theoretical coding', a concept at the heart of Glaser's account of 'theoretical sensitivity'. In his rejoinder to Strauss and Corbin, Glaser argues that this level of coding precludes need for the axial form, since it is during this process that the 'fractured story' produced by breaking up the initial findings into a plethora of open codes—subsequently reduced via focused coding—can be woven back together. In so doing the research findings are moved on to a higher conceptual level that leads in a theoretical direction. In his classic 1978 account of theoretical sensitivity, Glaser includes a complete chapter on theoretical coding, and in so doing outlines what he terms a series of 'Coding Families' incorporating analytic categories such as his 'Six Cs: Causes, Contexts, Contingencies, Consequences, Covariances, Conditions'. Charmaz argues that, if used skilfully, these can 'hone your work with a sharp analytic edge'.

Some users of GTM, as well as those whose only experience of the method is via their role as reviewers or editors, have pointed out that both Glaser's coding families and Strauss–Corbin's axial coding can be seen as responses to the need for guidance on coping with the outcomes of initial coding using GTM. Researchers often find themselves confronted by a multitude of codes, and this can prove an obstacle in the process of identifying core categories and higher conceptualization, eventually leading to genuine theoretical insights and innovations. As will be explained at further length in a subsequent section, a method is a tool and the effectiveness of that tool is dependent not only on the quality of the method itself, but also on the skill of those using it. Dogmatic and unquestioning use of either Glaser's coding families or Strauss–Corbin's axial coding is to be avoided at all costs; conversely, research reports should not be dismissed out of hand merely because the version of GTM under discussion is not the one favoured by the reviewer or reader.

6. Developing and reflecting upon research stages—memo-writing and memos

Given the iterative core at the heart of GTM—involving data gathering and analysis in intimate cycles—it is important that the researcher tracks the ways in which the analysis progresses through these iterations as they happen. This is a far more reliable manner of doing things, rather than trying to reconstruct the process once the research has been completed and the reports are being written. Keeping true to her stress on gerunds, Charmaz labels her chapter on this topic 'Memo-writing' (Charmaz, 2006), describing it as 'the pivotal intermediate step between data collection and writing drafts of papers'.

Researchers claiming use of GTM should be able to demonstrate their particular use of the method in the form of successive generations of memos. 'Remaining firmly grounded in the data, researchers use memos "to create social reality" (Richardson, 1998, p. 349—quoted by Lempert) by discursively organizing and interpreting the social worlds of their respondents' (Lempert, 2007). 'When memoing a topic analytically, the researcher generates a set of categories, contrasts, comparisons, questions, and avenues for further consideration which are more abstract than the original topic' (Lempert, 2007).

When describing the activity of memo-writing to general research audiences it is common to evoke responses along the lines of 'this is just like keeping a research diary', or 'action research and other forms of participative research demand the same thing'. To an extent, keeping contemporaneous notes should be part of any effective research practice, so memo-writing can be included in this category. But in the hands of an effective user of GTM memo-writing becomes something far more powerful and useful—Charmaz (2006) provides numerous examples of different forms of memo.

Lempert in her contribution to the Handbook refers to memos as 'asking questions of the data' (Lempert, 2007)—again note the gerund form. So memo-writing involves far more than merely noting down one's experiences or thoughts as the research progresses, although in the early stages of research memos may be based precisely around these sorts of input. The key to memo-writing is to use them to express in writing and then to develop one's ideas about codes and their inter-relationships. Charmaz offers some excellent examples of memos, as well as a memo on memo-writing itself (2006, Chapter 4). She also exemplifies the way in which memos can form the basis for written papers, and how memos can themselves be incorporated into published research accounts.

Memo-writing has always been a key aspect of GTM. In *TS* Glaser stresses the ways in which memos lie at the heart of the method. Writing theoretical memos is 'the core stage in the process of generating theory, the bedrock of theory generation'. A researcher who skips this stage 'is not doing grounded theory'. Similarly, all three editions of Strauss and Corbin's works contain extensive reference to the importance of memo-writing.

As Charmaz admirably demonstrates, there is no fixed format for memos. Early ones will often be very wordy, as researchers express overall ideas that come to mind as they begin to iterate between data-gathering and coding. As their ideas develop and take form around open codes and then focused codes, memos may become more terse, consisting largely or wholly of lists or diagrams to summarize key findings. For Charmaz memo-writing 'forms a space and place for exploration and discovery' (2006, pp. 81–82). But memo-writing is also preparatory to writing for publication, and Glaser argues that if researchers have developed their memos systematically and coherently then they form a firm basis for research outputs. He actually outlines a series of steps moving from theoretical coding, through theoretical memos and theoretical sorting, to theoretical writing (1978, Chapters 4–8).

In their initial GTM studies—*Awareness* and *Time*—Glaser and Strauss do not appear to use memos in their writing; indeed the style they have adopted is very different from what might now be regarded as the accepted GTM mode of writing. Kearney makes precisely this point, arguing that Glaser and Strauss 'were much more comfortable writing at a distance from the data' (2007, p. 132), something that is uncharacteristic of contemporary qualitative accounts which have to respond to the stringent demands of editors and reviewers. But a close reading of their founding texts indicates that many of the chapter headings and subheadings are in fact pointers to memos which have been woven together to produce the persuasive narrative accounts. In the ensuing years the skills used to move from 'fractured data' to theoretical insight has been encapsulated around the articulation of what is involved in memo-writing. Glaser's point about the core role of this activity retains its validity. Memo-writing is an essential but not sufficient aspect of GTM. Published accounts of GTM-based research must refer to memo-writing, and examples should be included in these accounts in some manner. A failure to do so provides genuine grounds for suspicion on the part of editors and reviewers that the claim for use of GTM is weak at best or specious at worst.

7. Theoretical saturation

Charmaz (2006) defines this as 'the point at which gathering more data about a theoretical category reveals no new properties nor yields any further theoretical insights about the emerging grounded theory'. Various commentators have pointed out that discussion of the ways in which researchers determined that they had reached this position is rarely evident in published accounts.

We have referred to this issue in our recent chapter in the APA Encyclopaedia (Bryant & Charmaz, 2012) using the example referred to by Bowen (2008)—the paper by Caelli et al. (2003, p. 13)—where they argue that 'evidence of saturation must be given in the presentation of the data and discussed via the forms in which it was recognized during the analysis' (p.137). This appears to offer some guidelines for presenting readers with an account of how theoretical saturation was determined.

Unfortunately the use of the passive voice in this extract effaces some of the key issues that ought to be clarified for readers and reviewers, and which can be indicated by adding the italicized inserts to the extract itself—'evidence of saturation must be given (*by whom*) in the presentation of the data (*to whom*) and discussed (*by and with whom*) via the forms in which it was recognized (*by whom*) during the analysis (*performed by*)'.

People find the concept of theoretical saturation difficult to grasp, and many critics of GTM see it as evidence of a weakness in the method since it appears to be so nebulous in many GTM texts and GTM-based research publications. Yet all research projects need to have regard for the issue of the point at which the decision is made that sufficient data has been gathered to provide a firm basis to move on to deeper analysis and subsequent conclusions and outputs. Many methods—qualitative and quantitative—do not really address this issue explicitly; so here we have not a weakness but a strength of GTM with its overt attention to the topic in the form of theoretical saturation. This provides an adequate and robust response to the question of when to stop gathering more data, provided that researchers clarify the bases for the decision to move on from the iterations between data gathering and coding to higher forms of conceptualization.

8. Categories and theories

For Glaser the result of a successful GTM research project should be a substantive grounded theory (see above) based on a single core category. This is not to suggest that during the research process only one category will be identified for such development. Indeed, in their founding project, Glaser and Strauss identified two potential categories—*awareness* and *trajectory*—but they specifically chose the former to develop further as the basis for their initial study; the latter being developed separately in a later work (*Time for Dying*—see Bryant, 2009, [67]).

Some GTM research results in more than a single core category, although usually no more than between two and four. (A larger number of categories would be seen as an indication of failing to offer a clear conceptual overview of a substantive topic.) In such cases the relationships between these categories must be explained—Do they fit together or not? As Charmaz correctly points out '[E]arly grounded theory studies stressed causal relationships but now many scholars aim for interpretive understandings' (2006, p. 120).

This leads on to the vexed question 'What is a theory?' For many methods this is not necessarily a central issue, but for GTM it certainly is given that the method is specifically meant to give rise to grounded theories. The problem is that the term theory itself is fraught with ambiguities, and those writing from within the GTM perspective have not always done justice to their understanding of the term. As I have written elsewhere (Bryant, 2009) a theory can apply to someone's highly personal supposition just as easily as it can to a far more well-founded view such as the theory of relativity. Charmaz makes similar points in her discussion of positivist versus interpretive accounts of the term (2006, Chapter 6). Glaser and Strauss, both jointly and in their separate accounts, argue that codes, categories, and concepts have to 'earn their way', and that grounded theories have to have 'grab', 'fit' with the context, and 'work'. All this seems somewhat vague until one understands that one of the key influences particularly on Strauss was the pragmatism of John Dewey. Dewey's view of theories, or any claims to knowledge, was that they had to be judged in terms of their usefulness rather than against some abstract criteria of truth or correspondence to reality. (See Bryant, 2009 for an extended discussion of the pragmatist thread in Strauss' work and GTM.)

For Dewey, theories are tools. A tool may be useful in some contexts and not in others, or some entities claiming to be tools may have no use whatsoever. GTM has always had a following among practitioners, particularly around healthcare and associated professions and practices. In part, this can be explained by the genesis of the method from UCSF, which specializes in this area, but over the long term this could only have been maintained by a fairly consistent set of outputs of GTM-based research that has had a beneficial impact of such practices. As a consequence, if researchers claim that they have developed a substantive grounded theory, they should be able to point to ways in which their research actually has led to changes in practice, or could be envisaged as doing so. Examples can be found in the collection edited by Glaser, *Examples of Grounded Theory: A Reader* (1993).

9. Getting beyond the mantras—the role of the researcher

Writers claiming use of GTM often resort to variations or verbatim quotes of one or more of what might best be termed 'the mantras of grounded theorists'—e.g. 'entering the research domain with an open mind', 'allowing the theory to emerge from the data', 'letting the data speak for themselves/itself'. Invocation of any or all of these should not be seen as inevitably leading to inadequate research, although as has already been pointed out, such statements inevitably lead many reviewers to suspect or discount whatever follows.

In our chapter in the Handbook we offer what we term an epistemological account of the history of GTM, pointing out that the initial publications by Glaser and Strauss coincided with the early stages of a sustained attack on positivism and its concepts of data and observation, in particular, in the work of Thomas Kuhn and those who published in his wake. In the ensuing decades neither Glaser nor Strauss made any concerted effort to respond to these developments, and it was really only with the publication of Charmaz's chapter in the second edition of the *Handbook of Qualitative Methods* that the issue was brought to the general attention of those concerned with research methods. Charmaz contrasted Glaser's *objectivist* form of GTM with her *constructivist* form. Essentially the former was based on a form of positivism, seeing data as given and the observer as neutral or objective; the latter saw data as far more problematic since the role of the observer was centred on being active, selective, and interpretive. Glaser responded to Charmaz in his article in FQS (Glaser, 2002), and in turn I responded to Glaser (Bryant, 2003).

There is no need at this juncture to offer further details of the debates themselves, interested readers can refer to the items listed in the section on Further Reading. But it is crucial that people understand that although it is important for researchers to indicate their stance with regard to core epistemological and ontological issues, this may have little or no bearing on the value and robustness of their research: a clear and strong statement of epistemological rectitude is no guarantee of good research findings, similarly highly questionable epistemological claims can precede convincing and valuable findings. The problem with many GTM-based research outputs is that they simply evade any engagement with these issues, which is a critical inadequacy at a time when research proposals and publications are deemed incomplete without clarity on method and, usually, epistemology.

As I have pointed out elsewhere (Bryant, 2009), both the objectivist/positivist and the constructivist/interpretivist accounts are flawed. The former cannot maintain the fiction of data as a given, and the neutrality of the researcher/observer. The latter, being based on a questioning of all claims to knowledge, cannot sustain its own knowledge claims that underlie its critique of positivism—i.e. that all knowledge is socially constructed. The irony is that GTM, even from its earliest formulations, contains the basis for a clear and cogent response to this paradox. In their justification and characterization of the method and the grounded theories so produced, Glaser and Strauss stressed that such theories had to fulfil several criteria—'fit', 'grab', 'work', 'relevance', and 'modifiability'. Stated in this stark manner these may not seem to offer a basis for justifying one's research, but as guidelines they are a potent starting point, particularly if underpinned by an appreciation of the pragmatist view of theories as tools to be judged by their usefulness and suitability. Charmaz develops a cogent set of criteria in her account (2006, pp. 182–183), incorporating 'credibility', 'originality', 'resonance', and 'usefulness'. So rather than seeing the claims of GTM-based research as weaker than those made by other approaches, I would argue that the method actually offers a far more cogent set of criteria that other non-GTM-based researchers, reviewers, and assessors should be encouraged to consider and adopt.

Further Reading

Readers looking for a clear and concise introductory text on GTM should start with Kathy Charmaz (2006) *Constructing Grounded Theory*, offering succinct accounts of the core features of the method. The first word of the title is indicative of her constructivist position.

Readers interested in the debates and wide-ranging insights across the method should then turn to Bryant, A. & Charmaz, K. (Eds.) (2007a) *The Handbook of Grounded Theory*. The contributors include Barney Glaser plus several of those who studied with Glaser and Strauss at UCSF in the 1960s and the 1970s, and also some younger researchers who have taken the method into new areas. There are also chapters by several German-speaking researchers, whose ideas emanate from Strauss' influence, including explicit links to pragmatism.

The founding trilogy of the method itself should be read, but these are not introductory texts. Glaser and Strauss *Awareness of Dying* (1965) is the earliest of these, followed by *The Discovery of Grounded Theory* (1967), then *Time for Dying* (1968). Both *Awareness* and *Time* contain brief methodological appendices that should not be ignored.

Glaser *Theoretical Sensitivity* (1978) is a key text. Strauss incorporated several large sections from it in his initial solo GTM book. As has been argued in earlier sections, the concept of theoretical sensitivity is critical to consideration of the nature of the role of the researcher. The move from data gathering to analysis and conceptualization that moves beyond simple re-description depends on the skills of the researcher. This is generic to all research. For GTM it is encapsulated in the term theoretical sensitivity, and researchers of any kind looking for guidance in this aspect should certainly read this book.

Those with an interest in the epistemological debates around GTM should read the following in the sequence suggested. (1) Charmaz, K. (2000) 'Constructivist and objectivist grounded theory'. In Denzin, N. K. & Lincoln, Y. S. (Eds.), *Handbook of Qualitative Research* (2nd ed., pp. 509–535). Thousand Oaks, CA: Sage. (2) Bryant, A. (2002). 'Re-grounding grounded theory'. *The Journal of Information Technology Theory and Application*, 4, 25–42. (3) Glaser, B. G. (2002). 'Constructivist grounded theory?' Forum Qualitative Sozialforschung/Forum: *Qualitative Social Research*, 3(3), Art. 12, http://nbn-resolving.de/urn:nbn:de:0114-fqs0203125 [accessed: July 27,

2009]. (4.) Bryant, A. & Charmaz, K. (2007). 'Grounded theory in historical perspective: An epistemological account'. In Bryant & Charmaz (Eds.), *The Sage Handbook of Grounded Theory* (pp. 31–57). London: Sage.

Strauss' work can be traced by starting with Strauss, A. *Qualitative Analysis for Social Scientists* (1987). New York: Cambridge University Press, then moving onto the joint work, Strauss, A., & Corbin, J. (1990 & 1998) *Basics of Qualitative Research: Grounded Theory Procedures and Techniques.* Newbury Park, CA: Sage. The third edition has been published as Corbin & Strauss.

Counterpoint Perspectives

As has already been indicated, there are several versions or variants of GTM. In some cases these variants have been seen by their critics as no longer incorporating the essential aspects of the method. Glaser has continued to produce a wide and stimulating series of accounts explaining the whys and wherefores of what he terms 'traditional' or 'classic' GTM. Publishing under the aegis of his own Sociology Press, he offers his own accounts as well as a range of edited texts exemplifying use of GTM. His 1992 book *Basics of Grounded Theory* offers a vigorous defence of his position, in the light of Strauss and Corbin's book. His later writings, particularly *The Grounded Theory Perspective* (2001) and *Jargonizing: Using the Grounded Theory Vocabulary* (2009), indicate his views of constructivist and other forms of GTM from which he wishes to distance his position.

The Strauss–Corbin variant has recently been updated by Julie Corbin in the third edition of their book (Corbin and Strauss, 2008). Although essentially based on the earlier editions, Corbin outlines the ways in which her own position has developed; partly as a response to changes in the field of research methods, and partly due to changes in her own understanding of the issues. Readers should start with her Preface, which outlines these developments.

Adele Clarke has introduced the idea of 'Situational Analysis' to GTM-oriented practice, terming this 'grounded theory after the postmodern turn' (Clarke, 2005). She summarizes this in the chapter in the Handbook (Clarke & Friese, 2007). The Handbook itself encompasses several variants and perspectives on the method, with contributions from Glaser and Holton that fall explicitly into the self-defined category of 'traditional GTM', also several contributions from the German-speaking tradition that is heavily influence by Strauss' teaching and specifically oriented towards pragmatism.

Author's Reflections on Quality

I first came across the work of Glaser and Strauss while studying social sciences as an undergraduate. But in those days reference was to their work on dying, rather than as an example of a new method for research. Many years later, in the 1980s and 1990s, I found several references to their work in research proposals from PhD students at my university. In many cases it seemed that students were submitting incomplete or incoherent research proposals, claiming that their chosen method— GTM—allowed them to start their research without clear research questions and also without a detailed literature review. In some cases, when challenged, the students revised their approach, but some defended their choice of method. This led me to a re-reading (actually a first, proper reading) of *Discovery* and some of the other GTM literature.

While being struck by the difference in the approach, I was also troubled by the ways in which those proposing to use the method often went no further in their explanation than offering a few short quotes from *Discovery*, followed by some brief discussion of data gathering from which they anticipated some conceptual advances would emerge at a later stage.

One of my students did, however, persevere with use of the method on a far more articulate basis, discovering along the way that many of those claiming use of the method in the area of information systems were seemingly unaware of the divergence of Glaser and Strauss in their later writings (see

Smit & Bryant, 2000; also Bryant, 2007). This led to my more detailed study of some of the early GTM writings, which led to publication of *Re-grounding Grounded Theory* (Bryant, 2002). It was only after the appearance of this paper that I discovered Kathy Charmaz' work, initially the chapter in the second edition of the *Handbook of Qualitative Research*. Kathy had anticipated the same critical points, albeit expressed far more cogently, but more importantly, she had a body of work attesting to the power of the method undertaken from a more epistemologically and methodologically aware position.

In the ensuing years we have worked together on several papers, and most notably on the Handbook, which brings together a wide range of perspectives from seasoned users of the method. One aspect which has become far clearer to me in that time has been the influence of pragmatism, an aspect of GTM of which many, particularly in the German-speaking community of GTM users, were already aware. The peculiar aspect of this is that many of the criticisms that beset GTM can be diffused with reference to pragmatist principles, something which Strauss clearly understood since in his last book he describes pragmatism as a continuous thread running through all his work.

The current situation with regard to GTM is that it is both highly popular and widely regarded with suspicion and misgivings. As I have stressed at several points in the preceding sections, it is imperative that when using or proposing to use GTM in a project, the researcher must understand the contentious and misunderstood aspects of the method. It is perfectly understandable that many editors of reputable journals feel uncomfortable when confronted by research papers claiming use of GTM. They will have come across far too many that seek to cover their methodological inadequacies by simply paying lip-service to GTM. The onus is on the writer to explain why the method was chosen, and how it has been used. This justification and use must extend beyond reiteration of some of the GMT mantras supplemented by some cursory form of coding. Writers must also demonstrate knowledge of the method that extends beyond the earliest writings, and offer at least some indication of the difference variants that now exist. (I suspect that *Discovery* is truly a classic book—i.e. referred to by many, but read by far fewer.)

Extending the pragmatist position on theories to apply equally to methods underlines the point that methods are tools and they should be judged by the ways in which they are used and the outcomes that result. To adapt one of Barney Glaser's favourite phrases, I no longer have a concern about 'worrisome epistemological accuracy'. I have read valuable and persuasive research accounts where the researcher states that the work develops from a positivist position. Similarly, I have come across poor research which is based on a constructivist one. This applies across all the variations of GTM, and regardless of the specific perspective the research outcomes must be judged in themselves, using the criteria discussed earlier.

Note

1. When editing the Handbook (Bryant & Charmaz, 2007) I deliberately added a 'Discursive Glossary' (Bryant & Charmaz, 2007a, 2010) incorporating the clear and concise set of definitions developed by Kathy Charmaz in her introductory and expository text 'Constructing Grounded Theory' (2006); supplementing these entries with extracts from some of the contributors to the Handbook itself. I noted that '[T]he terminology used with regard to GTM can be confusing, and any effort to produce a single authoritative and definitive set of definitions is certain to be contentious and self-defeating. Different authors refer to different exemplars, and sometimes even the same author will use or imply different definitions of a single term central to GTM.'

References

Bowen, G. A. (2008). Naturalistic inquiry and the saturation concept: A research note. *Qualitative Research, 8*(1), 137–152.

Bryant, A. (2002). Re-grounding grounded theory. *The Journal of Information Technology Theory and Application, 4*, 25–42.

Bryant, A. (2003). A constructive/ist response to Glaser. In *Forum Qualitative Sozialforschung/Forum: Qualitative Social Research, 4*(1). Retrieved 30 March, 2010 from www.qualitative-research.net/index.php/fqs/article/view/757.

Bryant, A. (2009). Grounded theory and pragmatism: The curious case of Anselm Strauss. In *Forum Qualitative Sozialforschung/Forum: Qualitative Social Research. 10*(3). Retrieved 30 March, 2010.

Bryant, A. & Charmaz, K. (Eds.) (2007a, 2010). *The Sage Handbook of Grounded Theory.* London: Sage.

Bryant, A. & Charmaz, K. (Eds.) (2007b). Editors' introduction grounded theory research: Methods and practices. In Bryant & Charmaz, 2007a.

Bryant, A. & Charmaz, K. (Eds.) (2007c). Grounded theory in historical perspective. In Bryant & Charmaz, 2007a.

Bryant, A. & Charmaz, K. (2012). Grounded theory and psychological research. In H. Cooper (Editor-in-Chief). *APA Handbook of Research Methods in Psychology Vol. 2. Foundations, Planning, Measures, and Psychometrics.* American Psychological Association.

Caelli, K., Ray, L., & Mill, J. (2003). "Clear as mud": Toward greater clarity in generic qualitative research. *International Journal of Qualitative Methods, 2,* 1–24.

Charmaz, K. (2000). Grounded theory: Objectivist and constructivist methods. In N. K. Denzin & Y. S. Lincoln (Eds.), *Handbook of Qualitative Research* (2nd ed., pp. 509–535). Thousand Oaks, CA: Sage.

Charmaz, K. (2006). *Constructing Grounded Theory: A practical guide through qualitative analysis.* London: Sage.

Charmaz, K. (2007). Constructionism and grounded theory. In J. A. Holstein & J. F. Gubrium (Eds.), *Handbook of Constructionist Research* (pp. 319–412). New York: Guilford.

Charmaz, K. (2008). Grounded theory as an emergent method. In S. N. Hesse-Biber & P. Leavy (Eds.), *The Handbook of Emergent Methods* (pp. 155–170). New York: Guilford.

Clarke, A. (2005). *Situational Analysis: Grounded theory after the postmodern turn.* Thousand Oaks, CA: Sage.

Clarke, A. & Friese, C. (2007). Clarke grounded theorizing using situational analysis. In Bryant & Charmaz, 2007a.

Corbin, J. & Strauss, A. (2008). *Basics of Qualitative Research (3rd ed.).* Thousand Oaks, CA: Sage.

Denzin, N. K., Lincoln, Y. S., & Tuhiwai Smith, L. (2008). *Handbook of Critical and Indigenous Methodologies.* Thousand Oaks, CA: Sage.

Glaser, B. (1978). *Theoretical Sensitivity.* Mill Valley, CA: Sociology Press.

Glaser, B. (1992). *Basics of Grounded Theory: Emergence vs. forcing.* Mill Valley, CA: Sociology Press.

Glaser, B. (Ed.) (1993). *Examples of Grounded Theory: A reader.* Mill Valley, CA: Sociology Press.

Glaser, B. (1998). *Doing Grounded Theory: Issues and discussions.* Mill Valley, CA: Sociology Press.

Glaser, B. (2001). *The Grounded Theory Perspective.* Mill Valley, CA: Sociology Press.

Glaser, B. (2002). Constructivist grounded theory? FQS. In *Forum Qualitative Sozialforschung/Forum: Qualitative Social Research.* 3(3). Retrieved 30 March, 2010 from www.qualitative-research.net/index.php/fqs/article/view/825.

Glaser, B. (2009). *Jargonizing Theory.* Mill Valley, CA: Sociology Press.

Glaser, B. & Strauss, A. (1965). *Awareness of Dying.* Chicago: Aldine.

Glaser, B. & Strauss, A. (1967). *The Discovery of Grounded Theory: Strategies for qualitative research.* Chicago: Aldine.

Glaser, B. & Strauss, A. (1968). *Time for Dying.* Chicago: Aldine.

Kearney, M. (2007). From the sublime to the meticulous. In Bryant & Charmaz, 2007a.

Kelle, U. (2007). The development of categories. In Bryant & Charmaz, 2007a.

Kuper, A., Lingard, L., & Levinson, W. (2008). Critically appraising qualitative research. *BMJ, 337,* 687–692. doi: 10.1136/bmj.a1035.

Lempert, L. (2007). Asking questions of the data. In Bryant & Charmaz, 2007a.

Reichertz, J. (2007). Abduction: The logic of discovery of grounded theory. In Bryant & Charmaz, 2007a.

Richardson, L. (1998). Writing: A method of critical inquiry. In N. K. Denzin & Y. S. Lincoln (Eds.) *Collecting and Interpreting Qualitative Materials* (pp. 345–371). Thousand Oaks, CA: Sage.

Smit, K. & Bryant, A. (2000). Grounded theory method in IS research: Glaser vs. Strauss. *Research in Progress Papers,* 2000–2007. www.leedsmet.ac.uk/inn/RIP2000.htm.

Star, L. (2007). Living grounded theory. In Bryant & Charmaz, 2007a.

Stern, P. (2007). On solid ground: Essential properties for growing grounded theory. In Bryant & Charmaz, 2007a.

Strauss, A. (1987). *Qualitative Analysis for Social Scientists.* Cambridge: Cambridge University Press.

Strauss, A. & Corbin, J. (1990). *Basics of Qualitative Research.* Thousand Oaks, CA: Sage.

Strauss, A. & Corbin, J. (1998). *Basics of Qualitative Research (2nd ed.).* Thousand Oaks, CA: Sage.

Strubing, J. (2007). Research as pragmatic problem-solving. In Bryant & Charmaz, 2007a.

Titscher, S., Meyer, M., Wodak, R., & Vetter, E. (2000). *Methods of Text and Discourse Analysis.* Thousand Oaks, CA: Sage.

Wiener, C. (2007). Making teams work in conducting grounded theory. In Bryant & Charmaz, 2007a.

9
Interview Research

Audrey A. Trainor

When researchers want to understand how people make meaning of their life experiences, they often go straight to the source and ask questions. Considered broadly, interview research includes a wide range of question and response strategies. This variety in strategies crosses multiple domains: variation in purpose (e.g., asking to better understand a range of responses or asking to gain a deep and complex understanding of a difficult-to-define concept), variation in organizing respondent opportunities (e.g., individual and group), variation in tools for data collection, variation in analytic perspectives, and variation in representation forms. Like Roulston (2010), I believe that variety in form and function reflects theoretical orientations that align with researchers' various ontological and epistemological stances. Qualitative touchstones, then, must be flexible and indicate alignment among form, function, and orientation. In this chapter, I consider methodological touchstones that serve as quality indicators for publishing research based on interviews that are not author-identified as narrative, life history, or other methodologies. The following selected key terms are included to help distinguish components among the variety of interview research approaches.

Select Terms

Active interview is a dynamic exchange of ideas based on interaction between participants and researchers; reflects a co-construction and evolution of knowledge on a content area of interest to researchers; area of interest can also be introduced by participants (Gubrium & Holstein, 2003; Holstein & Gubrium, 1995).

Conversation guide is a list of topics or a checklist of issues researchers intend to cover or ask about during an interview (Rubin & Rubin, 2005).

Focus group interview is a dynamic exchange of ideas based on questions and responses with a group of participants and researchers; ideal number of people per group ranges and depends on the purpose and nature of the research (Morgan, 1996, 2002).

In-depth interview is a conversational, lengthy, and interactive exchange of ideas, during which the researcher works to develop a close relationship with participants so that responses are deep and meaningful (Johnson, 2002); likely requires multiple interview sessions (Seidman, 2006). In-depth interviews are sometimes referred to as *phenomenological interviews* (Roulston, 2010).

Interview protocol is a formalized, written list of questions researchers predetermine or intend to ask prior to the interview; can be sent ahead to participants (Rubin & Rubin, 2005).

Semi-structured interview is a dynamic exchange of ideas based on researchers' open-ended questions or areas of interest with probes that are designed to elicit details and explanations (Roulston, 2010); questions are loosely sequenced and may be arranged or may change form in response to interviewee participation (Kvale, 1996).

Structured interview is a formalized, structured exchange of information based on questions and responses often in the form of a questionnaire or survey (Fontana & Frey, 2003); designed to elicit a set of predictable responses that correspond to a set of uniform prompts or questions (Bernard & Ryan, 2010). Qualitative data resulting from the use of surveys is often, but not always, quantified and analyzed accordingly. My focus in this chapter is reviewing qualitative approaches to interview methodologies.

Diversities in Perspective, Context, and Form

Using interviews to answer research questions has a rich history, including theorizing about this methodology, its scientific contributions, and the practice of method (Platt, 2005). The proliferation of interviewing to understand our world represents a shift in the conceptualization of who has knowledge worthy of consideration and how to use this knowledge to understand and address the problems of our time (Gubrium & Holstein, 2003). Interview research as methodology, rather than a method, is somewhat controversial. Despite qualitative approaches with more ethnographic leanings, interview research is common in some social science disciplines. Gathering, analyzing, and disseminating research based on this single type of data is also somewhat typical of qualitative research in medicine and health sciences (cf. Kuper, Lingard, & Levison, 2008; Schwarze, Bradley, & Brasel, 2010). Additionally, interviewing is a common method for data collection across methodologies and from within differing epistemological stances.

From qualitative inquiry traditions rooted in anthropology, interviews are considered but one of many complementary tools used for data collection (Spradley, 1979). In this view, interviews are thought to be limited in scope and should be accompanied by observations, document reviews, etc. Researchers who espouse this view may prioritize reliability or, in qualitative vernacular, authenticity (Silverman, 2001), in search of a single, discoverable truth or a clearly defined parameter surrounding a group of truths. Other researchers with similar epistemological dispositions may concur that interviews are insufficient for anchoring analysis and implications, but their concerns may be tied to conceptualizations of validity. Researchers in this vein speak about triangulation as a means to validate data (see, for example, Wray, Markovik, & Manderson, 2007). For researchers who embrace interpretivism and use a variety of representational strategies, qualitative research must encompass multiple methods of data collection to provide both thick description and deeply layered explanations of the phenomena being studied (Denzin, Lincoln, & Giardina, 2006). Triangulation, in this line of thinking, is a signifier of rigor that requires the consideration of multiple sources of data. Interview studies may lose traction from this point of view; however, triangulation can be established as a thumbnail of consistency and difference across multiple interviews with one participant or across interviews with multiple participants.

Another emergent concern about interview data is one that cautions against the privileging of voice, typically conceptualized as words and perspectives of participants, in qualitative inquiry (Jackson & Mazzei, 2009). Scholars who espouse these concerns have expressed reservation on multiple fronts, that such privilege facilitates problematic representation, that it excludes the experiences of people who communicate without voice (Snelgrove, 2005), and that it promises an undeliverable truth (Lather, 2009). Many of these concerns are conceptually tied to a postmodern episteme and skepticism of modern and structural theoretical frames, and/or are embraced by scholars who aim to deconstruct and critique.

Despite these concerns and controversies, interview research is discernable as a methodology (Kvale, 1996), and reviewers are commonly asked to evaluate its merit. Reviewers then must first determine their level of tolerance for interviewing as methodology. In my view, a reviewer intolerant of any particular method should probably decline the opportunity to review such a submission, or at the very least, disclose his/her discomfort or intolerance. Second, reviewers should read for the purpose of understanding the author's approach to interview research. If a researcher identifies her work within a particular methodology (e.g., ethnography, case study, and narrative), it is important to read to evaluate the congruency between the methodology and its representation. Embedded methodology guiding interview research, however, may not be explicitly identified. In either case, the following methodological touchstones should guide reviewers to enter a dialog with a text, seeking an understanding about the potential contributions of the work.

Qualitative Touchstones

1. The sample of participants generates a breadth and depth of interviews necessary to answer the research questions

Strategies for answering research questions through interview designs vary widely, and these influence the indicators for desirable or sufficient numbers of participants. In an oft-cited introductory text to qualitative methods, Patton (2002) focuses on pragmatic concerns of conducting research. In this view, the quantity of participants is sufficient when both the breadth and depth of data is judged by the researcher to be adequate, given the practical constraints of funding, logistics, and time. In the context of focus groups, the ideal size of a group has been represented by a range of numbers, from eight to twelve for large marketing-based approaches, to four to six for small in-depth approaches (Morgan, 1996, 2002).

Reviewers may question the number of participants in relation to the study's quality; however, a more adept way to critique the quality of an interview study at the level of the sample is to ask, *What is the sampling strategy and does it match the purpose of the study?* For example, whether the authors state the use of a criterion, snowballing, or any other in a myriad of sampling methods, it is appropriate for a reviewer to opine on the stated strategy and its congruence with the research questions. For a reviewer to argue that the number itself is not sufficient for some arbitrary reason, however, does not constitute a valid critique. Kvale (1996) points out that large, representative samples are not suited to meet the aim of qualitative studies and that these are too big to be analyzed for "penetrating observations" (p. 102). Further, Kvale (1996) notes that interview studies with just one participant are appropriate when the purpose and research questions align with the exploration of the experiences of a specific person.

Saturation, an indication that a concept has been thoroughly examined such that no new themes or points in need of further exploration emerge from the recursive process of data collection and analysis (Corbin & Strauss, 2008), has been suggested as a touchstone for quality of participant recruitment and/or opportunities for data collection with the total sample of participants (Lincoln & Guba, 1985). Within the tradition of clinical research in the medical and health fields, saturation is valued because it is a known practice that mirrors a patient–doctor interview where the former gives the latter enough information through a series of questions and answers to interpret a malady and suggest a treatment plan (Miller & Crabtree, 2005).

Authors who employ saturation as a criterion for a sufficient sample should explain how they conceptualize saturation (e.g., Are they employing *theoretical saturation*, whereby they stopped recruiting participants when analytic processes yield a repetition of coding categories and themes?

Are they employing *redundancy* of participants' responses as a parameter of the sample?). An example of the redundancy explication, taken from Kolb and Hanley-Maxwell's (2003) study of parents' perspectives of the social skills of adolescents' with disabilities, is, "Because theoretical saturation was achieved before completion of the 11 interviews, no additional parents were sought" (p. 165). For an additional example, see Wray and colleagues' (2007) study of women with gynecological cancers.

Saturation, however, is a disputed concept. Richardson and St. Pierre (2005) argue that saturation is positivistic and ignores the role of the researcher's interpretation of data, and, in particular, writing as an interpretive act. They argue that the object of inquiry is not the representation of participants, but rather the subjective interpretation that promulgates aesthetics, reflection, and/or impact. From this view, participant sampling and thus the question, *Are the included participants sufficient to answer the research question?* is not an important touchstone for the overall quality of a study. Rather, postmodernists and poststructuralists may emphasize researchers' interpretations, be they interpretations of one or many interviews.

Several qualitative touchstones emerge from this brief discussion of sample size. First, both the actual sample sizes and their significance to conclusions that can be drawn from qualitative studies vary. Also, the nature of the sample itself is an important factor to consider. Second, the ambiguity associated with defining sample sizes necessitates sophistication in the review process. Reviewers must ascertain the extent to which researchers provide a rationale for sample size that is congruent with their ontological and epistemological orientations. If researchers state that they approached the study from a postmodern perspective, for example, and then they lay out their strategy for generating a randomized sample, a reviewer should question the extent to which this is congruous in her critique.

2. The individuals interviewed are in positions of experience to respond to the types of interview questions that map to the research questions

A related yet separate sampling issue is whether the participants who are included have the appropriate experiences, knowledge, perceptions, and/or ability to provide rich data. As with discussions of the number of participants included in the study, the researchers' discussion of sampling should connect the rationale for the sample to the research questions. For example, in my interview research of parents of children who receive special education, I invited participants (i.e., parents) to invite adults with whom they shared responsibilities of decision making during school-based meetings (Trainor, 2010a, 2010b). My actions expanded the sample to include the parents' adult children as well as parents' siblings or parents, thus complicating interpretation. I believe my purpose to gather thick and rich descriptions of the types of cultural and social capital families used in school meetings was well served by this decision because together we generated extensive examples of capital based on our interactive discussions. Had I been more interested in interpreting the roles that specific family members (e.g., mothers) played in special education processes, this decision would have introduced a competing purpose to my interpretive job, potentially subtracting from my focus on the research question at hand.

While Kvale (1996) asserts that the most knowledgeable, motivated, articulate, and honest person would be the best interviewee, he concedes that this person likely does not exist. More importantly, the conceptualization of quality around participant selection begs a question about the inclusion or exclusion of research participants. A reviewer's deliberation of the quality of the pool of research participants should be mindful of the qualitative tradition that, despite the aforementioned controversies about voice acknowledged in the introduction of this chapter, is rooted in the relational and interpretive nature of this tradition of inquiry (Lincoln, 1995). In other words, should we select the most "motivated" group of participants, what would be lost in our interpretation by excluding unmotivated participants? Or, should we deem some participants "honest," how would our interpretation of truth work to exclude participants in patterned and/or implicit ways that reflected our own biases? Important for reviewers, then, is this consideration: *Do the researchers explain who was included, who was not, and how the sample relates to the interpretation of data for the purpose of answering the research question?*

As we discuss in the introduction to this reviewer's guide, one hallmark of qualitative research is innovation, making quality criteria challenging to identify. In terms of sample selection, reviewers should be familiar with the affordances that innovation, particularly when seen through the paradigmatic lenses of interpretivism and constructivism, lends to the research community (i.e., researchers and participants) writ large. For example, reviewers accepted both ambiguity and innovation inherent in Snelgrove's (2005) representation of her interpretation of research participation by youth with significant intellectual disabilities who did not use verbal language to communicate. In doing so, reviewers' questions about other aspects of quality may have superseded sampling for the simple fact that the question of participants' knowledge may have been impossible to answer considering their position of being labeled as having significant intellectual disabilities and their nonverbal methods of communication. Another key factor might have been the theoretical stance that children and youth can be key informants. That the paper was published is one indicator that its contribution outweighed its unconventional methods, in the minds of those who reviewed it.

3. The researchers establish relationships with participants who are congruent with both the interview design and paradigmatic ties to relational inquiry

For those who approach interviewing from a relational perspective, people are likely to be more willing to participate in an interview with someone with whom they are acquainted or someone they know well (Rubin & Rubin, 2005). From another view, interviewing involves interaction where the researchers and participants activate one another's participation and responses resulting in co-constructed experience (Gubrium & Holstein, 2003). Both of these explanations have, at their cores, an appreciation for the interactive process of establishing a relationship with another person for the purpose of construing meaning. Both also reject the notions that research is unbiased and that it represents an objective truth. From these and other interpretivist or constructivist views, relationships between researchers and participants are not something to be avoided, as would be the predilection of positivistic researchers and reviewers. Rather, reviewers from the former perspectives believe that quality is indicated through the establishment of ethical relationships that foster familiarity and contingency with participants.

Quality indicators of such relationships quickly become complicated as issues of ethics, power, and identity, to name only several, take on more or less importance. The ebb and flow of the importance of these embedded criteria (i.e., relational criteria) in the overall judgment of quality depends heavily on the epistemological perspective of both reviewer and researcher. Institutional review boards (IRBs) and professional organizations promulgate guidelines for ethical research that includes the interpersonal relationships between researchers and participants. For example, both the American Psychological Association (APA) and the American Educational Research Association (AERA) have published specific guidelines for assurances that such have been followed (AERA, 2006; APA, 2003). Such declarations may suffice for reviewers who value objectivity and thus distance between researchers and participants, but for those researchers anchored to the relational criteria such as fairness, mutual benefit, and "democratic sharing of knowledge" (Lincoln, 1995, p. 277) of the larger research project, obligation exceeds the enactment of IRB or professional guidelines (Rubin & Rubin, 2005).

Quality indicators of research relationships track rapport (Patton, 2002; Seidman, 2006), trust (Fine, Weis, Weseen, & Wong, 2003; Fontana & Frey, 2003; Rubin & Rubin, 2005), and reciprocity (Subedi, 2006; Trainor & Bouchard, in press; Zigo, 2001). Each of these criteria is inextricably related and complex; universal positions or clearly delineable definitions are elusive or illusory, depending on one's ontological and epistemological allegiances. For instance, both Patton (2002) and Seidman (2006) posit that limiting rapport is essential to maintaining neutrality and thus avoiding or minimizing participants' desire to please the researchers. Roulston (2010) associates this stance with a "neopositivist[ic]" (p. 86) desire to capture interpretation that accurately represents the interview. On the other hand, postmodernists assume researcher–participant "contamination" and interpretive biases to be inescapable, omnipresent, and necessary to interpretive processes (Gubrium & Holstein, 2003, p. 78). Despite controversies, most interview researchers appreciate the fact that in any dynamic exchange about a concept of import to researchers and participants mirrors the relationship between the two parties. Reviewers must ask, *Do the researchers and participants in this study have relationships that contribute to interview data with the depth necessary to address the research questions? Are the two parties sufficiently distant from one another so that coercion and pleasing do not unduly influence interviews? Do the researchers describe this relationship and its import on interpretation and analysis?*

4. The researchers present themselves and associated subjectivities (e.g., background, experience, and positionality) to supplement or aide the interpretation of the results and implications of interview data

Because qualitative research relies on relationships and the interpretation of them, a quality touchstone of interview research includes evidence of researchers' reflexivity with regard to position (Merriam et al., 2001) and subjectivity (Behar, 1996; Roulston, 2010). Reflexivity is the process of acknowledging, reflecting, and reporting how one's identities, beliefs, knowledge, and relationships to people, material, and concepts influence one's work. Reflexivity collides with conceptualizations of self, other, truth, and purpose in research (Merriam et al., 2001; Pillow, 2003). Epistemological differences are reflected in researchers' emphasis on the importance and promise of reflexivity, ranging from a phenomenologist's use of "bracketing," or holding one's positionality and subjectivity at bay, to a critical theorist's acceptance of the political self as interpreter and constructor of knowledge (Morrow, 2005). Feminist theorists have contributed much to the discussion of the roles position and identity play in interviewing, highlighting the integration of self, social position, and purpose throughout method, including, but not limited to, interviewing (Reinharz & Davidman, 1992).

Representation of self to gain access to people to interview, as well as subsequent efforts to analyze and report interviews, is complicated. Reviewers from diverse epistemological stances may share a common concern, *What/How do the researchers' relationships, positions, or biases afford or limit interview data collection and analysis?* For example, a researcher who wants to interview people from a specific socioeconomic background may draw on commonalities between herself and the target to "fit in" and gain access. Or, a researcher may tap into her existing social networks that will prompt and mediate introduction to, and sustained relationships with, potential participants. On the other hand, a researcher may work her outsider status as an affordance of near anonymity for participants. For a complex discussion of the multiple insider/outsider positionalities and their influence on the research process, see Schweber's (2007) discussion of the role of her religion, background, and related cultural capital as she gained entry into faith-based educational settings. Whatever the method of gaining access, insider/outsider status comes with expectations and obligations, as well as varied degrees of ease, comfort, and openness associated with shared knowledge or experience. Data collection, however, is only a part of the process. Interviews get interpreted on multiple levels: by researchers and participants while interviewing, by researchers during later stages of reflection and analysis, and later by the public audience. A researcher who gains access to a population because of perceived insider/outsider status may feel a sense of obligation to represent interviewees in ways that are amenable to them, to advance critical renditions outside the reach of participants, or any number of reactions in response to researcher–participant relationships. Once in the field in the form of disseminated texts, interpretation by the larger community may fall on a continuum of help/harm for participants.

Exactly what constitutes status as either an insider or an outsider, however, is difficult to define (Merriam et al., 2001). Extending the example above, the researcher may see obvious connections (i.e., indicative of insider status) at the level of socioeconomic status or background, but may find differences across other aspects of experience and identity (e.g., gender). Or, as Subedi (2006), an American academic with familial and cultural ties to his home country and research site of Nepal, problematizes, identifying as both insider and outsider can require a double consciousness that introduces numerous complications. Importantly, identities (i.e., insider/outsider signifiers) contribute to the negotiation of power in a relationship between researchers and participants that may come to bear before, during, and after interviews. Fine and colleagues (2003), in theorizing about research and social justice, were concerned about the power they held when depicting working-class participants and ways in which these depictions might both conflict with participants' voices and collude with stereotypical views and assumptions embedded in policy. Because one's status in relation to others is shifting and impossible to pin down, determining its significance on analysis and representation of interview data is largely left to researchers' reflective thinking (Subedi, 2006).

How reflexivity serves interviewing and analyzing, or later interpretation of related presentations, remains largely unexplored, unknown, and potentially unknowable. Despite inherent complications, researchers have a responsibility to be reflexive in such a way that complicates the analytic processes (Fine et al., 2003). While extensive discussion of reflexivity is beyond the scope of this guide, reviewers should expect some contextualized discussion of the researchers' position and subjectivities that does not overshadow the participants' interviews (Fine et al., 2003). *When and how is reflexivity sufficiently represented?* While no two reviewers may answer this question with the same response, the important point here is to recognize that researcher reflexivity should be addressed and that it is inherently complicated, casting a doubt on overly simplistic representation of its enactment. As importantly, reviewers should not eschew reflexivity as untenable because it somehow violates sacrosanct objectivity, as this view is incongruent with the qualitative paradigm.

5. Interview questions map to research questions

Whether using structured interview protocols or guides that range from semistructured questions to lists of general topics for discussion, researchers should identify a discernible relationship or pathway between the research questions and the interview questions. At times, the relationship or path will be obvious because the research questions are composed of uncomplicated language and concepts that are universally understood, at least on some basic level. At other times, the research topic includes terms and concepts that beg explanation, or even translation, as questions or prompts may be developed for people outside of the immediate and constructed research context. For instance, when interviewing parents about cultural and social capital used in special education processes, I avoided the terms "cultural," "social," and "capital," because these terms, born of theoretical discussions beyond the field of special education, were outside of the vernacular of people I was interviewing, at least as I experienced in the field of practice. Instead, I asked parents to discuss whose advice they sought when participating in special education (e.g., a potential conceptualization of social capital) or what types of information they found most valuable during these processes (e.g., a potential conceptualization of cultural capital). In this way, I was able to use the more commonsense definitional aspects of the terms during interviews, mapping these and participant responses to the research questions. The extent to which I, or any researcher, is able to map abstract and theoretical terms from the research questions to interview guides must be determined by examining the interview data, the interpretation, and representation.

Questions as tools for eliciting responses (i.e., data) take on multiple formats and these formats should align with the researchers' epistemological orientation. In the use of a structured interview protocol, a script is developed for the purpose of reducing the potential for variable question interpretation by participants (Fontana & Frey, 2005), while questions for an active interview may appear to be nothing more than a list of topics to elicit and co-construct meaning with participants (Gubrium & Holstein, 2003; Johnson & Weller, 2002). Additionally, a range of interviewing techniques requires researchers to respond to participants by using probes and subsequent question guides that are individualized and activate their knowledge of the topic (Gubrium & Holstein, 2003; Rubin & Rubin, 2005). Therefore, flexibility and capacity for responsiveness are additional indicators of quality in research questions. Because of this variability, reviewers should expect to find differences in presentation of interview questions that align with the tools used to collect interviews. For example, if the researcher states that the design of the study involved the use of structured interviews, a protocol of questions is appropriate to include in publication. If other strategies that foster variation among participant responses are used, researchers should present a broad description of interview questions rather than a verbatim reproduction of the question guide. Judgment of the alignment of the interview questions to the research questions supersedes the form of what is shared. Therefore, reviewers should ask, *Do the questions asked help answer the questions driving the inquiry?*

6. The researchers describe their approach to collecting and/or constructing interviews and related logistical decisions to the extent that these procedures fundamentally impact interpretation

Interview researchers make many decisions that converge to define and describe data collection. Constructing a rationale for implementing one approach to interviewing over another will set in motion a legion of logistical decisions (e.g., how to gain access to the research site; how to structure time, place, duration, and frequency of interviews; how/whether to record and transcribe interviews; how to follow through and exit the research site). Similarly, researchers must engage ethical considerations such as locating and pursuing opportunities for relationships with participants, garnering participant consent/assent, and maintaining trustworthy researcher–participant relationships. A detailed presentation of the sum total of these decisions (certainly a list that goes well beyond the aforementioned components) would be onerous for the researchers and of little use to reviewers.

Detailed reports may appease a reviewer's curiosity or mollify a need to validate or verify procedure, connecting this to perceptions of accuracy of data interpretation and reporting. Interpreting and/or constructing meaning based on interviews, however, requires recursive decision making that employs researchers' interpretive lenses and aptitudes throughout the design and implementation process, assuring that no two people, or perhaps not even the same person given an opportunity to "do over," would necessarily make the same interpretations and resulting decisions. Therefore, the goal in explicating data collection is to inform the reviewer of the ways in which researchers identify that these decisions influenced interpretation, analysis, and representation, as well as how these might influence the reviewers' interpretation of the study. For example, if I use a digital recording device, with permission, to capture all interviews, must I report this? If I have identified my methodological approach and it is one that accepts the use of recorded interviews, reporting this detail is superfluous. Alternatively, if I identify my methodological approach as one that eschews recording devices (i.e., emphasizing authenticity and concerns regarding the performative nature of communication), and I use the device, I need to explain both my rationale and how I interpret this departure from the methodology as having influence on interpretation. In another, alternative scenario, if I use the device during interviews with two participants, and a third participant disallows this, I need to describe and explain this difference in process only to the extent that it affected my interpretation and subsequent analysis of the interview.

On the point of detailed reporting of data collection methods and qualitative rigor, concerns about *methodolatry* (also spelled *methodolotry)* have emerged over time and across social science disciplines. Methodolatry is an overemphasis on procedure intended to address concerns of verification, replicability, and defense of interpretation that overshadows interpreted and co-constructed meaning, thus minimizing the contribution of the research (Chamberlain, 2000; Janesick, 2003; Schrag & Ramsey, 1994). Here again, a reviewer must understand the ontology and epistemology of the researchers to best answer the question, *Does the researcher describe data collection in such a way that adds to the interpretation and the construction of meaning of the interviews?*

7. The method of analyzing interviews is identified and explicated

Methods of analyzing interviews include the usual suspects: grounded theory, constructivist grounded theory, phenomenology, content analysis, discourse analysis, etc. (Bernard & Ryan, 2010; Roulston, 2010). Obviously, an exhaustive list of qualitative touchstones for each approach to analysis would result in a tome, and thus is beyond this compact discussion. Similar to my comments regarding the level of detail in the reporting of data collection activities (see Touchstone 6), researchers should divulge sufficient detail about analytic methods to demonstrate congruency between analysis and underlying epistemologies, ontologies, and methodologies (Caelli et al., 2003; Morrow, 2005; Roulston, 2010). For example, in the analysis of oral history interviews, Smith (2003) suggests employing not only some general tools used for interview analysis, but also specific tools to evince collective and cultural meaning constructs such as symbolic order and popular memory, of interest to historical analysts. To juxtapose another marker of quality, discourse about the use of voice, reflexivity, and literary elements as analytic tools in narrative research resulted in a diverse set of approaches converging at the point of purposeful and parsimonious use of any tool that has the potential to elevate researchers' voices at the expense of participants' stories (Barone, 2009; Clandinin & Murphy, 2009; Coulter, 2009; Coulter & Smith, 2009; Smith, 2009).

Depending on approach, the analysis of interviews may weigh what was said, how it was said, how what was said was interpreted, and what interactions transpired between and among researchers and participants to varying degrees. So what are the basic analytic tools used in the analysis of interviews and how do reviewers know researchers are using them adeptly? Researchers use inductive, deductive, and abductive reasoning to code data and emerge themes during and following repeated watching or listening to recordings of interviews or readings of transcripts (LeCompte & Schensul, 1999; Patton, 2002; Roulston, 2010). In part, reviewers are charged with judging the extent to which the analysis both resonates with the extant scholarship and introduces new knowledge. Various words have been used to describe this quality touchstone: credibility (Toma, 2006), trustworthiness (Lincoln & Guba, 1985; Morrow, 2005), and validity (Kvale, 1996; Lather, 1986; Maxwell, 1992).

Some qualitative scholars have argued for additional markers of analytic quality that align with the politicized, impassioned, and inherently biased nature of interpretivism. Lincoln (1995) emphasizes relational and action-oriented aspects of knowledge production. In this view, analysis, always incomplete and contextualized by the position of the researcher, centers on social justice and purpose, leading to shared knowledge and commitment to change for the common good (Denzin, 2005). The role of activism in decisions about quality is poorly understood and infrequently discussed. If researchers make the claim that their work is an exemplar of advocacy or action, reviewers may have a difficulty understanding whether the work exemplifies or fulfills this goal. What is important for reviewers to note is that clarity about authors' positions (philosophical, theoretical, personal, etc.) contributes to, rather than detracts from, interpretivist and constructivist approaches to interview research. Epistemological and ontological congruency is again underscored on this point. The reviewer, then, must be concerned with the question, *Do the researchers present an analysis that addresses the research questions?* And, *does the analysis align with epistemological stance of the researchers?* If, for example, researchers position themselves as postpositivists, the relationship between analysis and position and/or action will likely be unexplored in analysis and representation. While Lincoln, Denzin, and others may argue that this violates a fundamental tenet of qualitative research, a range of perspectives still prevails and consensus is difficult to identify.

8. The representation of the interview research project is an integration of interviews and their interpretation that results in new knowledge

The selection and representation of interview data (i.e., participants' quotes, whether verbatim or synthesized) is part of the analytic process. In the same vein, writing about interviews, or any other data, is an activity inextricable from analysis, "an interpretive process that can only partially represent complex social worlds. Writing is the scholarly instantiation of the cultural meaning making" (Graue, 2006, p. 519). This quality touchstone serves to remind reviewers that representation of interviews should ultimately produce new ways of thinking about the problem or question under consideration. Consideration of the potential contribution of the content likely will lead reviewers to additional questions about the form of the representation. Researchers make choices about how to represent interviews, attending to the quality and quantity of participant quotations and/or dialogue, in addition to descriptions of both the context of the research and the participants' lives.

Some researchers may emphasize participants' voice in the representation of counternarratives as a tool for destabilizing dominant truisms. Others may use interview data to illustrate first-person accounts of experience and perceptions or establish multiplicity in perspective. Still others may consider interviewing one way to present a snapshot of reality as experienced by participants. A shared concern across purposes is how to present the participants' words in text, particularly because the text must often adhere to length specifications for publications in journals. Quotations from interviews carry explicit and implicit meanings, both of which contribute to the production of knowledge (Rubin & Rubin, 2005). Therefore, reviewers should ask, *Are participant quotations paired with relevant interpretations?* When researchers present direct quotes absent of interpretation, the representation of interview data becomes belabored by what Kvale (1996) called "hyperempiricism" (p. 254).

Researchers' interpretation of participants' interviews, always at the root of representation, varies according to the philosophical underpinnings of the researchers' intentions to produce knowledge. Editing quotations for style is acceptable (Kvale, 1996; Rubin & Rubin, 2005), however, some researchers emphasize the verbatim textual representation of participants' words. Metaphor is frequently the representation of analysis, and an illustration of researcher-identified patterns. For reviewers, then, a central question addressing quality is *Does the researcher explain the relationship between the interview data and the metaphorical representation, often called a theme, in such a way that it communicates meaning and new knowledge?* This question might well be asked of other types of data interpretation such as document reviews and observations.

From a postmodern perspective, fact and fiction blur, thus leading some to produce innovative textual representations of participants' and researchers' words in the form of poetry, novels, and other artistic forms (Rosenblatt, 2003; Roulston, 2010). Acceptability of modes of interpretation is not only in purview of reviewers; journal mission statements and histories of publication are also indicators of tolerance for the breadth of representational formats. For example, the *International Review of Qualitative Research* (IRQR) seeks innovative and experimental forms of qualitative inquiry and thus may be amenable to fictive accounts of interview data (IRQR, 2011). On the other hand, journals that emphasize the publication of evidence-based forms of inquiry that directly link data with findings or conclusions would likely not be so. Because the range of acceptable representations is vast, it is important for the reviewer to understand the journal's mission and their own tolerance for what constitutes valuable representation in the production of knowledge.

Further Reading

The following texts provide a range of discussions about interviewing as a methodology. Most of these examples could be considered "how to" or methods texts; therefore, touchstones for judging the quality of interview research are often embedded in the authors' assertions about correct implementation of interviews.

Gubrium, G. F., & Holstein, J. A. (Eds.). (2002). *Handbook of Interview Research: Context and Method.* Thousand Oaks, CA: Sage.
This handbook provides a range of theoretical and practical approaches to interview research written from the perspectives of a diverse group of scholars with interviewing expertise. Sections of the book include descriptions of specific interview strategies, such as in-depth, life story, and focus group interviewing; respondent-specific considerations (e.g., suggestions for interviewing elderly people, people who are ill, and race and gender issues in interviewing); and technical procedures such as transcribing and using technology. Other sections address analytic and representational issues.

Gubrium, J. F., & Holstein, J. A. (2003). *Postmodern Interviewing.* Thousand Oaks, CA: Sage.
The authors tailor this text, an edited collection of writings from postmodern scholars, to explicate and discuss postmodern approaches and concerns within interview research methodology. The text focuses on innovation and the evolution of interviewing as a tool for meaning making; researcher reflexivity; analysis, and representation. As the title reveals, postmodern epistemologies, ontologies, and methodologies are its focus.

King, N., & Horrocks, C. (2010). *Interviews in Qualitative Research.* Los Angeles, CA: Sage.
The authors of this text focus on the implementation of both individual and group interviews throughout key stages of inquiry. Detailed assertions about logistics of interviewing, including recording interviews, interviewing from a distance, and question formulation contribute to the content of this book. The authors present specific approaches relative to phenomenology and narrative research designs.

Kvale, S., & Brinkmann, S. (2009). *InterViews: Learning the Craft of Qualitative Research Interviewing* (2nd ed.). Los Angeles, CA: Sage.
The second edition of Kvale's earlier, oft-cited reference on the implementation of interview research contains a continued focus on the methods and tools for use in interview research. The authors of this edition encompass a range of methodological and philosophical approaches. The authors' extended discussion of the concept of validity continues to comprise a standalone chapter; however, the previous edition's chapter on quality of interview research is now embedded in the contents of the entire book.

Roulston, K. (2010). *Reflective Interviewing.* Los Angeles, CA: Sage.
Roulston's text emphasizes the central problem of congruency between philosophy and approach in interview research. As such, chapter contents include the presentation of method from differing philosophical perspectives such as the neopositivist, the phenomenologist, and the postmodernist, to name only a few. Chapters are organized to loosely follow key stages in the research process, beginning with question design and walking the reader through data collection and analysis. The focus at each juncture is the act of interviewing; therefore, the book contains many detailed discussions of the logistics of implementing an interview study.

Rubin, H. J., & Rubin, I. S. (2005). *Qualitative Interviewing: The Art of Hearing Data* (2nd ed.). Thousand Oaks, CA: Sage.
Primarily a resource for implementing interviews, the authors focus on research and interview question formation, as well as strategies for the elicitation of participant responses. Additionally, analysis and presentation of data each comprise distinct chapters. The authors focus on the steps to implementation and provide examples from their research, focusing less on the philosophical underpinnings and varieties in approach.

Counterpoint Perspectives

Seidman, I. (2006). *Interviewing as Qualitative Research: A Guide for Researchers in Education and the Social Sciences* (3rd ed.). New York: Teachers College Press.
For an approach to interviewing that adheres more strictly to the philosophical and methodological tenets of phenomenology the 2006 edition of Seidman's *Interviewing as Qualitative Research* provides specific parameters for the implementation of interview research design, data collection, and, with a lesser focus, data analysis. Book chapters outline steps to follow in the implementation of interview research including participant selection, ethical considerations, and interviewing technique.

Author's Reflections on Quality

As a researcher, I often feel as though I am being pulled in multiple directions by my field's construction of quality in qualitative research methods and the underpinnings of my ontological, epistemological, and methodological preferences or "gut feelings" about how knowledge is constructed. From the field, I am pulled toward a positivistic epistemological stance whose ontology honors a discoverable and definable realist's truth, using the methodology of experiment and single-subject design. The current trend defining empirical evidence narrowly ignores, however, the legacy of special education and disability studies qualitative research that served both to document dehumanizing educational and social practices that have harmed individuals with disabilities, and to advocate for the eradication of such practices. I am comfortable with interpretation and its complexities, as well as explicit purposes to critique and to deconstruct. Further, I am skeptical of inquiry that does not consider the contextual, historical, and sociopolitical realities that embed and are embedded by our research questions and how we answer them. At the same time, my work is solidly situated in the field of special education, so I experience tension and ambivalence when defining quality indicators.

As I reflect on quality, I am reminded that while I may be "comfortable with interpretation" as I mention above, I am uncomfortable with not being heard in my field. I have, therefore, adopted a pragmatist's stance, trying to carefully document each decision of my research design (e.g., whether I transcribed verbatim, how many total hours I spent interviewing, providing examples of coding or thematic analyses of data) in an effort to disseminate my work. Of course, these efforts have had the effect of edging me back toward a positivistic stance that I purport to eschew. Like Kraus, a twentieth-century playwright who observed, "Language is the mother of thought, not its handmaiden," I have come to realize that this approach, that is, doing interpretive work and describing it in positivistic ways, can devolve the interpretive process with the head that begun to chase the tail quickly becoming the tail itself. In writing this chapter, I have had the luxury of reflection as I have argued for the qualitative touchstones herein. Mutually informing, narrow views of evidence harken to the desire in education to understand quality indicators of sound research that point to sound solutions, while qualitative scholars remind us that in flexibility we gain the capacity to expand the possibilities for solutions. Based on my recent pretenure experiences as a qualitative researcher, I have tried to consider quality broadly, maintaining an openness to the possibility for flexibility, variation, critique, and innovation that draws people into, rather than excludes from, the act and art of inquiry. Equally important, I have posited junctures where methodological detail might be able to serve the act of quality discernment.

References

American Educational Research Association. (2006). Standards for reporting on empirical social science research in AERA publications. *Educational Researcher, 35*(6), 33–40.

American Psychological Association. (2003). Guidelines on multicultural education, training, research, practice, and organizational change for psychologists. *American Psychologist, 58*, 377–402.

Barone, T. (2009). Comments on Coulter and Smith: Narrative researchers as witnesses of injustice and agents of social change? *Educational Researcher, 38*, 591–597.

Behar, R. (1996). *The Vulnerable Observer: Anthropology that breaks your heart*. Boston, MA: Beacon Press.

Bernard, H. R. & Ryan, G. W. (2010). *Analyzing Qualitative Data: Systematic approaches*. Thousand Oaks, CA: Sage.

Caelli, K., Ray, L., & Mill, J. (2003). "Clear as mud": Toward greater clarity in generic qualitative research. *International Journal of Qualitative Methods, 2*(2), 1–9.

Chamberlain, K. (2000). Methodolatry and qualitative health research. *Journal of Health Psychology, 5*(3), 285–296. doi: 10.1177/135910530000500306.

Clandinin, D. J. & Murphy, M. S. (2009). Comments on Coulter and Smith: Relational ontological commitments in narrative research. *Educational Researcher, 38*, 598–602.

Corbin, J. & Strauss, A. L. (2008). Writing theses, monographs, and giving talks about your research. In J. Corbin & A. L. Strauss (Eds.), *Basics of Qualitative Research: Techniques and procedures for developing grounded theory* (3rd ed., pp. 275–295). Los Angeles, CA: Sage.

Coulter, C. A. (2009). Response to comments: Finding the narrative in narrative research. *Educational Researcher, 38*, 608–611.

Coulter, C. A. & Smith, M. L. (2009). The construction zone: Literary elements in narrative research. *Educational Researcher, 38*, 577–590.

Denzin, N. K., Lincoln, Y. S., & Giardina, M. D. (2006). Disciplining qualitative research. *International Journal of Qualitative Studies in Education, 19*(6), 769–782.

Denzin, N. K. (2005). Emancipatory discourses and the ethics and politics of interpretation. In N. K. Denzin & Y. S. Lincoln (Eds.), *The Sage Handbook of Qualitative Research* (3rd ed., pp. 933–958). Thousand Oaks, CA: Sage.

Fine, M., Weis, L., Weseen, S., & Wong, L. (2003). For whom? Qualitative research, representations, and social responsibilities. In N. K. Denzin & Y. S. Lincoln (Eds.), *Handbook of Qualitative Research* (pp. 107–131). Thousand Oaks, CA: Sage.

Fontana, A. & Frey, J. H. (2003). The interview: From structured questions to negotiated text. In N. K. Denzin & Y. S. Lincoln (Eds.), *Collecting and Interpreting Qualitative Materials* (2nd ed.). Thousand Oaks, CA: Sage.

Fontana, A. & Frey, J. H. (2005). The interview: From neutral stance to political involvement. In N. K. Denzin & Y. S. Lincoln (Eds.), *The Sage Handbook of Qualitative Research* (2nd ed.). Thousand Oaks, CA: Sage.

Graue, B. (2006). Writing in education research. In C. F. Conrad & R. C. Serlin (Eds.), *The SAGE Handbook for Research in Education: Engaging ideas and enriching inquiry* (pp. 515–528). Thousand Oaks, CA: Sage.

Gubrium, J. F. & Holstein, J. A. (2003). *Postmodern Interviewing* (pp. 3–18, 67–80). Thousand Oaks, CA: Sage.

Holstein, J. A. & Gubrium, J. F. (1995). *The Active Interview*. Thousand Oaks, CA: Sage.

Jackson, A. Y. & Mazzei, L. A. (Eds.). (2009). *Voice in Qualitative Inquiry*. London: Routledge.

Janesick, V. J. (2003). The choreography of qualitative research design. In N. K. Denzin & Y. S. Lincoln (Eds.), *Handbook of Qualitative Research* (2nd ed., pp. 195–207). Thousand Oaks, CA: Sage.

Johnson, J. C. & Weller, S. C. (2002). Elicitation techniques for interviewing. In J. F. Gubrium & J. A. Holstein (Eds.), *Handbook of Interview Research: Context and method*. Thousand Oaks, CA: Sage.

Johnson, J. M. (2002). In-Depth interviewing. In J. F. Gubrium & J. A. Holstein (Eds.), *Handbook of Interview Research: Context and method*. Thousand Oaks, CA: Sage.

Kolb, S. M., & Hanley-Maxwell, C. (2003). Critical social skills for adolescents with high incidence disabilities: Parental perspectives. *Exceptional Children, 69*(2), 163–179.

Kvale, S. (1996). *InterViews: An introduction to qualitative research interviewing*. Thousand Oaks, CA: Sage.

Lather, P. (1986). Issues of validity in openly ideological research: Between a rock and a soft place. *Interchange, 17*(4), 63–84. doi: 10.1007/bf01807017.

Lather, P. A. (2009). Against empathy, voice, and authenticity. In A. Y. Jackson & L. A. Mazzei (Eds.), *Voice in Qualitative Inquiry* (pp. 17–26). London: Routledge.

LeCompte, M. D. & Schensul, J. J. (1999). *Analyzing & Interpreting Ethnographic Data*. Walnut Creek, CA: AltaMira Press.

Lincoln, Y. S. (1995). Emerging criteria for quality in qualitative interpretive research. *Qualitative Inquiry, 1*, 275–289.

Lincoln, Y. S. & Guba, E. G. (1985). *Naturalistic Inquiry*. Beverly Hills, CA: Sage.

Maxwell, J. (1992). Understanding validity in qualitative research. *Harvard Educational Review, 62*, 279–300.

Merriam, S. B., Johnson-Bailey, J., Lee, M.-Y., Kee, Y., Ntseane, G., & Muhamad, M. (2001). Power and positionality: Negotiating insider/outsider status within and across cultures. *International Journal of Lifelong Education, 20*, 405–416.

Miller, W. L. & Crabtree, B. F. (2005). Clinical research. In N. K. Denzin & Y. S. Lincoln (Eds.), *Handbook of Qualitative Research* (3rd ed., pp. 507–535). Thousand Oaks, CA: Sage.

Morgan, D. L. (1996). Focus groups. *Annual Review of Sociology, 22*, 129–152.

Morgan, D. L. (2002). Focus group interviewing. In J. F. Gubrium & J. A. Holstein (Eds.), *Handbook of Interview Research: Context and method* (pp. 141–160). Thousand Oaks, CA: Sage.

Morrow, S. L. (2005). Quality and trustworthiness in qualitative research in counseling psychology. *Journal of Counseling Psychology, 52*, 250–260.

Patton, M. Q. (2002). *Qualitative Research & Evaluation Methods* (3rd ed.). Thousand Oaks, CA: Sage.

Pillow, W. (2003). Confession, catharsis, or cure? Rethinking the uses of reflexivity as methodological power in qualitative research. *International Journal of Qualitative Studies in Education, 16*, 175–196.

Platt, J. (2005). The history of the interview. In N. K. Denzin & Y. S. Lincoln (Eds.), *The Sage Handbook of Qualitative Research* (3rd ed., pp. 33–54). Thousand Oaks, CA: Sage.

Reinharz, S. & Davidman, L. (1992). *Conclusions Feminist Methods in Social Research* (pp. 240–269). New York: Oxford University Press.

Rosenblatt, P. C. (2003). Interviewing at the border of fact and fiction. In J. F. Gubrium & J. A. Holstein (Eds.), *Postmodern Interviewing* (pp. 225–241). Thousand Oaks, CA: Sage.

Roulston, K. (2010). *Reflexive Interviewing: A guide to theory and practice*. Los Angeles: Sage.

Rubin, H. J. & Rubin, I. S. (2005). *Qualitative Interviewing*. Thousand Oaks, CA: Sage.

Schrag, C. O. & Ramsey, R. E. (1994). Method and phenomenological research: Humility and commitment in interpretation. *Human Studies, 17*(1), 131–137.

Schwarze, M. L., Bradley, C. T., & Brasel, K. J. (2010). Surgical "buy-in": The contractual relationship between surgeons and patients that influences decisions regarding life-supporting therapy. *Critical Care Medicine, 38*(3), 843–848. 810.1097/CCM.1090b1013e3181cc1466b.

Schweber, S. (2007). Donning wigs, divining feelings, and other dilemmas of doing research in devoutly religious contexts. *Qualitative Inquiry, 13*(1), 58–84.

Seidman, I. (2006). *Interviewing as Qualitative Research: A guide for researchers in education and the social sciences* (3rd ed.). New York: Teachers College Press.

Silverman, D. (2001). *Interpreting Qualitative Data: Methods for analysing talk, text and interaction*. Thousand Oaks, CA: Sage.

Smith, M. W. (2009). Comments on Coulter and Smith: The issue of authorial surplus in narrative research. *Educational Researcher, 38*, 603–607.

Smith, R. C. (2003). Analytic strategies for oral history interviews. In J. F. Gubrium & J. A. Holstein (Eds.), *Postmodern Interviewing* (pp. 203–223). Thousand Oaks, CA: Sage.

Snelgrove, S. (2005). Bad, mad, and sad: Developing a methodology of inclusion and a pedagogy for researching students with intellectual disabilities. *International Journal of Disability Development and Education, 9*(3), 313–319.

Spradley, J. P. (1979). *The Ethnographic Interview*. New York: Holt, Rinehart, and Winston.

Subedi, B. (2006). Theorizing a "halfie" researcher's identity in transnational fieldwork. *International Journal of Qualitative Studies in Education, 19*, 573–593.

Toma, J. D. (2006). Approaching rigor in applied qualitative research. In C. F. Conrad & R. C. Serlin (Eds.), *The SAGE Handbook for Research in Education: Engaging ideas and enriching inquiry* (pp. 405–423). Thousand Oaks, CA: Sage.

Trainor, A. A. (2010a). Diverse approaches to parent advocacy during special education home–school interactions: Identification and use of cultural and social capital. *Remedial and Special Education, 31*, 34–47.

Trainor, A. A. (2010b). Reexamining the promise of parent participation in special education: An analysis of cultural and social capital. *Anthropology & Education Quarterly, 41*, 245–263.

Trainor, A. A. & Bouchard, K. A. (in press). Exploring and developing reciprocity in research design. *International Journal of Qualitative Studies in Education.*

Wray, N., Markovic, M., & Manderson, L. (2007). "Researcher saturation": The impact of data triangulation and intensive-research practices on the researcher and qualitative research process. *Qualitative Health Research, 17*(10), 1392–1402. doi: 10.1177/1049732307308308.

Zigo, D. (2001). Rethinking reciprocity: Collaboration in labor as a path toward equalizing power in classroom research. *International Journal of Qualitative Studies in Education, 14*, 351–365.

10
Mixed Methods

Donna M. Mertens

An old Italian proverb reads, "What's old is new, what's new is old" (Melfi, 2011). This quote could be used to characterize the story of mixed methods in the research community in that mixed methods have been used by researchers for many years, but attention to the specifics of mixed methods research is relatively new. Many researchers intuitively came to the conclusion that research on complex social issues can be enhanced by the use of multiple methods; hence the combination of both quantitative and qualitative data in the same studies is nothing new. Even the pioneer constructivists, Lincoln and Guba (1985) did not exclude the use of quantitative data in qualitative research designs, with the caveat that the constructivist philosophical assumptions were not violated. While some might interpret Lincoln and Guba's position to mean that mixed methods are legitimate, this caveat does raise some thorny issues for researchers. Is the mixing of paradigms possible or desirable? Are there paradigms that are amenable to exploring the meaning of mixed methods? The exploration of answers to these questions provides the basis for the qualitative touchstones discussed in this chapter.

Select Terms

Mixed methods: In mixed methods research, a researcher or team of researchers combines elements of qualitative and quantitative research approaches (e.g., use of qualitative and quantitative viewpoints, data collection, analysis, and inference techniques) for the broad purposes of breadth and depth of understanding and corroboration (Johnson et al., 2007, p. 123). Teddlie and Tashakkori (2009) add that mixed methods research includes the selection and synergistic integration of the most appropriate techniques from a myriad of qualitative, quantitative, and mixed strategies to investigate the phenomenon of interest.

Multiple methods are typically used to describe studies in which more than one quantitative or more than one qualitative method is used in the same study or program of research. These are not considered mixed methods studies because they do not combine quantitative and qualitative data in the same study or program of research.

Paradigm: Building on the work of Guba and Lincoln, a paradigm is a meta-physical construct that provides an organizing framework for the philosophical assumptions that guide researchers in their theorizing and practice.

Convergent/Parallel mixed methods design: The convergent design involves collecting and analyzing two independent stands of qualitative and quantitative data in a single phase, merging the results of the two strands, and then looking for convergence, divergence, contradictions, or relationships between the two databases (Creswell & Plano Clark, 2010, p. 116). Similar definitions are provided by Mertens (2010) and Teddlie and Tashakkori (2009) who call it a parallel design.

Sequential mixed methods designs involve research conducted in two (or more phases). The researcher first collects one type of data and then uses that data to inform the collection of the second type of data (Creswell & Plano Clark, 2010; Mertens, 2010). This can be quantitative first, followed by qualitative, or vice versa.

Cyclical mixed methods designs: Data collection activities are conducted over several phases that may overlap, take place simultaneously, or be iterative in nature (Gorard, 2010). For example, researchers may start with a qualitative analysis of extant literature and a quantitative analysis of existing data sets. This could be followed by a revision of the research questions and then subsequent data collection on the specific needs of a community and the appropriateness of interventions for specific contexts.

Transformative mixed methods designs typically use a cyclical pattern in data collection, with each cycle of data collection vetted through representatives of the community. The goal of this design is to facilitate the furtherance of social justice and human rights (Mertens, 2009).

Diversities in Perspective, Context, and Form

As the field of mixed methods has emerged as a distinct approach in the research community, a variety of reactions have surfaced that represent different viewpoints on the role and importance of paradigms as philosophical frameworks in social science research. Discussions about paradigms generally build on Lincoln and Guba's conceptualization of paradigms as metaphysical frameworks that are made up of four philosophical assumptions, including axiology (ethics), ontology (reality), epistemology (knowledge), and methodology (systematic inquiry) (Lincoln, Lynham, & Guba, 2011).

Some researchers claim that they use mixed methods a-paradigmatically, that is, the researcher operates based on responsiveness to the research question and funder requirements without consideration of philosophical assumptions. Greene (2007) and Mertens (2010) caution that operating in such a manner does not mean that the researcher is paradigm-free, rather it means that the researcher is operating without critical examination of the philosophical assumptions that guide their work.

Positions have also arisen that are based on a dichotomy between constructivist and postpositivist paradigms, to wit:

- *Incompatibility*: Mixed methods are impossible because different methodological assumptions lead to different methods choices.
- *Complementary*: Researchers can use both quantitative and qualitative methods if they adhere rigorously to the tenets associated with each paradigm.
- *Dialectical*: Both constructivist and postpositivist have something to offer; research will advance through the deliberate and critical dialogues that occur among scholars who situate themselves in different paradigms (Greene, 2007; Lincoln, 2010).

A third category of mixed methods from a paradigmatic perspective encompasses the territory of mixed methods specific paradigms. These include:

- *Pragmatic paradigm*: The research question dictates the method; quantitative and qualitative methods are used because they are best suited to answer the research questions. The results of both types of data are integrated for each study (Biesta, 2010).
- *Transformative paradigm*: Mixed methods enhance the researcher's ability to capture the complexity of issues of human rights and social transformation (Mertens, 2009, 2010).

As can be inferred from the plethora of positions with regard to mixed methods, they provide fertile ground for controversy as well as for intellectual growth. Voices from the constructivist paradigm have suggested that mixed methods is dominated by postpositivists who do not have an understanding of the rich traditions in qualitative research (Denzin, 2010). Giddings (2006) even went so far as to question whether mixed methods were not just postpositivism in drag. It is not surprising that researchers who hold strong constructivist beliefs would find grounds for criticizing those who use mixed methods from a strongly postpositivist position. However, there are mixed methods researchers who situate themselves within paradigms that provide for broader opportunities to be responsive to cultural issues through the use of mixed methods. For example, Howe (2004) offered a democratic framework he called mixed methods interpretivism; Hesse-Biber (2010) provided a feminist framework for mixed methods; and Mertens (2009, 2010) contributed the transformative paradigm that posits that mixed methods can be used to illuminate injustices in society and enhance the potential of researchers to contribute to social transformation. Other mixed methods researchers have delineated ways in which typically qualitative designs can incorporate mixed methods, such as Christ (2010) on action research, Nilsen and Brannen (2010) on biographical research, and Bergman (2010) on hermeneutical analysis.

A natural consequence of having so many different paradigmatic stances associated with mixed methods is that there is no single set of criteria that would be appropriate to use for the evaluation of all mixed methods research studies. Hence, in the mixed methods touchstones, a number of different values are discussed in the context of the researcher's philosophical assumptions. The guiding principle throughout the mixed methods touchstones is that the research should consistently reflect the researcher's assumptions in the chosen methods, analysis, and interpretation.

Another issue of importance in preparing to review mixed methods research is the need for reviewers to draw on their knowledge of criteria for quality as understood for individual quantitative or qualitative studies, as well as to be aware of the unique characteristics of mixing these methods in a single study. The following section focuses on the touchstones for review at the intersection of quantitative and qualitative methods, which is the hallmark of mixed methods research.

Qualitative Touchstones

1. The researcher makes clear the assumptions that provide the philosophical frame for the research by providing explicit explanations of the axiological, epistemological, ontological, and methodological assumptions

Researchers have a responsibility to make clear their paradigmatic stance when writing about their mixed methods studies. For example, researchers who situate themselves in the constructivist paradigm should consistently adhere to the criteria for quality associated with the qualitative design of their study, even when their research involves mixing methods. The chapters in this book provide guidance for researchers who choose to use various qualitative designs. In addition, Lincoln (2009) reiterated criteria for qualitative research that include credibility, confirmability, transferability, and dependability as parallel criteria to the postpositivists validity, reliability, objectivity, and generalizability. The addition of quantitative data in such studies should be achieved in ways that are commensurate with the constructivist's criteria for quality.

Reviewers of research that is conducted from a complementary (Morse, 2010) or dialectical stance (Greene, 2007) should note the extent to which the researchers adhere to the criteria for quality for the individual approaches. Again, the chapters in this book provide guidance for a multitude of qualitative approaches that are conducted within the constructivist paradigm. For the quantitative approaches, there are multiple sources that provide guidance in terms of assessing the quality of research that is conducted within the postpositivist paradigm. For example, Mertens (2010) provides specific criteria for assessing the quality of experimental and quasi-experimental designs, comparative and correlational research, survey methods, and single-case designs. Morse (2010) supports the complementary use of mixed methods that gives priority to keeping the quantitative and qualitative parts of the study separate in order to maintain the integrity of the paradigmatic assumptions associated with each. Greene and Hall (2010) agree that researchers must be clear about the assumptions that guide each approach used in their studies. In contrast to Morse, they urge researchers from different traditions to engage in respectful and dialectical "dialogue toward enhanced, reframed, or new understandings" (p. 123). Reviewers of dialectical mixed methods research should focus on the extent to which the researchers demonstrate "meaningful engagement intended to be fundamentally generative of insight and understanding that are of conceptual and practical consequence" (p. 124).

The pragmatic paradigm has been invoked as providing the guiding philosophical base for mixed methods research by a number of prominent researchers in the field (Creswell & Plan-Clark, 2010; Teddlie & Tashakkori, 2009). Biesta (2010) makes the helpful distinction between everyday pragmatism and philosophical pragmatism. The former can be seen in discussions in which a pragmatic stance is claimed and justified by the practice of choosing the right tool for the right purpose. Philosophical pragmatism, on the other hand, does not provide a "paradigmatic underpinning or wholesale justification of mixed methods research, but rather a set of insights that can help us to have a more precise discussion about the strengths and weaknesses of mixed methods approaches" (p. 97). Morgan (2007) argued against conceptualizing pragmatism as a paradigm, and argued for a pragmatic approach to avoid the strictures placed on mixed methods researchers that a metaphysical paradigm might impose. Even in arguing against pragmatism as paradigm, he argued for clarity about the epistemological and methodological assumptions that lead to decisions about the use of mixed methods. Researchers might characterize their mixed methods research as either based in the pragmatic paradigm or the product of a pragmatic approach. The differences between claiming the use of an everyday pragmatic paradigm, a pragmatic approach, or a philosophical pragmatic paradigm have implications for criteria used to assess their quality.

Reviewers who encounter an everyday pragmatic stance should inquire as to the adequacy of the critical thinking that is demonstrated in the authors' explanations of how their work reflects pragmatism. Do the researchers go beyond the superficial argument that it is legitimate to claim that their work reflects the pragmatic paradigm because the purpose and questions determined the methods chosen? If one adopts a philosophical pragmatic paradigm, then researchers have a responsibility to support their assertions in research on the basis of careful observation and control. Thus, the researcher needs to address the combination of action and reflection that resulted in the knowledge represented in the research and also the tension between the concept of knowledge as objective, waiting to be discovered, and knowledge as social construction. Reviewers should note how the researchers incorporate thinking about how their "different approaches generate different outcomes" (Biesta, 2010, p. 113). They should discuss how their "knowledge claims resulted from the processes and procedures through which the knowledge has been generated so as not to make any assertions that cannot be warranted on the basis of the particular methods and methodologies used" (p. 113).

Researchers who work within the transformative paradigm hold philosophical assumptions that call upon them to directly engage members of culturally diverse groups with a focus on increased social justice. The transformative paradigm provides a metaphysical umbrella that encompasses research conducted within a wide range of theoretical frameworks, including critical theories, feminist theories, human rights-based, indigenous/postcolonial, and culturally responsive research. The transformative philosophical assumptions can be characterized as follows:

- Axiology
  - Identification and respect for cultural norms that support human rights and social justice;
  - Identification and challenge of cultural norms that sustain an oppressive system;
  - Reciprocity—what evaluators give back to communities;
  - Resilience—recognition and validation of the knowledge, expertise, and strengths in the community;
  - Sustainability—facilitating conditions such that actions to continue to enhance social justice and human rights are feasible once the evaluator leaves the community;
  - Recognition of limitations—not overstepping the evaluator's boundaries or over-promising.

- Ontology
  - Recognizes that different versions of reality exist;
  - All versions of reality are not equal;
  - Recognizes privilege given to what is perceived to be real based on social, political, cultural, economic, ethnic, gender, religion, and disability positionality;
  - Interrogates versions of reality that sustain oppressive systems;
  - Makes visible versions of reality that have the potential to further human rights.

- Epistemology
  - Establishment of an interactive link between the evaluator and participants;
  - Acknowledges that knowledge is socially and historically located;
  - Explicit acknowledgment of power inequities;
  - Development of a trusting relationship.

- Methodology
  - Researchers need to report about the qualitative/dialogic moments that they used in the beginning of their study in order to ascertain the cultural context in which they worked;
  - Qualitative and quantitative data facilitate responsiveness to different participants and issues;
  - Methods used need to capture the contextual complexity and be appropriate to the cultural groups in the research study;
  - A cyclical design can be used to make use of interim findings throughout the research study.

The transformative philosophical assumptions have implications for reviewers at all stages of the research process. Initially, reviewers should examine transformative mixed methods studies to determine the extent to which the researchers demonstrated that their work reflects the spirit of the assumptions associated with the transformative paradigm. For example, how did the researchers demonstrate their knowledge of and responsiveness to the cultural norms and beliefs of the different stakeholder groups? How did the researcher identify who needed to be involved and appropriate strategies for their involvement? How did the researcher identify the cultural norms and beliefs that were operating in the community? How did they appropriately engage with members of the community? How did the researchers determine those cultural norms and beliefs that might further social justice or those that might sustain an oppressive status quo? How did they take into account the expertise, knowledge, and strengths of the community in order to provide a platform for authentic engagement between the evaluator and the community?

As a corollary to the need for the researcher to be explicit about their paradigmatic assumptions, reviewers should also be aware of their own assumptions and how those assumptions might influence their critical review of a manuscript. Reviewers may feel conflicted if their paradigmatic views differ from that of the researcher. This is an opportunity to be frank about the assumptions that the reviewers themselves are using when critiquing a manuscript. The topic of self-reflexivity is widely discussed in the qualitative literature and has important implications for the review of mixed methods research as well (Mertens, 2009).

2. Researchers should be explicit about the theoretical frameworks that inform their work and how the frameworks influence the research process and findings

Hesse-Biber (2010) argues that theory should come before method because theories lead "the researcher to ask certain research questions and prioritize what questions and issues are most important to study" (p. 11). Just as paradigms inform methodological choices, some theories inform the focus of the research by stressing the researcher's social situatedness in terms of race, class, gender, and other relevant characteristics (also known as positionality). Other theories guide the researcher's thinking about the phenomenon under study (e.g., theories of literacy or theories of motivation). Transformative and constructivist researchers have identified many positional theories that are commensurate with their philosophical assumptions, for example, feminist theories, Critical Race Theories, critical theories, human rights theories, disability rights theories, indigenous theories, deafness rights theories, and queer theories (Mertens, 2009, 2010; Mertens & Ginsberg, 2009).

In order to critique a study that uses a positionality theory, the reviewer needs to be cognizant of the implications of that theory for the research process and findings. For example, Hesse-Biber (2010) suggests that reviewers of mixed methods research that is framed by feminist theory should consider the extent to which the research "probes questions of power, difference, silence, and oppression, with the goal of moving toward a more just society for women and other oppressed groups . . . [Do the] researchers study women's issues by listening to their voices, exploring and thus empowering their experiences, and examining connections between power and knowledge?" (p. 129). Similar questions could be raised for research that uses other positionality theories, such as Critical Race Theory (Stanfield, 2011), indigenous theory (Chilisa, 2011), and deafness rights theory (Harris, Holmes, & Mertens, 2009).

Researchers who use positionality or substantive theories need to provide a clear articulation of the theory and its implications, as well as demonstrate that they have integrated those implications consistently throughout the research study.

3. Researchers should make explicit their mixed methods design, including the design of both the quantitative and qualitative parts of the study and the points of intersection

The definition of terms section of this chapter includes explanations of various design options for mixed methods research. Mixed methods designs can be somewhat simplistic when researchers collect both qualitative and quantitative either at the same time (concurrent designs) or sequentially (Nastasi, Hitchcock, & Brown, 2010). They can also be quite complex and appear in the form of iterative approaches in "which the design evolves during multiple phases of research process" (Nastasi, et al., p. 311). It is the latter complex design that is most common in transformative mixed methods research.

As noted in the section on paradigms, different methodological assumptions lead to different criteria for judging the quality of designs. However, the overall criterion for judging design quality is the extent to which it allows the researcher to make valid inferences (Nastasi et al., 2010). Depending on the researcher's paradigmatic stance, the criteria for design might be those for postpositivists (Mertens, 2010; Morse, 2010), constructivists (Lincoln, 2009), or transformative researchers (Mertens, 2009). Greene (2007) adds that criteria that are specific to different paradigmatic stances are not sufficient; reviewers must also judge the integration of the design (i.e., methods are integrated throughout the study) and the extent to which mixing occurs at the inference level.

O'Cathain (2010) argues that different criteria for determining the quality of mixed methods designs might need to be considered for different designs. However, she does provide generic criteria for assessing the quality of mixed methods designs, including:

- *Design transparency*: Description of design type from known typology, or key aspects of design, if known typologies do not describe the design used. Essentially, the researcher needs to provide details of the design in terms of which groups engaged in what types of interventions and what types of data collection methods were used for each group at specific stages in the study.
- *Design suitability*: The design is appropriate for addressing the overall research question, matches the reason for combining methods, and is appropriate for the stated paradigm.
- *Design strength*: The strengths and weaknesses of methods are considered to minimize shared bias and optimize the breadth and depth of the study.
- *Design rigor*: Methods are implemented in a way that remains true to the design (p. 541).

For transformative mixed methods studies (Mertens, 2009, 2010b) and others who use cyclical mixed methods designs (Nastasi et al., 2010), reviewers can ask the following questions to evaluate their designs:

- How did the researchers build into the design ways to demonstrate that they are leaving the community better off than when they began the research study—in terms of increased knowledge, capacity, or changes in policies or practices?
- Did the researchers use qualitative/dialogic moments in the beginning of the planning in order to ascertain the cultural context in which they are working?
- Did the researchers include both qualitative and quantitative data to facilitate responsiveness to different participants and issues?
- What methods did the researchers use to capture the contextual complexity and be appropriately responsive to the cultural groups in the research study?
- How did the researcher use a cyclical design to make use of interim findings throughout the research study?

4. Mixed methods research involves having samples for both the qualitative and quantitative portions of the study, hence researchers need to clarify their rationale for the samples selected, the methods they used for the different samples, and the implications of the similarities and differences between the samples

Teddlie and Yu (2007) described five different sampling strategies for mixed methods research: (1) purposive or quota for both parts of the study; (2) sequential sampling in which the results of the first phase of the study influences sampling decisions for the second phase; (3) probability-based sampling for the quantitative portion and purposive sampling for the qualitative portion; (4) multilevel sampling based on various strategies such as random selection of locations with purposive sampling of participants at selected locations; and (5) combinations of mixed methods sampling throughout the course of the study. Researchers should give a clear explanation of the sampling strategies that they used, the rationale for their selection, and the implications of the sampling plan for the quality of the study. For example, do unequal sample sizes threaten the researchers' ability to draw inferences from either portion of the study? Does shared variance between the quantitative and qualitative samples threaten the ability to make inferences?

Reviewers of research conducted within the transformative paradigm should also address queries related to the representation of marginalized groups, for example, how did the researcher:

- identify, support, and include diverse participants?
- reveal different versions of reality, including their basis in terms of privilege and power?
- contribute to the change in participants' understandings of what is real?

5. Data collection procedures need to be explained for both the quantitative and qualitative portions of the study; adherence to quality in data collection needs to be demonstrated for each type of data

By definition, mixed methods studies involve the collection of both quantitative and qualitative data. With quantitative data, researchers should demonstrate the quality of the data collection by discussing its psychometric properties, such as validity, reliability, and objectivity. If a researcher contends that these characteristics are not relevant, then they should provide a justification for that stance. With qualitative data, researchers can provide evidence that they adhered to the criteria for quality as outlined by Lincoln (2009). In terms of mixed methods, reviewers should be aware of the data transparency (i.e., the extent to which each method is described in sufficient detail and its role is made clear within the study) and data rigor (i.e., the extent to which methods are implemented with rigor) (O'Cathain, 2010). Reviewers should be aware that in the qualitative portion of a study, the researcher may have used an unstructured interview format, and therefore, not be able to provide an interview protocol because it was individualized for each respondent.

Creswell and Plano Clark (2010) suggest that reviewers consider the following questions in assessing the quality of data collection in mixed methods studies:

1. Are the same constructs being measured in the quantitative and qualitative portions of the study? If so, how does the researcher demonstrate that consistency? If not, what are the implications of measuring different constructs?
2. If one of the approaches is dominant in the study and the other approach constitutes a much smaller portion of the study, what are the implications in terms of resources devoted to data collection? How does the researcher demonstrate quality in data collection, particularly if the one approach is given significantly fewer resources?

Transformative mixed methods researchers are encouraged to acknowledge their own positions of power and privilege when it is time to select data collection methods (Mertens, 2009). They need to demonstrate that they understand their own power and privilege and the way that communities understand their roles in the research in terms of data collection decisions. Reviewers should be aware of the extent to which these power and privilege issues were explored in the study and the implications of this process for data collection decisions. How responsive are the data collection processes to the needs of subgroups within the participant groups? Were materials adapted as necessary to address issues of language, literacy, traditions, and disabilities? How were data collection strategies used to address the power differentials in the stakeholder groups? How did the data collection give voice to members of marginalized communities? Was there evidence of sufficient trust between the researcher and the community members to support claims that the data provided were accurate?

6. Data analysis in mixed methods studies should adhere to standards for quality for analysis of both quantitative and qualitative data; tensions between the outcomes of the different analyses must be addressed; inferences should be clearly linked with the data analysis

O'Cathain (2010) provides the following criteria for assessing the quality of mixed methods data analysis:

- *Analytic adequacy*: Data analysis techniques are appropriate for the research question and are undertaken properly.
- *Analytic integration*: Any integration taking place at the analysis stage of a study is robust, for example, data transformations are defensible (p. 542).

Creswell and Plano Clark (2010) add that researchers need to clearly explain the nature of the data integration and its strengths and weaknesses. Reviewers should be aware of the strategies used for data integration and should be sensitive to potential privileging of one type of data over another. What is lost or gained when quantitizing qualitative data? To what extent do the data from different methods converge or diverge? How do researchers address discrepancies that surface between the quantitative and qualitative data analyses?

In terms of inference, O'Cathain (2010) draws our attention to the following criteria:

- *Interpretive transparency*: It is clear which findings have emerged from which methods.
- *Interpretive consistency*: Inferences are consistent with the data on which they are based.
- *Theoretical consistency*: Inferences are consistent with current knowledge and theory.
- *Interpretive efficacy*: Meta-inferences from the whole study adequately incorporate inferences from the qualitative and quantitative findings and inferences.
- *Inference transferability*: Transferability to other contexts and settings (pp. 542–543).

Reviewers should also be aware of potential bias in the interpretation of the results. For example, does the researcher reach conclusions related to quantitative and qualitative findings that favor one type of data over another? How do the researchers involve community members in the interpretation of the findings? How are the data interpreted through appropriate cultural lenses?

At this point in the review, reviewers are in a good position to make judgments about the overall congruence throughout the manuscript between philosophical assumptions and theoretical tenets and the design, implementation, and reporting of the research.

Further Reading

Tashakkori, A. & Teddlie, C. (2010). *Sage Handbook of Mixed Methods in Social and Behavioral Research.* Thousand Oaks, CA: Sage.
This handbook includes an overview of the status of mixed methods research in the social and behavioral science communities. It contains sections on philosophy and theory, methodology, and applications in practice. Several chapters specifically address criteria for determining the quality of mixed methods research. Other chapters examine mixed methods research from constructivist standpoints.

Mertens, D. M. (2009). *Transformative Research and Evaluation.* New York: Guilford.
The author explains the philosophical assumptions of the transformative paradigm and provides guidance for researchers who have a goal of addressing issues of human rights and social justice in their work. Examples of

transformative mixed methods research are provided from many different countries and in many different disciplines. Specific focus can be found on marginalized communities, such as people with disabilities, those who are deaf, indigenous communities, and women.

Hesse-Biber, S. N. (2010). *Mixed Methods Research: Merging theory with practice*. New York: Guilford.
Mixed methods are presented from a qualitative framing with an emphasis on the importance of theory as a predecessor to methods decisions. Hesse-Biber presents examples from international contexts that demonstrate the role of feminist theory and a postmodern stance in mixed methods.

Creswell, J. & Plano Clark, V. (2010). *Designing and Conducting Mixed Methods Research*. Thousand Oaks, CA: Sage.
This textbook provides a basic introduction to mixed methods research. Its focus is on designing mixed methods studies, with additional guidance in implementing these studies. Other chapters address the analysis and interpreting of mixed methods data.

Counterpoint Perspectives

Denzin, N. (2012). Triangulation 2.0? *Journal of Mixed Methods Research*, 6(2), 80–88.
For a discussion of mixed methods that is based on a critical evaluation of the philosophical positioning of mixed methods in the pragmatic paradigm, see Denzin who argues that this stance misinterprets the meaning of pragmatism and ignores the fundamental epistemological assumptions associated with pragmatism as a philosophy. By ignoring these assumptions, he contends that much of mixed methods research reflects the assumptions of the postpositivist paradigm without giving credence to the rich methodological principles found in the constructivist paradigm. Furthermore, he argues that researchers have an ethical responsibility to work toward furthering social justice that requires appropriate involvement at the community level. He makes the controversial proposal that a moratorium should be declared on mixed methods until we can understand how research can be used as a catalyst for social change.

Author's Reflections on Quality

My graduate training in research focused entirely on quantitative approaches as they are viewed by proponents of the postpositivist paradigm. When I began conducting research in the mountainous Appalachian region on solutions to poverty in the early 1970s, I realized like many researchers that quantitative data only told part of the story. I educated myself on constructivism and qualitative approaches in order to fill that void. At the same time, I was becoming aware of the contributions that feminist scholars were making to uncovering biases in research topics and methods, especially as they applied to gender-based discrimination. As I grew in consciousness, I realized that many marginalized groups in society were being denied access to privileges on the basis of some inherent or socially determined characteristic. After conducting primarily quantitative work at Ohio State University with various marginalized communities, I looked around to find a context in which I could work with members of such a community and employ research methods that were responsive to the complexity of cultures that I might find there.

This search led me to my present position at Gallaudet University, the only university in the world that has the mission to serve deaf and hard-of-hearing students and communities. I entered this community without having met a deaf person, but with an open heart and an open mind and a willingness to figure out if it was possible to establish relationships that would lead to research opportunities together in the service of social justice. I learned (and continue to learn) a great deal from this quest. First, I realized that even my knowledge of quantitative and qualitative methods was inadequate to the task of undertaking such research. I began exploring the work of feminist and racial minority writers as a source to understand better the ideas needed to work in marginalized communities. With support from my students, I came to the conclusion that marginalized communities are very heterogeneous and that an umbrella was needed to address the differences in power relations in research context based on gender, race, ethnicity, language, disability, deafness, and other markers that are used as a basis of discrimination and oppression.

From this experience, the transformative paradigm has evolved as reflecting my philosophical beliefs. The assumptions of the transformative paradigm are explained elsewhere in this chapter; therefore, they are not repeated here. However, positioning myself in the transformative paradigm leads me to base my judgments about research quality on the extent to which it is geared to address issues of discrimination and oppression and to facilitate social change.

I am not swayed by those who argue that paradigms are not necessary because in practice, many researchers report that they do not consider their philosophical assumptions when practicing their craft. I hold the position that everyone has philosophical assumptions. These are either made explicit and used to guide the research, or they are critically unexamined assumptions that are also guiding research, but possibly and unconsciously in a pernicious manner.

References

Bergman, M. (2010). Hermeneutic content analysis: Textual and audiovisual analyses within a mixed methods framework. In A. Tashakkori & C. Teddlie (Eds.), *Sage Handbook of Mixed Methods in Social and Behavioral Research* (2nd ed., pp. 379–396). Thousand Oaks, CA: Sage.

Biesta, G. J. J. (2010). Pragmatism and the philosophical foundations of mixed methods research. In A. Tashakkori & C. Teddlie (Eds.), *Sage Handbook of Mixed Methods in Social and Behavioral Research* (2nd ed., pp. 95–118). Thousand Oaks, CA: Sage.

Chilisa, B. (2011). *Indigenous Research Methodologies*. Thousand Oaks, CA: Sage.

Christ, T. W. (2010). Teaching mixed methods and action research: Pedagogical, practical, and evaluative consideration. In A. Tashakkori & C. Teddlie (Eds.), *Sage Handbook of Mixed Methods in Social and Behavioral Research* (2nd ed., pp. 643–676). Thousand Oaks, CA: Sage.

Creswell, J. W. & Plano Clark, V. L. (2010). *Designing and Conducting Mixed Methods Research* (2nd ed.). Thousand Oaks, CA: Sage.

Denzin, N. K. (2010). Moments, mixed methods, and paradigm dialogs. *Qualitative Inquiry, 16*(6), 419–427.

Giddings, L. S. (2006). Mixed-methods research: Positivism dressed in drag? *Journal of Research in Nursing, 11*, 195–203.

Gorard, S. (2010). Research design, as independent of methods. In A. Tashakkori & C. Teddlie (Eds.), *Sage Handbook of Mixed Methods in Social and Behavioral Research* (2nd ed., pp. 237–253). Thousand Oaks, CA: Sage.

Greene, J. C. (2007). *Mixed Methods in Social Inquiry*. San Francisco: Jossey-Bass.

Greene, J. & Hall, J. (2010). Dialectics and pragmatism: Being of consequence. In A. Tashakkori & C. Teddlie (Eds.), *Sage Handbook of Mixed Methods in Social and Behavioral Research* (pp. 119–144). Thousand Oaks, CA: Sage.

Harris, R., Holmes, H., & Mertens, D. M. (2009). Research ethics in sign language communities. *Sign Language Studies, 9*(2), 104–131.

Hesse-Biber, S. N. (2010). *Mixed Methods Research: Merging theory with practice*. New York: Guilford Press.

Howe, K. R. (2004). A critique of experimentalism. *Qualitative Inquiry, 10*, 42–61.

Johnson, R. B., Onweugbuzie, A., & Turner, L. (2007). Toward a definition of mixed methods research. *Journal of Mixed Methods Research, 1*, 112–133.

Lincoln, Y. S. (2009). Ethical practices in qualitative research. In D. M. Mertens & P. Ginsburg (Eds.), *Handbook of Social Research Ethics* (pp. 150–169). Thousand Oaks, CA: Sage.

Lincoln, Y. S. (2010). "What a long, strange trip it's been . . .": Twenty-five years of qualitative and new paradigm research. *Qualitative Inquiry, 16*(1), 3–9.

Lincoln, Y. S. & Guba, E. G. (1985). *Naturalistic Inquiry*. Beverly Hills, CA: Sage.

Lincoln, Y. S., Lynham, S. A., & Guba, E. G. (2011). Paradigmatic controversies, contradictions, and emerging confluences, revised. In N. K. Denzin & Y. S. Lincoln (Eds.), *The Sage Handbook of Qualitative Research* (4th ed., pp. 97–128). Thousand Oaks, CA: Sage.

Melfi, M. (2011). Italy revisited: Folk sayings on aging. www.italyrevisited.org. Accessed July 27, 2011.

Mertens, D. M. (2009). *Transformative Research and Evaluation*. New York: Guilford.

Mertens, D. M. (2010). *Research and Evaluation in Education and Psychology: Integrating diversity with quantitative, qualitative, and mixed methods* (3rd ed.). Thousand Oaks, CA: Sage.

Mertens, D. M. & Ginsberg, P. (Eds.) (2009). *Handbook of Social Research Ethics*. Thousand Oaks, CA: Sage.

Morgan, D. L. (2007). Paradigms lost and pragmatism regained: Methodological implications of combining qualitative and quantitative methods. *Journal of Mixed Methods Research, 1*, 48–76.

Morse, J. (2010). Procedures and practice of mixed method design: Maintaining control, rigor and complexity. In A. Tashakkori, & C. Teddlie (Eds.), *Sage Handbook of Mixed Methods in Social and Behavioral Research* (2nd ed., pp. 339–352). Thousand Oaks, CA: Sage.

Nastasi, B. K., Hitchcock, J. H., & Brown, L. M. (2010). An inclusive framework for conceptualizing mixed methods design typologies: Moving toward fully integrated synergistic research models. *Sage Handbook of Mixed Methods in Social and Behavioral Research* (2nd ed., pp. 305–338). Thousand Oaks, CA: Sage.

Nilsen, A. & Brannen, J. (2010). The use of mixed methods in biographical research. In A. Tashakkori & C. Teddlie (Eds.), *Sage Handbook of Mixed Methods in Social and Behavioral Research* (2nd ed., pp. 677–724). Thousand Oaks, CA: Sage.

O'Cathain, A. (2010). Assessing the quality of mixed methods research: Toward a comprehensive framework. In A. Tashakkori & C. Teddlie (Eds.), *Sage Handbook of Mixed Methods in Social and Behavioral Research* (pp. 531–557). Thousand Oaks, CA: Sage.

Stanfield, J. H. (2011). *Rethinking Race and Ethnicity in Research Methods*. Walnut Hills, CA: Left Coast Press.

Teddlie, C. & Tashakkori. A. (2009). *Foundations of Mixed Methods Research*. Thousand Oaks, CA: Sage.

Teddlie, C. & Yu, F. (2007). Mixed methods sampling: A typology with examples. *Journal of Mixed Methods Research, 1,* 77–100.

11
Oral History, Life History, and Biography

Valerie J. Janesick

We tell ourselves stories in order to live.
Joan Didion

Oral history, life history, and biography are three approaches to qualitative inquiry that share certain characteristics. At the same time, each has a unique flavor and set of goals and meaning. Narrative in style, all three approaches can often use video or photography and more recently use found data poetry, and thus multiple text analysis is often warranted. These three sister approaches have in common the end result of capturing the lived experience of an individual or a collective of individuals by telling stories. In other words, we are investigating subjectivity that is human lived experience. My reference point to distinguish among the three approaches is that of the theoretical approach of the researcher, and the statement of the researcher defining the selected approach. In this chapter I will describe and explain the three approaches and discuss the relative merits and generous contributions of each approach. Next I will discuss the touchstones and criteria for reviewing oral history, life history, and biography. In fairness I will also need to talk about narrative storytelling, a technique closely associated with these three approaches and with qualitative work in general. In addition, since this is the digital era, near the end of this chapter I will list some resources available for free on the internet through listservs, blogs, YouTube, and other sites that can enhance our understanding of oral history, life history, and biography. Finally, I look at the power and possibility of all three approaches in terms of informing social justice projects in the social sciences. Likewise, wherever possible I will add web resources for understanding these approaches because the internet is exploding with oral history and life history projects on YouTube, Myspace, Second Life, and Facebook. Wherever possible I will also include relevant blogs such as the one on institutional review, www.institutionalreviewblog.com. The requirements of any institutional review board become critical when doing oral history, life history, or biography because of the debates within the field of oral history over whether or not oral history is research. In fact, there is a federal statement on this excluding oral history from IRB review. As a result, many oral historians have taken to writing about this and as you might imagine there is a wide range of opinions. Some say all one needs is a signed consent form and others say just do the IRB review or both.

Select Terms

Oral history is the collection of stories and reminiscences of those who have firsthand knowledge of particular experiences (Janesick, 2010). There are many definitions of oral history available and I have used this particular definition because it casts a wide net. At the heart and soul of oral history we find the testimony of someone telling a story. In this chapter, the term testimony is used to indicate its general meaning, that is giving testimony, oral or written, as a firsthand authentication of any event. Oral history and testimony provide us with an avenue of thick description, analysis, and interpretation of people's lives through probing the past in order to understand the present. The postmodern and interpretive appreciation of the study of people and their stories, those stories from the outside or periphery of society, offer a unique opportunity to view oral history as a social justice project. For example, women, minorities, and any person or group categorized as "the other" may find a benefit just from actually recording their stories for themselves and for future generations. As a social justice record is kept, the stories cannot be lost. While oral history as a genre is most often associated with the field of history, since the past century it has been readily used by the social sciences and most recently in the field of education. Many oral histories are written to describe firsthand witness accounts of traumatic events such as Hurricane Katrina survivors' oral histories or the first responders to the 9/11 World Trade Center attacks.

Life history is about gaining insights into the broader human conditions by coming to know and understand the experiences of humans (Cole & Knowles, 2001). In the area of life history as in oral history, researchers document the nuance, texture, complexity, and meaning in a given life. By extension, when we understand one person's life story, we understand the context, the community, and the collective. As Cole and Knowles (2001) have elegantly argued, to understand an individual life in its context is to understand the complexities of lives in communities. Life history has been used widely in the social sciences and health and medical fields. In this approach, many life histories begin with a traumatic event or series of events such as child abuse stories, witnessing a natural disaster, etc. Many writers call these events turning points.

Biography is a written account of a person's lived experience. In most cases the biographer may research the person's life through written records and historical documents if the person is deceased. In addition, turning point moments often define certain biographies. In fact, traumatic events are often turning points and become the beginning of many a biography. If the person is still living, the biographer may do extensive interviewing in addition to reviewing documents. One could say that the biographer uses the techniques of both the oral historian and the life historian. For example, recently the biographer and historian Susan Shiff (2010) has written a biography of *Cleopatra* based on written documents, photographs of artifacts, and sculpture. Biography has been a genre used in many fields including medicine, the social sciences, education, business, and the arts and sciences. Many writers today use biography as a component of historical fiction. Here writers use the basic historical details and embroider them within a fictional context as true to the details of the time as is possible given the written record.

Overall the difference in oral history, life history, and biography depends on the researcher's training, background, and theoretical frames of their respective fields. I used the text by Shiff to illustrate a biography about Cleopatra. If, however, Cleopatra had been interviewed by someone while she was alive and they had documented that in writing that could be an oral history if it met the criteria and if the researcher defined it as such. However, it could also be a life history if it met certain criteria set by the individual researcher. The criteria selected by individual researchers to name their approach to the project may include:

1. The theoretical framework selected for the project, such as phenomenology or hermeneutics;
2. The methods chosen such as interviews plus or minus documents, documents alone, or any other combinations of research techniques; and
3. The viewpoint of the researcher in terms of interpretation of multiple data collection techniques versus the culturally produced artifact of the researcher and participant together sharing interpretation. The discipline of history, for example, utilizes oral history in most cases. Life history, however, grew out of literature and the arts and thus researchers in these traditions would surely tap into the traditions of their particular discipline. As with any research project, it is the researcher's responsibility to identify, describe, define, and explain the approach used in the research. In addition, the research needs to identify the theory that guides the research. Once those are known it is not problematic.

Researcher reflective journal is a journal kept during the entire research process whether the researcher is using oral history, life history, or biography. Journal writing may also be used by the person who is participating in the research project. Some writers call this co-researching and this acknowledges the active role and reflection of the participant in the research project, that is, the person whose story is being told. Journal writing also allows the researcher to focus the study more acutely, remain close to the data, and imagine alternative explanations for the evidence at hand. Furthermore, the journal may be an outlet for creative renderings of data such as drawings, photos, collages, installations of materials, etc. (see Janesick, 2004, 2007, 2011).

Document review offers oral historians, life historians, and biographers a rich source of data to augment interviews or written testimonials. Usually the researcher has a theoretical lens explicitly identified from which to view the documents. Likewise, the researcher explains that theoretical lens and any selected methods of analysis. Documents are a rich resource for any qualitative researcher. They are critical in providing the context for oral histories, life histories, and biographies. They add to the story. For example, in a recent study on female leaders, their vitae, sample correspondence, and their own photographs were used to document their average day. This type of data helps to inform any other data such as interviews or observations.

Subjectivity in this chapter is defined as human lived experience and the physical, political, historical context of that experience (see Ellis & Flaherty, 1992). In a sense, oral history, life history, and biography are remarkably sociological from the idea that sociology is about understanding human experience. If we use any of these three approaches we are concerned with investigating subjectivity, more particularly the lived experience of one or more individuals.

Diversities in Perspective, Context, and Form

In a sense, you may think of oral history, life history, and biography as emergent and thus representing a diversity of perspectives, context, and form. This emergent set of methodologies is part of a growing body of literature on emergent qualitative methods (see Hesse-Biber & Leavy, 2008; Frisch, 2008), especially in the field of education. These authors and many others define emergent methods as those methods that attempt to modify or adapt existing methods. For example, researchers who employ oral history, life history, or biography often rely on interviewing as a major data collection technique. This is a traditional technique. However, in this technology-driven global cultural space, an interviewer may use the World Wide Web through SKYPE to do an interview with someone across continents. So a traditional technique, interviewing, is adapted and emerges as a new strain of interviewing. Likewise, emergent methods usage may result in emergent data representation techniques such as creating poetry from interview transcripts, that is, found data poetry. Educators have a long history of solidly positivist and neopositivist views and predominantly quantitative educational research. Since the 1970s, more emphasis has been placed on opening the repertoire of techniques in research to include the qualitative techniques. These approaches to research widen our understanding of schools and society by incorporating voice. Since qualitative work in general and oral history, life history, and biography in particular often include the voices and stories of those on the margins of society, I hope this chapter contributes to some awareness of social justice. Because women have regularly been excluded from oral history projects in the past century, obviously the feminist research methods texts offer us something in our understanding of feminist oral history (Reinharz, 1992; Hesse-Biber & Leavy, 2007). These three techniques of oral history, life history, and biography offer possibilities not available in more codified approaches at this point in time. The major possibility here is focusing on social justice stories or at least stories that contribute to our understanding of social justice. Nonetheless, the rigor required of qualitative work traces back to a long and dependable historic chain. The checks and balances in qualitative work such as staying in a setting over time; having an outside reader of field notes, transcripts, and initial findings; keeping a researcher reflective journal; and the discipline of writing itself speaks well for the future of the three approaches described in this chapter. Thus it is apparent that diversity of perspectives in data collection, data representation, and analysis is part of the toolkit for oral historians, life historians, and biographers.

The power of oral history, life history, and biography lies in the power of storytelling. Whether the researcher embraces and describes the story of one person's life or a collection of individual stories told together, the power resides in the *meaning made of the storytelling* and what we learn from the stories. For example, the oral histories of firefighters first to respond to the World Trade Center on 9/11 individually tell the unique story of many an individual. Taken together as you read the collective of this unique community, even more power is evident in the storytelling. In addition, since these approaches capture the lived experience of a person or persons, the social justice goals become more definite when capturing the stories of those left on the periphery of society. Oral history, life history, and biography then become vehicles for any individual to tell the story that needs to be told. In recent history, for example, traumatic events such as 9/11 and Hurricane Katrina became important sites for completing transformative oral histories and life histories. Many survivors of Katrina have written autobiographically and visiting researchers captured the biographies, oral histories, and/or life history of many Katrina victims. Many of the projects that described Hurricane Katrina survivors serve to punctuate the underlying social justice implications of doing this type of research. These stories captured issues of race, class, gender, inequality, and power. What these three approaches have in common is *telling stories* through spoken text, written text, video text, or all of these media.

Qualitative Touchstones

Oral history, life history, and biography as qualitative approaches to inquiry share some common touchstones. In addition, it is natural and a given that one person's life is as important as many lives. Thus, it can easily be said that oral history, life history, and biography offer a path to a personal and individual story of a person's life or a snapshot of it. As such, the preoccupation of other postpositivist traditional approaches that look for generalization, large samples sizes, prediction, and control are out of place here in these three genres. Thus the single qualitative case study is often a common description of these three approaches. It is the uniqueness of the individual case that makes us desire to read and understand the story behind it. Likewise, in these three genres it is already assumed that the individual story will give us a glimpse of something new. Thus the touchstones here are constructed from an understanding of the arts, classic sociology, anthropology, and history. They do not rely on statistics as such although they often employ demographic date to round out the cases or portraits of the lives under study. Here the touchstones rely on qualities related to investigating the researcher's and participant's subjectivities. Likewise, when using any of these genres it is already assumed that we embrace subjectivity, and we honor the description and explanation of all the messiness of human life. We welcome the opportunity to deconstruct the contradictions, vulnerabilities, complexity, and problems of participants. We take in the story being told with openness to the whole person, body, senses, soul, spirit, and cognition. As a result, in these approaches, I wish to pose the following questions as touchstones for understanding oral history, life history, and biography. I am using the touchstones often used in choreography and the dance world, my favorite metaphors, as frames. These frames are design, balance, composition, and harmony. Let us now turn to these touchstone questions in order to assist in the understanding of how to make sense of oral history, life history, and biography.

1. Design: Is the story told cohesive and coherent?

Few people will read the accounts of a given life if they are not well written structurally, artfully, and beautifully. The participants' own words are important and the mainstay of the story told. In addition, the researcher/writer of the oral history, life history, or biography must craft the case with sensitivity to meaning. What did the participant mean in this or that sentence? If other media are used, are the media authentic? How are the media integral to the story? To do this kind of work, the researcher must be a skilled and accomplished writer and interpreter. For example, it is important to interpret the colloquialisms, metaphors, language, slang, and stereotypes that may come up in an interview or documents. For example, the recent biography of Cleopatra (Shiff, 2010) is written with great detail as to what that time period was like. Key phrases used, the gender issues of the day, and a powerful female leader are all explained in context. Thus the writer is scientist and artist rolled into one in terms of presentation, meaning given, and interpretation of that data all done in a narrative style that carries the reader along. In addition and, obviously, in choosing to read a given oral history, life history, or biography, a reader must have an interest in the topic to a great extent. Likewise, when reviewing historical documents, the researcher must be sensitive to their historical context.

Furthermore, cohesiveness is connected to coherence. All elements of the work should cohere: the title of the work and the actual data story presented, the abstract, the research questions, and the methodology selected. In the reporting of oral history, life history, and/or biography, the researcher must be coherent not just in presenting and analyzing data, but also in interpreting for the reader the meaning of the data and the analysis. In this way, a coherent and cohesive final report has a way of getting to the heart of the story and so designing that story, like choreographing a dance, becomes pivotal, substantial, creative, and illuminating in my view.

2. Balance: Is the story told trustworthy?

So many writers have written about trustworthiness that I will focus here only on the team of Rubin and Rubin (2005) as a starting point and my own work (Janesick, 2011). Throughout the long and elegant history of qualitative work, there are many checks and balances in the process to assure trustworthiness. For one thing, qualitative researchers must hold to the ethical codes of conduct agreed on within a discipline to insure trustworthiness. Also, Institutional Review Boards (IRBs) of any institution follow the federal requirements and may add additional requirements if working with protected populations. Some rules of thumb are also balancing mechanisms (Janesick, 2011, pp. 185–188). Thus, as a reviewer, you might look for:

1. *Did the researcher study her own group? It is regularly advised not to study one's own group in the immediate sense.* If a doctoral student, for example, wishes to study perspectives on teaching by life histories of teachers, go to a faculty other than one's own. The social world being what it is, gives one pause to move away from the immediate sphere to go elsewhere. There are many teachers who will be happy to tell their stories. If you are too close to home, this could end up haunting you for life. For example, what happens when a participant

denies saying something, or five years later has a falling out with the researcher? Here I would caution anyone on this issue. Now that we live in a digital era, with blogs as data, and social network statements as data, what is said in one's youth may not feel so positive later on in life. While this generation admits there is no privacy, there are many who still wish to keep some things private. Especially when writing about race, class, gender, and power, the researcher is already more scrutinized than the researcher who elects the safer route. A good way to handle this is to make explicit the role of the researcher somewhere in the final reporting of the project. In addition, this is an ongoing conversation in many disciplines and will most likely not be settled one way or another in our lifetimes. The point is to be aware of the tradeoffs involved in such a situation. Being too close to a culture or setting may result in missing something obvious in the telling of the final story.

2. *Did the researcher use an outside reader?* Many researchers in this tradition have an outside reader of field notes, transcripts, and initial categories and codes for a fresh viewpoint, to have a critical sounding board, and for support if nothing else. In fact, on the web there are many opportunities to study and write with feedback groups if a person cannot get feedback immediately from a peer or colleague.

3. *Is the study designed to understand a person's life?* A good example of case life histories is the work of Oliver Sacks (1995). As he takes the reader through life histories of rare and paradoxical cases, there is no missing the fact that he writes to understand the lived experience and make sense of it. This contrasts with other approaches designed for prediction and control.

4. *Was enough time spent in the field, or reviewing documents?* A good rule of thumb is time in the field needs equal or more time in analysis. Is the oral history, life history, or biography one that exemplifies enough time in the research process to warrant the conclusions and interpretations presented? In our fast-paced world, this polished rule of thumb from the history of more than one discipline is a good one to follow.

5. *Have points of tension and conflict been uncovered?* It is also wise to look for all points of tension, conflict, that which does not ring true, and so on. A one-sided report does not convince. A rich and nuanced report contains the whole picture, warts and all. There is no need to present an incomplete picture of the participant. Here the biographer is intrepid in painting full pictures, such as the recent biography of Cleopatra mentioned earlier.

6. *Has a pilot study been completed?* One other major checkpoint is the faithful and steadfast pilot study. I cannot say too much about the need to test questions in interviews, observations, double checking one's own reflection through the researcher reflective journal, and trying out initial themes, categories, and/or codes. This alone offers dependable confidence in the entire design and conduct of research.

7. *Have ethical issues been addressed as needed?* All ethical issues that may evolve must be addressed in the final reporting. For example, in a recent dissertation study, a participant was tired of interviews and dropped out. The researcher then wrote a small section on the implications of this for the study and viewed this as an ethical issue. She described what she learned from this and explained how she selected another participant. Another ethical challenge might be to decide what should be done when the participant says, "please turn off the tape for a few minutes so I can disclose something I do not want in the transcript." Here again, it is illuminative for the reader to know that such an event occurred and it is the judgment call of the researcher to explain what this means for the context of the study. Finally, before a study is undertaken, all consent forms must be current and appropriate clearance must be obtained.

In addition, consider for balance the points made by Rubin and Rubin (2005). They offer thoroughness, believability, and transparency as additional checks and balances in a given narrative. All of these qualities assist in a rigorous approach to a well-rounded story. Obviously, in the case of oral history when oral histories are recorded immediately following traumatic events such as 9/11 and hurricane Katrina, while the focus is often on the immediacy of the event, when one steps back to look at the big contextual picture, the stories told reveal many more layers about the person being interviewed. They carry trustworthiness through the experience of the trauma. In the case of oral history, life history, and biography the story is told in a given historical context. It is from this context that a sense of empowerment evolves. For example, let us review this example from an oral history of the firefighters on the scene at ground Zero on September 11, 2001.

Retrieved from: Oral histories from September 11 compiled by NY Firefighters

From John Amato Interview Date: January 2, 2002

A. . . . At that point we were walking towards the building. We still didn't know it was a total collapse. As we get closer and closer, we notice that the smoke is clearing. We don't see the south tower. Now we're starting to talk to each other and started to actually worry what's in for us next. As we approached Chambers Street, kept walking, still no one had told us about the total collapse. We get down to about Barclay and Vesey Street, which is a block away from the overpass, the bridge overpass that goes across the West Side Highway. All you hear is a rumbling in the street. It sounded like an earthquake. When I was a younger kid, I was in an earthquake and it felt like the same exact feeling. I looked, and I could see the antenna on the top of the roof coming straight down. We all turned and just threw our rollups down and started running as fast as we could. I took about five steps, I turned back to look behind me, and the debris was on my heels. Guys were just scrambling through the streets. Finally the debris overcame us, and you couldn't see anymore. It was like pitch-black, total darkness. I kind of ran into a building. I hit the building. One of the gentlemen working in the building I think I see was an engineer pulled me over towards the entrance. I went into the entrance. You couldn't see. It was dark as night. Finally a few minutes went by, about four or five minutes went by, it started clearing, and we started looking for members of Engine 68 as well as all the other engines that had driven down with us. We found everyone. We were told to stay at Chambers Street until further notice. That's about it. We stayed at Chambers Street. They didn't give us permission to go back in there, since we had already been involved with the collapse.

Q. So you stayed there for some period of time at Chambers, the staging area?
A. The staging area, yeah.
Q. And then from there you left? You took your rig back to 68 at some point?
A. Oh, yeah, I'd say about 11 p.m. that Night . . . Yeah, we stayed there the whole day.
Q. The whole day, and they never put you work?
A. No. . . . They just didn't want anyone involved with the immediate collapse back in there. That was their idea. Since we were on paper as one of the companies, they didn't want us to go.
Q. Is everybody from 68 okay?
A. Yeah.

Here, we are drawn immediately to John's response. The transparency, immediacy, believability, and thoroughness take us to the level of trustworthiness. While we all watched the news reports as this tragic and traumatic event unfolded, hearing the actual testimony of a firefighter brings us right to the heart of the experience at his personal level and at the macro level of the event.

A sense of history and a sense of context serve to illuminate the present situation with an eye to some past experience or set of experiences (Janesick, 2010). A sense of history requires us to face ourselves, to define who we are, and to write down our histories. This sense of history empowers the researcher with respect for other stories as well. The stories unlike our own enable us to see additional interpretations of the social world and our experience with it. This, along with the early points made in this section, brings us to trustworthiness.

3. Composition: Are the roles of the researcher and participant clearly described and all ethical considerations revealed?

Critics of qualitative research often assert that qualitative researchers need to be more explicit about the design used, the process used throughout the design, the rationale for selection of the participants, and the exact relationship of the researcher and the participant. I wholeheartedly agree. In fact, it would be helpful for all researchers to tell their stories about the process of any given research project. The more we can be clear, descriptive, and forthcoming about these matters, the better the state of the art. Of course, there are some situations that you simply cannot imagine. Let us take the instance of the federal government overseers who outright state that oral history is not for generalizing, and therefore not research. In this situation, the U. S. Office for Human Research Protection (OHRP), which is part of Health and Human Services (HHS), has determined that oral history interview projects do not involve the type of research defined by HHS regulations and are therefore excluded from IRB oversight. (See 45 CFR part 46 of the OHRP regulations.) Another good statement for a reviewer's understanding of the complexity of the issue on oral history as research is the statement on IRB's from the American Historical Association. (See www.historians.org/Perspectives/Issues/2004/0403/0403newl.cfm.) To summarize briefly, Federal regulations have a definition that includes generalizability. Since one's lived experience is unique and all individual stories are just that, oral history was not included as research. Several universities and professional historical societies debated over this and this is well documented in the literature and summaries are available on the websites of the Oral History Association and the American Historical Society. Some universities require IRB approval for oral histories; others elect not to go that route and both sides offer strong and credible arguments. Consequently, there is a great deal of elasticity here as far as interpretation of seeking IRB approval.

Institutions vary as to how they interpret this and professional organizations have also weighed in on this. In this chapter, I will not take a side bar here to talk about conflicting conceptions of research. That is available in many textbooks, journals, annual meetings of professional organizations proceedings, and so on. Also, the original IRB regulations were set up for medicine and that is a different type of research, though it is also ironically, case by case. The point for consideration here is to err on the side of safety and be sure that informed consent is given in any oral history project, life history, or biography. Oral history in particular is a fascinating case. The people interviewed are not anonymous. The power of documenting a story holds. Many legal scholars have written that oral history is like journalism and English, where you tell one person's story and that is that. In our multimedia age, there is a sense in journalism that anything goes. One has only to look at YouTube to see this played out. On the other hand, oral history as a field has always held to the requirement for permission for informed consent and for any photographs, videos, or documents used in a given reported story. The oral historian may be perplexed by the IRB regulations but they have always used consent forms. In any event, for oral history, life history, and biographical research, it is wise to take advantage of an expedited review for ethical and humane considerations. Furthermore, dissertations, typically the first step in research career, obviously should have IRB approval.

An additional ethical issue that emerges in the postmodern era is that of social justice and the research process. In viewing oral history as a social justice process one has the opportunity to look at the stories of individuals usually excluded from mainstream research. By documenting their stories, we get a fuller picture of social life and the practices of society. For example, Venkatesh (2008), in his study of gangs in Chicago, uses a combination of a life history of a gang leader and ethnography to document what it means to be a member of a gang through the lens of critical theory. He tried to get at what policies help some people and not others, among many other questions. By shadowing a gang leader, interviewing him, and in fact taking on the role of gang leader for a day, the researcher deconstructed hierarchies in this subsociety, its relationship to some public policy implementation, how gangs function in a neighborhood, and the personal leadership struggle of a gang leader reflecting values of the community itself. He also exposed the graft and corruption in the Chicago Housing Authority as part of the story. He describes and explains the many injustices that lead to social justice in an ironic way. In this example, life history and biography become vehicles for enriching the knowledge base of both qualitative research methods and social justice. Also from this example we learn testimony, a key component of life history, oral history, and biography, and it provides us with an avenue of thick description, analysis, and interpretation of people's lives through probing the past and present.

The postmodern appreciation of the study of people and their stories, those stories from persons generally on the outside or periphery of society, offer a unique opportunity to view oral history as a social justice project. For women, minorities, anyone who is categorized as "the other," or at least not a member of the mainstream, may benefit from actually recording their stories. As a social justice record is kept, the stories cannot be lost. As we trace someone's life journey, or a portion of it, to the present, qualitative researchers may find a way to analyze and interpret these stories to advance social justice. One of the useful prototypes of oral history is testimony.

Testimony is also used as a form of biography, oral history, and life history. Globally, testimony has been used to document the stories of victims and those perpetrators who committed crimes against them. Testimony of individuals allowed for the written record of a catalog of misdeeds, which then facilitated some part of social justice. To use a prime example, let us consider the case of South Africa and the Truth and Reconciliation Commission (TRC). The TRC was a vehicle for capturing the witnesses' stories of the events occurring in South Africa under the earlier system of apartheid. Testimony allowed all of us to more fully understand the political, cultural, emotional, and psychological aspects of apartheid as never before. Since Africa retains storytelling as part of its culture, the brave individuals who took part in the TRC testimony gave straightforward descriptions, often emotional and jarring, of what had occurred. This was the first step toward forgiveness, and reconciliation. In fact, Desmond Tutu (1999) has argued that one cannot arrive at forgiveness without truth as a starting point. Tutu and other writers often catalog four types of truth:

1. *Factual and forensic truth*, that is, the actual evidence of what occurred.
2. *Personal or narrative truth*, that is, the person's story and narrative of how something occurred.
3. *Social or cultural truth*, which is basically the social context and history of what occurred.
4. *Healing or restorative truth*, that is, what is needed to heal the wounds of the three previously listed types of truth.

Thus, disciplines that are practice based, including education, nursing, business, medical studies, and social work, for example, stand to benefit immensely. By conducting oral histories, life histories, and biographies with key members of groups typically outside the mainstream, we have a perfect way to document society's injustice, cruelty, and thoughtlessness. Oral history, life history, and biography provide critical techniques in the qualitative toolbox for those researchers with the strength to tackle race, class, and gender inequities. In addition, testimony in any format furthers our knowledge of the lived experience of any number of individuals on the edges of society. These four approaches to documentation can only assist us in a more rigorous practice.

4. Harmony: Are the conclusions and interpretations based on the data presented for study and is the narrative coherent, nuanced, and layered? Are the voices of marginalized individuals included?

Any research report needs to convince the reader of its meaning both in the details that shape that story told and in the overall implications of the particular work in relation to the big picture. In this type of work, as in the arts, context is everything. So life history, oral history, and biographical researchers need to be good writers and persuaders. By laying out the details of the story, the thick description to set the scene and the details of the words of the participants, we have the beginning of the documentation of lived experience. But what do we do with these details? Here we come to the crux of writing up oral history, life history, and biography. Today, in this postmodern moment as researchers, we have many media available and many approaches to create new ways of representing the data. By postmodern I refer to research that examines race, class, gender, and power. Here I will discuss two of these major approaches, found data poems or any type of poetry, and performance research. Performance research may include digital video stories, drama, poetry, and photography.

Found data poems are literally poems created from the actual words in the transcripts, documents under review, and any other written data collection method such as the researcher's reflective journal. Yes it is possible to find and create poetry despite any objections to the contrary. I am always amazed by the fact that students say to me, "I can't write poetry." It is more amazing to see their own surprise and delight in finding poems in the actual data. To illustrate, see this found poem I created from the statement of purpose of the journal, *The Qualitative Report*, which recently celebrated twenty years-plus online. The reader may go to the site to find that statement at www.nova.edu/ssss/QR/index.html.

WE Are the Qualitative Report
By Valerie J. Janesick
We are peer reviewed with
Passionate ideas and critical collaboration
Debates, and topics, and research possibilities
The hallmark is assisting.
Not rejection rates but
Manuscript as centerpiece in the development process.
Assigned a team to weave collective comments
We grow as authors and mentors
We are a learning community
We give back, we trust, we are.

So here we have the example of a poem created from the actual text data. Another type of poem, a haiku (Japanese poetry), followed from this regarding the meaning of the celebratory anniversary of the journal also written by me.

Meaning comes with solitude
Like the egret on the water
Silence again.

All in all, poetry is a tried and true method to be considered for data representation. Another popular and current way to represent data is to perform research through poetry, drama, video, or photography. Since we live in a digitally saturated environment, students are often digital natives and actually prefer digital formats and they think digitally. It only makes sense to make use of this strength in the representation of qualitative research data. Oral history, life history, and biography in particular already have a large collection of video archives at major university oral history centers, online, and of course on YouTube. In a recent search on Google with the terms oral history, life history, and biography, nearly two million videos popped up in the search. Here one can find straightforward interviews on video with graphics overlaid for extracting meaning, photo montages overlaid with a narrator, or several other performance examples to get one thinking about new ways of representing lived experience.

Many qualitative researchers use photography on a regular basis. In these three idioms, photography is a serious and often needed piece of the data. For example, on YouTube there is a Second World War veteran who is 94 years old and as he speaks about his memories of certain moments in that war, the viewer of the oral history can see actual news clips, photos, and documents from the era. He has a multipart oral history and the effect is powerful. One comes away with a new appreciation of his lived experience. That is, the harmony component of any research of this nature. Here we describe and explain the lived experience but we think about new and powerful techniques to represent the data. By using the digital tools available to all we now can create a space and keep it forever on a public forum site, YouTube.

I invite the reader of this chapter to jump into viewing selected examples of visual narratives, written narratives, poetic narratives, and performance narratives. In some cases, this is referred to as arts-based research. A good beginning to understand performance research and arts-based research is the work of Denzin (1997) and Barone and Eisner (2012). These are powerful books, which cover theory, practice, examples, and controversies. These writers look for the nuance and the layers of meaning as reviewers, artists, and writers often do. The media themselves used in performance and arts-based research act as part of the research process. What is also striking about new approaches to data presentation is the obvious visual space for all voices to be included; thus a social justice theme is ever present.

Further Reading

Web Resources that Help Illuminate Approaches through Digital Media

1. Oral History Association, OHA

www.dickinson.edu/organizations/oha
The Oral History Association, established in 1966, seeks to bring together all persons interested in oral history as a way of collecting human memories. With an international membership, the OHA serves a broad and diverse audience. Local historians, librarians and archivists, students, journalists, teachers, and academic scholars from many fields have found that the OHA provides both professional guidance and collegial environment for sharing information. The OHA encourages standards of excellence in the collection, preservation, dissemination, and uses of oral testimony. The OHA has established a set of goals, guidelines, and evaluation standards for oral history interviews. The association also recognizes outstanding achievement in oral history through an awards program. This site is packed with information and resources.

2. H-Oralhist

www.h-net.org/~oralhist
H-Oralhist is a member of the H-Net, Humanities & Social Sciences On-Line initiative. H-Oralhist is a network for scholars and professionals active in studies related to oral history. It is affiliated with the OHA. It is a wealth of information. It contains updated lists of the many thousands of individual oral histories on file in hard text, tape, video, multimedia, and the centers where they reside.

3. HistoricalVoices.org

www.historicalvoices.org

The purpose of Historical Voices is to create a significant, fully searchable online database of spoken word collections spanning the twentieth century—the first large-scale repository of its kind. Historical Voices will both provide storage for these digital holdings and display public galleries that cover a variety of interests and topics. Check out this site if you wish to store your digital tales.

4. American Historical Association

www.historians.org

The American Historical Association (AHA) is a nonprofit membership organization founded in 1884 and incorporated by Congress in 1889 for the promotion of historical studies, the collection and preservation of historical documents and artifacts, and the dissemination of historical research. As the largest historical society in the United States, the AHA provides leadership and advocacy for the profession, fights to ensure academic freedom, monitors professional standards, spearheads essential research in the field, and provides resources and services to help its members succeed. The AHA serves more than 14,000 history professionals, representing every historical period and geographical area. AHA members include K–12 teachers, academics at two- and four-year colleges and universities, graduate students, historians in museums, historical organizations, libraries and archives, government and business, as well as independent historians.

5. Digitales

www.digitales.us/

This site introduces the viewer to digital storytelling in multiple formats and catalogs many such stories. By inclusion of voices there is a social justice component to many of the life histories, oral histories, and biographies.

6. Center for Digital Storytelling

www.storycenter.org

This center is dedicated to the art of personal storytelling. The center offers workshops, programs, ad services, all focused on capturing personal voice and facilitating teaching methods. Their motto is: listen deeply, tell stories.

7. Stories for Change

www.storiesforchange.net

This site is an online meeting place for community digital storytelling and advocates for social change. It is a wealth of information and offers many models and exemplary storytelling. They offer resources and a curriculum and to use this site you need to open an account to upload your digital stories.

8. Center for Studies in Oral Tradition

www.oraltradition.org

Founded in 1986 with the approval of the University of Missouri Board of Curators, the Center for Studies in Oral Tradition stands as a national and international focus for interdisciplinary research and scholarship on the world's oral traditions. Our long-term mission is to facilitate communication across disciplinary boundaries by creating linkages among specialists in different fields. Through our various activities we try to foster conversations and exchanges about oral tradition that would not otherwise take place. It has established a series of paper and web publications aimed at serving a broad academic constituency. They sponsor a number of events, offer bibliographic information, and resources for someone wanting to get started in oral history and life history work.

Key Books for Further Understanding

Literally, there are thousands of journal articles, books, YouTube videos on oral history, life history, and biography. I have selected these texts for their nuance, texture, and layers of understanding. Also, the authors have a lifetime of doing this type of research.

Denzin, N. (1989). *Interpretive Biography.* Thousand Oaks, CA: Sage.

This text is one of the best in terms of learning about biographical research. Denzin manages to lay out an argument for interpretive biography as a key technique of the postmodern era. He also describes and defines the assumptions involved in studying personal life documents, stories, memories, accounts, and narratives.

Ellis, C. & Flaherty, M. (Eds.) (1992). *Investigating Subjectivity: Research on lived experience.* Thousand Oaks, CA: Sage.

One of the major reasons to read this book is to understand the complexity and nuance of investigating subjectivity that is the work of all qualitative researchers. Specifically in the arenas of oral history, life history, and biography, we work in the area of subjectivities and welcome the emotionality, the authenticity, the diversity and the relevance of human lived experience as told in the form of a story.

Clandinin, D. J. & Connelly, M. (2000). *Narrative Inquiry: Experience and story in qualitative research.* San Francisco, CA: Jossey-Bass.

This book takes narrative work to a new level and is user friendly. It argues for thinking narratively and is a guide through the processes of life history work and all narrative approaches. Topics covered include composing research texts and persistent concerns such as ethics and anonymity.

Cole, A. L. & Knowles, J. G. (2001). *Lives in Context: The art of life history research.* New York: AltaMira Press.

The authors of this text are well known for a lifetime of defining the importance of arts-based approaches to research and narrative inquiry. They explore the method of writing life history research and deconstruct the relationships of researcher and researched. The inclusion of sections on imagery, ethics, care, respect, and capturing lived experience make this a must-read book for all potential life history, oral history, or biographical researchers.

Janesick, V. J. (2010). *Oral History for the Qualitative Researcher: Choreographing the story.* New York: Guilford Press.

This book describes and explains the multiple approaches and uses of oral history as a qualitative technique and uses the metaphor of choreography to discuss the practice, foundations, and ethical issues involved in doing oral history. Many case examples are used to illustrate the strategies for collecting data, representing, analyzing, and interpreting oral history data. Using artistic approaches to representation of data, the author uses found data poetry, photography, and video to capture lived experience.

Hess-Biber, S. N. & Leavy, P. (Eds.) (2008). *Handbook of Emergent Method.* New York: Guilford Press.

This extensive handbook is a crucial resource for those looking to push the methodological boundaries of the tired postpositivist approaches used in the past century to little effect. The authors have constructed a solid group of scholars dealing with emergent methods since the world is changing at warp speed due to but not limited to the internet, globalization, social networks, and other societal facts of life. Individual scholars here describe ways to push beyond the previous century and argue for getting to the heart of lived experience. Performance-based research, found data poetry, photography, metaphor analysis, internet inquiry, and much more are part of this provocative and rigorous work. For oral historians, life historians, and biographers as well as other qualitative researchers, the authors provide a vocabulary for change and an alternative to sleepy approaches of the past.

Counterpoint Perspectives

The best I can do on counter perspectives is to say that I am sure a traditionalist positivist looking at oral history, life history, and biography might use other criteria. It may be enough just to get the story, which is how oral history began. If you go to your nearest public library, chances are high that there are many tapes filed away with stories from community members. In fact, you may find neopositivists and others who say oral history, life history, and biography are not research at all because they are not generalizable. Here they miss the meaning of individual carefully crafted cases. The value of all these one-of-a-kind stories is just that: they are one of a kind. They teach us through their unique elements something about humanity in a particular period of time. Likewise, another theorist from any frame would be guided by that favored framework. Here I have been clear about my critical pedagogy and how I approach oral history, life history, and biography. The reader is always invited to offer other opinions.

Author's Reflections on Quality

Obviously, these touchstones grow out of my lifetime as a scholar and that work is influenced by my life in the arts and the study of critical pedagogy. In the past as a dancer and choreographer and now a student of yoga and meditation, I see my work as part of contributing to social justice through documenting oral histories. Since storytelling is the essences of oral history, life history, and biography, the topic of this chapter, there is a remarkable fit between storytelling as dance and storytelling as a written text in the form of a journal article or book. In dance, the dancer/choreographer works to get to the heart of what needs to be stated in movement. In narrative research approaches, especially the three outlined in this chapter, the researcher works to get to the heart of what needs to be stated in terms of the story told. This is a basic principle of choreography as well.

Similarly, the work of Paulo Freire and others led me early in my academic career to an understanding of the pedagogy of the oppressed. Freire's ideas are similar to those of many an artist, so a marriage was born here for me between the artistic and the socially relevant use of education and research for achieving a social justice action and/or discussion at the very least. Qualitative work in particular by documenting the stories of lived experience from all walks of society has a crack at getting to some part of social justice. While there will always be debates about the purposes of research, many qualitative researchers see our research as contributing to social justice for changing the inequities of the status quo. I throw my hat in with this group. We have many opinion pieces, questionnaires, and surveys in educational research over the past eighty-five years or so in the field of educational research. That provides one side of the coin so to speak. The other side of the coin is the research that documents a person's lived experience. Here oral history, life history, and biography bring the human side of the research act to the forefront. We can learn a great deal about society through these approaches to research and say with ease that we see research as a tool for making the schools and society better places. I am a critical pedagogy practitioner, a feminist, an artist, and a postmodern thinker. So for me quality boils down to the emotional, psychological, and visual representation of the story told. Does it capture the lived experience to the extent that I feel I am walking in those shoes? Does the story capture the whole picture, warts and all? I notice that recently in the field of qualitative research, researchers are shy of presenting warts so to speak. They are fearful of telling the whole story. That which does not seem to fit and the ruptures are often as important as the smooth set of words and pictures. Derrida (1972) pointed out that when we try to capture a person's life story in any form we always filter through language and signs, hidden meanings, and thus we are always unstable as all languages are in flux. Here I consider the digital and the poetic as languages. I do not think this should deter anyone from trying to capture the lived experience of our participants. The qualitative methods used in oral history, life history, and biography are time tested and rigorous. These methods include interviews, documents, the research reflective journal, and observation. They reveal all the concerns of the postmodern researcher such as race, class, and gender issues. They force us to see other ways of knowing. Basically we are researching subjectivity and we are proud of that. We welcome documenting the rigor in the process and we embrace the ambiguities and contradictions in anyone's story. We as researchers then tell the entire story as best we can with our tools, our processes, our minds, and our artistry. Oral history, life history, and biography offer solid vehicles to knowledge and understanding. By their design we are all richer.

References

Barone, T. & Eisner, E. (2012). *Arts Based Research.* Los Angeles, CA: Sage.

Clandinin, D. J. & Connelly, M. (2000). *Narrative Inquiry: Experience and story in qualitative research.* San Francisco, CA: Jossey-Bass.

Cole, A. L. & Knowles, J. G. (2001). *Lives in Context: The art of life history research.* New York: AltaMira Press.

Derrida, J. (1972). Structure, sign and play in the discourse of the human sciences. In R. Macksey & E. Donato (Eds.), *The Structuralist Controversy* (pp. 247–265). Bloomington IN: Indiana University Press.

Denzin, N. (1989). *Interpretive Biography.* Thousand Oaks, CA: Sage.

Denzin, N. (1997). *Interpretive Ethnography.* Thousand Oaks, CA: Sage.

Ellis, C. & Flaherty, M. (Eds.). (1992). *Investigating Subjectivity: Research on lived experience.* Thousand Oaks, CA: Sage.

Frisch, M. (2008). Three dimensions and more: Oral history beyond the paradoxes. In S. N. Hesse-Biber & P. Leavy (Eds.), *Handbook of Emergent Methods* (pp. 221–238). New York: Guilford Press.

Hesse-Biber, S. N. & Leavy, P. (2007). *Feminist Research Practice: A primer.* Thousand Oaks, CA: Sage.

Hess-Biber, S. N. & Leavy, P. (Eds.). (2008). *Handbook of Emergent Methods.* New York: Guilford Press.

Janesick, V. J. (2004). *Stretching Exercises for Qualitative Researchers (2nd ed.).* Thousand Oaks, CA: Sage.

Janesick, V. J. (2007). Oral history as a social justice project: Issues for the qualitative researcher. *The Qualitative Report, Vol. 12*, 1. Retrievable at: www.nova.edu/ssss/QR/QR12-1/janesick.pdf.

Janesick, V. J. (2010). *Oral History for the Qualitative Researcher: Choreographing the story.* Thousand Oaks, CA: Sage.

Janesick, V. J. (2011). *Stretching Exercises for Qualitative Researchers (3rd ed.).* Thousand Oaks, CA: Sage.

Rubin, H. J. & Rubin, I. S. (2005). *Qualitative Interviewing: The art of hearing data (2nd ed.).* Thousand Oaks, CA: Sage.

Sachs, O. (1995). *An Anthropologist on Mars.* New York: Alfred A. Knopf.

Shiff, S. (2010). *Cleopatra: A life.* New York: Little, Brown, and Company.

Tutu, D. (1999). *No Future Without Forgiveness.* New York: Image Books.

Venkatesh, S. (2008). *Gang Leader for a Day: A rogue sociologist takes to the streets.* New York: Penguin Books.

Yow, V. (1994). *Recording Oral History: A practical guide for social scientists.* Thousand Oaks, CA: Sage.

12
Narrative Inquiry

D. Jean Clandinin and Vera Caine

> People shape their daily lives by stories of who they and others are and as they interpret their past in terms of these stories. Story, in the current idiom, is a portal through which a person enters the world and by which their experience of the world is interpreted and made personally meaningful. Narrative inquiry, the study of experience as story, then, is first and foremost a way of thinking about experience.
>
> (Connelly & Clandinin, 2006, p. 375)

Narrative inquiry is, first and foremost, a way of understanding experience. It is also a research methodology. It is, then, both a view of the phenomena of people's experiences and a methodology for narratively inquiring into experience (Clandinin & Connelly, 2000). As such it allows for the intimate and in-depth study of individuals' experiences over time and in context. The introduction of narrative inquiry as a research methodology has reshaped the field of qualitative research through its close attention to experience as narrative phenomena; through the importance of the relational engagement of researchers and participants; and through the attention to relational ethics which are at the heart of the inquiry.

Narrative inquiry is a way to study experience. In studying and understanding experience narratively, researchers recognize the centrality of relationships among participants and researchers studied through, and over, time and in unique places and multilayered contexts. Amidst these relationships, participants tell and live through stories that speak of, and to, their experiences of living. The process of narrative inquiry is composed of engaging with participants in the field, creating field texts and writing both interim and final research texts (Clandinin & Connelly, 2000). Throughout this process ethical considerations require that researchers remain attentive to ethical tensions, obligations and responsibilities in their relationships with participants.

Select Terms

Field texts refer to the records, including, for example, field notes, transcripts of conversations, and artifacts such as photographs and journal that are composed or co-composed by researchers and participants. We use the term field texts rather than data to signal that these texts are experiential, intersubjective texts rather than objective texts. Field texts are co-compositions reflective of the experiences of researchers and participants and need to be understood as telling and showing those aspects of experience that the relationship allows (Caine, 2002).

Research texts can be either interim or final texts. Field texts are embedded within research relationships and reflect multiple nested stories (Murphy, 2004). Field texts are shaped into interim research texts, which are shared and negotiated with participants prior to being composed into final research texts. Final research texts are written with public audiences in mind.

Three-dimensional narrative inquiry space: Field texts are composed with attention to the three-dimensional narrative inquiry space (Clandinin & Connelly, 2000). *Temporality* comes into play in two ways: the first is that field texts are composed over multiple interactions with participants, and the second is that field texts are co-composed through participants' and researchers' reflections on, and of, earlier life experiences. *Sociality* directs attention inward toward the participants' and researchers' thoughts, emotions, and moral responses and outward to events and actions. *Place* directs attention to places where lives were lived as well as to the places where inquiry events occur.

Relationships are central to understanding the work of narrative inquirers. Not only is the relational space between researchers and participants integral to understanding the composition or co-composition of field texts and research texts, but relationships also are a central way of making sense of the temporal and contextual aspects of narrative inquiry.

Negotiation refers to the ongoing relational work of narrative inquirers with participants as they live together in the field, co-compose field texts, and co-compose interim and final research texts. Negotiation involves a continuous dialogue, in which both participants and researchers are equally engaged and that is reflected in the conversations, actions, and commitments to the ongoing relationship.

Conversation: While interviews are one way that field texts are composed with participants, conversation is a far more common method of co-composing field texts. Conversations create a space for the voices and stories of both participants and researchers to be heard and composed. In narrative inquiry, conversations are shaped by both the participants and researchers; they are not guided by predetermined questions, or happen with the intention to be therapeutic, resolve issues, or answer problems.

Response: The term response is frequently used in narrative inquiry to refer to the ways in which researchers and participants work in relational ways. Taken from the same root as responsibility, it signals the importance of making spaces for telling and listening to stories as well as to the responsibility researchers and participants have to sustaining each other (Lopez, 1991; Schultz, 1997). A response is guided by relational ethics and an ethics of everyday life (Charon & Montello, 2002). Response also refers to the community in which each researcher is embedded; it is the response community, which supports each researcher throughout the inquiry.

Ethics: A relational ethical stance is founded in an ethics of care (Noddings, 1984) and is the starting point and stance that narrative inquirers take throughout a narrative inquiry. A commitment to relationships and reciprocal respect (Bruno, 2010) are key elements; to live in collaborative ways in which we can co-compose and negotiate stories. The ethics of care also calls forth social responsibilities, with an attention to equities and social justice.

Personal, practical, and social justifications: Narrative inquirers need to justify their inquiries in personal, practical, and social ways. Throughout the inquiry, researchers continuously revisit these justifications and engage in negotiations with participants to clarify, substantiate, or shift justifications.

Diversities in Perspective, Context, and Form

Since the late 1980s and early 1990s, social science researchers have taken a narrative turn to understanding experience (Pinnegar & Daynes, 2007). While there is a history of narrative work within the traditions of narratology (the theory and study of narrative) and narrative research, researchers (Connelly & Clandinin, 1990) began to specifically develop a research methodology called narrative inquiry. Narrative inquiry and narrative research, terms used almost interchangeably in the current research literature, signify a research methodology. As there were important and subtle distinctions being highlighted in the early years of the development of the methodology, what became apparent was how interwoven narrative ways of thinking about phenomena are with narrative inquiry as research methodology. It was "the interweaving of narrative views of phenomena and narrative inquiry that marks the emerging field and that draws attention to the need for careful uses and distinctions of terms" (Clandinin & Rosiek, 2007, p. 36). This careful attention to terms has led to considerable debate within the emerging methodology. For example, within the broad field of qualitative research, there are many analytic methods or forms of narrative analysis (Polkinghorne, 1988; Josselson & Lieblich, 1995; Josselson, Lieblich, & McAdams, 2003; Reissman, 2008). Some forms of narrative analysis are used as methods within other qualitative research methodologies, such as thematic analysis, linguistic analysis, structural analysis, and more recently visual analysis (Riessman, 2008). Stories or narratives are also used as data in other qualitative methodologies such as phenomenology and case study. Narrative or story forms of representation are also used as ways of representing results or findings in various qualitative and quantitative methodologies and are increasingly seen as a way for knowledge translation in health science and other professional disciplines. Narrative inquiry, as its own methodology, has developed important terms and distinctions that have become more apparent and well recognized as guiding what counts, or what fits, within the field of narrative research. While there is no one way of engaging in narrative inquiry, there is now a fairly well-established view of narrative inquiry as both methodology and phenomenon (Clandinin, 2007).

Dewey's theory of experience (1938) is most often cited as the philosophical underpinning of narrative inquiry (Clandinin & Connelly, 2000). Dewey's two criteria of experience, interaction and continuity enacted in situations, provide the grounding for attending to a narrative conception of experience through the three-dimensional narrative inquiry space with dimensions of temporality, place, and sociality. Bruner's (1986) ideas (psychology) about paradigmatic and narrative knowing, Carr's (1986) ideas (philosophy) about the narrative structure and coherence of lives, Bateson's (1989, 1994) ideas (anthropology) about continuity and improvisation as a response to the uncertainties in life contexts, and Coles' (1989) ideas (medicine) about narrative in life and teaching practice also add to the philosophical bases for narrative inquiry. As Clandinin and Rosiek (2007) point out:

> Framed within this view of experience, the focus of narrative inquiry is not only on individuals' experience but also on the social, cultural, and institutional narratives within which individuals' experiences are constituted, shaped, expressed, and enacted. Narrative inquirers study the individual's experience in the world, an experience that is storied both in the living and telling and that can be studied by listening, observing, living alongside another, and writing, and interpreting texts.
>
> (pp. 42–43)

Within this ontological and epistemological stance, narrative inquiry is a way of understanding and inquiring into experience. Within this stance we also situate narrative inquiry in relationships and in community, attending to notions of expertise and knowing in relational and participatory ways.

Qualitative Touchstones

We outline twelve qualitative touchstones for narrative inquiry. The meaning of touchstone, and how we used it in our chapter, has been an educative process. While one meaning directs our attention to a touchstone as a quality or example that is used to test the excellence or genuineness of others, we were also drawn to a touchstone as a hard black stone, such as jasper or basalt, which was used to test the quality of gold or silver by comparing the streak left on the stone by one of these metals with that of a standard alloy. We wondered if we metaphorically touched or scratched a narrative inquiry, what kinds of streaks or marks would be left. In what follows we lay out the kinds of streaks or marks that might be become visible as we used our touchstones to mark narrative inquiry.

1. Relational responsibilities

> We have to pay the closest attention to what we say. What patients say tells us what to think about what hurts them; and what we say tells us what is happening to us—what we are thinking, and what may be wrong with us. [. . .] Their story, yours, mine—it's what we all carry with us on this trip we take, and we owe it to each other to respect our stories and learn from them.
>
> (Coles, 1989, p. 30)

In narrative inquiry we are attentive to what it means to live as researchers in relationships, to live in collaborative ways in which we can co-compose and negotiate the living, reliving, telling, and retelling of stories. It is important to understand narrative inquiry spaces as spaces of belonging for both researchers and participants; spaces that are always marked by ethics and attitudes of openness, mutual vulnerability, reciprocity, and care.

Ethical matters pervade narrative inquiry and are marked by a relational ethics, an ethics of care (Noddings, 1984; Bergum, 1999). Relational ethics are marked by responsiveness, as well as marked by short- and long-term responsibilities (Huber, Clandinin, & Huber, 2006). As we attend to our relational responsibilities, we attend to issues of equity and social justice, which inform the significance of our work. While narrative inquiry opens up a relational knowing and understanding of experience, each relationship between researcher and participant opens up a relational world. This relational world allows us to attend to the lives in relation, that is, the lives of participants and researchers, within the three-dimensional inquiry space (Clandinin & Connelly, 2000). The three-dimensional narrative inquiry spaces are reflective of a continuous process of interplay and engagement between researchers and participants as they live in the field, compose and co-compose field texts, and as they engage in the inquiry into the field texts that moves them towards co-composing research texts. While questions of ownership of stories often surface in the writings of interim and final research texts, Clandinin and Connelly remind us that we might better think of this as relational responsibilities. Indeed, narrative approaches recognize that in the act of hearing and retelling, ethical responsibilities are paramount (Charon & Montello, 2002). These ethical responsibilities are, in many ways, the ethics of everyday life (Charon & Montello, 2002); they guide all interactions with participants, including the negotiations of relationships with participants. Ethical understandings in narrative inquiry are marked by living in relational spaces that bring forth researchers' and participants' lived ethical understandings, complexities, and tensions. Living and being in a relational space brings forth responsibilities where issues of attentiveness, presence, and response matter (Lugones, 1987; Bateson, 1994). It is marked by a process of self-reflection, contemplation, openness, and uncertainty (Bergum, 1999).

2. In the midst

Narrative inquirers always enter into research relationships in the midst. We mean this in several ways: in the midst of researchers' own ongoing lives, both personal and professional; in the midst of researchers' lives enacted within particular institutional narratives such as funded projects, graduate student research, and personally compelling studies; in the midst of institutional narratives such as university or other organisational narratives; in the midst of social, political, linguistic, and cultural narratives. Our participants are always in the midst of their lives and their lives are shaped by attending to past, present, and unfolding social, cultural, institutional, linguistic, and familial narratives (as an example, see Clandinin et al., 2006).

As we design narrative inquiries, we need to imaginatively place ourselves amidst possible lives of potential participants. In so doing, we are attentive to the imagined temporality, sociality, and places of participants' lives. With our lives as researchers we need to engage in intensive autobiographical narrative inquiries (Chung, 2008; Cardinal, 2010; Clandinin, 2010), inquiring into a range of field texts (such as photographs, journals, or memory box artifacts) that allow us to understand who we are and are becoming in relation to potential participants and particular phenomenon. Autobiographical narrative inquiry allows us to compose our research puzzles as we begin the processes of justifying our inquiries personally, practically, and socially. Sometimes the entire inquiry is an autobiographical narrative inquiry. However, in studies involving participants other than the researcher alone, autobiographical narrative inquiry is only the first part of the inquiry. As participants' and researchers' lives meet in the midst of each of our unfolding complex and multiple experiences, we begin to shape time, places, and spaces where we come together and negotiate ways of being together and ways of giving an account of our work together.

Understanding that we are meeting in the midst has implications for imagining and living out a narrative inquiry. There are implications for how we think of negotiating entry, how we negotiate the relational living alongside or the spaces of story telling, as well as implications for negotiating research texts, and eventually negotiating exit. Of course, exit, for narrative inquirers, is never a final exit as we continue to carry long-term relational responsibilities for our participants, for ourselves, and for the work we have done together (Huber, Clandinin, & Huber, 2006).

3. Negotiation of relationships

Entering the field begins with negotiation of relationships, and the research puzzles to be explored. Negotiations of purpose, transitions, intentions, and texts are ongoing processes throughout the inquiry. Narrative inquirers also negotiate ways they can be helpful to participant(s) both in, and following, the research. In the moments of negotiating ways to be helpful narrative inquirers often call on, and are called, to live out professional responsibilities and to express personal practical knowledge (Connelly & Clandinin, 1988) and social positioning. While our intent is to enter the relationships with participants as researchers, participants come to know and see us as people in relation with them; a reminder that we always carry ethical responsibilities. As we are guided by relational ethics and always remain aware of our short- and long-term responsibilities, we try hard to negotiate ways in which we can be helpful; we do not turn away from participants' needs and wishes. This, too, means that we spend sustained time with participants, their families, and/or communities.

Thinking within the three-dimensional narrative inquiry space throughout the narrative inquiry means that we share Andrews' (2007) wonder: "[h]ow is our own sense of identity affected by opening ourselves to the very different realities that are encountered by others?" (p. 489). This wonder opens the sense, as we live within the three-dimensional narrative inquiry space with our participants throughout the inquiry, of the importance of acknowledging that neither researchers nor participants walk away from the inquiry unchanged. Even though our lives meet in the midst as we begin the inquiry together and even though we leave in the midst as final research texts are composed, we realize that the relational space of telling and retelling stories has shifted who we are as we continue to relive and retell our stories long after the inquiry in the field ended. As researchers attend to how we have changed throughout the inquiry we are often drawn back to considerations of the practical and social justifications of the inquiry. Listening deeply and inquiring into our changed lived and told stories calls forth the possibility to attend differently, to shift practices, and to create possible social–political or theoretical places we can impact as narrative inquirers.

4. Narrative beginnings

As noted in the personal justification that is initiated at the outset of the study is the process of autobiographical narrative inquiries (Clandinin, 2006; Chung, 2008; Cardinal, 2010). Our research begins with inquiring into researchers' own stories of experience. Because narrative inquiry is an ongoing reflexive and reflective methodology, narrative inquirers need to continually inquire into their experiences before, during, and after each inquiry.

In writing and inquiring into our narrative beginnings as researchers, we attend through the three-dimensional narrative inquiry space to our own experiences. This may mean that we reach as far back as our childhoods to understand, and, at times, to name our research puzzle; it also means that we attend to the places in which our stories have unfolded; and we make evident the social and political contexts that shaped our understandings. While our narrative beginnings are an important part of our research puzzle, they do not necessarily become, in their entirety, part of the final, public research texts; we share those parts that help audiences better understand our research puzzles and findings of our research.

5. Negotiating entry to the field

What we mean by field is perhaps different from what is seen as the field in other qualitative or arts-based research methodologies. As noted, in narrative inquiry, we negotiate with participants an ongoing relational inquiry space. This relational space is what we most commonly call the field. There are two starting points for narrative inquiry: listening to individuals tell their stories and living alongside participants as they live and tell their stories (Connelly & Clandinin, 2006). The most frequently used starting point is with telling stories and the methods most commonly used are conversations, or interviews as conversations. Some narrative inquirers also use artifacts (Taylor, 2007) to trigger the telling of stories. In the second starting point, narrative inquirers begin with living alongside participants. In beginning with living alongside participants, researchers may be embedded within a community that participants belong to prior to the inquiry, or they may use visual media (Caine, 2007; Caine & Lavoie, 2011), policy or practice documents, and/or participant observation. For narrative inquirers who begin with living stories, telling stories using methods such as conversations, oral histories, and interviews also play a part (Clandinin & Connelly, 2000). However, when we situate our inquiries primarily in the living of stories, we often go wherever participants take us; we meet their families, lovers, past family members, friends, and/or colleagues. It is in the moments of living alongside our participants that we begin to enter places that are important to our participants and, in this way, we, too, enter the social milieu of which they are a part. The places and relationships we become part of when we begin with living alongside participants call forth the stories we tell. On the other hand, when we situate our inquiries first in the telling of stories, we, too, can be drawn into participants' places, and participants' other relationships. Whether the beginning point is living or telling stories, inquirers need to attend to the ways individual narratives of experience are embedded in social, cultural, familial, linguistic, and institutional narratives. Each inquiry reflects the ambiguities, complexities, difficulties, and uncertainties encountered by the inquirer as she/he lives in the field and writes field texts and interim and final research texts.

6. Moving from field to field texts

As we co-compose the relational three-dimensional narrative inquiry space with participants, narrative inquirers begin to compose or co-compose field texts. Field texts, commonly called data, are composed from conversations, interviews, participant observations, as well as artifacts. Artifacts that may become part of the field texts include artwork, photographs, memory box items, documents, plans, policies, annals, and chronologies. Sometimes, however, artifacts serve only as triggers for telling stories and are not, themselves, part of the field texts. As we negotiate relational spaces with participants, including places and times to meet, and events to become part of, we also negotiate a diversity of field texts. Some participants may write, collect, or develop their own field texts and these may include journals, poetry, fictional stories, or the collection of artifacts. It is important as researchers to stay awake to the multiple ways to tell and live experiences. Each form of field text, and each negotiation of the same, tells us about how others make sense or meaning from experience, and might also point us to possibilities of diverse final research texts, that is, the representations of retold stories.

7. Moving from field texts to interim and final research texts

Moving from field texts to interim and final research texts is a complicated and iterative process, full of twists and turns. In many quantitative and qualitative research methodologies, when data are collected, there is a process of member checking for accuracy of the data and a linear unfolding of data gathering to publishing research findings. This is not how narrative inquirers move from field texts to interim and final research texts.

Narrative inquirers continue to live in relational ways with participants throughout the process of making their findings public. This means that field, interim, and final research texts are negotiated with participants, as well as with those who have become part of the research journey. As part of interim research texts, researchers, or researchers and participants, may write narrative accounts of the experience as it relates to the initial research puzzle. The interim research texts, such as narrative accounts, are ways to make sense of multiple and diverse field texts. Often interim research texts call forth the telling and living of additional field texts, that is, they call forth further experiences to be told or lived. Interim research texts are a way to engage in a retelling and reliving of research relationships.

As part of the interim research texts, we continue to live within the three-dimensional narrative inquiry space. Field texts are read and reread, looked at and relooked at, and attention is paid simultaneously to temporality, sociality, and place. It is the attention to the three-dimensional narrative inquiry space that then moves deeper into the meaning of the experiences. While there are three dimensions in the inquiry space, these dimensions are often intertwined and knotted. In some ways the three dimensions form the fabric of life experience. The knots tie stories to place, people, and time, and one dimension cannot be understood without the others. It is in this way that our interim research texts point us to new field texts, and the wonders that remain as we make sense of our negotiated research puzzle.

While interim research texts are the beginning place of attending to our research puzzles, a place to begin to make meaning of our field texts, we eventually need to move to final research texts. Final research texts are often difficult to write, in part because researchers and participants now need to turn their attention to public audiences, audiences they may not know, and audiences who may be far removed from the lived and told experiences of participants. In the composing of final research texts, it is important to attend again to the personal, practical, and social justifications of the collaborative work. While final research texts include traditional academic publications, dissertations, thesis, and presentations, often participants, and our attention to practical and social implications, call us to also write final research texts for nonacademic audiences. When writing for nonacademic audiences, final research texts may include theater plays, art exhibits, websites, poetry, policy briefs, as well as other forms of public texts.

8. Representing narratives of experience in ways that show temporality, sociality, and place

While final research texts can be written in scholarly papers and presentations, or with attention to nonacademic audiences, they always need to reflect temporality, sociality, and place. It is important in each narrative inquiry to attend to the three dimensions of the narrative inquiry spaces in the unfolding and iterative research process. It is in the attending to these dimensions that insight into experiences relevant to the research puzzle can be brought forth in all of their complexity. There may be times where one dimension foregrounds the inquiry, but all dimensions are attended to.

It is often when we attend to all of the dimensions that we begin to see disruptions, fragmentations, or silences in participants' and our own lives. The inquiry space opens up a space to see the knots that live within each of our lives' fabrics, and how these are interwoven into the experiences under study. While our intention is not to engage in therapeutic processes or to heal, the process of narrative inquiry can be therapeutic, that is, it can draw attention to the difficult places, times, or contexts in which we all live.

By making all three dimensions of the inquiry space visible to public audiences, the complexity of storied lives also becomes visible. In this way, we avoid presenting smooth or cover stories (Clandinin & Connelly, 1995). Avoiding cover stories and layering the complexity of the inquiry also helps to draw readers into the stories, to lay their own experiences alongside the inquiry, to wonder alongside participants and researchers who were part of the inquiry. Final research texts are never meant to have final answers, as we did not come with questions; rather they are intended to engage audiences in rethinking, retelling, and inquiring into experiences in collaborative and ethical ways, to look at the ways in which they practice and the ways in which they relate to others.

9. Relational response communities

Narrative inquirers are always strongly encouraged to participate within a response community. Within a response community, the initial research puzzle, works in progress (interim research texts), and final research texts can be shared and discussed. Response communities are critical elements within the inquiry, as they help inquirers recognize how they shape both the experiences of their participants and their research puzzles. These communities often consist of people the researcher values and trusts to provide responsive and responsible dialogue about his/her unfolding inquiry. Response communities, marked by diversity, can enrich the research, particularly if they are composed of interdisciplinary, intergenerational, cross-cultural, academic, and nonacademic members. It is amidst response communities that narrative inquirers also continuously learn about methodological and theoretical development, learn about ethical and responsive ways to be in relationships, and learn to listen again and again. As others attend to us as researchers and as participants in our own inquiries, we also come to understand the complexities embedded with our own journeys as researchers. Response communities intentionally need to be set up to come together over time and on an ongoing and regular basis. Short-term obligations and long-term responsibilities need to be negotiated continuously within response communities in order to maintain trust, respect, and a sense of care.

Given the iterative nature of narrative inquiries, there is a continuous interplay among field texts, interim research texts, and final research texts. It is through a response community that narrative inquirers are often reminded to engage in this interplay and iterative process, to inquire into, and to revisit field texts, to address issues of personal, practical, and social significance, and to inquire into new research puzzles. Response communities, while providing insights and wonders, also sustain members, and celebrate achievements and relationships in ways that are supportive and responsive.

10. Justifications—personal, practical, and social

As we begin to imagine and design narrative inquiries, it is important to hold in mind the need narrative inquirers share with all social science researchers, that is, the need to be able to justify the research through responding to the questions of "so what?" and "who cares?" As narrative inquirers we need to be able to justify narrative inquiries in three ways: personally, practically, and socially. These justifications are imagined at the outset of the inquiry, revisited throughout the inquiry, and are addressed again as interim and final research texts are composed.

Personal justification. In order to personally justify a narrative inquiry as well as to position ourselves in relation to the phenomenon under study, narrative inquirers begin with what we call narrative beginnings. Beginning with an autobiographical narrative inquiry allows the researcher to study who they are and are becoming in relation to the phenomena, to consider who they see themselves as being in relation to participants, and to locate themselves in the research literature. The autobiographical narrative inquiries are the starting points for initially shaping and deepening the research puzzle. Our personal justification for this work also often fuels the passion and dedication to our work, and it is an important element in the long-term work each narrative inquiry calls forth. Throughout an inquiry our personal justifications might shift, calling us to relive and retell our autobiographical stories, and to inquire more deeply into the knowing called forth by our engagement with participants and in a response community.

Practical justification. Another kind of justification that is important to consider early in the design of the narrative inquiry that will begin to shape the response to the "so what" question is the practical justification. It is the practical justification that often brings us close to the experiences of others and the social contexts in which they are positioned. Here we often ask questions about teaching, care, or social practices. As part of the practical justification, narrative inquirers consider issues of social justice and equity. We wonder, alongside participants, how their and our experiences might be shaped differently in the future. As narrative inquirers we share borderland spaces with social scientists, who come from a constructivist or critical social science perspective, spaces that call forth a deeper understanding on how social contexts shape experiences. As we compose final research texts it is important for narrative inquirers to discuss the practical significance of their work. As Connelly and Clandinin (1990) point out:

> Seeing and describing story in the everyday actions of teachers, students, administrators, and others requires a subtle twist of mind on behalf of the inquirer. It is in the tellings and retellings that entanglements become acute, for it is here that temporal and social, cultural horizons are set and reset.
>
> (p. 4)

Theoretical justification. A third justification that is also necessary to consider at the outset of the study is the question of theoretical or social justification.

> We can think of social justification in two ways: theoretical justification as well as social action and policy justifications. Theoretical justification comes from justifying the work in terms of new methodological and disciplinary knowledge.
>
> (Clandinin & Huber, 2010, p. 436)

Given that narrative inquiry is a relatively new research methodology, it is important that each researcher considers the methodological contributions they make. These could be contributions to making visible epistemological and ontological understandings, the development of methods, as well as the explorations of the uses of narrative inquiry in fields outside of education, where narrative inquiry has been predominately utilized. While methodological contributions are at times harder to recognize by beginning researchers, it is important to recognize that questions or wonders unanswered for novice researchers can equally propel the further development of the methodology.

As pointed out by Clandinin and Huber (2010), it is social actions and policy justifications that form significant contributions to the theoretical justification of a narrative inquiry. Narrative inquirers add both to the public discourse, as well as to particular policies at any given time. While narrative inquirers do not generalize from the experiences of their participants, they add to policy development by pointing out the complexities, contradictions, and inconsistencies often inherent in policies and their implementation. One of the significant contributions is frequently to the ways in which others understand the lives of people, in the assumptions and values they place on lived experiences, and making visible the silences, disruptions, and complexities inherent in people's experiences.

11. Attentive to audience

Narrative inquirers have to balance issues of voice, signature, and audience. Within each inquiry, researchers attempt to represent the multiplicity of voices and signatures, which are reflected in the importance of diverse textual structures and accounts. Narrative inquiries are always filled with rich, temporally unfolding, narrative accounts as they represent the lived and told experiences of participants and researchers. Research texts can take multiple forms, including textual, visual, and audible forms.

In narrative inquiry it is imperative to address the questions of how larger social, institutional, and cultural narratives inform our understanding and shape the researchers' and participants' stories to live by (Connelly & Clandinin, 1999). Paying attention to these contextual narratives enables researchers to further deepen the complexity of the living and telling of stories.

During the composition of research texts, narrative inquirers are attentive to both participants and possible public audiences. Research texts are negotiated with participants, who remain the most influential voice in the move to final research texts. Research texts need to reflect the narrative quality of the experiences of both participants and researcher, and the ways these stories of experiences are embedded within social, cultural, familial, linguistic, and institutional narratives.

While research texts are negotiated between researcher and participants, researchers also owe responsibility to the scholarly community and must compose research texts that answer the questions of "so what?" or "who cares?" These questions speak to the social and theoretical significance of each narrative inquiry. Ultimately, research texts develop out of repeated asking of questions concerning the significance of the research. Research texts also attend to the personal and practical significance of the research, paying attention to the growth for researchers and participants that can occur in the (re)living and (re)telling of the experience. As narrative inquirers come to know in relational ways, the inquiries also become an intervention, which requires the researcher to remain attentive to ethical issues long after leaving the field and final research texts have been composed.

12. Commitment to understanding lives in motion

As narrative inquirers we enter into the research in the midst, in the midst of our own lives and in the midst of our participant's lives. Recognizing this also means that there will never be a final story, that each story and experience begs for a new story to be told, for the experience to be retold and also relived. When we, as researchers, understand this, we also bring a commitment to understanding lives in motion, a commitment to seeing, and representing lives always in the making (Greene, 1995). In all our interim and final research texts we pay attention to the temporal unfolding of experience, and to the unfolding of our relationships. Each telling shifts, as each time the composition of the audience or the experience of the audience changes. Our retold and relived stories are composed in the tensions of telling, living, and retelling, tensions that hold the fabric of our lives together, that allow us to recompose and restory our experiences in new ways. Understanding lives in motion needs to create openings for new relationships to emerge, for lives to unfold in unexpected ways, and for an element of surprise to remain; it too means that there is no final telling, no final story, and no one singular story we can tell. While this is troubling to researchers who rely on the truth or accuracy and verifiability of data, it is opening the possibility for narrative inquirers to continuously inquire into the social fabric of experience and to not lose sight that people are always becoming.

Further Readings and Counterpoint Perspectives

There is a history of narrative work within the traditions of narratology (Bal, 1997), narrative analysis, and life writing. All of these approaches place the emphasis on the structure and content of stories or narratives. The term narratives and stories are often used interchangeably and often signify in the above approaches a discrete unit of text. Unlike narrative inquiry as described in the previous pages, the textual units are often seen as independent from people's experiences and are often analyzed outside of their detailed social context, place, and time, and are, thus, removed from an individual life lived. While the epistemological and ontological foundations of narrative analysis, narratatology, and life writing are substantively different from narrative inquiry, they can, and do, inform the work of narrative inquiry. It is also important that, while the terms narrative inquiry and narrative research are used almost interchangeably in the current research literature (Clandinin, 2007), they signify research methodologies in contrast to the myriad forms of narrative analysis.

To further understand narrative inquiry, it is important to note that Dewey's (1938, 1958) view of experience is cited most often as the philosophical underpinnings of narrative inquiry (Clandinin & Rosiek, 2007). Dewey's criteria of experience, interaction, and continuity, enacted in situations, provide the grounding for the attention in the three-dimensional narrative inquiry space to temporality, place, and sociality (Clandinin & Connelly, 2000). Narrative inquiry is further grounded in the ideas of Bruner (1986), Carr (1986), Bateson (1989, 1994), and Coles (1989).

Narrative inquiry reflects a deeply relational inquiry and the relationship of teller and listener has to be taken into account because meanings shift in varying situations and historical contexts (Cruikshank, 1998). Each story is embedded in context (Mishler, 1979; Ochberg, 1994). Without the contexts of lives, field texts become meaningless (Ayres & Poirier, 1996). It has been helpful to us to read the works of scholars who have worked with oral traditions or indigenous people such as Cruickshank (1998), Basso (1996), King (2003), and Young (2005), among others. Their work, in particular, points out the significance of the narratives told is not always in the latent recalling of the experience but in the process of the telling or articulation and fabrication, which gives rise to a kind of embodied theory and understanding of experience.

It is also helpful to understand that other narrative scholars have situated narrative research close to interpretive methodologies.

> Narrative research, rooted in interpretive hermeneutics and phenomenology, strives to preserve the complexity of what it means to be human and to locate its observations of people and phenomena in society, history and time.
>
> (Josselson, 2006, p. 3)

While we can see the relationship to narrative inquiry in their emphasis on history and time, it misses the importance of relationship between the research and research participants, as well as the long-term relational responsibilities. As narrative inquirers we do not remove ourselves from our research puzzles and observe phenomena or analyze people, but, rather, we become part of the ongoing negotiation of making meaning of experience. While Josselson is a clinical psychologist, we also see this in others who are closely drawn to phenomenology and hermeneutic inquiry.

The work of Mishler (1991) and others, such as Bamberg and Georgakopoulou (2008), also remain important, all of whom place an emphasis on the narrative context, pragmatics, and analytic framework of narrative. Mishler (1999) proposes an analytic framework that looks at narratives as a way of interpersonal, social, and cultural positioning and sees narratives as a way to express and negotiate these positions. Bamberg and Georgakopoulou, on the other hand, focus on what they have termed small stories and includes analysis of smaller segments of texts and conversations.

> we advance our lines of argumentation by sketching out a five-step analytical operation for tapping into small stories as sites of identity work. These five steps grow out of the model of positioning (as put forward by Bamberg, 1997, and elaborated in Bamberg, 2004a, 2004b; cf. also Georgakopoulou, 2000) that succeeds in navigating between the two extreme ends of fine-grained micro-analysis and macro-accounts.
>
> (p. 377)

While a focus on content as well as structure can further advance narrative research, in narrative inquiry this is only one aspect of the inquiry.

Authors' Reflections on Quality

As we look back across the twelve touchstones, we are reminded that these were developed across time, across multiple studies and contexts, and that these continue to evolve. While we have chosen to name twelve, there might be others, but for now these seem to be key and we anticipate that they will remain key for some time. The touchstones we selected reflect our becoming narrative inquirers, and also the importance of methodological and relational commitments. We hope that readers can sense the marks that are left as people engage these touchstones against their own narrative inquirers.

Michael Connelly and Jean began this work on narrative inquiry many years ago, in part because they were trying to give an account of teachers' experiential knowledge. They wanted to find a way to build on what Dewey (1938) wrote of experience and to use his ideas to think about teacher knowledge as both personal and practical and lived out in practice. It was Mark Johnson, in the early 1980s, who turned their attention to how thinking narratively could help them do this work. In the spring of 1999 Vera attended a workshop on narrative inquiry facilitated by Jean and Janice Huber. Vera was drawn into their stories as researchers as they spoke of their relationships with participants in ways that reminded Vera of the ways in which her family had gathered around the family table. It was at the family kitchen table that Vera first learned about the sustained commitment that drew forth difficult to tell and challenging to live stories. Vera was particularly drawn to the living of narrative inquiry, of entering lives in the midst, lives always in progress. With time Vera recognized that she was pulled to narrative inquiry through the stories and experiences of her childhood, and now through her experiences as a registered nurse. It was, and continues to be, the *attending to* and the *attending with* that shapes Vera's relationships with her research participants.

As Jean and Vera worked together through Vera's graduate work, alongside others, it became important to attend to the reverberations of the stories we noticed in our own lives. It continues to be these reverberations that remind us of the importance of a narrative community, a response community that is diverse, and responds with curiosity and care.

To think about quality in narrative inquiry is to think about multiple commitments. The most significant commitments and obligations are methodological and relational commitments. As with other methodologies, it is important to show commitment to a methodology, which involves extensive reading, engagement with other scholars and, in narrative inquiry, it also involves an extensive commitment to writing as a way to inquire (Richardson, 2003). A methodological commitment also precludes taking short cuts, avoiding the complex process of co-composing interim and final research texts. A methodological commitment calls forth a continuous attending to lives in the midst, filled with complexities and ongoing negotiations. As Clandinin and Connelly (2000) point out, narrative inquiry is both methodology and phenomena under study. Narrative inquirers recognize that it is a way of living narratively, of living the phenomena that shapes their lives, their teaching, nursing, or other practices, and that calls forth a relational commitment to participants.

While we enter and leave lives in the midst, as narrative inquirers we continue to have long-term relational responsibilities and a commitment to the lives we have been privileged to become a part of. As we sit here and write this chapter we recount the ways in which we too have become part of our participants' lives, how our dissertations have become wedding gifts, birthday gifts, accounts that trace the last days and hours of participants' lives. Our work is significant to participants and they, too, tell us that our relationships, and inquiry into their unfolding lives, matter; they call upon us to remember them, to engage with them and to celebrate their, and our, achievements. It is perhaps, as King (2003) points out, that "the truth about stories is that's all that we are" (p. 2), and through inquiring narratively into our storied lives and experiences we are able to attend and live differently, to attend in relational ways to the everyday lives of others.

References

Andrews, M. (2007). Exploring cross-cultural boundaries. In D. J. Clandinin (Ed.), *Handbook of Narrative Inquiry. Mapping a methodology* (pp. 489–511). Thousand Oaks, CA: Sage.

Ayres, L. & Poirier, S. (1996). Virtual text and the growth of meaning in qualitative analysis. *Research in Nursing & Health, 19*, 163–169.

Bal, M. (1997). *On Narratology: Introduction to the theory of narrative (2nd ed.).* Toronto, ON: University of Toronto Press.

Bamberg, M. & Georgakopoulou, A. (2008). Small stories as a new perspective in narrative and identity analysis. *Text and Talk, 28*(3), 377–396.

Basso, K. (1996).*Wisdom Sits in Places. Landscape and language among the Western Apache.* Albuquerque, NM: University of New Mexico Press.

Bateson, M. C. (1989). *Composing a Life.* New York: Atlantic Monthly Press.

Bateson, M. C. (1994). *Peripheral Visions: Learning along the way.* New York: HarperCollins.

Bergum, V. (1999). Ethics as question. In T. Kohn & R. McKechnie (Eds.), *Extending the Boundaries of Care: Medical ethics and caring practices* (pp. 167–180). New York: Oxford.

Bruner, J. (1986). *Actual Minds, Possible Worlds.* Cambridge, MA: Harvard University Press.

Bruno, S. (2010). *NehiyawiskwewAcimowina: Attending to the silences in the lives of Cree women in university.* Unpublished doctoral dissertation, University of Alberta, Edmonton, Alberta, Canada.

Caine, V. (2002). *Stories Moments: A visual narrative inquiry of Aboriginal women living with HIV.* Unpublished master's thesis, University of Alberta, Edmonton, Alberta, Canada.

Caine, V. (2007). *Dwelling with/in Stories: Ongoing conversations about narrative inquiry, including visual narrative inquiry, imagination, and relational ethics.* Unpublished doctoral dissertation, University of Alberta, Edmonton, Alberta, Canada.

Caine, V. & Lavoie, M. (2011). Places inarticulately close. *International Journal of Nursing Philosophy, 12*(3), 229–235.

Cardinal, T. (2010). *For All my Relations: An autobiographical narrative inquiry into the lived experiences of one aboriginal graduate student.* Unpublished master's thesis, University of Alberta, Edmonton, Alberta, Canada.

Carr, D. (1986). *Time, Narrative, and History.* Bloomington, IN: Indiana University Press.

Charon, R. & Montello, M. (2002). *Stories Matter: The role of narrative in medical ethics.* New York: Routledge.

Chung, S. (2008). *Coming a Curriculum of Lives: A narrative inquiry into the interwoven intergenerational stories of teachers, children and families.* Unpublished master's thesis, University of Alberta, Edmonton, Alberta, Canada.

Clandinin, D. J. (2006). Narrative inquiry: A methodology for studying lived experience. *Research Studies in Music Education, 27,* 44–54.

Clandinin, D. J. (Ed.). (2007). *Handbook of Narrative Inquiry: Mapping a methodology* (pp. 35–75). Thousand Oaks, CA: Sage.

Clandinin, D. J. (2010). Potentials and possibilities for narrative inquiry. In M. Campbell & L. Thompson (Eds.), *Issues of Identity in Music Education: Narratives and practices* (pp. 1–11). Charlotte, NC: Information Age Publishing.

Clandinin, D. J. & Connelly, F. M. (1995). *Teachers' Professional Knowledge Landscapes.* New York: Teachers College Press.

Clandinin, D. J. & Connelly, F. M. (2000). *Narrative Inquiry: Experience and story in qualitative research.* San Francisco, CA: Jossey-Bass.

Clandinin, D. J. & Huber, J. (2010). Narrative inquiry. In B. McGaw, E. Baker, & P. P. Peterson (Eds.), *International Encyclopedia of Education* (3rd ed.). New York: Elsevier.

Clandinin, D. J., Huber, J., Huber, M., Murphy, M. S., Murray-Orr, A., Pearce, M., & Steeves, P. (2006). *Composing Diverse Identities: Narrative inquiries into the interwoven lives of children and teachers.* London/New York: Routledge.

Clandinin, D. J. & Rosiek, J. (2007). Mapping a landscape of narrative inquiry: Borderland spaces and tensions. In D. J. Clandinin (Ed.), *Handbook of Narrative Inquiry: Mapping a methodology* (pp. 35–75). Thousand Oaks, CA: Sage.

Coles, R. (1989). *The Call of Stories: Teaching and the moral imagination.* Boston: Houghton Mifflin.

Connelly, F. M. & Clandinin, D. J. (1988). *Teachers as Curriculum Planners: Narratives of experience.* New York: Teachers College Press.

Connelly, F. M. & Clandinin, D. J. (1990). Stories of experience and narrative inquiry. *Educational Researcher, 19*(5), 2–14.

Connelly, F. M. & Clandinin, D. J. (1999). *Shaping a Professional Identity: Stories of educational practice.* New York: Teachers College Press.

Connelly, F. M. & Clandinin, D. J. (2006). Narrative inquiry. In J. Green, G. Camili, & P. Elmore (Eds.), *Handbook of Complementary Methods in Education Research* (pp. 375–385). Mahwah, NJ: Lawrence Erlbaum.

Cruikshank, J. (1998). *The Social Life of Stories: Narrative and knowledge in the Yukon Territory.* Vancouver, BC: University of British Columbia Press.

Dewey, J. (1938). *Experience and Education.* New York: Collier Books.

Dewey, J. (1958). *Experience and Nature.* New York: Dover.

Greene, M. (1995). *Releasing the Imagination: Essays on education, the arts, and social change.* San Francisco, CA: Jossey-Bass.

Huber, M., Clandinin, D. J., & Huber, J. (2006). Relational responsibilities of narrative inquirers. *Curriculum and Teaching Dialogue, 8*(1/2), 209–223.

Josselson, R. (2006). Narrative research and the challenge of accumulating knowledge. *Narrative Inquiry, 16*(1), 3–10.

Josselson, R. & Lieblich, A. (Eds.). (1995). *Interpreting Experience: The narrative study of lives* (Vol. 3). Thousand Oaks, CA: Sage.

Josselson, R., Lieblich, A., & McAdams, D. P. (Eds.). (2003). *Up Close and Personal: The teaching and learning of narrative research.* Washington: American Psychological Association.

King, T. (2003). *The Truth about Stories: A native narrative.* Toronto, ON: House of AnansiPress.

Lopez, B. (1991). *Crow and Weasel.* New York: North Point Press.

Lugones, M. (1987). Playfulness, "world"-travelling, and loving perception. *Hypatia, 2*(2), 3–19.

Mishler, E. G. (1979). Meaning in context: Is there any other kind? *Harvard Educational Review, 49,* 1–19.

Mishler, E. (1991). *Research Interviewing: Context and narrative.* Cambridge, MA: Harvard University Press.

Mishler, E. (1999). *Storylines: Craftartists' narratives of identity.* Cambridge, MA: Harvard University Press.

Murphy, M. S. (2004). *Understanding Children's Knowledge: A narrative inquiry into school experiences.* Unpublished doctoral dissertation, University of Alberta, Edmonton, Alberta, Canada.

Noddings, N. (1984). *Caring: A feminine approach to ethics and moral education.* Berkley, CA: University of California Press.

Ochberg, R. L. (1994). Life stories and storied lives. In A. Lieblich & R. Josselson (Eds.), *The Narrative Study of Lives* (Vol. 2, pp. 113–144). Thousand Oaks, CA: Sage.

Pinnegar, S. & Daynes, J. G. (2007). Locating narrative inquiry historically: Thematics in the turn to narrative. In D. J. Clandinin (Ed.), *Handbook of Narrative Inquiry: Mapping a methodology* (pp. 3–34). Thousand Oaks, CA: Sage.

Polkinghorne, D. E. (1988). *Narrative Knowing and the Human Sciences.* New York: State University of New York Press.

Richardson, L. (2003). *Writing: A method of inquiry.* San Francisco, CA: Rowman AltaMira.

Riessman, C. K. (2008). *Narrative Methods for the Human Sciences.* Thousand Oaks: Sage.

Schultz, R. (1997). *Interpreting Teacher Practice: Two continuing stories.* New York: Teachers College Press.

Taylor, S. (2007). *A Narrative Inquiry into the Experience of Women Seeking Professional Help with Severe Chronic Migraines.* Unpublished doctoral dissertation, University of Alberta, Edmonton, Alberta, Canada.

Young, M. (2005). *Pimatisiwin: Walking in a good way, a narrative inquiry into language as identity.* Winnipeg, MB: Pemmican Publications.

13
Phenomenology

Eileen J. Porter and Marlene Z. Cohen

Phenomenological research is work inspired by the philosophical traditions that Spiegelberg (1994) called "the Phenomenological Movement" (p. 2). In the typical fashion of a phenomenologist, Spiegelberg, a scholar of the history of those traditions, characterized the movement as more like "an unfolding plant than . . . a river" (p. 2). The tradition germinated in an early work of the German philosopher Edmund Husserl, *Ideas: General Introduction to Pure Phenomenology*, first published in 1913. Husserl later expanded, modified, and even ignored some of his original ideas—strategies also adopted by some of his students and by Martin Heidegger, who worked at the University of Frieburg. Husserl was born into a Jewish family, and the notorious 1933 race laws of the Nazi regime took away Husserl's academic standing and privileges. Following an illness, he died at Freiburg, Germany, in 1938. Phenomenology in Germany ended for all practical purposes with the Nazi years. In the 1930s, the movement flourished in France, where Husserl's papers were transferred shortly after his death. New hybrids developed, especially through the work of Jean-Paul Sartre (1963), Maurice Merleau-Ponty (1962), and Paul Ricoeur (1981). Thus, the metaphor of a plant is an apt descriptor of the phenomenological movement (Spiegelberg); it developed over time in various climates, flowering profusely and yielding unique philosophical fruits.

Neither Husserl (1913/1962) nor Heidegger (1927/1962) sought to develop a research method as that term is understood today. However, because some of their key beliefs remain basic to methods that emerged from those traditions, we review the key differences in their views. Husserl's philosophy grew in part out of his critiques of the psychological studies of his day, which in his view, were insufficiently grounded in understanding of the nature of experience. Husserl sought to recognize what was evident in experience ("the real"), but without referring to such particulars, to grasp the essence or the "irreal" (p. 263). Kohak (1978) compared "arbitrary 'facts' . . . [to] principles which order them and which are not themselves arbitrary" (p. 19). Husserl believed that a person was constituted by consciousness, the basic tool used to explore experience. In contrast, in *Being and Time*, his major work, Heidegger (1927/1962) emphasized Being over consciousness. According to Spiegelberg (1994), Heidegger viewed "Being as the decisive part of human being" (p. 364). He viewed truth as a property of Being, Being as temporal, and time as a potential framework for understanding Being (Spiegelberg). Husserl (1913/1962) sought, through reflection, to discern the nature and structure of experience, "the thought formations of the higher and lower" (p. 232). In contrast, Heidegger viewed Being as inherently particular and nongeneralizable. Thus, for Heidegger, it was not only useless but impossible for a human being to grasp the essence of an experience. Spiegelberg drew another key comparison of the overall aims of the two philosophers. Although Husserl's goal was to foster science by "strengthening it internally" (Spiegelberg, p. 75), Heidegger sought to "uncover hidden meanings by anticipatory devices" (Spiegelberg, p. 385).

Methodologists and researchers have applied these varied philosophical beliefs in different ways, resulting in three major research approaches (Cohen & Omery, 1994). These traditions share many similarities and some differences, which we consider later in our discussion of variations in perspective, form, and context. Despite differences among the philosophies of phenomenology, Spiegelberg (1994) pointed to a core thread that carries over into method, noting that "The common concern is that of giving the phenomena a fuller and fairer hearing than traditional empiricism has accorded them" (p. 680). Having presented this background about the phenomenological movement (Spiegelberg, 1994), we continue in light of that "common concern" (Spiegelberg, p. 680). We define key terms pertaining to the philosophy, the methods, or both. After reviewing the basic phenomenological research methods and the extent of their use in recent years, we highlight touchstones for publishing phenomenological research. We view the touchstones as indicators that illustrate the value of aligning the various phases of the work with the philosophical tradition that inspired it, while recognizing the need for flexibility to capture the essence of the experience, its meaning, or both.

Select Terms

Eidetic reduction is a careful process of transitioning from a focus on particulars or facts to the more general essence of experience (Husserl, 1913/1962; Spiegelberg, 1994).

Hermeneutic circle is a metaphor that guides inquiry on several levels. Analysis begins as parts of the text are understood in relation to the whole text and vice versa. Individual texts are then understood in relation to all the texts and vice versa. Researchers begin with a vague and tentative notion of the meaning of the whole of the data and with the reflexive awareness that this notion is an anticipation of meaning. This awareness causes a dialectical examination of the parts of the data to understand better the whole. With a better understanding of the whole, examination of different data or the same part of the data at a deeper level drives the analysis forward. This is the hermeneutic circle as it continues throughout analysis (Cohen, Kahn, & Steeves, 2000). Ideally, the hermeneutic circle suggests a continuous dialectic in analysis. Geertz (1988) described the process as focusing attention alternatively "between the most local of local detail and the most global [of theoretical] structure in such a way as to bring them into simultaneous view" (p. 69).

(Lived) experience "is essentially something that flows, and starting from the present moment we can swim after it, or gaze reflectively turned towards it, whilst the stretches we leave in our wake are lost to our perception" (Husserl, 1913/1962, p. 127). Husserl viewed experience as the beginning point for all knowledge of the world as well as the repository within which that knowledge remains. Although Husserl used different German words, with different meanings, to refer to experience in *Ideas* (1913/1962), Kohak (1978) emphasized that Husserl sought "to stress that experience, as such, in principle, is a subject's experience" (p. 158). Although the adjective "lived" is not consistently used in the literature, there is agreement among descriptive phenomenologists that "it is to experience as lived by a subject . . . that we need to return" (Kohak, 1978, p. 6).

Lifeworld is a frame of reference for understanding the context of experience, based on Husserl's (1913/1962) philosophy and proposed by the phenomenological sociologists, Schutz and Luckmann (1973). Lifeworld is both the "stock of knowledge . . . that is fundamentally and typically familiar"

[. . . and the] "taken-for-granted frame in which all the problems which I must overcome are placed" (Schutz & Luckmann, 1973, p. 7, p. 4).

Phenomenological reduction (bracketing) refers to setting aside the usual or scientific points of view about an experience in favor of focusing on describing what remains of the experience (Husserl, 1913/1962; Spiegelberg, 1994). Husserl (1913/1962) used the mathematical metaphor of bracketing for reduction. Researchers begin each study by examining their prejudices, commitments, and such to "bracket" them out so that phenomena can be seen as they are, not as they are as reflected through preconceptions.

Diversities in Perspective, Context, and Form

As noted earlier, there are three primary approaches to phenomenological research. They are descriptive phenomenology, interpretive phenomenology, and hermeneutic phenomenology. We discuss each in turn, reviewing the key methodologists associated with each approach.

Descriptive Phenomenology

This approach is based on Husserl's (1913/1962) philosophy. Researchers working from this tradition aim to explore and describe the essential structure of an experience in terms of phenomena. Early methodological prototypes were developed by psychologists at Duquesne University, including Colaizzi (1978) and Giorgi (1985). Many researchers from a variety of disciplines (including education, psychological sciences, and health sciences) have used the methods of Giorgi (1985) and Colaizzi (1978). Of the descriptive methods, theirs are the most commonly used. Since 2000, there have been about 200 citations of Giorgi's method and about 300 citations of Colaizzi's method in research articles cited in ERIC, PsychInfo, or CINAHL. Accordingly, we briefly characterize the main steps of Colaizzi's method, followed by a similar description of Giorgi's method.

Although Colaizzi's (1978) method is widely characterized as consisting of seven steps, Colaizzi preceded an explanation of those steps by recounting particular preliminary activities associated with the "approach of phenomenological psychology" (p. 54). Colaizzi said that the phenomenologist must obtain a description of the experience from participants by direct questions. However, Colaizzi emphasized that the researcher could develop those questions only by examining and documenting personal assumptions about the topic and discussing those presuppositions with others. After generating "research questions . . . to tap the subjects' experiences" (Colaizzi, 1978, p. 58), the researcher could obtain a sample of persons who had experienced the phenomenon and "collect the subject's descriptive responses" (p. 58) of it. Colaizzi referred to those responses as "protocols" (p. 58).

Only after discussing those preliminary activities did Colaizzi (1978) present the data analysis steps with which his method has long been associated. Those steps involve (1) reading all protocols; (2) extracting "significant statements" (Colaizzi, 1978, p. 59); (3) "formulating meanings" (p. 59) of those statements; (4) organizing meanings into "clusters of themes" (p. 59); (5) validating themes by referring back to the protocols; (6) deriving an "exhaustive description" (p. 61) of the topic; (7) formulating a statement that captures the structure of the phenomenon; and (8) returning to each participant to discuss findings in a "final validating step" (p. 61), prepared to incorporate any new data into the findings.

The aim of Colaizzi's (1978) method is to achieve "a descriptive understanding of psychological phenomena by reflectively disclosing their meanings" (p. 68). Colaizzi's approach has been linked primarily with Husserl's (1913/1962) philosophy. However, Colaizzi referred to Heidegger (1927/1962) as "the germinal phenomenologist" (p. 53) and emphasized Heidegger's "method of phenological [sic *description* as the "only method . . . to achieve understanding of human experience as it is given" (Colaizzi, 1978, p. 53). In presenting a new phenomenological method, Colaizzi was "devoted to developing the meaning of . . . [this] complicated statement" (p. 53) of Heideggerian philosophy: "to let that which shows itself be seen from itself in the very way in which it shows itself from itself" (Heidegger, 1927/1962, p. 58). Thus, it could be argued that Colaizzi's (1978) approach was influenced more by the philosophy of Heidegger (1927/1962) than by that of Husserl (1913/1962).

Colaizzi (1978) was also influenced by early methodological musings of Giorgi (1970), who like Husserl (1913/1972), had criticized traditional psychological methods for failing to study phenomena appropriately. Like Colaizzi (1978), Giorgi (1985) later proposed specific research activities for a psychological phenomenological method. As Colaizzi (1978) had done, Giorgi (1985) emphasized the importance of Husserl's (1900/1970) maxim, to "return to the things themselves" (p. 252). Although Giorgi did not cite Heidegger (1927/1962), both "meaning" and "structure" are important in Giorgi's (1985) method, as in Colaizzi's approach. Giorgi's (1985) method is typically associated with four "steps" (p. 10) of data analysis. However, like Colaizzi, Giorgi preceded the list of steps by explaining preliminary activities. To carry out Giorgi's method, the researcher obtains from participants a description of an everyday situation that is relevant to the phenomena of interest. The description is to be written, that is, documented. At that point, analysis can begin. The researcher reads the description to obtain a basic grasp of it before rereading it to extract "'meaning units' from within a psychological perspective" (Giorgi, 1985, p. 10). After reviewing the meaning units to ascertain their "psychological insight" (Giorgi, p. 10), the researcher draws upon the meaning units to devise a descriptive statement about the person's experience. Giorgi characterized that culminating statement as "the structure of the experience" (p. 10). This approach is particularly suited for psychological phenomenological analyses of existing texts in which participants have been asked one question—to describe a situation that pertains to the phenomenon of interest.

Since the groundbreaking work of Colaizzi (1978) and Giorgi (1985), other scholars have developed descriptive phenomenological methods. Porter (1998b), a nurse-researcher, who was inspired by Husserl's book, *Ideas* (1913/1962), and the methodological reflections of Omery (1983) and Oiler (1982), found discrepancies between Husserl's philosophy and psychological methods of descriptive phenomenology including those of Colaizzi (1978) and Giorgi (1985). Porter developed a new method to describe health-related experiences (1994, 1998b) and their personal–social context as lifeworld (1995), drawing on the perspectives of the phenomenological sociologists, Schutz and Luckmann (1973). The thrust of Porter's (1998b) method is conveyed in this phrase: "making clearer . . . [while] glancing towards" (p. 19, citing Husserl [1913/1962, p. 180, p. 109]).

In contrast to other descriptive phenomenological methodologists, Porter (1998b) engages in preliminary critique of constructs relevant to the experience of interest (2000, 2007b), as Husserl (1913/1962) advised. Those constructs and relevant personal experiences are bracketed or set aside during data gathering, which occurs over time by interview and observation in the setting where the experience is lived. Intentions of each participant and elements of lifeworld, the most specific levels of findings, are labeled in vernacular language and compared to discern similarities, resulting in broader categories. From most specific to most general, findings are reported in a taxonomy of experience (intention, component phenomenon, and phenomenon) (Porter, 1994, 1998b) and a taxonomy of lifeworld (element, descriptor, and feature) (Porter, 1995). Participants and co-investigators are involved in ongoing dialogue about findings, which are refined and compared with bracketed concepts and other relevant literature in the discussion of findings. Finally, the researcher is to propose uses for findings. That is, descriptive phenomenological research should lead to insights about enhancing empirical validity of relevant constructs. Such insights are viewed as grist to the scientific mill and reported to enhance valid measurement of constructs. Second, the work should yield ideas for grounding practice in intentions of clients who share key characteristics with participants (Porter, 1998b).

The recursive activities of Porter's (1998b) method have been used to describe health-related experiences of older women in lifeworld context, relative to individuals (Porter, 2008; Porter,

Ganong, & Armer, 2000), subsamples (Porter, 2005b, 2007a; Porter, Matsuda, & Lindbloom, 2010), and samples of seven to forty women (Porter, 1994, 2005a; Porter, Ganong, & Matsuda, in press). Porter's students have explored a broad range of experiences, including teen pregnancy (Burns, 2008; Burns & Porter, 2007), lymphedema management (Fu, 2005), and maternal care of young adult children with traumatic brain injury (Wongvatunyu & Porter, 2005, 2008). Scholars of family studies have drawn on Porter's (1998b) method to elaborate experiences of unmarried young women (Sharp & Ganong, 2007), remarried stepfathers (Hans & Coleman, 2009), and teen fathers of Mexican origin involved in the justice system (Parra-Cardona, Sharp, & Wampler, 2008). In keeping with the goal of the method, those scholars have contributed knowledge, shed empirical light on constructs, and recommended uses for findings in health care and human services.

Interpretive Phenomenology

The second tradition, which is interpretive, has also been called "Heidggerian hermeneutics" (Benner, 1985, 1994; Diekelmann, 2001; Diekelmann, Allen, & Tanner, 1989). The intent is to reveal frequently taken-for-granted shared practices and common meanings. Both Benner (1985) and Diekelmann and her colleagues (1989, 2001) labeled their work as "Heideggerian hermeneutical phenomenology." Diekelmann and her collaborators, whose primary focus has been on educational research, later developed and conducted what they call a "new phenomenological pedagogy, Narrative Pedagogy" (Diekelmann, 2001) based on an interpretive phenomenological approach. She described her approach as reflexive and reflective (Diekelmann, 2001). It begins with the study of philosophic texts. After nonstructured audiotaped interviews were complete, texts are read in their entirety, and then common themes are identified. A theme is a category that reflects shared experiences and practices. Themes are compiled using MARTIN, computer software that assists in retrieving and documenting the thinking throughout the analysis. When teams are used, team members identify themes within each interview and themes that are across interviews. Weekly team sessions are held to read interpretations and supporting excerpts, followed by dialogue to clarify the analysis. This process continues, clarifying discrepancies and refining the analysis, sometimes reinterviewing participants. The researchers also read widely to bring insights to the interpretations.

One example of this method is from one of Diekelmann's (2001) collaborators who used Heideggerian hermeneutical phenomenology to study the lived experiences of chronic illness (Ironside et al., 2003). This work was conducted as part of a research course. Students in a two-semester course began talking informally to community members about what nurses need to know to provide them with better care. Descriptions were collected, nursing literature was reviewed, and themes were identified. Issues surrounding chronic illness arose and students designed a study to investigate how chronic illness is experienced.

Benner (1985) described a hermeneutic process similar to that of Diekelmann (2001). After participants describe a lived experience, the researcher seeks commonalities in meaning, situations, practices, and bodily experiences. Analysis involves interpretation of the whole text and parts of the text and comparison of those interpretations. Three strategies are used to present findings: paradigm cases, exemplars, and thematic analysis. Benner (1994) also described interpretive phenomenology and provided examples of interpretive phenomenological studies.

Hermeneutic Phenomenology

The third approach combines features of descriptive and interpretive methods; it has been called hermeneutic phenomenology and the Utrecht School of phenomenology. This approach has been used and developed by Cohen, Kahn, and Steeves (2000) and van Manen (1997). These research methods are based on phenomenological philosophy and are used to determine how people interpret their lives and make meaning of what they experience. As is usual with hermeneutic phenomenological designs (Cohen, Kahn, & Steeves, 2000), data analysis begins during data collection. Interviews are conducted using open-ended questions about an experience with someone who has had that experience. These interviews are audio-taped and transcribed verbatim, and the transcription's accuracy is verified by the interviewer. Phenomenological analysis begins by reading each transcript several times to get a sense of each interview as a whole. Themes are identified in each transcript by examining it line by line and underlining and labelling passages with tentative theme labels. Passages from interview text and labels, or theme labels, for each interview were compared with passages and themes among and between all other interviews (Cohen, Kahn, & Steeves, 2000). In the hermeneutic circle, the researcher starts uncovering a tentative notion of the meaning of an experience using reflective awareness. This awareness leads to dialectical examination of parts of the data to better understand the whole. When the whole is understood, different data or the same parts of the data are examined at a deeper level. Then the analysis is repeated. The process helps the researcher to understand the statements in relation to the larger context of the individual's experience. Examples of research using Cohen, Kahn, and Steeves's approach (2000) include studies of experiences of patients and their family members at end of life (Cohen, Pace, Kaur, & Bruera, 2009), experiences of cancer treatment (Cohen et al., 2007), the experience of cancer survivors (Fletcher, Cohen, Schumacher, & Lydiatt, 2012), and experiences of illness in international settings (for instance, in Thailand, Kitrungrote, Wongkongkul, Chanprasit, Suttharangsee, & Cohen, 2008, and in Italy, Vellone, Piras, Talucci, & Cohen, 2008). Additional studies using Cohen, Kahn, and Steeves' approach have included understanding support needs of men with prostate cancer (Jones et al., 2011), experiences of boys who experienced intraparental homicide (i.e., one parent killing the other parent) (Steeves, Laughon, Parker, & Weierbach, 2007), and experiences with diabetes (Jones et al., 2008; Wenzel, Utz, Steeves, Hinton, & Jones, 2005).

Qualitative Touchstones

Despite the availability of these three specific phenomenological approaches (descriptive phenomenology, Heidggerian hermeneutics, and hermeneutic phenomenology), our survey of peer-reviewed research literature cited since 2000 in PsychInfo, CINAHL, and ERIC revealed a surprising fact. The majority of researchers who reported using a "phenomenological method" did not mention a specific approach or cite a methodologist. Given that fact and the diversity of phenomenological methods, we faced an interesting challenge in presenting quality indicators that would guide manuscript reviewers. Within each touchstone below, we offer an overall suggestion for phenomenological method (regardless of its underlying tradition), as well as specific notions pertaining to each tradition, as indicated.

1. The particular philosophical tradition underlying the chosen method is explained, and original sources are cited. If sources from another phenomenological tradition are cited, they are contrasted with the tradition of the chosen method, rather than viewed as compatible with it

Qualitative inquiry is often viewed as generic in form rather than as composed of specific traditions (Dixon-Woods, Shaw, Agarwal, & Smith, 2004). That generalization also characterizes the more circumscribed arena of phenomenological inquiry, in that many researchers proceed directly to method without acknowledging a debt to any of the diverse philosophical traditions we highlighted above. Thus, in proposing this touchstone, we buck another trend that emerged from our review of peer-reviewed research articles. That is, most researchers who used a "phenomenological" method did not state that the work was informed or inspired by a philosophical tradition. That oversight is in contradiction to Spiegelberg's (1994) critical point: "What distinguishes phenomenology from other methods is not so much any particular step it develops or adds to them but the spirit of philosophical reverence as the first and foremost norm of the philosophical enterprise" (p. 717).

Thus, in manuscripts, researchers should show that a decision to use a certain phenomenological method was grounded in recognition of its underlying philosophical premises. Reviewers should carefully consider not only whether a researcher mentions philosophical premises, but which premises are mentioned and whether those premises are accurate reflections of the philosophy. In view of the fact that relatively few researchers refer to original philosophical sources in their manuscripts, it behooves a reviewer to comment favorably when primary sources are cited. However, the accuracy of the researcher's citations should be appraised; a researcher who emphasizes that Husserl (1913/1962) was primarily interested in the "meaning of an experience" is likely referring to Heidegger (1927/1962) or Ricoeur (1981) instead. Furthermore, the reviewer can appraise the way in which the researcher has interpreted the philosopher whose work is cited. For instance, a researcher who cites Husserl but refers to phenomena as "objects" or "concepts" could be advised to review the original source for more information about the nature of phenomena.

Reviewers of phenomenological manuscripts find it necessary to appraise a researcher's references to philosophical premises because those premises should inform methodological decisions. A reviewer should appraise consistency between philosophy and method and raise questions when a manuscript is characterized by contradictory statements. For instance, if an aim of the work is to "uncover meaning using an interpretive method," a reviewer should expect to see clear explanations of how meaning was uncovered. An example of how this was described in a recent paper (Fletcher, et al., 2012), is:

> Using the phenomenological process, the investigator began the analysis by listening to each audio tape and reading each transcript several times to get a sense of the interview as a whole. Then using the hermeneutic circle, the researcher uncovered an idea of the meaning of the experience expressed by the survivor in the interview and used reflective awareness to further the process with dialectical examination of parts of the data to better understand the whole.
> (Cohen, Kahn, & Steeves, 2000)

This process led to a deeper understanding as the analysis was repeated.

The reviewer should not expect to see hints that a descriptive method was actually used instead, including the absence of any actual explanation of how meaning was uncovered, coupled with statements such as "Analysis ceased when description was complete." Instead, the author of an interpretive work could conclude findings by offering a data excerpt to illustrate that the meanings articulated as findings were evident, allowing the reviewer (and readers) to determine whether additional meanings were evoked.

We also believe that reviewers should expect researchers who cite more than one methodologist to compare and contrast the underlying philosophies of those methods, if any, as well as the methods themselves. We realize that this rejoinder is inconsistent with the practice of researchers, some who have relied on more than one phenomenological method concurrently. That strategy could be appropriate if the methods arise from the same philosophical tradition. However, it is problematic if researchers cite the descriptive method of Giorgi (1985) and the hermeneutic method of van Manen (1997), because those methods emerge from disparate philosophical traditions. However, van Manen's (1997) approach does include descriptive work, so the author should be clear about the philosophical basis of the method when complementary sources are used. Reviewers of phenomenological manuscripts should expect to see evidence that researchers understand hallmarks of the different traditions and that they take those nuances into consideration in selecting and using a given method or in devising an approach from several methods. In phenomenological research, creativity and flexibility of approach must emerge from knowledge of the traditions on which each approach is based.

Finally, although we have focused on citation of primary philosophical sources, many researchers tend to cite secondary or even tertiary sources about phenomenological philosophy, including recent research reports by other researchers. We have recommended that reviewers check the accuracy of ideas that authors draw from original philosophical sources. This is also important when secondary or tertiary sources are cited. If a reviewer finds, for instance, that an author relied on a secondary or tertiary source for methodological guidance but finds that guidance wanting, the reviewer can give the author specific rationale for accessing primary sources instead. A distinction should be made between primary sources of philosophy (such as Husserl, 1913/1962) and sources for methods. Sources such as Porter (1998b), Cohen, Kahn, and Steeves (2000), or van Manen (1997) are useful guides, whereas citations of basic research textbooks might reveal that an author has limited familiarity with phenomenological research methods.

2. To establish the rationale for pursuing a phenomenological study of a particular
experience, relevant literature is reviewed. Evidence is provided that the empirical essence
of the experience has not been carefully explored in prior research. That is, the researcher
should describe any prior work about the experience that has been (1) designed to
measure constructs relevant to the experience without exploring the experience itself, or
(2) undertaken using qualitative methods other than phenomenology. The researcher
reprises the contributions of prior quantitative and qualitative work while building an
argument that critically important, basic knowledge in the field can be attained through
phenomenological work

In phenomenological manuscripts, there is no substitute for what Kline (2008) characterized as a "persuasive rationale for the research" (p. 213). We believe it is important for phenomenological researchers to present a literature review relevant to the experience of interest, although many phenomenological researchers have not done so, based on the stated or unstated rationale that one should approach the experience naively. Although it is difficult to argue persuasively that a naïve posture is possible for an investigator, even prior to data-gathering, a scholar who does not present a literature review should offer a rationale for that decision. Failure to review the extant literature likely means the context of what is known and what is new may be difficult to understand, which is seldom useful in advancing knowledge.

3. For a descriptive phenomenological study, the research question (or purpose of the study) is
based on an interest in understanding the essence of an experience (what it is like) and (in
most cases) its context, with context defined. For an interpretive phenomenological study, the
research question (or purpose) is grounded in an interest in understanding the meaning of the
experience and (in most cases) its context

In a phenomenological study, authors typically present a statement of purpose or a research question, rather than both. However, a reviewer should expect to see clear evidence of one or the other, occasionally at the outset of the work or following the literature review and preceding the method. As with any qualitative study (Clark, 2003), the disciplinary relevance of the research question in a phenomenological study should be clearly explained by the author and evident to the reviewer. In framing the purpose or question of a phenomenological study of an experience, authors typically explain whether or not the context of the experience is also to be explored or described. Furthermore, the way in which context is understood from a phenomenological perspective is typically explained either in conjunction with the purpose statement or within the methods section.

4. The approach is referenced with methodological works grounded in descriptive phenomenology or interpretive phenomenology as appropriate, rather than generic qualitative methods or another qualitative method such as grounded theory. Particular constructs or theories that are held in abeyance or bracketed during data collection should be stated. The approach is exemplified by specific activities, related in sufficient detail and with data examples to illustrate rationale for ongoing methodological decisions

When researchers use a phenomenological method, a reviewer should expect that the terms used to refer to method are consistent with phenomenology. Many such manuscripts include references to terms associated with other methods, including "saturation" (associated with grounded theory), "key informant" (linked to ethnography), and "clarification of concepts" (basic to content analysis). The appearance of such terms in a phenomenological manuscript raises questions about the researcher's understanding of key differences between phenomenology and other qualitative methods and the extent to which the method was actually phenomenological in nature. For instance, with regard to saturation, Husserl (1913/1962) advised that one is never finished considering a phenomenon, that new data can always be obtained, and that one's understanding is always open to new insights. As the term is typically understood, saturation is not an aim of descriptive phenomenology, because there is no end to the new data that can be obtained or to the new insights that can emerge from extant data. Porter (1998b) has relied on that perspective as a rationale for statements that despite efforts to "fully develop a phenomenon" (p. 21), the work reflects the understanding of the researcher at the time. That viewpoint necessitates ongoing modifications of and additions to extant taxonomies of the structure of an experience and its personal–social context as related experiences are explored and described (Porter, 1998a, 2005a; Porter & Lasiter, 2008).

Reviewers should expect to see that authors offer a concise but complete explanation of how they used a particular method. For instance, Giorgi's (1985) method involves a precise series of activities that are to be carried out systematically. Because the reader cannot be placed in the position of taking any of those activities for granted, the reviewer should ask for more detail about any methodological activity that lacks a sufficient explanation. Each activity must be explained thoroughly to justify findings and enable appraisal of rigor. When there is more than one author, an explanation of involvement in the various research activities is also important to include. Although reviewers might not have knowledge of the authors, when a team project is described, more than one author should have both accountability and credit for the work.

Some researchers use software to assist with analysis. This is appropriate and sometimes necessary with a large dataset, particularly when the emphasis is placed on the value of the software with data management, rather than the data analysis. Reviewers should be aware that novice researchers sometimes confuse this assistance with having the "computer do the analysis," which is of course neither appropriate nor possible.

5. In-depth interviews with individuals and observation are the primary sources of data; the researcher's experience can be integrated as data in certain situations. Actual data (remarks of participants) are presented in enough detail to provide empirical support to findings (the author's presentation of the essence of the experience, its meaning, or both). When employed, numerical data support but do not overshadow the narrative about the essence of the experience

Because the basic focus of phenomenology is the experience of the individual, the in-depth interview with an individual is considered the most appropriate approach to data collection. Whereas some methodologists advise a single interview with each participant, followed by another session to seek feedback (Colaizzi, 1985), others advise a series of interviews over time to more fully capture the essence of that person's experience (Porter, 1998b). A series of interviews may not be possible, as in the example of research conducted with persons who were at the end of their life and were not alive when the analysis was complete (Cohen et al., 2007). Regardless of the number of interviews or the span of time involved, the emphasis is on understanding each participant's experience sufficiently to enable comparison with the experiences of other persons in the study. Such a goal might be rendered problematic if data collection for a phenomenological study is attempted in a focus-group format. By its very nature, a group format precludes in-depth exploration of the experiences of any given individual. If an author reports that data for a phenomenological study were obtained in focus groups, the reviewer should expect a clear rationale for that decision and evidence that the experiences of all participants were truly explored during data gathering. For example, a phenomenological study of Filipino American patients with cancer used a focus group format primarily because members of the research team who were Filipino Americans noted that members of this culture are most open to group interactions (Harle et al., 2007).

When thinking about space constraints, it is important to consider what reviewers of grants and manuscripts need to see to understand the quality of the data and analysis. Most authors note that interviews were audio-recorded and transcribed verbatim. Such a statement is important to many reviewers as an assurance that data were accurately recorded. In addition, the quality of interviews is central to the quality of the data. Several words are used appropriately to describe interviews: narrative, tell a story, open/semi-structured/in depth/unstructured. Some authors note they did not raise specific questions, and many note the importance of not influencing informants during data gathering. All of these details help the reviewer to know that the interviews were likely to yield a thick description, which is one that accurately captures the experience from the perspective of the informant in its fullest and richest complexity (Denzin, 1989; Geertz, 1973). Other details are less consistently included. For instance, when interviews were not conducted in English but were published in English, the translation process is not consistently discussed but needs to be described. This also applies if a coauthor who assisted with the analysis did not speak the language in which interview data were obtained. International researchers might appropriately cite international methodologists and sources in languages other than English.

Finally, contradiction is a feature of experience. Accordingly, one hallmark of a valid phenomenological study is the researcher's attention to the idiosyncrasies and nuances of individual experiences and the ways in which those variations emerge across a sample. The manuscript should demonstrate with evidence of the researcher's "close contact and connection" (Freeman, deMarrais, Preissle, Roulston, & St. Pierre, 2007, p. 30) with participants. Some phenomenological researchers further demonstrate the pervasive influence of their interactions with participants by documenting and incorporating facets of their own experience as data (Drew, 1989).

6. Findings are presented in a narrative manner reflecting an underlying structure drawn from the experience, rather than in keeping with a prescribed or proscribed theoretical framework

A reviewer should be particularly attentive if a phenomenological researcher emphasizes a particular theoretical framework in the introduction, the literature review, or both, and fails to set aside or bracket that perspective during data gathering and analysis. In some manuscripts, findings are framed in keeping with key terms of particular theories, rather than emerging empirically from participant data. This is a possible indication that the author entered the work with a mindset and selected data to support that point of view. In some such manuscripts, the researcher concludes by purporting that the work "confirms" a particular theory. Such an outcome is consistent with one goal of certain quantitative studies, but it is quite inconsistent with the qualitative paradigm. Any of these circumstances raises questions about the accuracy of the work, because there is insufficient evidence that the researcher was influenced by spending time with persons who were living the experience (Morse, Barrett, Mayan, Olson, & Spiers, 2002).

7. The report of findings should be sufficiently aesthetic in nature so as to draw the reader in to the experience of participants. A logical style of presentation should be coupled with the careful selection of pithy remarks from participants that evoke a sense of understanding on the part of the reader. A description of ways in which participants were involved in discussing emergent findings should be included

Because "the first objective of the phenomenological approach is the enlarging and deepening of the range of our immediate experience" (Spiegelberg, 1994, p. 679), conducting a phenomenological study is necessarily a rich and artistic endeavor. The essence of the researcher's creative experience should ooze from the manuscript in a variety of ways, including selection of intriguing data excerpts, derivation or creation of unique metaphors to characterize findings, and unusual or unpredictable juxtapositions of dialectical ideas. In a general discussion of aesthetics of qualitative research, Sandelowski (1995) emphasized the need to consider both "artistic and scientific canons of criticism" (p. 205). We view a phenomenological manuscript as a special case of Sandelowski's (1995) general point that a manuscript should reveal something about the person who created it. That is, we also argue that a phenomenological manuscript should illustrate the care the author–creator took to weave a resonating narrative from data of participants, such that some of their personal uniqueness is revealed as well. However, the nature of an art form cannot always be readily discerned, and reviewers, like other patrons of fine art, can and do welcome guideposts. For instance, it is useful when authors envision and articulate an organizing framework for findings (such as a chronology or specific to general); if findings that are nonetheless compelling appear to be shared in a random manner, a reviewer can offer a recommendation to the author to consider adopting an organizational principle.

In a rare methodological treatise focused solely on phenomenology, Bradbury-Jones, Irvine, and Sambrook (2010) recently reviewed the literature associated with the pros and cons of seeking "participant feedback" or conducting "member checks" (p. 25) about findings. After providing a short overview of descriptive and hermeneutic phenomenology, they presented an extensive rationale for using such feedback in hermeneutic and interpretive studies. However, Bradbury-Jones and colleagues did not reconsider the potential utility of such feedback in descriptive work, despite a stated intention to do so. This approach is an example of a problematic trend in the field, in which scholars provide overviews of both phenomenological traditions, present conclusions drawing on literature and personal experience with only one tradition, and then draw generic conclusions that span both traditions.

The conclusion that "participant feedback has a legitimate place in phenomenology" (Bradbury-Jones, 2010, p. 32) was not based on appraisal of its relevance in descriptive studies as well as interpretive studies. The predilection to conjoin the descriptive and interpretive traditions is a specific instance of the general "tendency to treat it [qualitative research] as a unified field, both at the level of data collection . . . and at the level of methodological approach" (Dixon-Woods et al., 2004, p. 224).

However, involving participants in ascertaining the credibility of analysis is particularly critical in descriptive phenomenology, although its emphasis and style varies with the method. In Colaizzi's (1985) method, the researcher interviews each participant once and then asks each participant this question, "How do my descriptive results compare with your experiences?" (p. 62). Colaizzi emphasized that new data arising from that dialogue "must be worked into the final product of the research" (p. 62), although there is no explanation as to how this should be done. In contrast, Porter (1998b) recommended that the researcher engage in frequent, focused discussions over time, accumulating evidence about each person's experience and, during most encounters, engaging in conversation about whether an emergent label for an intention captures what the person is trying to do with the experience. The nascent description of the experience is carried back and forth anonymously among different participants, so that all are engaged in considering some facet of the experiences of persons other than themselves (Porter, 1998b). Findings are honed as well in ongoing dialogue with coinvestigators, contributing to a nonproscriptive "'harmonious filling out' (Husserl, 1313/1962, p. 356) of the phenomena" (Porter, 1998b, p 21). That is, although participants' feedback about findings is considered and often reported in the manuscript, there is no mandate that it be incorporated in its entirety into the research product. Thus, because each phenomenological method has particular perspectives about soliciting and incorporating participant views on findings, we advise reviewers (again) to access the original report of the method while reviewing the manuscript. In addition, reviewers (as all readers) can and should judge for themselves how well the labels fit data provided to support or illustrate the label.

8. The discussion of findings should address the extent and nature of relationships between the present work and any prior work about the experience. The discussion of findings should interface with any bracketed literature, so as to more completely illuminate extant knowledge about the experience of interest gleaned through other research traditions as well

There is a distinction between findings and discussion of findings, and it is important that the two be presented separately, so that the reviewer can better judge the validity of findings. Although the findings of a phenomenological study should shed new light on the nature or meaning of an experience or both, a reviewer can raise legitimate questions about an author's statement that the work evokes or captures "the truth" about an experience. Such a goal is inconsistent with the aims of qualitative research in general and phenomenological research, in particular, regardless of the philosophical tradition with which it is associated.

Further Reading

Cohen, M. Z., Kahn, D., & Steeves, R. (2000). *Hermeneutic Phenomenological Research: A practical guide for nurse researchers.* Thousand Oaks, CA: Sage.

This short text is meant to provide practical guidance to those undertaking phenomenological research using the philosophical underpinnings of hermeneutics. The book was based on the authors' experiences conducting research and clarifies some of the approaches each "invented" to conduct their studies. It includes an overview of phenomenological research, its historical antecedents, and "how to" do research using this approach. This can be used by those who are using this method for the first time or for advanced researchers.

Husserl, E. (1962). *Ideas: General introduction to pure phenomenology* (W. R. B. Gibson, Trans.). London: Collier-Macmillan. (Original work published 1913.)

Although *Ideas* was not the first of Husserl's works, it was an extremely influential presentation of the key thrusts of descriptive phenomenology, a branch of philosophy that he founded. The "Author's Preface to the English Edition," which he wrote after completing the book in 1913, is a very useful overview of his views of science and how it could be further developed through the philosophical investigations that he characterized as "descriptive phenomenology" (p. 21).

Kohak, E. (1978). *Idea & Experience: Edmund Husserl's project of phenomenology in Ideas I.* Chicago, IL: The University of Chicago Press.

For new students of descriptive phenomenology, Kohak's rather short book is probably the best source of information and inspiration. Kohak provided useful, concrete explanations of some of Husserl's more difficult ideas, noting for instance, that the "essence" in which Husserl sought to describe is not like "a hidden core," but rather "an overt, characteristic way of being, what an X is 'in principle'" (p. 9). Kohak continued by explaining, then, that "Husserl is concerned with the relationship of particulars and principles in ordinary experience" (p. 9).

Schutz, A., & Luckmann, T. (1973). *The Structures of the Life-world* (R. M. Zaner & H. T. Engelhardt, Jr., Trans.). Evanston, IL: Northwestern University Press.

Alfred Schutz, who visited Husserl often during the last few years of Husserl's life, developed the subdiscipline of phenomenological sociology, in part by elaborating Husserl's notion of *Lebenswelt* or lifeworld, while incorporating ideas of other scholars and disregarding or disputing other of Husserl's philosophical thrusts. When Schutz died in 1959, his widow approached his student, Thomas Luckmann, and asked him to complete the book on which Schutz had worked for years. The basic thrust of the work is that the reality people take for granted is of a shared and social nature, with a structure that can be stratified into "spatial, temporal, and social structures of everyday experience" (Schutz & Luckmann, 1973, p. 36).

Spiegelberg, H. (with Schuhmann, K.) (1994). *The Phenomenological Movement: A historical introduction* (3rd revised and enlarged ed.). Dordrecht, The Netherlands: Kluwer Academic Press.

This extensive volume is the definitive source of information about the historical development and ongoing impact of the phenomenological movement and the various traditions that have emerged from it. Spiegelberg (1994) provided detailed information about the relationships and interactions of the key players in the movement over time—a strategy that enables students to grasp how the philosophers influenced each other's ideas. In "Part Five: The Essentials of the Phenomenological Method," Spiegelberg noted that "interpreting concealed meanings" (p. 712) be viewed as a "final step in the phenomenological procedure" (p. 712). Thus, he recommended that scholars "investigate general essences and their relationships" before undertaking studies designed to "interpret the meaning of phenomena" (p. 682).

Counterpoint Perspectives

Popay, J., Rogers, A., & Williams, G. (1998). Rationale and standards for the systematic review of qualitative literature in health services research. *Qualitative Health Research*, 8, 341–351.

Each of the Qualitative Touchstones presented above is grounded in a strong emphasis on rigor, regardless of which particular phenomenological approach is used. We recognize that rigor is not the only basic criterion of interest in qualitative research, regardless of method. Popay et al. (1998) emphasized flexibility, aptness, and clarity of description, and subjectivity as critical.

Dougherty, M. C., Freda, M. C., Kearney, M. H., Baggs, J. G., & Broome, M. (2011). Online survey of nursing journal peer reviewers: Indicators of quality in manuscripts. *Western Journal of Nursing Research*, 33(4), 506–521.

Just as rigor is not the only basic criterion of interest or importance in qualitative research, other factors must be considered in reviewing phenomenological manuscripts. In their survey of 1,675 peer reviewers of nursing journals, Dougherty et al. (2011) did not ask respondents to differentiate between qualitative and quantitative works; hence, there are no specific references to phenomenological manuscripts. However, the general findings are relevant here. Among eight options offered as potential priorities when writing a review, these four options were selected most often: (1) providing a critique of organization and clarity (61.7%), (2) making a recommendation on publication (59.6%), (3) offering a critique of "rigor and validity" (p. 512) (53.1%), and (4) "judging clinical relevance and importance" (p. 512) (46.9%). Thus, those respondents typically viewed clarity and organization of a manuscript as more important than rigor, which, in turn, is viewed as comparable in importance to clinical relevance. As Dougherty and colleagues observed those findings were tempered by several key facts. That is, some major nursing journals focus on clinical scholarship, and 30 percent of respondents did not have a doctoral degree; clinicians with masters' degrees are more likely to emphasize clinical relevance of a study over the fine points of any particular research approach, including phenomenological methods.

Thorne, S. (1991). Methodological orthodoxy in qualitative nursing research: Analysis of the issues. *Qualitative Health Research, 1*(2), 178–199. doi:10.1177/104973239100100203.

An additional important criterion for evaluating research is to examine the traditions in light of their relationship to the larger projects of disciplines. In this classic paper, Thorne examined phenomenology, in addition to grounded theory and ethnography, in relationship to anthropology, philosophy, sociology, and nursing. With regard to phenomenology, Thorne noted that nurses who conduct phenomenological research are often not interested in the deeper structures of "being," which interested phenomenological philosophers, but rather variations of meaning in shared experiences, such as pain or grief. Whereas Thorne clearly did not advocate "sloppy research" (p. 195), she suggested that scholars in practice disciplines (nurses, educators, and others) depart from traditional phenomenological assumptions. Questions are shaped by practical implications. For example, because subjective experience is highly contextualized: perceptions of persons with a chronic illness such as diabetes would not be the same as perceptions of persons with an acute illness. Thus, research questions should reflect this practice orientation.

Authors' Reflections on Quality

Having worked together throughout to prepare the content of this chapter, we take this opportunity to offer our personal perspectives on quality. We each address the question of ways in which the touchstones we proposed arise from our own lives as scholars.

Porter: In devising touchstones, rather than criteria for reviewing phenomenological manuscripts, we have nonetheless focused on features of the manuscript—as though the work was an object to be scrutinized, well, objectively. However, engaging with a manuscript as a reviewer is itself an experience—one that can be understood reflexively in keeping with the emphasis of phenomenological inquiry. During the review process the relationships between a reviewer's personal experiences (including methodological expertise) and the content and methodology of a given manuscript are critically important. Just as each individual's experience is viewed as unique in every phenomenological study, each reviewer brings a unique perspective to the review of every manuscript. When I prepare a manuscript review, I always share those individualized perspectives with the editor in the box for "comments for editor only" that is typically provided in on-line manuscript review centers. For instance, I have explained that my opinion about a certain methodological issue or approach is likely tempered by my own prior research work with a particular population group. Editors can weigh those personal and professional factors that are contextual to the review to better discern when one type of bias or another might affect the tenor of the review. I believe it is important, then, for reviewers of phenomenological manuscripts to reveal that the review process has engendered the sort of self-reflection that is a critical facet of the phenomenological method.

Cohen: Both quality standards and practical considerations are important to me when planning, conducting, writing, and reviewing research. These practical considerations include requirements from both grant funders and journals. In writing grant proposals, it is important of course to follow the funding agencies directions. In addition, it is essential in planning to specify the number of participants and the number of interviews in order to have an accurate timeline and budget for the project. This is when a concept such as "saturation" might be invoked. While it is a term from grounded theory, it concisely describes the idea that no new ideas are found in interviews after a certain point, that is, that a "complete" description has been obtained. More "orthodox" may object to using this language, but the label "saturation" is a short way of describing the idea, which may be useful considering the page limits for most grants and manuscripts. Although some journals do not limit length, many journals limit manuscripts to fifteen pages, which can necessarily limit the amount of space that can be devoted to describing methods. When reviewers find the results resonate, questions about the methods seem less important.

Another "compromise" I am comfortable with is acknowledging that many similarities, as well as differences, exist among qualitative methods. Consistency in references and language are more important to some than others. Another example is the word validity, which has been linked with quantitative research traditions. Some have "translated" this standard for phenomenological research to mean accuracy and trustworthiness. Using the word validity may evoke assumptions that do not fit with phenomenological methods. However, the word applies to the standards of quality that are important in all research, and some advocate using the terms reliability and validity to discuss rigor in qualitative research to link qualitative methods with mainstream science (Morse et al., 2002), while others simply discuss standards of rigor and use the same language for social science and natural science (Moss et al., 2009).

References

Benner, P. (Ed.). (1994). *Interpretive Phenomenology*. Thousand Oaks, CA: Sage.

Benner, P. (1985). Quality of life: A phenomenological perspective on explanation, prediction, and understanding in nursing science. *Advances in Nursing Science, 8*(1), 1–14.

Bradbury-Jones, C., Irvine, F., & Sambrook, S. (2010). Phenomenology and participant feedback: Convention or contention? *Nurse Researcher, 17*(2), 25–33.

Burns, V. E. (2008). Living without a strong father figure: A context for teen mothers' experience of having become sexually active. *Issues in Mental Health Nursing, 29*(3), 279–297. doi:10.1080/01612840701869692.

Burns, V. E. & Porter, E. J. (2007). The experience of having become sexually active for teen mothers. *Journal of Community Health Nursing, 24*(4), 215–236. doi: 10.1080/07370010701645877.

Clark, J. P. (2003). How to peer review a qualitative manuscript. In F. Godlee & T. Jefferson (Eds.), *Peer Review in Health Sciences* (2nd ed., pp. 219–235). London: BMJ Books.

Cohen, M. Z., Kahn, D., & Steeves, R. (2000). *Hermeneutic Phenomenological Research: A practical guide for nurse researchers*. Thousand Oaks, CA: Sage.

Cohen, M. Z. & Omery, A. (1994). Schools of phenomenology: Implications for research. In J. M. Morse (Ed.), *Critical Issues in Qualitative Research* (pp. 136–156). Thousand Oaks, CA: Sage.

Cohen, M. Z., Pace, E., Kaur, G., & Bruera, E. (2009). Delirium in advanced cancer patients leading to distress in patients and their family caregivers. *Journal of Palliative Care, 25*(3), 164–171.

Cohen, M. Z., Slomka, J., Pentz, R., Flamm, A., Gold, D., Herbst, R., & Abbruzzese, J. (2007). Phase I participants' views of quality of life and trial participation burdens. *Supportive Care in Cancer, 15*(7), 885–890. doi: 10.1007/s00520–007–0216–0.

Colaizzi, P. (1978). Psychological research as the phenomenologist views it. In R. Walle & M. Kings (Eds.), *Existential Phenomenological Alternatives for Psychology* (pp. 48–71). New York: Oxford University Press.

Denzin, N. K. (1989). *Interpretive Interactionism*. Newbury Park, CA: Sage.

Diekelmann, N. (2001). Narrative pedagogy: Heideggerian hermeneutical analyses of lived experiences of students, teacher, and clinicians. *Advances in Nursing Science, 23*(3), 53–71.

Diekelmann, N., Allen, D., & Tanner, C. (1989). *The NLN Criteria for Appraisal of Baccalaureate Programs: A critical hermeneutic analysis*. New York: The National League for Nursing Press.

Dixon-Woods, M., Shaw, R. L., Agarwal, S., & Smith, J. A. (2004). The problem of appraising qualitative research. *Quality and Safety in Health Care, 13*(3), 223–225. doi: 10.1136/qshc.2003.008714.

Dougherty, M. C., Freda, M. C., Kearney, M. H., Baggs, J. G., & Broome, M. (2011). Online survey of nursing journal peer reviewers: Indicators of quality in manuscripts. *Western Journal of Nursing Research, 33*(4), 506–521. doi: 10.1177/0193945910385715.

Drew, N. (1989). The interviewer's experience as data in phenomenological research. *Western Journal of Nursing Research, 11*(4), 431–439. doi: 10.1177/019394598901100405.

Fletcher, B., Cohen, M. Z., Schumacher, K., & Lydiatt, W. (2012). Blessing and a curse: Head and neck cancer survivors' experiences. *Cancer Nursing: An International Journal for Cancer Care, 35*(2), 126–132. doi: 10.1097/NCC.0b013e31821bd054.

Freeman, M., deMarrais, K., Preissle, J., Roulston, K., & St. Pierre, E. A. (2007). Standards of evidence in qualitative research: An incitement to discourse. *Educational Researcher, 36*(1), 25–32. doi: 10.3102/0013189X06298009.

Fu, M. (2005). Breast cancer survivors' intentions of managing lymphedema. *Cancer Nursing, 28*(6), 446–457.

Geertz, C. (1973). *The Interpretation of Culture*. New York: Basic Books.

Geertz, C. (1988). *Works and Lives: The anthropologist as author*. Stanford, CA: Stanford University Press.

Giorgi, A. (1970). *The Approach to Psychology as a Human Science*. New York: Harper & Row.

Giorgi, A. (1985). *Phenomenology and Psychological Research*. Pittsburgh, PA: Duquesne University Press.

Hans, J. D. & Coleman, M. (2009). The experiences of remarried stepfathers who pay child support. *Personal Relationships, 16*(4), 597–618. doi: 10.1111/j.1475–6811.2009.01241.x.

Harle, M., Dela Cruz, R., Velosa, G., Rock, J., Faulker, J., & Cohen, M. Z. (2007). The experience of Filipino American Patients with cancer. *Oncology Nursing Forum, 34*(6), 1170–1175. doi: 10.1188/07.ONF.1170–1175.

Heidegger, M. (1962). *Being and Time* (J. Macquarrie & E. Robinson, Trans.). New York: Harper & Row. (Original work published 1927.)

Husserl, E. (1962). *Ideas: General introduction to pure phenomenology* (W. R. B. Gibson, Trans.). London: Collier-Macmillan. (Original work published 1913.)

Husserl, E. (1970). *Logical Investigations* (Vol. 1) (J. Finley, Trans.). New York: Humanities Press. (Original work published 1900.)

Ironside, P. M., Scheckel, M., Wessels, C., Bailey, M. E., Powers, S., & Seeley, D. K. (2003). Experiencing chronic illness: Co-creating new understandings. *Qualitative Health Research, 13*(2), 171–183. doi: 10.1177/1049732302239597.

Jones, R., Utz, S., Williams, I., Hinton, I., Alexander, G., Moore, C., Blankenship, J., Steeves, R. H., & Oliver, N. (2008). Family interactions among African Americans diagnosed with type 2 diabetes. *The Diabetes Educator, 34*(2), 318–326. doi:10.1177/0145721708314485.

Jones, R., Wenzel, J., Hinton, I., Cary, M., Jones, N., Krumm, S., & Ford, J. (2011). Exploring cancer support needs for older African-American men with prostate cancer. *Supportive Care in Cancer, 19*(9), 1411–1419. doi: 10.1007/s00520–010–0967-x.

Kitrungrote, L., Wongkongkul, T., Chanprasit, C., Suttharangsee, W., & Cohen, M. Z. (2008). Experiences of caregivers of spouses with head and neck cancer undergoing radiation therapy. *Thai Journal of Nursing Research, 12*(3), 207–219.

Kline, W. B. (2008). Developing and submitting credible qualitative manuscripts. *Counselor Education and Supervision, 47*(4), 210–217.

Kohak, E. (1978). *Idea & Experience: Edmund Husserl's project of phenomenology in Ideas I.* Chicago, IL: The University of Chicago Press.

Merleau-Ponty, M. (1962). *Phenomenology of Perception* (C. Smith, Trans.). New York: Humanities Press. (Original work published 1945.)

Morse, J. M., Barrett, M., Mayan, M., Olson, K., & Spiers, J. (2002). Verification strategies for establishing reliability and validity in qualitative research. *International Journal of Qualitative Methods, 1*(2), 13–22.

Moss, P. A., Phillips, D. C., Erickson, F. D., Floden, R. E., Lather, P. A., & Schneider, B. L. (2009). Learning from our differences: A dialogue across perspectives on quality in education research. *Educational Researcher, 38*(7), 501–517. doi:10.3102/0013189X09348351.

Oiler, C. (1982). The phenomenological approach in nursing research. *Nursing Research, 31*(3), 178–181.

Omery, A. (1983). Phenomenology: A method for nursing research. *Advances in Nursing Science, 5*(2), 49–62.

Parra-Cardona, J. R., Sharp, E. A., & Wampler, R. J. (2008). "Changing for my kid": Fatherhood experiences of Mexican-origin teen fathers involved in the justice system. *Journal of Marital & Family Therapy, 34*(3), 369–387. doi: 10.1111/j.1752–0606.2008.00078.x.

Popay, J., Rogers, A., & Williams, G. (1998). Rationale and standards for the systematic review of qualitative literature in health services research. *Qualitative Health Research, 8*(3), 341–351. doi: 10.1177/104973239800800305.

Porter, E. J. (1994). Older widows' experience of living alone at home. *Image: Journal of Nursing Scholarship, 26*(1), 19–24. doi: 10.1111/j.1547–5069.1994.tb00289.x.

Porter, E. J. (1995). The life-world of older widows: The context of lived experience. *Journal of Women & Aging, 7*(4), 31–46. doi: 10.1300/J074v07n04_04.

Porter, E. J. (1998a). Older widows' intention to keep the generations separate. *Health Care for Women International, 19*(5), 395–410. doi: 10.1080/073993398246179.

Porter, E. (1998b). On "being inspired" by Husserl's phenomenology: Reflections on Omery's exposition of phenomenology as a method for nursing research. *Advances in Nursing Science, 21*(1), 16–28.

Porter, E. J. (2000). Research on home care utilization: A critical analysis of the preeminent approach. *Journal of Aging Studies, 14*(1), 25–38. doi:10.1016/S0890–4065(00)80014–6.

Porter, E. J. (2005a). Older widows' experience of home care. *Nursing Research, 54*(5), 296–303.

Porter, E. J. (2005b). Wearing and using personal emergency response system buttons: Older frail widows' intentions. *Journal of Gerontological Nursing, 31*(10), 26–33.

Porter, E. J. (2007a). Problems with preparing food reported by frail older women living alone at home. *Advances in Nursing Science, 30*(2), 159–174. doi: 10.1097/01.ANS.0000271106.42043.be.

Porter, E. J. (2007b). Scales and tales: Older women's difficulty with daily tasks. *Journal of Gerontology: Social Sciences, 62B*(3), S153–S159.

Porter, E. J. (2008). Home care as a complex experience: A chronological case study. *Home Health Care Services Quarterly, 27*(3), 167–183. doi: 10.1080/01621420802317260.

Porter, E. J. & Lasiter, S. (2008). Reducing my risk of intrusion: An intention of old homebound women who live alone. *Nursing Research, 57*(5), 351–359. doi: 10.1097/01.NNR.0000313503.30346.e7.

Porter, E. J., Ganong, L. H., & Armer, J. A. (2000). The "church family" and kin: An older rural black woman's support network and preferences for care providers. *Qualitative Health Research, 10*(4), 452–470. doi: 10.1177/104973200129118570.

Porter, E. J., Matsuda, S., & Lindbloom, E. J. (2010). Intentions of older homebound women to reduce the risk of falling again. *Journal of Nursing Scholarship, 42*(1), 101–109. doi: 10.1111/j.1547–5069.2010.01334.x.

Porter, E. J., Ganong, L. H., & Matsuda, S. (in press). Intentions of older homebound women with regard to reaching help quickly. *Western Journal of Nursing Research*.

Ricoeur, P. (1981). *Hermeneutics and the Human Sciences.* (J. B. Thompson, Trans. & Ed.). New York: Cambridge University Press.

Sandelowski, M. (1995). Qualitative analysis: What it is and how to begin. *Research in Nursing & Health, 18*(4), 371–375. doi: 10.1002/nur.4770180411.

Sartre, J.-P. (1963). *Search for a Method.* New York: Vintage Books.

Schutz, A. & Luckmann, T. (1973). *The Structures of the Life-World* (R. M. Zaner & H. T. Engelhardt, Jr., Trans.). Evanston, IL: Northwestern University Press.

Sharp, E. A. & Ganong, L. H. (2007). Living in the gray: Women's experiences of missing the marital transition. *Journal of Marriage & the Family, 69*(3), 831–844. doi: 10.1111/j.1741-3737.2007.00408.x.

Spiegelberg, H. (with Schuhmann, K.) (1994). *The Phenomenological Movement: A historical introduction* (3rd revised and enlarged ed.). Dordrecht, The Netherlands: Kluwer Academic Press.

Steeves, R. H., Laughon, K., Parker, B., & Weierbach, F. (2007). Talking about talk: The experience of boys who survived intraparental homicide. *Issues in Mental Health Nursing, 28*, 899–912. doi: 10.1080/01612840701493576.

Thorne, S. (1991). Methodological orthodoxy in qualitative nursing research: Analysis of the issues. *Qualitative Health Research, 1*(2), 178–199. doi: 10.1177/104973239100100203.

Van Manen, M. (1997). *Researching Lived Experience: Human science for an action sensitive pedagogy (2nd ed.).* London, England: The Althouse Press.

Vellone, E., Piras, G., Talucci, C., & Cohen, M. Z. (2008). Quality of life for caregivers of people with Alzheimer's disease. *Journal of Advanced Nursing, 61*(2), 222–231. doi: 10.1111/j.1365-2648.2007.04494.x.

Wenzel, J., Utz, S. W., Steeves, R. H., Hinton, I., & Jones, R. A. (2005). Plenty of sickness: Description by African Americans living in rural areas with type 2 diabetes. *The Diabetes Educator, 31*(1), 98–107. doi:10.1177/0145721704273242.

Wongvatunyu, S. & Porter, E. J. (2005). Mothers' experience of helping young adults with traumatic brain injury. *Journal of Nursing Scholarship, 37*(1), 48–56. doi: 10.1111/j.1547-5069.2005.00015.x.

Wongvatunyu, S. & Porter, E. J. (2008). Helping young adult children with traumatic brain injury: The life-world of mothers. *Qualitative Health Research, 18*(8), 1062–1074. doi: 10.1177/1049732308320111.

14

Poetics and Performance

Monica Prendergast and George Belliveau

The past decade or so has led to a flourishing of poetic and performance-based qualitative research (for bibliographies on each approach, see Prendergast, 2009a, 2009b; Beck, Belliveau, Lea, & Wager, 2011). Researchers have turned to these arts-based approaches for many reasons and from varied theoretical perspectives. However, the majority of poetic and performance studies could be seen as engaging in the work of art and also in carrying out the work of social science in innovative and interdisciplinary ways. The challenges inherent to the review process of poetic or performance-based inquiries, or creative submissions in other related alternate forms, is one that has been debated in conference settings, between colleagues, and in the literature (Ackroyd & O'Toole, 2010; Faulkner, 2007, 2010; Gallagher, 2007; Piirto, 2002; Saldaña, 2003, 2005; Sullivan, 2009). In all cases, however, we believe that it is imperative for reviewers to attend to both scholarly and aesthetic aspects of the work.

Reviewers less familiar with poetic or performance approaches will find this chapter useful in presenting selected key terms and qualitative touchstones that attend to the necessary vigor required of a peer-reviewed publication and the attendant aesthetic qualities present in a successful poetry- or performance-based study. As researchers who have made numerous contributions to each arts-based range of methods under discussion here—and who have also surveyed these approaches through meta-analyses—we are well placed to consider the challenges of reviewing poetic and performance research studies (see relevant citations under Belliveau and Prendergast in References).

Select Terms

Ethnotheater and *ethnodrama* are defined most often as modes of dissemination of data gathered and analyzed using traditional qualitative research tools such as action research, narrative, interviews, and field notes. It is essentially the dramatization of ethnographically gathered data.

Found poems are poems crafted from preexisting texts of some kind and creating found poems is a key strategy in poetic inquiry when working with interview or other participant data, or with texts of various kinds (Butler-Kisber, 2002; Molnar, 2010; Prendergast, 2004b, 2006; Pryer, 2005, 2007; Sullivan, 2000; Walsh, 2006). In a research context, these texts are most often either interview or focus group data or theoretical texts. Found poetry has a history in literature and is created by many poets as both a writing exercise and as poems for publication (see Angelou, 1991; Colombo, 1966; Dillard, 1995; Moody, 2001).

Performed research (Ackroyd & O'Toole, 2010) consists of a number of possible practices and shares common approaches to ethnotheater, verbatim theater, performance ethnography, performative inquiry, research-based theater, among others. Each context that includes performed research is unique; as such the approach will vary. Essentially, performed research includes researchers and/or artists making use of both artistic and research approaches to bring particular research phenomena to life for outside and/or inside witnesses/audiences.

Poetic inquiry is an umbrella term coined by Prendergast, Leggo, and Sameshima (2009a, 2009b; see also Thomas, Cole, & Stewart, 2012) to cover the forty-plus discrete terms found in Prendergast's (2007) meta-analysis of peer-reviewed social science publications incorporating poetry as a methodological approach. A summary of findings from this survey (Prendergast, 2009a, 2009b) lists these terms and groups poetically informed studies according to the dominant voice presented: *researcher-voiced* (autobiographical or autoethnographical studies dominate here); *participant-voiced* (poetic transcriptions or poetic representations of participant data); or, *literature-voiced* (theoretical poems usually crafted as found poems from other texts).

Poetic transcription (Freeman, 2006; Glesne, 1997, 2010; Whitney, 2004) refers to the process of transcribing data in poetic as opposed to prosaic ways. As Glesne (1997) defines it, "Poetic transcription approximates poetry through the concentrated language of interviewee, shaped by researcher to give pleasure and truth" (p. 213).

Poetic representation (MacNeil, 2000; Richardson, 1992a, 1992b, 1994, 1997; Ward, 2011; Waskul & van der Riet, 2002) is an indicator of how data will be represented in a study. Sociologist Laurel Richardson (1993) describes this process and its critical purpose:

> By settling words together into new configurations, the relations created through echo repetition, rhythm, rhyme let us see and hear the world in a new dimension. Poetry is thus a practical and powerful means for reconstitution of worlds. It suggests a way out of the numbing and deadening, disaffective, disembodied, schizoid sensibilities characteristic of phallocentristic social science.
>
> (p. 705)

Research-based theater generally incorporates theater throughout the research process with an aim to enhance "understanding of lived experience in different groups and communities." This understanding of research-based theater does not restrict the approach to creating theater from disseminated research or data involving an ethnographic approach (Belliveau & Lea, 2011).

Research poems or research poetry (Cannon Poindexter, 2002; Faulkner, 2007, 2010) is the term favored by Sandra Faulkner and others to indicate poems written in a research context. Faulkner's (2010) book *Poetry as method: Reporting research through verse* employs this terminology throughout.

Verbatim theater (Anderson & Wilkinson, 2007; MacCleave, 2006; Paget, 1997) is a form of documenting research through the creation of theater by using specific dialogue generally yielded from interviews on a specific topic. A verbatim script makes use of the precise words offered by the research subjects, yet the creative team may cut or reorder the wording in the development of dialoguing the data.

Diversities in Perspective, Context, and Form

Poetics

In the 182 peer-reviewed social science journal articles incorporating poetic methods analyzed in Prendergast's 2007 annotated bibliography, an abundance of diverse perspective, contexts, and forms were apparent. Here we sketch out some of the more common approaches taken.

Autobiographical/autoethnographical studies employing poetic methods are the dominant form of poetic research, as almost exactly half of the surveyed studies fall under this heading in whole or in part. These studies use poetry to highlight life stories and experiences of interest to a field or discipline. For example, social worker Richard Furman writes poems about his father's battle with cancer (2004a), memories of adolescent identity formation (Furman et al., 2007), and the trauma of a hospital emergency room visit (2006) as contributions to health research. Poet and language and literacy researcher Carl Leggo has spent much of his career on "speculations" (2004b, 2005b) and "ruminations" (1999, 2002, 2004a, 2005a) on how to live poetically in the world. His insistence on finding the sense of wonder in memory and everyday life through poetry makes up a significant part of his contribution to language arts education (Leggo, 2008; Prendergast & Leggo, 2007). Prendergast (2011a) writes autoethnographic poems about her experience of working at a long distance from her home and family. She reflects on how this fact of life for many academics is akin to the experiences of migrant workers worldwide, albeit in very different socioeconomic conditions. Thus, Prendergast follows the example of Weems (2009) who insists that research poetry elicit empathetic responses in readers and listeners. Empathy is just one possible emotional response to poetic forms, which may manifest as feelings of anger or advocacy in readers, depending on the intentions of the autobiographical poet and the context of the resulting poems.

Participant-voiced poetic inquiry studies are also plentiful and make up one-third of the 182 studies in Prendergast's meta-analysis of this method. These studies appear most often in education, health studies (predominantly in nursing), social work, sociology, and anthropology journals. While the range of topics covered in these studies is broad, a common focus on *affect* is fairly consistent; that is, these participant-voiced poetic inquiry studies are interested in some emotional aspect of participants' experience. In health studies, for example, poetic transcriptions/representations of participants dealing with illness, addiction, or impending death are seen (Cannon Poindexter, 2002; Galvin & Todres, 2009; Kendall & Murray, 2005; Öhlen, 2003; Philip, 1995; Sameshima, Vandermause, & Chalmers, 2009). Clearly, these topics lend themselves to the powerful emotional expression that poetic language facilitates so well. Other studies involving poetic transcription or representation through found poetry (although that literary term and practice is rarely acknowledged by researchers), focus on the following assortment of research questions:

How do managers feel about losing their jobs (Brearley, 2000)?
How do young Batswanians (sic) feel about their gender roles (Commeyras & Montsi, 2000)?
How do primary elementary students feel about their relationship with their teacher (Butler-Kisber, 2002)?
How do parents of autistic children feel about their interaction with the health and education systems (Beatson & Prelock, 2002)?
How does it feel to be a mother (Barg, 2001), an art teacher (Buttignol et al., 2001), a parent with school-aged children (Freeman, 2001), a girl (Gannon, 2001), a gay teacher (Grace, 2001; Guiney Yallop, 2005), a teacher of color (Santoro & Kamler, 2001), a refugee (Hones, 1998)?
(Prendergast, 2009b, pp. xxii–xxiii)

For us, a readily apparent affective component is highly desirable in an effective poetic inquiry employing participant-voiced research poetry.

Literature-voiced poetic inquiry is the smallest set of studies seen, making up only 13 percent of the citations in Prendergast's bibliography. However, the *Vox Theoria* section of Prendergast, Leggo and Sameshima's edited collection of poetic inquiry (2009b, pp. 3–144), offers a number of significant contributions to this less common area of poetic inquiry practice. Contributions here include reprintings of Cahnmann's (2003) and Piirto's (2002) influential essays, a theorization of poetic inquiry in relation to the cut-up methods of experimental modern writers such as William S. Burroughs

(James, 2009), a theorization extending from the work of Deleuze and Guattari (Shidmehr, 2009), and a theorization drawing on the qualities of effective literary poetry (Sullivan, 2009; see following text for more on this latter contribution). While theories on and of poetic inquiry are welcome indicators of a growing robustness as an arts-based method, there are also examples of poetic inquiry studies that draw on theoretical texts to elucidate/interpret them through poetic transcription/ representation (Prendergast, 2004, 2006, 2011; Prendergast & Leggo, 2007; Sullivan, 2000).

In sum, poetically informed studies range widely in disciplinary locations and voices employed. In the majority of cases, however, a clearly delineated affective component is present to allow for the creation of effective poems. More theoretical poetic inquiry may not have actual poetry present in the text, yet the theorization may be deemed significant for the development of the methodology by the research community interested in qualitative arts-based approaches. Or, when drawing specifically on theoretical texts in the creation of found poems as a poetic inquiry method, it is advised that the original texts, dense and abstruse though they may be, contain sufficient qualities of imagery and emotionality to make them worth rendering into poetic forms.

Performance

We have chosen *performance-based research* as the umbrella term to encompass research that integrates aspects of performance, which involves a wide spectrum of human social interactions (Schechner, 1988/2003), but for our purposes will focus on theater-based performance practices. Scholarly writings from arts-based researchers from various arts disciplines, aside from the ones we cite in poetry and theater in this chapter, have informed our thinking: that is, *Dance*: Blumenfeld-Jones, 2008; Snowber, 2007; *Music*: Bresler, 2008; Gouzouasis, 2008; *Visual Art*: Sullivan, 2005; O'Donoghue, 2009. It is also important to note the seminal work from scholars, such as Butler (1997), Madison & Hamera (2006), and Schechner (1985), to name but a few who have expanded and enriched understandings of performance by making use of the term outside the arts and into community settings and everyday life. As such performance reaches widely beyond music, dance, poetry, art, and drama.

Nonetheless, to focus our discussion and reflect the authors' expertise, the approaches shared in this chapter reflect theater-based models within performance-based research. Approaches within this realm—research-based theater—have been variously named: verbatim theater (Anderson, 2007; Paget, 1997), performance/performed ethnography (Alexander, Anderson, & Gallegos, 2005; Denzin, 1997, 2003), performed research (Ackroyd & O'Toole, 2010), documentary theater (Dawson, 1999), performative inquiry (Fels & Belliveau, 2008; Fels, 2009), or ethnotheater/ethnodrama (Mienczakowski & Moore, 2008; Saldaña, 2003). These various research-based theater approaches have individual nuances and intentions, yet they all share the potential to expand understandings, engage audiences, and provoke new learning experiences through the dramatization and performing of research.

Over the past two decades, arts-based researchers have been providing insights on the scope and breadth of (theater) performance-based research, helping readers/viewers to better understand the place and meaning of this approach. To address the various modes and forms of performance-based research, Beck, Belliveau, Lea, & Wager (2011) developed a comprehensive spectrum, describing research projects that involve theatre to help situate the range of work being done in this genre. The spectrum of performance-based research provides markers and exemplars for readers/viewers to appreciate the variety of possibilities within this artistic-research approach, and to better understand ways to evaluate the intent and outcomes. In *Performing Research: Tensions, triumphs and trade-offs of ethnodrama*, Ackroyd and O'Toole (2010) bring together various authors describing particular projects and offering insights about working approaches, ethical issues, and reception of the work. Using theater approaches to playwriting and rehearsing, Saldaña (2005) provides specific suggestions as to how researchers can work with artists to create pieces that "entertain" ideas as well as provide an aesthetic experience. Saldaña also showcases full scripts so that readers can be exposed to the written outcome of pieces of performance-based research. The body of literature on the reception and evaluation of research-based theater is growing but authors are still working toward trying to address the uniqueness and nuanced nature of theater as a form of research. Cox, Kazubowski-Houston, and Nisker (2006), Gray et al. (2003), and Mitchell et al. (2011) have written about the reception of audiences' reactions and insights of viewing research-based theater, seeking to find the efficacy of this approach. Arguments that playwriting (MacKenzie and Belliveau, 2011) and play-building (Norris, 2009) are forms of qualitative analysis have been theorized, offering academics ways as to how theater can be used critically during the analysis phase.

This growing critical body of literature on research-based theater is providing researchers, artists, and reviewers insights on the development, conditions, and receptions of this research approach. However, it is very timely to develop a more comprehensive framework, a set of guidelines to assess and comment on performance-based research, enabling creators and reviewers with benchmarks to consider while developing and/or reviewing the work.

Qualitative Touchstones

The touchstones shared below offer important considerations for reviewers while they assess scholarly/artistic work that describes, shares, and/or evaluates poetic- or performance-based research. We are presenting our qualitative touchstones separately by discipline here, although there is some overlapping between poetry and performance, as both are forms of arts-based qualitative research. Thus, for example, the question of balance between aesthetic and instrumental elements is addressed in both sections, but sources are listed from different literature. Our decision to present separate sections is intended to assist reviewers who are seeking guidelines on either one of the two approaches.

Poetics

1. Effective contextualization and application of poetic forms

As a number of poetic inquirers have argued, poetry should only be employed within a research study when there is an apparent "good fit" between topic and method (Faulkner, 2007, 2010; Piirto, 2002; Prendergast, 2009a, 2009b; Sullivan, 2009). Faulkner (2007) recommends that researchers write an *ars poetica* that expresses why they are drawn to poetic inquiry and who has influenced this decision:

> One entrée into writing your own *ars poetica* is to read, study, and borrow other poet researchers' work and *ars poetica* to define, refine, and test your own conceptualizations. Who are your favorite poets? Why are they your favorite? What are they doing in their poems that make you excited?
>
> (p. 223)

Certainly, there are many poetic inquiry studies extant that do little more than cite a small number of methodological sources and present poetic representations or transcriptions with little or no discussion of poetic form. A reviewer of such studies is making a reasonable request, in our view, when asking writers to contextualize and clarify their choice of poetry as an approach.

Qualification also comes into play here. A poetic inquirer may not be a literary poet as well. In the absence of an MFA or other qualification in poetry writing, a researcher should be honest in expressing his or her background and experiences in working with and through poetry. As Piirto (2002) pointedly states:

To observe heartfelt efforts by researchers [at an arts-based educational research conference] with little or no background in the art being demonstrated was sometimes painful, especially to those who worked in, were trained in, knew, and loved the art being demonstrated. Is not the concept of quality and qualification to be taken seriously in arts-based research?

(p. 443)

Experimentation and innovation are welcomed in arts-based research, which is a relatively new range of methods in qualitative research (Butler-Kisber, 2010; Cahnmann-Taylor & Siegesmund, 2008; Irwin & de Cosson, 2004; Knowles & Cole, 2008; Leavy, 2009; Springgay, Irwin, Leggo, & Gouzouasis, 2007). Yet, experimentation and innovation cannot occur in a void. At a minimum, a poetic inquirer should articulate a brief *ars poetica* that effectively locates his or her interest in and focus on poetry as methodology.

2. Affective and/or imagistic elements present in the work

Poetry works in very distinctively different ways than prose. Poetry has key elements of metaphor in the form of imagery, and rhythm in the use of repetition, line breaks, and even in the visual appearance of words on the page. We turn to poetry because it allows us to express something that feels inexpressible in prose. When poetry is brought into a social science context, all of these qualities and characteristics should ideally be apparent. In the literature on poetic inquiry, there are examples seen wherein the data transcribed into poetic forms are lacking in affect, imagery, and/or metaphor, and the resulting poems suffer aesthetically as a result. Mundane data can only lead to mundane poems crafted from that data. A reviewer with little or no background in poetry can still determine if these basic elements are woven into a poetically informed study through a researcher's attention to the question being addressed having some inherent quality of lived experience, preferably with a heightened emotional aspect or aspects of some kind. We have read poetic transcriptions that read as narratives, and only the use of line breaks makes these narrative "poetic" in the way they look, if in no other way at all.

Fortunately, literary poet and poetic inquirer Anne Sullivan (2009) addresses these concerns in her essay "On poetic occasion in inquiry: Concreteness, voice, ambiguity, tension, and associative logic." Sullivan presents these qualities of poetry reframed for the purposes of inquiry, asking:

What happens when the material is arrayed in front of us and we have to decide what to do with it, whether or not to make poetry of it? Some materials are more welcoming of poetic rendering than others, and most of us who do this work probably recognize these materials intuitively or by knowledge so deeply internalized that it feels intuitive. We recognize the occasions for poetry as easily as we recognize a familiar road.

(p. 111)

Sullivan goes on to present each of these "occasions for poetry" (p. 112) by defining and illustrating each one with one or more poems, some her own and some from her students or from the literature of poetic inquiry. Her criteria for poetic occasions include *concreteness*, *voice*, *emotion*, *ambiguity*, *associative logic*, and *tension*.

Any reviewer of a poetic inquiry study will be well served by drawing on Sullivan's terminology. Nevertheless, while it may be possible to determine the effectiveness of poems based on interview or other types of participant data, it is another matter entirely if the poems offered are original. How is one to "judge" this kind of autobiographical or autoethnographical poetry? We address this question next.

3. Reflexivity and presence of researcher and/or participants

Richardson (2000) creates review criteria for what she calls "creative analytic practice ethnography" (p. 929) that have proven adaptable for arts-based research methods, as each range of methods shares common interests in aesthetic rendering of interpretive inquiries. Richardson lists reflexivity as one of her criteria, asking:

> How did the author come to write this text? How was the information gathered? Are there ethical issues? How has the author's subjectivity been both a producer and a product of this text? Is there adequate self-awareness and self-exposure for the reader to make judgments about the point of view? Does the author hold him- or her-self accountable to the standards of knowing and telling of the people he or she has studied?
>
> (p. 937)

These questions are useful when applied to poetic inquiry studies, as they address the importance of the role of the researcher in intersubjective relation to the topic under investigation and with the participants (if any are involved). Transparency is a key criteria here for peer reviewers: How visible is the author in the work, or is s/he "hiding" behind the data analysis, masking (perhaps) invisible intentionalities? How clearly and ethically represented are the participants? In our view, these kinds of reflexively oriented questions are valuable ones to ask of any poetic inquiry.

4. Overall impact in aesthetic and disciplinary terms

This final touchstone for poetic inquiry asks reviewers to assess a submission based on two separate but related criteria: How well do the poetic elements work within the study as poetry? How well does the study overall work as a scholarly contribution? Again, Richardson (2000) provides much-needed support in her review criteria:

> *Substantive contribution:* Does this piece contribute to our understanding of social life? Does the writer demonstrate a deeply grounded (if embedded) social scientific perspective? How has this perspective informed the construction of the text? [. . .]
>
> *Aesthetic merit:* [. . .] Does this piece succeed aesthetically? Does the use of [poetic] practices open up the text, invite interpretive responses? Is the text artistically shaped, satisfying, and not boring?
>
> (p. 937)

Arts-based research can be seen as a doubled enterprise; the researcher not only is charged with creating something worthy of peer-reviewed publication, but is also responsible for creating an aesthetically rich and rewarding piece of writing (or other artistic creation). Poetic inquiry is one step further away from standardized academic report writing than creative nonfiction, auto-ethnography, or narrative inquiry, as poetry is one step removed from prose. Due to the very particular demands of poetry (such as concision, description, imagery, emotion, lyricism, and so on), a successful poetic inquiry study is necessarily held to fulfill all the qualitative touchstones criteria offered in this section, concerned as they are with the particularities of poetry and its application in social science research.

Performance

1. Instrumental and the aesthetic balance in the work

A number of scholars working in research-based theater have discussed the balance of integrating the instrumental (research) and the aesthetic (theater) in their work, as this weaving impacts the audience's reception and understanding (Beare & Belliveau, 2008; Saldaña, 2010; White & Belliveau, 2010). When the work is presented with too strong an emphasis on the didactic (research findings), the audience engagement tends to be lessened (Cox, Kazubowski-Houston, & Nisker, 2006), yet by the same token if the artistic is too dominant, a lack of credibility and research integrity can be experienced (Mienczakowski, 2001). Jackson (2005) shares his perspective on the ability of researcher/artists to balance the instrumental and artistic without compromising either. He argues that the higher the artistic quality the more chances of engagement with the subject matter (or research). Thus, performance-based research's ultimate strength is when art and research inform one another, working in tandem, neither taking precedence over the other. The performance-based research spectrum offered by Beck Belliveau, Lea, and Wager (2011) acknowledges that researchers come with varying levels of experience in artistic ability. As such the artistic piece will vary depending on the experience and expertise of those working on the research. The spectrum's goal is to provide a framework to position the work and intentions of the researchers using arts-based approaches, rather than making value judgments.

2. Sharing the artistic in the academic article to provide the reader entry points inside the work

Research articles that include performance-based research should aim to find the balance of describing, analyzing, and theorizing their approach to research along with sharing/integrating some of the actual artistic, theatrical work (when possible). The blending of the artistic and instrumental found in the performance representation should exist in the scholarly article (Belliveau, 2006), otherwise the reader is left without being able to appreciate the aesthetic experience that might have occurred between performers and audience. A/r/tography scholars (Irwin & Springgay, 2008) have been publishing research that weaves in examples of their art works, and artistically represents the connections and spaces between the artistic and academic. Just as important, placing the artistic representation on its own as self-explanatory can be problematic and limiting for the purposes of scholarly writing. Creating an exegesis and/or scholarly discussion to situate the underpinnings of the work is a vital consideration to further growth in the field.

3. Using all the elements of the theater (or other performance genres) to share the research

Individuals working with research-based theater are encouraged to capitalize on the various elements of theater to increase the audience experience. For instance, when only text or dialogue is used, such as in a verbatim piece between interviewer and interviewee, the invitation for the audience to enter can be limited. Researchers and artists are encouraged to consider sound, visuals, pacing of dialogue, character intents, plot-line, among other theater considerations, to help create a vivid world for audience members to enter. (See Mackenzie and Belliveau (2011) for a full discussion on this matter from a playwright and researcher's perspective.) Ideas should merge with emotions, inviting the audience to think and feel, experiencing the research-based theater on multiple levels. The artistic aspects generate potential for a more layered understanding and experience of the research shared.

4. Honoring the research context, the fact–fiction balance

When researchers and artists engage in research-based theater, a key question throughout the process should include: How does the artistic representation honor and inform the research? Research-based theater's intent is to bring research to life for targeted audiences, which usually consists of the research participants themselves, other academics, policy makers, and sometimes the general public. Individuals working with research-based theater have a responsibility to the research context and participants first and foremost. As such, no matter what artistic choices are taken, the intent needs to honor what was found in the research, the process, and/or findings. If the artistic strays too far from the actual research, it then moves away from the original intent of research-based theater, which is to theatricalize data collection, and/or analysis and/or findings.

Further Reading

Ackroyd, J. & O'Toole, J. (2010) *Performing Research: Tensions, triumphs and trade-offs of ethnodrama.* Stoke-on-Trent, UK: Trentham.

The two authors provide key issues researchers and/or artists might encounter while integrating performance (theater) into a research process. They also draw upon six case studies that demonstrate various approaches to research-based theater.

Butler-Kisber, L. (2010). *Qualitative Inquiry: Thematic, narrative and arts-informed perspectives.* Thousand Oaks, CA: Sage.
This text draws on the author's work with graduate students over a number of years. Approaches include collage, narrative, and found poetry. In her chapter on poetic inquiry, Butler-Kisber offers a useful overview of poetic transcription including an activity showing how a poem was crafted from interview data (pp. 86–88). She also presents the strategy of writing "poetry clusters" (pp. 95–96) on a theme or event as "a powerful and compelling way of getting a prism-like rendition of the subtle variations of a phenomenon" (p. 95).

Faulkner, S. (2009). *Poetry as Method: Reporting research through verse.* Walnut Creek, CA: Left Coast.
Faulkner lays out her approach to writing research poetry with chapters on reasons for engaging with poetry in research contexts, on the development of craft, and on effective criteria for assessing research poetry. Faulkner also provides examples from her own poetic inquiry practice.

Fels, L. & Belliveau, G. (2008). *Exploring Curriculum: Performative inquiry, role drama and learning.* Vancouver: Pacific Educational Press.
Fels and Belliveau offer theoretical and methodological approaches to their work and then share six detailed examples of performative inquiries that cut across several disciplinary areas. Personal narratives are shared as well as ways to assess performative inquiry.

Knowles, J. G. & Cole, A. (2008). *Handbook of the Arts in Qualitative Research.* Thousand Oaks, CA: Sage.
This Sage handbook is a significant marker in the development and acceptance of arts-based research. The collection has chapters on both poetry (Leggo, 2008; Neilsen, 2008) and dramatic performance (Donmoyer & Donmoyer, 2008; Kerry-Moran, 2008; Mienczakowski & Moore, 2008; Pelias, 2008; Saldaña, 2008).

Leavy, P. (2008). *Method Meets Art: Arts-based research practice.* New York: Guilford Press.
Leavy offers a useful overview of the possibilities available in arts-based approaches to research. Reprints of previously published articles by prominent arts-based researchers provide strong examples of practice.

Norris, J. (2009). *Playbuilding as Qualitative Research: An arts-based approach.* Walnut Creek, CA: Left Coast.
Norris presents educational research carried out over a twenty-year period using collective playbuilding processes as a way of both generating and representing data.

Prendergast, M., Leggo, C., & Sameshima, P. (2009). *Poetic Inquiry: Vibrant voices in the social sciences.* Rotterdam: Sense.
This collection contains over thirty poetic inquiry studies and provides an effective survey of this methodology.

Saldaña, J. (Ed.). (2005). *Ethnodrama: An anthology of reality theatre.* Walnut Creek, CA: AltaMira.
Saldaña's anthology offers a wide range of scripted ethnodramatic texts, providing the breadth and possibilities of using theater to inquire as well as disseminate research data.

Counterpoint Perspectives

Poetics

The most thorough debate on the use of poetry in research seen in the literature dates back to 1995–1996 in the journal *Qualitative Sociology*. Michael Schwalbe (1995) argues that "we can't meet our aims and responsibilities as qualitative sociologists by writing poetry" (p. 393). Schwalbe insists that sociologists have certain responsibilities, such as accessing social worlds and uncovering and interpreting the frameworks of those worlds, which poetry simply cannot address: "Poetry fails at these things because it keeps its foundations hidden, functions as a restricted code, and gives primacy to form over analytic content" (p. 393). He uses the poetic works of Laurel Richardson to make his claims for the failure of poetry as a sociological method, concluding that "the only way to meet the aims and responsibilities that define our craft and discipline is to write better prose" (p. 393).

In an issue of the same journal, published exactly one year after Schwalbe's essay, a number of prominent sociologists write rebuttals to his methodological position against the uses of poetry. These essays by Richardson (1996) herself, Norman Denzin (1996), and Elizabeth St. Pierre (1996) (among others), indicates the high level of interest at that time in the development of more innovative approaches to qualitative inquiry, including poetic ones.

Performance

In her article "Master versus servant: Contradictions in drama and theatre education" (2005), Schonmann shares how researchers working in various modes of theater research have tipped the scale too far, making the message, research, instrumental to the focus and driving force. Her call is to reestablish theater, the art within this work. She argues that many theater-based projects are diluted of practically all artistry, and thus the message is the "Master," with the art-form falling behind as the mere "Servant." She urges researcher/artists working in theater education to focus on and develop the art form, not allowing the instrumental aspects of the work to be at the forefront. Jackson makes a similar yet different argument in *Theatre, Education and the Making of Meanings: Art or instrument?* (2008), where he carefully chronicles this debate over the past century. Jackson acknowledges the delicate balance and challenges of weaving art and instrument, yet he proposes that it is possible to honor both in a piece of theater.

Authors' Reflections on Quality

Poetics

Monica

I am always seeking new ways to engage poetically with research topics of interest, when and if those topics open themselves to poetic investigation. I continue to employ found poetry as a way to represent my understandings of participant data (Prendergast *et al.*, 2009a, 2009b) or theoretical texts (Prendergast, 2011b). But I have also begun to publish poetic inquiries that fall into the autobiographical/autoethnographical area, inspired (and challenged) as I am by those who do their work so well in these blended studies of the self and/in society through poetry (Prendergast, 2008, 2009b, 2011a).

When I read and/or review poetically informed studies, I am looking for all the criteria listed above in this chapter under Qualitative Touchstones. I expect the author to locate his or her work in and among the ongoing methodological body of literature that is poetic inquiry. I want to see a harmonious relationship between topic and approach; that the issue at-hand provides what Sullivan (2009) calls the poetic "occasion." Ideally, I want to read poems that do the twofold job of illuminating the topic under investigation and also of being effective poems. I am often disappointed, left feeling that this goal has fallen short, in my own work as well as in the work of others. However, like any passionate pursuit—closely akin in my mind to panning patiently for gold through much muck and mud—when I read a poem published (or hear it presented) that succeeds in its twinned tasks, the glimmer of gold is a surprising and rewarding delight.

Performance

George

Over the past decade I have committed myself as a researcher to seek meaningful ways to bring theater in the research process (Belliveau, 2007; Beare & Belliveau, 2008; Medina, Belliveau, & Weltsek, 2008; Wager, Belliveau, Lea, & Beck, 2009; White & Belliveau, 2011). This has opened up many considerations and questions as to how, when, and why researchers might make use of theater approaches in collecting, analyzing, and disseminating research. Ethical issues, aesthetic choices, responsibilities to data and participants, as well as evaluation considerations have been at the forefront of my critical thinking about this work. Immersing myself artistically in this work with colleagues and graduate students has allowed our collective thinking to move forward from practice to theory and back again. I have now been involved in six fully realized pieces of research-based theater and through the doing and reflecting new questions continue to arise, yet a sense of the landscape and parameters have emerged as suggested in the considerations and touchstones shared above.

When reviewing work in the area of research-based theater (performance-based research) I look for pieces that provide deeper understanding on the data through the art form in ways that may not have been possible otherwise. How has space, time, silence, movement, voice, images, dialogue, and sound been used to bring new meaning to the data analysis? How was theater/performance honored as an art form within the research sharing? How was research attended to in the performance sharing? Attention and integrity to both research and artistry is imperative to create meaningful and impactful performance-based research.

References

Ackroyd, J. & O'Toole, J. (2010). *Performing Research: Tensions, triumphs and trade-offs of ethnodrama.* Stoke on Trent, UK: Trentham Books.

Alexander, B. K., Anderson, G. L., & Gallegos, B. P. (Eds.). (2005). *Performance Theories in Education: Power, pedagogy and the politics of identity.* Mahwah, NJ: Lawrence Erlbaum.

Anderson, M. & Wilkinson, L. (2007). A resurgence of verbatim theatre: Authenticity, empathy and transformation. *Australasian Drama Studies, 50,* 153–169.

Angelou, M. (1991). Preacher, don't send me. In *I Shall Not Be Moved* (pp. 38–40). New York: Bantam Books.

Barg, Rose. (2001). Rebirthing mother. In L. Neilsen, A. L. Cole, & J. G. Knowles (Eds.), *The Art of Writing Inquiry* (pp. 115–124). Halifax, NS: Backalong Books.

Beare, D. & Belliveau, G. (2008). Dialoguing scripted data. In S. Springgay, R. Irwin, & C. Leggo (Eds.), *Being with A/R/Tography* (pp. 141–149). Rotterdam: Sense Publishers.

Beatson, J. E. & Prelock, P. A. (2002). The vermont rural autism project: Sharing experiences, shifting attitudes. *Focus on Autism and Other Developmental Disabilities, 17*(1), 48–55.

Beck, J., Belliveau, G., Lea, G., & Wager, A. (2011). Delineating a spectrum of research-based theatre. *Qualitative Inquiry.* Published online before print August 15, 2011, doi: 10.1177/1077800411415498.

Belliveau, G. (2007). Dramatizing the data: An ethnodramatic exploration of a playbuilding process. *Arts & Learning Research Journal, 23*(1), 31–51.

Belliveau, G. (2006). Collective playbuilding: Using arts-based research to understand a social justice drama process in teacher education. *International Journal of Education & the Arts, 7*(5). http://ijea.org/v7n5/index.html.

Belliveau, G. & Lea, G. (2011). Research-based theatre in education. In S. Schonmann (Ed.), *Key Concepts in Theatre Drama Education* (pp. 332–338). Rotterdam: Sense Publishers.

Blumenfeld-Jones, D. S. (2008). Dance, choreography, and social science research. In J. G. Knowles & A. Cole (Eds.), *Handbook of the Arts in Qualitative Research: Perspectives, methodologies, examples, and issues* (pp. 175–184). Thousand Oaks, CA: Sage.

Brearley, L. (2000). Exploring the creative voice in an academic context. *The Qualitative Report, 5*(3&4), online at www.nova.edu.ssss/QR/QR5-3/brearley.html.

Bresler, L. (2008). The music lesson. In J. G. Knowles & A. Cole (Eds.), *Handbook of the Arts in Qualitative Inquiry: Perspectives, methodologies, examples, and issues* (pp. 225–237). Thousand Oaks, CA: Sage.

Butler, J. (1997). *Excitable Speech: A politics of the performative.* London: Routledge.

Butler-Kisber, L. (2010). *Qualitative Inquiry: Thematic, narrative and arts-informed perspectives.* London: Sage.

Butler-Kisber, L. (2002). Artful portrayals in qualitative inquiry: The road to found poetry and beyond. *The Alberta Journal of Educational Research, XLVIII*(3), 229–239.

Buttignol, M., Diamond, C. T. P., & "Eleanor" (2001). Longing to be free: A trilogy of arts-based self-portraits. In L. Neilsen, A. L. Cole, & J. G. Knowles (Eds.), *The Art of Writing Inquiry* (pp. 44–55). Halifax, NS: Backalong Books.

Cahnmann, M. (2003). The craft, practice, and possibility of poetry in educational research. *Educational Researcher, 32*(3), 29–36.

Cahnmann-Taylor, M. & Siegesmund, R. (Eds.). (2008). *Arts-based Educational Research: Foundations for practice.* New York: Routledge.

Cannon Poindexter, C. (2002). Research as poetry: A couple experiences HIV. *Qualitative Inquiry, 8*(6), 707–714.

Colombo, J. R. (1966). *The Mackenzie Poems/William Lyon Mackenzie & John Robert Colombo.* Toronto: Swan Publishing.

Commeyras, M. & Montsi, M. (2000). What if I woke up as the other sex? Batswana youth perspectives on gender. *Gender & Education, 12*(3), 327–347.

Cox, S., Kazubowski-Houston, M., & Nisker, J. (2006). Genetics on stage: Public engagement in health policy development on preimplantation genetic diagnosis. *Journal of Social Science and Medicine, 68*(8), 1472–1480.

Dawson, G. F. (1999). *Documentary Theatre in the United States: An historical survey and analysis of its content, form, and stagecraft.* Westport, CT: Greenwood.

Denzin, N. K. (2003). *Performance Ethnography: Critical pedagogy and the politics of culture.* Thousand Oaks, CA: Sage.

Denzin, N. K. (1997). *Interpretive Ethnography: Ethnographic practices for the 21st century.* London: Sage.

Denzin, N. K. (1996). Punishing poets. *Qualitative Sociology, 19*(4), 525–528.

Dillard, A. (1995). *Mornings Like This.* New York: Harper Collins.

Donmoyer, R. & Donmoyer, J. Y. (2008). Readers' theater as data display strategy. In J. G. Knowles & A. Cole (Eds.), *Handbook of the Arts in Qualitative Inquiry: Perspectives, methodologies, examples, and issues* (pp. 209–224). Thousand Oaks, CA: Sage.

Faulkner, S. L. (2010). *Poetry as Method: Reporting research through verse.* Walnut Creek, CA: Left Coast.

Faulkner, S. L. (2007). Concern with craft: Using ars poetica as criteria for reading research poetry. *Qualitative Inquiry, 13*(2), 218–234.

Fels, L. (2009). Performative inquiry: Arresting the villains in Jack and the Beanstalk. *Journal for Learning through the Arts.* Irvine, CA: University of California. http://repositories.cdlib.org/clta/lta/vol4/iss1/art2.

Fels, L. & Belliveau, G. (2008). *Exploring Curriculum: Performative inquiry, role drama and learning.* Vancouver, BC: Pacific Education Press.

Freeman, M. (2006). Nurturing dialogic hermeneutics and the deliberative capacities of communities in focus groups. *Qualitative Inquiry, 12*(1), 81–95.

Furman, R. (2004a). Using poetry and narrative as qualitative data: Exploring a father's cancer through poetry. *Families, Systems, & Health, 22*(2), 162–170.

Furman, R., Langer, C. L., Davis, C. S., Gallrado, H. P., & Kulkarni, S. (2007). Expressive, research and reflective poetry as qualitative inquiry: A study of adolescent identity. *Qualitative Research, 7*(3), 301–315.

Gallagher, K. (2007). *The Theatre of Urban: Youth and schooling in dangerous times.* Toronto, Buffalo, London: University of Toronto Press.

Galvin, K. & Todres, L. (2009). Invitation to resonance. In M. Prendergast, C. Leggo, & P. Sameshima (Eds.), *Poetic Inquiry: Vibrant voices in the social sciences* (pp. 307–316). Rotterdam: Sense Publishers.

Gannon, S. (2001). (Re)presenting the collective girl: A poetic approach to a methodological dilemma. *Qualitative Inquiry, 7*(6), 787–800.

Glesne, C. (2010). Disappearing into another's words through poetry in research and education. *Learning Landscapes, 4*(1), 29–37. Available at www.learninglandscapes.ca.

Glesne, C. (1997). That rare feeling: Re-presenting research through poetic transcription. *Qualitative Inquiry, 3*(2), 202–221.

Gouzouasis, P. (2008). Music research in an a/r/tographic tonality. *Journal of the Canadian Association for Curriculum Studies, 5*(2), 33–58.

Grace, A. P. (2001). Poetry is narrative inquiry. In L. Neilsen, A. L. Cole, & J. G. Knowles (Eds.), *The Art of Writing Inquiry* (pp. 26–31). Halifax, NS: Backalong Books.

Gray, R. E., Fitch, M. I., LaBrecque, M., & Greenberg, M. (2003). Reactions of health professionals to a research-based theatre production. *Journal of Cancer Education, 18*(4), 223–229.

Guiney Yallop, J. (2005). Exploring an emotional landscape: Becoming a researcher by reawakening the poet. *Brock Education, 14*(2), 132–144.

Hones, D. F. (1998). Known in part: The transformational power of narrative inquiry. *Qualitative Inquiry, 4*(2), 225–248.

Irwin, R. L. & de Cosson, A. (Eds.). (2004). *A/r/tography: Rendering self through arts-based living inquiry.* Vancouver: Pacific Educational Press.

Irwin, R. L. & Springgay, S. (2008). A/r/tography as practice-based research. In S. Springgay, R. L. Irwin, C. Leggo, & P. Gouzouasis (Eds.), *Being with a/r/tography* (pp. xix–xxxiii). Rotterdam: Sense Publishers.

Jackson, A. (2005). The dialogic and the aesthetic: Some reflections on theatre as a learning medium. *Journal of Aesthetic Education, 39*(4), 104–118.

James, K. (2009). Cut-up consciousness and talking trash: Poetic inquiry and the spambot's text. In M. Prendergast, C. Leggo, & P. Sameshima (Eds.), *Poetic Inquiry: Vibrant voices in the social sciences* (pp. 59–74). Rotterdam: Sense Publishers.

Kendall, M. & Murray, S. A. (2005). Tales of the unexpected: Patients' poetic accounts of the journey to a diagnosis of lung cancer: A prospective serial qualitative interview study. *Qualitative Inquiry, 11*(5), 733–751.

Kerry-Moran, K. J. (2008). Between scholarship and art: Dramaturgy and quality in arts-related research. In J. G. Knowles & A. Cole (Eds.), *Handbook of the Arts in Qualitative Inquiry: Perspectives, methodologies, examples, and issues* (pp. 493–502). Thousand Oaks, CA: Sage.

Knowles, J. G. & Cole, A. L. (Eds.). (2008). *Handbook of the Arts in Qualitative Research: Perspectives, methodologies, examples, and issues*. Thousand Oaks, CA: Sage.

Leavy, P. (2009). *Method Meets Art: Arts-based research practice*. New York: Guilford.

Leggo, C. (2008). Astonishing silence: Knowing in poetry. In J. G. Knowles & A. Cole (Eds.), *Handbook of the Arts in Qualitative Inquiry: Perspectives, methodologies, examples, and issues* (pp. 165–174). Thousand Oaks, CA: Sage.

Leggo, C. (2005a). Pedagogy of the heart: Ruminations on living poetically. *The Journal of Educational Thought, 39*(2), 175–195.

Leggo, C. (2005b). Autobiography and identity: Six speculations. *Vitae Scholasticae: The Journal of Educational Biography, 22*(1), 115–133.

Leggo, C. (2004a). The curriculum of joy: Six poetic ruminations. *JCACS (Journal of the Canadian Association of Curriculum Studies), 2*(2), 27–42. Available at: www.csse.ca/CACS/JCACS/V2N2.html.

Leggo, C. (2004b). The poet's corpus: Nine speculations. *JCT: Journal of Curriculum Theorizing, 20*(2), 65–85.

Leggo, C. (2002). A calling of circles: Ruminations on living the research in everyday practice. *Networks: On-line Journal for Teacher Research, 5*(1). Available at: www.oise.utoronto.ca/~ctd/networks/journal/Vol%205(1).2002march/index.html.

Leggo, C. (1999). Research as poetic rumination: Twenty-six ways of listening to light. In L. Neilsen, A. L. Cole, & J. G. Knowles (Eds.), *The Art of Writing Inquiry* (pp. 173–195). Halifax, NS: Backalong Books.

MacCleave, A. (2006). Incommensurability in cross-disciplinary research: A call for cultural negotiation. *International Journal of Qualitative Methods, 5*(2), Article 8. Retrieved May 4, 2010 from www.ualberta.ca/~iiqm/backissues/5_2/pdf/maccleave.pdf.

MacKenzie, D. & Belliveau, G. (2011). The playwright in research-based theatre. *Canadian Journal of Practice-based Research, 3*(1). Available at: http://cjprt.uwinnipeg.ca/index.php/cjprt/article/viewFile/30/19.

MacNeil, C. (2000). The prose and cons of poetic representation in evaluation reporting. *American Journal of Evaluation, 21*(3), 359–368.

Madison, D. S. & Hamera, J. (Eds.). (2006). *The Sage Handbook of Performance Studies*. Thousand Oaks, CA: Sage.

Medina, C., Belliveau, G., & Weltsek, G. (2008). Reflective practices in drama teacher preparation. *Theatre Research in Canada, 28*(2), 130–143.

Mienczakowski, J. (2001). Ethnodrama: Performed research—limitations and potential. In P. Atkinson, A. J. Coffey, S. Delamont, J. Lofland, & L. H. Lofland (Eds.), *Handbook of Ethnography* (pp. 468–476). Thousand Oaks, CA: Sage.

Mienczakowski, J. & Moore, T. (2008). Performing data with notions of responsibility. In J. G. Knowles & A. L. Cole (Eds.), *Handbook of the Arts in Qualitative Research: Perspectives, methodologies, examples, and issues* (pp. 451–458). Thousand Oaks, CA: Sage.

Mitchell, G., Dupuis, S., Jonas-Simpson, C., Whyte, J., Carson, J., & Gillis, J. (2011). The experience of engaging with research-based drama: Evaluation and explication of synergy and transformation. *Qualitative Inquiry, 17*(4), 379–392.

Molnar, T. (2010). Hospitality and the hôte: Revealing responsibility through found poetry. *Learning Landscapes, 4*(1), 157–173. Available at: www.learninglandscapes.ca.

Moody. R. (2001). Three poems. *CrossXconnect, 5*(2), unpaginated. Retrieved November 28, 2011 from http://ccat.sas.upenn.edu/xconnect/v5/i2/t/contents.html.

Neilsen, L. (2008). Lyric inquiry. In J. G. Knowles & A. Cole (Eds.), *Handbook of the Arts in Qualitative Inquiry: Perspectives, methodologies, examples, and issues* (pp. 93–102). Thousand Oaks, CA: Sage.

Norris, J. (2009). *Playbuilding as Qualitative Research: A participatory arts-based approach*. Walnut Creek, CA: Left Coast Press.

O'Donoghue, D. (2009). Are we asking the wrong questions in arts-based research? *Studies in Art Education, 50*(4), 352–368.

Öhlen, J. (2003). Evocation of meaning through poetic condensation of narratives in empirical phenomenological inquiry into human suffering. *Qualitative Health Research, 13*(4), 557–566.

Paget, D. (1997). Verbatim theatre: Oral history and documentary techniques. *New Theatre Quarterly, 12*, 317–336.

Pelias, R. J. (2008). Performative inquiry: Embodiment and its challenges. In J. G. Knowles & A. Cole (Eds.), *Handbook of the Arts in Qualitative Inquiry: Perspectives, methodologies, examples, and issues* (pp. 185–194). Thousand Oaks, CA: Sage.

Philip, C. E. (1995). Lifelines: A journal and poems. *Journal of Aging Studies, 9*, 265–322.

Piirto, J. (2002). The question of quality and qualifications: Writing inferior poems as qualitative research. *International Journal of Qualitative Studies in Education, 15*(4), 431–445.

Prendergast, M. (2011a). In exile/in flight: Two poems from a poetic autoethnography of academic banishment. *Cultural Studies↔Critical Methodologies, 11*(3), 303–305.

Prendergast, M. (2011b). Utopian performatives and the social imaginary: Toward a new philosophy of drama/theater education. *Journal of Aesthetic Education, 45*(1), 58–73.

Prendergast, M. (2009a). "Poem is what?" Poetic inquiry in qualitative social science research. *International Review of Qualitative Research, 1*(4), 541–568.

Prendergast, M. (2009b). "Poem is what?" Poetic inquiry in qualitative social science research. In M. Prendergast, C. Leggo, & P. Sameshima (Eds.), *Poetic Inquiry: Vibrant voices in the social sciences* (pp. xix–xlii). Rotterdam: Sense Publishers.

Prendergast, M. (2009c). The scholar dances. *Qualitative Inquiry, 15*(8), 1373–1375.

Prendergast, M. (2008). *Teaching Spectatorship: Essays and poems on audience in performance*. Amherst, NY: Cambria Press.

Prendergast, M. (2007). *Poetic Inquiry: An annotated bibliography*. Vancouver, BC: Centre for Cross-Faculty Inquiry, Faculty of Education, University of British Columbia. [1082 page annotated bibliography.]

Prendergast, M. (2006). Found poetry as literature review: Research found poems on audience and performance. *Qualitative Inquiry, 12*(2), 369–388.

Prendergast, M. (2004). "Shaped like a question mark": Found poems from Herbert Blau's *The Audience Research in Drama Education, 9*(1), 73–92.

Prendergast, M. & Leggo, C. (2007). Astonishing wonder: Spirituality and poetry in educational research. In L. Bresler (Ed.), *International Handbook of Research in Arts Education* (pp. 1459–1480). New York: Springer.

Prendergast, M., Leggo, C., & Sameshima, P. (Eds.). (2009a). Poetic inquiry: Special issue. *Educational Insights, 13*(3). Available at www.educationalinsights.ca.

Prendergast, M., Leggo, C., & Sameshima, P. (Eds.). (2009b). *Poetic Inquiry: Vibrant voices in the social sciences.* Rotterdam: Sense Publishers.

Prendergast, M., Gouzouasis, P., Leggo, C., Irwin, R., & Grauer, K. (2009a). A haiku suite: The importance of music-making in the lives of secondary school students. *Music Education Researcher, 11*(3), 303–317.

Prendergast, M., Lymburner, J., Grauer, K., Leggo, C., Gouzouasis, P., & Irwin, R. (2009b). Pedagogy of trace: Poetic representations of teacher resilience/resistance in arts education. *Vita Scholasticae: The Journal of Educational Biography, 25,* 58–76.

Pryer, A. (2007). Two found poems. *Language and Literacy, 9*(1), unpaginated. Available at: www.langandlit.ualberta.ca/Spring2007/Pryer.html.

Pryer, A. (2005). Six found poems. *Language and Literacy 7*(2), unpaginated. Available at: www.langandlit.ualberta.ca/archivesDate.html.

Richardson, L. (2000). Writing: A method of inquiry. In N. K. Denzin & Y. S. Lincoln (Eds.), *Handbook of Qualitative Research* (2nd ed., pp. 923–948). Thousand Oaks, CA: Sage.

Richardson, L. (1997). *Fields of Play: Constructing an academic life.* New Brunswick, NJ: Rutgers University Press.

Richardson, L. (1996). A sociology of responsibility. *Qualitative Sociology, 19*(4), 519–524.

Richardson, L. (1994). Nine poems. *Journal of Contemporary Ethnography, 23*(1), 3–13.

Richardson, L. (1993). Poetics, dramatics, and transgressive validity: The case of the skipped line. *The Sociological Quarterly, 34*(4), 695–710.

Richardson, L. (1992a). The poetic representation of lives: Writing a postmodern sociology. *Studies in Symbolic Interaction, 13,* 19–29.

Richardson, L. (1992b). The consequences of poetic representation: Writing the other, rewriting the self. In C. Ellis & M. G. Flaherty (Eds.), *Investigating Subjectivity: Research on lived experience* (pp. 125–140). Newbury Park, CA: Sage.

Saldaña, J. (2010). Writing ethnodrama: A sampler from educational research. In M. Savin-Baden & C. H. Major (Eds.), *New Approaches to Qualitative Research: Wisdom and uncertainty* (pp. 61–69). New York: Routledge.

Saldaña, J. (2008). Ethnodrama and ethnotheatre. In J. G. Knowles & A. L. Cole (Eds.), *Handbook of the Arts in Qualitative Research: Perspectives, methodologies, examples, and issues* (pp. 195–207). Thousand Oaks, CA: Sage.

Saldaña, J. (Ed.). (2005). *Ethnodrama: An anthology of reality theatre.* Walnut Creek, CA: AltaMira Press.

Sameshima, P., Vandermause, R., Chalmers, S., & "Gabriel". (2009). *Climbing the Ladder with Gabriel: A methamphetamine addict in recovery.* Rotterdam: Sense Publishers.

Santoro, N. & Kamler, B. (2001). Teachers talking difference: Teacher education and the poetics of anti-racism. *Teaching Education, 12*(2), 191–212.

Schechner, R. (1988/2003). *Performance Theory (2nd ed.).* London: Routledge.

Schechner, R. (1985). *Between Theater and Anthropology.* Philadelphia, PA: University of Pennsylvania Press.

Schonmann, S. (2005). "Master" versus "servant": Contradictions in drama and theatre education. *Journal of Aesthetic Education 39*(4), 31–39.

Schwalbe, M. (1995). The responsibilities of sociological poets. *Qualitative Sociology, 18*(4), 393–413.

Shidmehr, N. (2009). Poetic inquiry as minor research. In M. Prendergast, C. Leggo, & P. Sameshima (Eds.), *Poetic Inquiry: Vibrant voices in the social sciences* (pp. 101–109). Rotterdam: Sense Publishers.

Snowber, C. (2007). The soul moves: Dance and spirituality in educative practice. In L. Bresler (Ed.), *International Handbook of Research in Arts Education* (pp. 1449–1456). Dordrecht: Springer.

St. Pierre, E. A. (1996). The responsibilities of readers: Toward an ethics of responses. *Qualitative Sociology, 19*(4), 533–538.

Sullivan, A. M. (2009). On poetic occasion in inquiry: Concreteness, voice, ambiguity, tension, and associative logic. In M. Prendergast, C. Leggo, & P. Sameshima (Eds.), *Poetic Inquiry: Vibrant voices in the social sciences* (pp. 111–126). Rotterdam: Sense Publishers.

Sullivan, A. M. (2000). The necessity of art: Three found poems from John Dewey's art as experience. *International Journal of Qualitative Studies in Education, 13*(3), 325–327.

Sullivan, G. (2005). *Art Practice as Research: Inquiry in the visual arts.* Thousand Oaks, CA: Sage.

Thomas, S., Cole, A. C., & Stewart, S. (Eds.). (2012). *The Art of Poetic Inquiry.* Big Tancook Island, NS: Backalong Books.

Wager, A., Belliveau, G., Lea, G., & Beck, J. (2009). Exploring drama as an additional language through research-based theatre. *International Journal for Drama and Theatre in Foreign and Second Language Education, 3*(2), 50–64.

Walsh, S. (2006). An Irigarayan framework and resymbolization in an arts-informed research process. *Qualitative Inquiry, 12*(5), 976–993.

Ward, A. (2011). "Bringing the message forward": Using poetic representation to solve research dilemmas. *Qualitative Inquiry, 17*(4), 355–363.

Waskul, D. D. & Van der Riet, P. (2002). The abject embodiment of cancer patients: Dignity, selfhood, and the grotesque body. *Symbolic Interaction, 25*(4), 487–513.

Weems, M. (2009). The E in poetry stands for empathy. In M. Prendergast, C. Leggo, & P. Sameshima (Eds.), *Poetic Inquiry: Vibrant voices in the social sciences* (pp. 133–144). Rotterdam: Sense Publishers.

White, V. & Belliveau, G. (2011). Multiple perspectives, loyalties and identities: Exploring intrapersonal spaces through research-based theatre. *International Journal of Qualitative Studies in Education, 24*(2), 227–238.

White, V. & Belliveau, G. (2010). Whose story is it anyway? Exploring ethical dilemmas in performed research. *Performing Ethos International Research Journal, 1*(1), 85–95.

Whitney, S. L. (2004). Don't you wish you had blond hair? *Qualitative Inquiry, 10*(5), 788–793.

15

Positional and Identity-Based Theories of Research

Adrienne D. Dixson and Vanessa Dodo Seriki

"We cannot know everything, nor can we survey power as if we can fully understand, control or redistribute it. What we may be able to do is something rather more modest but, perhaps, rather more radical: to inscribe into our research practices some absences and fallibilities while recognizing that the significance of this does not rest entirely in our own hands."

(Rose, 1997)

In many ways, the "moments" of qualitative research have helped to clarify the importance of and indeed create a mandate for researchers to locate and situate themselves within their research (Denzin & Lincoln, 2000). In essence, all research is informed by the "positions" and "identities" of the researcher. These qualitative research moments, in many ways, are a result of the "postmodern turn" that helped to facilitate the proliferation of scholarship by scholars who locate themselves within particular perspectives and communities. As a result, positionality and identity-based approaches to research have become even more visible. This chapter will attempt to provide some suggestions for how reviewers might consider quality aspects of qualitative research that is explicit about positional and identity-based theories.

Select Terms

Essentialism is a contested idea but for philosophers, essentialism is the notion that an object or a group of people have an "essence" or a set of characteristics that we can observe, know, identify and name. In the social sciences, we understand essentialism as the "characterisations of people, practices, institutions and other social phenomena as having fixed identities which [are] deterministically produce fixed, uniform outcomes" (Sayer, 1997).

Context refers to not only the physical and geographic location of the research, but also the socio-historical, socio-political, socio-emotional environment in which we engage in research. We develop this definition by drawing on Ryle's (1968) notion of "thick description" as presented by Geertz (1973) in which the researcher richly and vividly describes the setting or context, if you will, of the research project.

Transparency, simply stated, is the view that the research process is made clear for and to participants, colleagues, and the intended audience. We agree with other scholars who view transparency and reflexivity as intricately connected to each other and fundamental aspects of the research process (Hiles & Cermák, 2007; Seale, Gobo, Gurbrium, & Silverman, 2004).

Reflexivity is the notion that researchers will do more than merely think about and "reflect" on the research process but as feminist scholar, Pamela Moss posits, reflexivity is much more purposeful, 'by reflexivity I mean those introspective aspects of thought that are self-critical and self-consciously analytical' (Moss as cited in Rose, 1997).

Intersectionality is a concept that originates in Black feminist theories, most notably in the Critical Race Theory and suggests that scholars (and activists) take into consideration the simultaneity of race, class and gender and how they work in concert to shape and/or impact (or subordinate) people's lives and experiences (Crenshaw, 1989).

Diversities in Perspective, Context, and Form

Positional and identity based theories are situated within the critical theory or emancipatory paradigm of qualitative research (Guba & Lincoln, 2008). The purpose or aim of this paradigm is the "... critique and transformation of the social, political, cultural, economic, ethnic, and gender structures that constrain and exploit humankind, by engagement in confrontation, even conflict" (Guba & Lincoln, 1994, p. 113). A few positional and identity based theories that share this aim include, Black feminism, Feminism, Queer Theory, and Critical Race Theory to name a few. Each perspective seeks to provide a space for the voices of the marginalized group (Somekh & Lewin, 2005) they represent while also seeking social justice.

While the particular standpoint differs for scholars who engage Feminism, Queer Theory, Black feminism, and Critical Race Theory as their theoretical framework, a shared idea is the notion of the importance of lived experience. Both CRT and Black feminism advance the notion of the intersectionality of oppression by arguing that race, class, and gender, among other social identities, intersect and impact the lives and experiences of women of color and people of color (Crenshaw, 1989; King, 1988). This notion of intersectionality is also an emerging idea in feminist studies (McCall, 2005).

Researchers operating from the critical theory paradigm have a particular ontological and epistemological perspective. Ontologically, researchers assume reality is understandable but is shaped, over time, by societal structures such as politics, culture, economics, etc. (Guba & Lincoln, 1994). It is important to note, however, that these structures impact groups differently, and thus multiple realities exist. The construction of multiple realities, invariably, generates dominate constructions of reality which lead to inequalities. Researchers operating within this paradigm also recognize that their mere presence, within the research setting, has an impact on the constructed reality of the participants. Therefore, epistemologically, knowledge is formed through the interactions between the researcher and the researched and is dependent on what the values of each are (Guba & Lincoln, 1994).

Qualitative Touchstones

In thinking about specific qualitative touchstones for positional and identity-based theories of research, the primary relevant aspects focus on issues of epistemology and representation, rather than discrete and specific data collection methods. However, when reviewing articles that name a specific social location and/or identity-based theory, i.e., Black feminisms, Critical Race Theory, among others, we offer some ideas to consider that may help reviewers determine the integrity and "quality" of the project. We frame our particular examination of these issues of quality within Black feminist theories and Critical Race Theory and believe that they can speak across disciplinary foci to offer ideas for reviewers:

1. Researcher shares a common experience and/or identifies with the participants and/or the communities that are the focus of the study

Scholars who engage positional and identity-based theories generally identify or are a member of the communities they endeavor to study. For example, researchers who identify as feminist generally engage in and develop projects that examine issues that impact women and girls (Crenshaw, 1989; Collins, 2000). Collins (2000) suggests that Black women scholars have a "unique angle of vision" on their own lives and experiences. While certainly scholars who are not Black women can and have examined and written about Black women, feminists of color and White feminist scholars have argued that given both the invisibility and misrepresentation of women and their experiences, it is important that feminist scholars engage in projects that document and analyze women's experiences. Collins suggests that Black feminist thought necessitates the need for Black women scholars to engage in projects that focus on Black women's experiences:

> A third key theme characterizing Black feminist thought involves efforts to redefine and explain the importance of Black women's culture. In doing so, Black feminists have not only uncovered previously unexplored areas of the Black female experience, but they have also identified concrete areas of social relations where Afro-American women create and pass on self-definitions and self-valuations essential to coping with the simultaneity of oppression they experience.
>
> (p. 524)

It is quite possible, however, that researchers can study in communities where they do not share a gender or ethnic/cultural (or some other social identity) background; however, to make a claim for a particular position or identity, that necessitates naming the project as one premised on a particular positionality or identity, ideally, the researcher should have substantive experiences that gives him/her an "insider" perspective so as to speak with some authority on what it means to be positioned in a particular way, e.g., an African American mother or a Latina teacher.

2. Research project is premised on the notion that the participants and their communities are healthy and whole

A number of scholars argue that people and communities of color hold a cultural wealth that scholars and researchers often ignore or overlook (Gay, 2009; Gonzalez, Moll, & Amanti, 2005; Irvine, 2006; Ladson-Billings, 2009; Lawrence-Lightfoot & Davis, 1997; Lee, Beale, & Harpalani, 2003). Research projects premised on positional or identity-based theories are premised on these same ideas that communities of color hold a vast amount of cultural wealth and are whole and healthy. The challenge for researchers and scholars is to uncover the health and wealth found in those communities and translate it for the academic community in an effort to build on and strategize with community members and/or research participants on ways to maximize their assets.

3. Framing research question(s) probe structural issues that construct essentialized images of participants, obstruct opportunities or maintain and/or perpetuate subordination

The design of the research questions is significant. In light of the claims made by white feminist scholars, feminist scholars of color and scholars who engage in race-based research, positional and identity-based research is born out of the desire to redress and make more visible the experiences of marginalized people. In framing research questions, researchers should consider designing research questions that will allow them to interrogate the processes and practices that have rendered people from marginalized groups invisible; make oppressive and subordinating processes and practices more visible; document the ways in which people from marginalized groups resist and attempt to disrupt oppressive and subordinating processes and practices (Collins, 2000; Zuberi & Bonilla-Silva, 2008).

In essence, positional and identity-based research has, to a certain extent, an implicit social justice mission in that researchers who engage in positional and identity-based research are *always already* focused on examining inequity and subordinating processes. For example, scholars who specifically engage CRT should consider the CRT tenet of social change as an ultimate goal of their research. For example, research drawing on or claiming a CRT focus may not only identify the ways that racial inequity manifests in particular educational practices and policies, but it may also offer interventions or be designed to intervene in those practices and policies. While CRT focuses on the way race manifests in particular policies and practices, its primary aim is to "look to the bottom" (Matsuda, 1987) to both understand subordination and inequity and think about strategies to resist and disrupt them. The design of the research questions can be a collaborative endeavor in that the researcher engages community members to understand the issue and/or "problem" they want to understand, examine, or challenge.

4. Data analysis is transparent

In light of the implicit social justice mission of positional and identity-based research and the challenge and disruption to the status quo, it is imperative that the researcher makes the data analysis process transparent. In addition, given that some projects may be collaborations with community members and/or members of marginalized groups, it is important that the researcher makes plain her/his process for making claims. Moreover and in the case of collaborative projects, researchers need to consider ways in which the analysis process takes into consideration the epistemological perspectives of the collaborators. Researchers can engage specific analytic methods, i.e., grounded theory, document analysis, among others. It is important to note that for scholars who engage CRT, there are specific tenets of the theory that help to frame the analytical process (DeCuir & Dixson, 2004; Dixson & Rousseau, 2005).

Feminist researchers argue that the analysis phase include a rigorous and substantive reflexive process. Donna Haraway (1988) suggests that the researcher understands her role as one that is situated and therefore she must not only engage in *reflection* on the research process, but also be *reflexive* about her role in the field, relationship with participants, and relationship to the data she collected.

5. Representing the data captures the experiences and perspectives of the participants

Representing the data in positional and identity-based research can take a number of forms and formats but must reflect and capture the experiences and perspectives of the participants. In CRT research, scholars often use narrative and first-person accounts of participants' experiences with race and racism (Delgado, 1989; Matsuda, 1989). In other cases, CRT scholars use storytelling and counter-narrative wherein they craft fictionalized accounts of real events (Bell, 1999). Thus, although the narratives center the stories of participants, they blend these stories with policy, legislation, and other events to make visible the processes and practices that perpetuate and maintain oppression and subordination.

White feminist scholars have engaged in and called for multi-layered textual renderings of the data and the data analysis (Lather & Smithies, 1997). "Alternative" formats for representing data are an attempt by White feminist scholars and scholars of color to challenge static notions of neutrality and objectivity that fail to capture the contextual issues, complexity, and nuances of the experiences of people from marginalized groups. Moreover, alternative renderings are an attempt to provide spaces for the voices of participants that are often foreclosed in traditional academic discourse and documentation.

Researchers are thus encouraged to find creative ways to represent the data but we caution them to ensure that they take care that the alternative formats maintain the integrity of the experiences and voices of the participants. In other words, the creative format of the data representation should not mute the voices of the participants nor distort the experiences of the participants. The data should not fit the format, but the format should fit to represent the data. We acknowledge that this may be a difficult balance for researchers but reviewers should note that researchers should make the process for selecting a format and its creation as clear and transparent as possible. That is, while the creative process is unique and personal, it should not be mystical especially as researchers communicate it for readers, their participants and ultimately for reviewers who have to evaluate and assess manuscripts.

6. Sampling and negotiating the research site

In positional and identity-based research, indeed, with all "good" qualitative research, negotiating entry, cultivating and maintaining relationships, and making decisions about sampling are all important issues to consider and represent as transparently as possible. As noted by Young (2004), research premised on "insider" status, may take for granted issues of access and thus, it is important for researchers to explain the nature and extent of their relationship to and with participants and the research site. Identifying those spaces where the researcher has become an outsider or is outside adds to understanding the insights they offer. Moreover, how a researcher selected and omitted or disqualified participants is important to explain in light of the desire to challenge static notions of identity within the context of research from a positional and standpoint perspective.

Further Reading

The following texts provide a range of perspectives and discussions about the position and identity based theories. Many of the sources focus on feminist research given the important contributions feminist scholars have offered relative to positionality and identity in research. These sources stimulate thoughtful consideration of the researcher's position and identity, thereby encouraging reviewers to look for the researcher's explication of their position and identity throughout the research process. These listed sources clarify this and provide reviewers with considerations as they undertake the task of evaluating position and identity based research.

Abu-Lughod, L. (2006). Writing against culture. In H. L. Moore & T. Sanders (Eds.), *Anthropology in Theory: Issues in Epistemology* (pp. 466–479). Malden: Blackwell Publishing.
Abu-Lughod provides an anthropological view of positionality, in regards to feminism, which was overlooked by Clifford & Marcus (1986) in *Writing Culture*. Abu-Lughod posited that feminist anthropologists and "halfies" blur the boundary between self—the researcher and other—the researched.

Chiseri-Strater, E. (1996). Turning in upon ourselves: Positionality, subjectivity, and reflexivity in case study and ethnographic research. In P. Mortensen & G. E. Kirsch (Eds.), *Ethics and Responsibility in Qualitative Studies of Literacy* (pp. 115–133). Urbana: NCTE.
The author identified identities that position researchers relative to those they study, and how descriptions of this position, by the researcher, depends upon the paradigm to which they ascribe. This article helps reviewers understand that they must consider the researchers position as it determines what they know or do not know.

Collins, P. H. (1986). Learning from the outside within: The sociological significance of Black feminist thought. *Social Problem*, *33*(6), S14–S33.
Collins provides an exploration of the three characteristic themes in Black feminist thought, and how Black women negotiate their outsider position within in their research.

England, K. V. L. (1994). Getting personal: Reflexivity, positionality, and feminist research. *Professional Geographer*, *46*(1), 80–89.
England offers advice on how to approach research with marginalized groups, when the researcher does not share the identity of those being researched. It also provides insight into dealing with the power relation between

the researcher and the marginalized group, and promotes thoughtful examination of the researcher's position and identity.

Gilbert, M. R. (1994). The politics of location: Doing feminist research at "home." *Professional Geographer*, 46(1), 90–96.

This article calls attention to the fact that feminism does not posit that women are a monolithic group. For instance, using feminist research methodology does not necessarily lead to women researchers having an insider position among researched women.

Labaree, R. V. (2002). The risk of "going observationalist": Negotiating the hidden dilemmas of being an insider participant observer. *Qualitative Research*, 2(1), 97–122.

Labaree explores researcher position in qualitative research by examining the value, motivation, negotiation, and hidden dilemma of being an "insider."

Merriam, S. B., Johnson-Bailey, J., Lee, M.-Y., Kee, Y., Ntseane, G., & Muhamad, M. (2001). Power and positionality: Negotiating insider/outsider status within and across cultures. *International Journal of Lifelong Education*, 20(5), 405–416.

The authors use "tales from the field" to explore issues related to positionality and power when studying your own culture. They substantiate that both positions, insider and outsider, are and provide legitimate representation of those being studied.

Scheurich, J. J. & Young, M. D. (1997). Coloring epistemologies: Are our research epistemologies racially biased? *Education Researcher*, 26(4), 4–16.

This article extends the conversation about racially biased epistemologies as presented by Stanfield (1993), and provides examples of what the author terms, "new" race based epistemologies and their use.

Counterpoint Perspectives

Tinker, C. & Armstrong, N. (2008). From the outside looking in: How an awareness of difference can benefit the qualitative research process. *The Qualitative Report*, 13(1), 53–60.

Within this chapter, we have discussed feminism, particularly Black feminism, which often positions the researcher as an insider. As some of the further readings suggest, women researchers do not always hold an insider position when working with women since other social identities (Dwyer & Buckle, 2009), such as race, class, sexual orientation among other social identities, may mediate shared gender identity. In contrast, scholars have examined both the benefits and challenges of the insider positionality in qualitative research (Tinker & Armstrong, 2008; Young, 2004).

Tinker and Armstrong (2008) highlight the benefits extended to the qualitative research process when there is great distance between the researcher and researched, thus the researcher holds an outsider position. The authors highlight and explain four potential benefits of positioning oneself as an outsider to those they are studying. These benefits include eliciting detailed responses, minimizing participants' fear of being judged, asking comprehensive interview questions, and maintaining criticality in analysis. They also acknowledge some disadvantages to being an outsider, primarily the issues of rapport and trust. Their aim, however, was to illustrate that the dichotomy between insider/outsider positioning is too simplistic and does not account for the oscillation between insider/outsider in any research setting.

Similarly, sociologist Alford Young, Jr., an African American male whose body of scholarship has examined the experiences of African American men across a number of contexts, argues that his positionality as an African American male and, by extension, the insider status as a researcher, can sometimes complicate the qualitative research process. Where rapport and trust may be spaces more easily navigated because of insider status, Young argues that rapport can be "threatened, if not altogether ruptured, by certain kinds of insider statuses" (p. 188). Further, Young offers that given the proliferation of scholarship in qualitative research that takes up this idea of insider-outsider status, researchers inhabit a number of positions rather than a singular status of insider or outsider (p. 192). Young goes on to identify ways that this rupture in rapport occurs citing a researcher's failure to follow the "implicit rules of dialogue" as a primary slippage that can compromise the research process. In particular, it can frustrate participants when the researcher who has "insider" status fails to acknowledge an understanding of particular ideas that participants believe are intrinsic to that identity. Moreover, Young argues that outsiders might have an advantage because they can push on issues and ideas in ways that insiders cannot because participants assume they already know and understand. Young offers examples of his challenges interviewing low-income African American males despite his "extreme insider" status. Further, Young suggests that researchers may not probe further because they inaccurately assume that they understand underlying ideas that their participants communicate, thereby compromising their analyses. Ultimately, Young concludes, and we agree ". . . good research may be achieved in part by the researcher committing to sincere reflexive thought about how and why the researcher may be regarded as an outsider by the people under study" (p. 200).

Author's Reflection on Quality

How does your presentation of qualitative touchstones in this chapter reflect your life and work as a scholar?

Our common experiences as Black women scholars and mothers significantly inform this chapter. That is to say, that growing up in the United States as members of a group (African American women) that has been and is marginalized, we have often been in the uncomfortable position of reading and listening to research that not only misrepresents African Americans and African American communities but also has tended to blame underachievement, poverty, and crime on the Black family structure in general and Black mothers specifically. In educational research, research on African American education has tended to focus on failure rather than success and ignore the cultural wealth found in African American communities. Given our separate, yet common experiences growing up in African American households and communities, these misrepresentations and absences did not capture what we believed to be a more accurate representation of African Americans or explain our success as Black women entering and navigating the academy. Thus, for us, quality research that emanates from gender or race-based positions should be premised on the notion that African Americans, male and female, are "good" (Lawrence-Lightfoot, 1997).

Similarly, for both of us, our experiences with racism both personally and as divorced and single mothers of African American sons forced/helped us to develop an understanding of the ways in which inequity functions at a level beyond individual actors. That is, while we understand that individual actors may behave in racist and other discriminatory ways, we have become more aware of how structural and institutional processes perpetuate subordination that impact people of color in an intersecting manner. From our experiences, Black mothers are particularly vulnerable to the intersecting nature of racial and gender subordination. Thus, for us, quality research that examines the experiences of people of color, substantively and rigorously engages intersectionality.

Yet, given this history of negative portrayals of African Americans generally and African American women specifically, we were concerned about presenting qualitative touchstones that read like absolutes. In many ways, constructing absolutes about what constitutes "good" positional and identity-based research contradicts the very premise of this research and recreates a hierarchy and the potential to reify stereotypes that do not represent the variety, nuance, and complexity found in communities and people of color. Thus, we attempted to offer ideas that reviewers might consider that we believe are flexible and malleable enough to help reviewers make judgments about research, but also make more informed decisions about what constitutes quality research premised on these ideas of positionality and identity.

References

Abu-Lughod, L. (2006). Writing against culture. In H. L. Moore & T. Sanders (Eds.), *Anthropology in Theory: Issues in epistemology* (pp. 466–479). Malden, MA: Blackwell Publishing.

Bell, D. A. (1999). The power of narrative. *Legal Studies Forum, 23*(3), 315–348.

Chiseri-Strater, E. (1996). Turning in upon ourselves: Positionality, subjectivity, and reflexivity in case study and ethnographic research. In P. Mortensen & G. E. Kirsch (Eds.), *Ethics and Responsibility in Qualitative Studies of Literacy* (pp. 115–133). Urbana, IL: NCTE.

Clifford, J. & Marcus, G. E. (Eds.). (1986). *Writing Culture: The poetics and politics of ethnography.* Berkeley, CA: University of California Press.

Collins, P. H. (1986). Learning from the outside within: The sociological significance of Black feminist thought. *Social Problem, 33*(6), 14–33.

Collins, P. H. (2000). *Black Feminist Thought: Knowledge, consciousness, and the politics of empowerment.* Routledge Classics.

Crenshaw, K. (1989). Demarginalizing the intersection of race and sex: A Black feminist critique of anti-discrimination doctrine, feminist theory and anti-racist politics. *University of Chicago Legal Forum,* 139–167.

DeCuir, J. & Dixson, A. D. (2004). "So when it comes out, they aren't that surprised when it's there": Using critical race theory as a tool of analysis of race and racism in education. *Educational Researcher, 33,* 26–31.

Delgado, R. (1989). Storytelling for oppositionists and others: A plea for narrative. *Michigan Law Review, 87,* 2411–2443.

Denzin, N. K. & Lincoln, Y. (Eds.). (2000). *Handbook of Qualitative Research* (2nd ed., pp. 1–30). London: Sage.

Dixson, A. D. & Rousseau, C. K. (2005). And we are still not saved: Critical race theory in education ten years later. *Race, Ethnicity and Education, 8*(1), 7–27.

England, K. V. L. (1994). Getting personal: Reflexivity, positionality, and feminist research. *Professional Geographer, 46*(1), 80–89.

Gay, G. (2010). *Culturally Responsive Teaching: Theory, research and practice.* New York: Teachers College Press.

Geertz, C. (1973). *Interpretation of Cultures.* New York: Basic Books.

Gilbert, M. R. (1994). The politics of location: Doing feminist research at "home." *Professional Geographer, 46*(1), 90–96.

Gonzalez, N., Moll, L. C., & Amanti, C. (2005). *Funds of Knowledge: Theorizing practices in households and classrooms.* New York: Lawrence Erlbaum Associates.

Guba, E. G. & Lincoln, Y. S. (1994). Competing paradigms in qualitative research. In N. K. Denzin & Y. S. Lincoln (Eds.), *Handbook of Qualitative Research* (pp. 105–117). Thousand Oaks, CA: Sage.

Guba, E. G. & Lincoln, Y. S. (2008). Paradigmatic controversies, contradictions, and emerging confluences. In N. K. Denzin & Y. S. Lincoln (Eds.), *The Landscape of Qualitative Research* (pp. 255–286). Thousand Oaks, CA: Sage.

Haraway, D. (1988). Situated knowledges: The science question in feminism and the privilege of partial perspectives. *Feminist Studies, 14*(3), 575–599.

Hiles, D. & Cermák, I. (2007). Qualitative research: Transparency and narrative oriented inquiry. In C. Willig & W. Stainton-Rogers (Eds.), *The SAGE Handbook of Qualitative Research in Psychology* (pp. 147–164). London: Sage.

Irvine, J. J. (2003). *Educating Teachers for Diversity: Seeing with a cultural eye* (Multicultural Education, 15). New York: Teachers College Press.

King, D. K. (1988). Multiple jeopardy, multiple consciousness: The context of a Black feminist ideology. *Signs, 14*(1), 42–72.

Labaree, R. V. (2002). The risk of "going observationalist": Negotiating the hidden dilemmas of being an insider participant observer. *Qualitative Research, 2*(1), 97–122.

Ladson-Billings, G. (2009). *The Dreamkeepers: Successful teachers of African-American students.* San Francisco, CA: Jossey-Bass.

Lather, P. A. & Smithies, C. S. (1997). *Troubling the Angels: Women living with HIV/AIDS.* Boulder, CO: Westview Press.

Lawrence-Lightfoot, S. & Hoffman Davis, J. (1997). *The Art and Science of Portraiture.* San Francisco, CA: Jossey-Bass.

Lee, C. D., Beale Spencer, M., & Harpalani, V. (2003). "Every shut eye ain't sleep": Studying how people live culturally. *Educational Researcher, 32*(5), 6–13.

McCall, L. (2005). The complexity of intersectionality. *Signs: Journal of Women in Culture and Society, 30*(3): 1771–1800.

Matsuda, M. (1987). "Looking to the bottom: Critical legal studies and reparations," 22 Harvard Civil Rights—Civil Liberties L. Rev. 323, pp. 323–399.

Matsuda, M. (1989). Public response to racist speech: Considering the victim's story. *Michigan Law Review, 87,* 2320–2381.

Merriam, S. B., Johnson-Bailey, J., Lee, M.-Y., Kee, Y., Ntseane, G., & Muhamad, M. (2001). Power and positionality: Negotiating insider/outsider status within and across cultures. *International Journal of Lifelong Education, 20*(5), 405–416.

Rose, G. (1997). Situating knowledge: Positionality, reflexivities and other tactics. *Progress in Human Geography, 21*(3), 305–320.

Ryle, G. (1968). Thinking and reflecting. *Royal Institute of Philosophy Lectures, 1,* 210–226. doi:10.1017/S0080443600011511.

Sayer, A. (1997). Essentialism, social constructionism and beyond. *The Sociological Review, 46,* 453–487.

Scheurich, J. J. & Young, M. D. (1997). Coloring epistemologies: Are our research epistemologies racially biased? *Education Researcher, 26*(4), 4–16.

Seale, C., Gobo, G., Gubrium, J. F., & Silverman, D. (Eds.). (2004). *Qualitative Research Practice.* London: Sage.

Somekh, B. & Lewin, C. (2005). *Research Methods in the Social Sciences.* Thousand Oaks, CA: Sage.

Stanfield, J. H. (1993). Epistemological considerations. In J. H. Stanfield & R. M. Dennis (Eds.), *Race and Ethnicity in Research Methods* (pp. 6–36). Newbury Park: Sage.

Tinker, C. & Armstrong, N. (2008). From the outside looking in: How an awareness of difference can benefit the qualitative research process. *The Qualitative Report, 13*(1), 53–60.

Young, A. L. (2004). Experiences in ethnographic interviewing about race: The inside and outside of it? In J. Solomos & M. Bulmer (Eds.), *Researching Race and Racism* (pp. 187–202). London: Routledge.

Zuberi, T. & Bonilla-Silva, E. (Eds.). (2008). *White Logic, White Methods: Racism and methodology*. New York: Rowman & Littlefield.

Notes on Contributors

George Belliveau is associate professor in the Faculty of Education at the University of British Columbia where he teaches undergraduate and graduate courses in Theater/Drama Education. His research primarily focuses on exploring and developing the field of research-based theater, where researchers (from various fields) and artists collaborate to generate theater informed by research. Other areas of research include drama and social justice, Shakespeare and children, drama and literacy, and drama and L2 learning. George completed his PhD in Theater Studies at the University of British Columbia. Prior to his graduate work, George worked as an actor and spent seven years as a secondary teacher.

Antony Bryant is currently Professor of Informatics at Leeds Metropolitan University, Leeds, UK. His current research includes investigation of the ways in which the Open Source model might be used more widely, and in particular how it can be developed as a contributory feature for the reconstructed financial sector in the wake of the economic meltdown; coining the term *Mutuality 2.0* and developing the concept in various contexts—for example, www.opendemocracy.net/article/email/mutuality-2-0-open-source-the-financial-crisis. He has written extensively on research methods, being senior editor of *The SAGE Handbook of Grounded Theory* (SAGE, 2007)—co-edited with Kathy Charmaz with whom he has worked extensively within the area of grounded theory and research methods in general.

Mary Brydon-Miller, PhD, directs the University of Cincinnati's Action Research Center and is Professor of Educational Studies and Urban Educational Leadership in the College of Education, Criminal Justice, and Human Services. She is a participatory action researcher who engages in both community-based and educational action research. Her current scholarship focuses on ethics and action research.

Vera Caine is an assistant professor in the Faculty of Nursing at the University of Alberta and Affiliate Member of the CRTED. Her research interests center on theoretical issues in narrative inquiry and visual methodologies. During the past twelve years Vera has worked alongside Aboriginal communities in Northern Canada, as well as urban Aboriginal women living with HIV/AIDS and their families. Most recently Vera has engaged alongside youth who leave school early, as well as Aboriginal youth and their families in urban public schools.

D. Jean Clandinin is Professor and Director of the Centre for Research for Teacher Education (CRTED) and Development at the University of Alberta. A former teacher, counsellor, and psychologist, she is author or co-author of ten books. Four books and many chapters and articles were published with Michael Connelly. Their latest book, *Narrative Inquiry*, was published in 2000. She also authored two other books: the first based on her doctoral research and the second based on research from an experimental teacher education program. A 2006 book co-authored with seven former students, *Composing Diverse Identities: Narrative Inquiries into the Interwoven Lives of Children and Teachers*, drew on several years of research with children and teachers in urban schools. This book has been awarded the 2006 Narrative Research Special Interest Group Outstanding Book award and the 2007 AERA Division B Outstanding Book Award. She edited the handbook of *Narrative Inquiry: Mapping a methodology* (Sage, 2007). Her most recent book titled *Places of Curriculum Making* was published in 2011. She is currently working on a new book with Pam Steeves and Vera Caine about the experiences of youth who leave school without graduating.

Marlene Z. Cohen is the Associate Dean for Research, a Professor, and the Kenneth E. Morehead Endowed Chair in Nursing at the University of Nebraska Medical Center, College of Nursing. Her research focus has been on understanding how the world is perceived by clients and patients, by their family members, and by professionals, defining and promoting health and preventing disease, examining the influences of social and physical environments on health and illness, and addressing the effects of nursing care on patients and their families. Cancer-related behaviors and symptom management have also been a primary focus. Her PhD is from the University of Michigan in Clinical Nursing Research.

Catherine Compton-Lilly is an associate professor in Curriculum and Instruction at the University of Wisconsin Madison. She is the author of *Reading Families: The Literate Lives of Urban Children* (Teachers College Press, 2003), *Confronting Racism, Poverty and Power* (Heinemann, 2004), *Rereading Families* (Teachers College Press, 2007), the editor of *Breaking the Silence* (International Reading Association, 2009), and co-editor of *Bedtime Stories and Book Reports: Complexities, Concerns, and Considerations in Fostering Parent Involvement and Family Literacy* (Teachers College Press, 2010). Dr. Compton-Lilly has authored articles in several journals. Dr. Compton-Lilly engages in longitudinal research projects that last over long periods of time. In her most recent study, she followed a group of eight inner-city students from grade one through grade eleven. Her interests include examining how time operates as a contextual factor in children's lives as they progress through school and construct their identities as students and readers.

Adrienne D. Dixson, PhD, is an Associate Professor in the Department of Education Policy, Organization and Leadership in the College of Education at the University of Illinois at Urbana-Champaign. Her primary research interest focuses on how issues of race, class, and gender intersect and impact educational equity in urban schooling contexts. Her research is located within two theoretical frameworks: Critical Race Theory and Black feminist theories. Her current research examines how educational equity is mediated by school reform policies in the urban south. She is engaged in a long-term research project on school reform in post-Katrina New Orleans examining how local actors make sense of and experience reform policies and how those policies become or are "racialized." Her book publications include, *Critical Race Theory in Education: All God's Children Got a Song* (Routledge, 2006, co-edited with Celia K. Rousseau), *Integration Betrayed: Race, Education, and Inequity in the 21st Century* (Routledge, forthcoming, with Jamel K. Donnor), *The Handbook of Critical Race Theory and Education* (Routledge, forthcoming, with Marvin Lynn), and several journal articles.

Vanessa Dodo Seriki is an assistant professor of Science Education at the University of Houston–Clear Lake. As a graduate of an urban school, Dr. Dodo Seriki has dedicated her work to empowering the often voiceless, urban students who yearn to engage in science learning. Using a critical lens, Dr. Dodo Seriki's research examines the engagement in and access to science learning by urban students, particularly students of color. Before earning a doctorate, she worked as a secondary science teacher in Virginia and Maryland.

Valerie J. Janesick (PhD Michigan State University) is professor of Educational Leadership and Policy Studies, University of South Florida, Tampa. She teaches classes in Qualitative Research Methods, Curriculum Theory and Inquiry, Foundations of Curriculum, Ethics and Educational Leadership. She has written numerous articles and books in these areas including her recently completed third edition of *Stretching Exercises for Qualitative Researchers* (2011), which is reorganized around habits of mind and includes new sections on internet inquiry and constructing poetry from interview data. She uses dance and the arts as a metaphor for understanding research, evaluation, and assessment. Her book, *Oral History Methods for the Qualitative Researcher: Choreographing the Story* (Guilford Publications, 2010) argues for artistic representations of data and oral history as a social justice project. Find her website at: http://sites.google.com/site/valeriejjanesick. Correspondence to: vjanesic@usf.edu.

Anne Karabon has been an early childhood teacher in a variety of capacities and has worked with students ranging from children to adults. A graduate student at the University of Wisconsin–Madison in early childhood education, Anne is interested in professional development, funds of knowledge, and home school relations.

Nancy Kendall is an assistant professor of Educational Policy Studies, Comparative and International Education concentration, at the University of Wisconsin–Madison. Her research utilizes multisite, comparative ethnographic methods to explore issues related to schooling, gender, sexuality, and childhood and youth vulnerability in sociocultural and political economic perspectives. Most of her work has been done in Malawi and the US. She received her PhD from Stanford University in International and Comparative Education in 2004.

Donna M. Mertens, PhD, is a professor in the Department of Educational Foundations and Research at Gallaudet University, where she teaches advanced research methods and program evaluation to deaf and hearing students. She also serves as editor for the *Journal of Mixed Methods Research*. The primary focus of her work is transformative mixed-methods inquiry in diverse communities that prioritizes ethical implications of research in pursuit of social justice. Her recent books include *Program Evaluation Theory to Practice: A Comprehensive Guide*; *Transformative Research and Evaluation*; *The Handbook of Social Research Ethics*; *Research and Evaluation in Education and Psychology: Integrating Diversity with Quantitative, Qualitative, and Mixed Methods (3rd ed.)*; *Research and Evaluation Methods in Special Education*; and *Parents and Their Deaf Children: The Early Years*. She is widely published in the *Journal of Mixed Methods Research, American Journal of Evaluation, American Annals of the Deaf*, and *Educational Evaluation and Policy Analysis*.

Eileen J. Porter earned a PhD in Nursing at the University of Wisconsin–Milwaukee. Her research program is focused on describing the health-related experiences of older women who live alone at home. The overall aims are to grasp the essence of the health-related intentions of older women and to set that awareness in personal–social–environmental context. She developed a descriptive phenomenological method that she has used in a series of NIH-funded longitudinal studies. She is especially interested in describing experiences that evoke risks that older women associate with living alone (such as falling, being unable to reach help, dealing with intrusion of unwanted visitors, and causing worry or burden to helpers). A Fellow of the Gerontological Society of America, she is Professor Emerita of Nursing, University of Missouri, and Professor of Nursing at the University of Wisconsin–Madison.

Christopher N. Poulos is associate professor and head of the Communication Studies Department at the University of North Carolina at Greensboro. An ethnographer and philosopher of communication, he teaches courses in relational and family communication, autoethnography, dialogue, and film. His book, *Accidental Ethnography: An Inquiry into Family Secrecy*, was published by Left Coast Press in 2009. His work has appeared in Qualitative Inquiry, Communication Theory, Southern Communication Journal, International Review of Qualitative Research, Qualitative Communication Research, and in several edited books.

Monica Prendergast is an assistant professor of Drama/Theatre Education at the University of Victoria. Her research interests include arts-based research, critical pedagogies, performance theories, and innovative interpretive inquiry methods, particularly those using poetry. Her scholarly work has appeared in numerous books, handbooks, and journals. She is co-editor of *Poetic Inquiry: Vibrant voices in the social sciences* (Sense, 2009), of two special journal issues on poetic inquiry methods (*Educational Insights* [2009] and *Creative Approaches to Research* [2012]), and of the *Canadian Journal of Practice-Based Research in Theatre*.

Rebecca Rogers is an associate professor of Literacy and Critical Discourse Studies at the University of Missouri–St. Louis. Her scholarship focuses on the sociopolitical contexts of literacy and language education and situates critical discourse analysis within an ethnographic tradition. She has published widely in journals such as *Reading Research Quarterly, Linguistics & Education, Discourse, Critical Inquiry into Language Studies*, the *Journal of Literacy Research, Review of Research in Education*, and *Race, Ethnicity and Education*. Her books include *An Introduction to Critical Discourse Analysis in Education* (second edition; Routledge, 2011); *Designing Socially Just Learning Communities: Designing Critical Literacy Education across the Lifespan* (Routledge, 2009); *A Critical Discourse Analysis of Family Literacy Practices* (Lawrence Erlbaum, 2003); *Adult Education Teachers Designing Critical Literacy Practices* (Routledge, 2008). She was recently a Fulbright Scholar in Critical Discourse Studies at the Universidad de San Martín in Buenos Aires, Argentina.

Jim Scheurich is a professor at Texas A&M University. His research interests include equity in education, schools that are successful with diverse students, race and racism, and qualitative research methodologies. He is the editor of a research journal (*International Journal of Qualitative Studies in Education*) and associate editor of another (*Educational Administration Quarterly*), serves on several research journal editorial boards, and has published over nearly fifty articles in peer-reviewed research journals and seven books. He has served on several committees for national research organizations, including the Executive Committee for the University Council for Educational Administration (UCEA). In 2006, he received the Master Professor Award from UCEA, and he was a 2008 nominee for President of the American Educational Research Association (AERA).

Randy Stoecker is a professor in the Department of Community and Environmental Sociology at the University of Wisconsin, with a joint appointment in the University of Wisconsin-Extension Center for Community and Economic Development. He moderates/edits COMM-ORG: The On-Line Conference on Community Organizing (http://comm-org.wisc.edu), and does research and training in the areas of community organizing and development, community-based participatory research/evaluation, higher education community engagement, and community information technology. He has facilitated numerous participatory action research projects, community technology projects, and empowerment evaluation processes with community development corporations, community-based leadership education programs, community organizing groups, and other nonprofit organizations in North America and Australia.

Miriam Thangaraj is a doctoral student at the Department of Educational Policy Studies, University of Wisconsin–Madison, with a concentration in Comparative and International Education. Her research interests encompass global education and development discourses on schooling, childhood, and vulnerability. Currently, she is working on an ethnography of children and childhoods in a crafts-based community undergoing rapid, export-oriented industrialization in India.

Index